ASPECTS OF TOURISM
Series Editors: Chris Cooper, *Oxford Brookes University, UK,*
C. Michael Hall, *University of Canterbury, New Zealand* and
Dallen J. Timothy, *Arizona State University, USA*

Accessible Tourism
Concepts and Issues

Edited by
Dimitrios Buhalis and Simon Darcy

CHANNEL VIEW PUBLICATIONS
Bristol • Buffalo • Toronto

Library of Congress Cataloging in Publication Data
A catalog record for this book is available from the Library of Congress.
Accessible Tourism: Concepts and Issues/Edited by Dimitrios Buhalis and Simon Darcy.
Aspects of Tourism
Includes bibliographical references.
1. People with disabilities–Travel. 2. Tourism. I. Buhalis, Dimitrios. II. Darcy, Simon, 1964-
HV3022.A2215 2011
910.68'40-dc222010041488

British Library Cataloguing in Publication Data
A catalogue entry for this book is available from the British Library.

ISBN-13: 978-1-84541-161-9 (hbk)
ISBN-13: 978-1-84541-160-2 (pbk)

Channel View Publications
UK: St Nicholas House, 31–34 High Street, Bristol BS1 2AW, UK.
USA: UTP, 2250 Military Road, Tonawanda, NY 14150, USA.
Canada: UTP, 5201 Dufferin Street, North York, Ontario M3H 5T8, Canada.

Typeset by The Charlesworth Group
Printed and bound in Great Britain by Charlesworth Press.

Contents

Acknowledgements

Like any project this book has a history that brought it to fruition. Back in 2005 Ivor Ambrose put a team together to work on improving the information provision for accessible tourism through the European project OSSATE. He included Dimitrios Buhalis as an information management expert in tourism and a handful of disability and tourism experts, many of whom had disabilities themselves and were passionate about making a difference. At the outset of this project it was immediately evident that there was a body of research already in the area, primarily instigated by Simon Darcy and his collaborators. A couple of trips to Sydney and a few beers later, a close friendship and partnership were developed, fuelled by a passion for research on accessible tourism. A global network of friends/ collaborators emerged rapidly to harness the best conceptual developments in the topic. Discussions were always about making a positive difference and taking this area forward and to the mainstream academic enquiry and industry practice. As a result the idea of these books emerged as a way to achieve this and to assist the area to grow.

When we are discussing accessible tourism, all around the world, there is a realisation that several issues emerge immediately. People with access requirements are often frustrated with the lack of facilities and also information that would make travel planning and, hence, travelling easier. They are dissatisfied with the public sector for the lack of regulation, control and implementation. They are also critical of the private sector for not understanding their needs as they would for any other consumer group and for being unwilling to invest in facilities that can improve accessibility. When talking to tourism operators, especially in countries where accessibility is not at the forefront of legislation and practice, they are unable to understand the complexity that is inherent to disability and access: they want simple practical guidelines and worry about the extra cost they will bear to adapt their facilities. In the centre of this mismatch in the marketplace, there are a number of misunderstandings or misconceptions from both sides that prevent the development and the implementation of accessible tourism.

This book then brings together key issues and themes to provide a comprehensive resource for positive dialogue. It aims to explore and demonstrate the key concepts of accessible tourism and in this way to bring together all stakeholders in the international debate. It also brings accessibility into the mainstream of tourism inquiry and encourages all relevant stakeholders to engage in the discussion and negotiation towards universal design. This will not only allow a much more inclusive approach for clientele but will also enable tourism suppliers to open their doors to new markets which have a great potential, as well as acting appropriately, or effectively and efficiently, to improve their operational bottom line.

The editors were conscious of the need to make the material 'research driven'. Each of the contributing authors has attempted to honour the intent of the editors and we thank them for their collegiality and enthusiasm. As editors we also wanted to ensure the overall quality of the manuscript and subjected the chapters to blind external review in addition to our own editorial processes. These processes have been important to ensure that the book has coherence and continuity in the development of the concepts and issues.

The editors would like to express their gratitude to Ivor Ambrose for his contribution in various parts of the book and also for his collaboration and support. They would also like to thank Stephen Schweinsberg who has overseen most of the reviewing process, as well as assisting the editorial work in each stage. We would also like to thank all our contributors for engaging in the debate and contributing to the project, and our publishers Elinor Robertson and Tommi Grover for their trust and support.

Dimitrios Buhalis and Simon Darcy
March 2010

Contributors

Editors

Dimitrios Buhalis is a Strategic Management and Marketing expert with specialisation in Technology and Tourism. He is currently Established Chair in Tourism and Deputy Director of the International Centre for Tourism and Hospitality Research (ICTHR) at the School of Services Management at Bournemouth University and Professorial Observer at the Bournemouth University Senate. Professor Buhalis is leading eTourism research and is working with the Bournemouth team on introducing technology in all aspects of tourism research and teaching. He represents Bournemouth University as the BU representative to the United Nations World Tourism Organisation and he is a Fellow of the International Academy for the Study of Tourism. He is currently the President of the International Federation of Information Technology for Travel and Tourism (IFITT).

Simon Darcy is an Associate Professor in Events, Sport and Tourism at UTS, Sydney. He is a core member of the UTS' Cosmopolitan Civil Societies Research Centre. Simon is an interdisciplinary researcher with expertise in developing inclusive organisational approaches to diversity groups. His research has spanned a variety of contexts including sport, tourism, events, volunteers, transport and the built environment. Simon has held grants with the Australian Research Council, Sustainable Tourism Cooperative Research Centre, the United Nations ESCAP, and has carried out research studies for all levels of government and the private sector. Over the last decade, his body of work on accessible tourism has gained national and international recognition. Simon is actively involved in changing government and industry practice through implementing the outcomes of his research. Since incurring a spinal injury in 1983 Simon is a power wheelchair user and passionately believes in the rights of all people to fully participate in all aspects of community life.

Authors

Ivor Ambrose is the Managing Director and co-founder of ENAT, the European Network for Accessible Tourism, a Belgian non-profit association of organisations working in tourism development, disability, education, research and access consulting. With a background in Environmental

Psychology he has worked for over 30 years as a researcher, project manager, developer and policy adviser in the fields of building design and evaluation, public housing, accessibility and assistive technologies for disabled and elderly people, and information systems. His has previously held positions at the European Commission DG Information Society in Belgium, the Danish Building Research Institute and the University of Surrey, UK. He now acts as an international consultant on accessible tourism development projects for regions, destinations, enterprises and funding programmes of the European Union.

Esa Arola(†) was a Principal Lecturer at the School of Tourism and Services Management at Jyväskylä Polytechnic in Central Finland, following a successful career in the hospitality industry. He was instrumental in developing the Tourism Industry and Education Symposium. His PhD concentrated on the encounters of disabled customers on the tourism stage. Esa is remembered by colleagues and friends for his kindness and great humor as well as for his professionalism and passion for research on disability and tourism.

Yael Brandt is a graduate of the Department of Business Administration, Guilford Glazer School of Business and Management, Ben-Gurion University of the Negev, Israel. Her thesis centres on the tourist experience for people with disabilities.

Bruce Cameron is Director of Easy Access Publishing, he has a Bachelor of Economics Degree (1980) and he is a Certified Practising Accountant (CPA). Following an extended trip to the United Kingdom and Europe in 1992, he left the finance industry to research, write and publish Easy Access Australia, Australia's only travel guide for people with a disability.

Chris Cooper is the Dean of Oxford Brookes Business School in the UK. He was previously Director of the Christel DeHaan Tourism and Travel Research Centre at the University of Nottingham Business School and Professor and Head of the School of Tourism at the University of Queensland, Australia. His early career was in the travel industry and the Universities of Surrey and Bournemouth. He is a member of the United Nations World Tourism Organization Leadership Forum and Panel of Experts and he is a Fellow of the International Academy for the Study of Tourism. He served as Chair of the UNWTO's Education Council and in 2009 he received the UNWTO Ulysses Award.

Robyn Cooper is currently a PhD student in the School of Historical Studies at the University of Leicester. She completed her undergraduate honours degree at the University of Queensland, Australia. The focus of her research is travel to the British Empire in the late 19th and early 20th centuries.

Larry Dwyer is Qantas Professor of Travel and Tourism in the School of Marketing, Australian School of Business, University of New South Wales. His primary research interests are in the areas of Tourism Economics and Tourism Management. Larry is a member of the International Advisory Board of the Business Enterprises for Sustainable Tourism Education Network (BESTEN). He is a founding member and President of the International Association for Tourism Economics. Larry is a Fellow of the International Academy for Study of Tourism, the world's peak academic tourism association and is now its second Vice President.

Victoria Eichhorn is Lecturer in Tourism at the Faculty of Management and Law at the University of Surrey, UK, where she mainly teaches issues related to destination management and marketing, the business of tourism and exclusion/ inclusion in tourism. Before joining the university, Victoria worked for the German National Tourism Board in Madrid, Spain, as Press Officer and Internet Marketing Manager. Victoria also worked as Research Officer for accessible tourism, where she focused on research-ing barriers to tourism participation, the market potential and size for accessibility as well as business models and plans for establishing an accessible information service. Victoria's research focuses on exclusionary practices in tourism, particularly in relation to disability, identity and the discourse of 'social exclusion'.

Beth Foggin is an independent consultant and educator in both academic and travel industry milieux – with particular emphasis on the socio-cultural history and geography of the Australasian and North American regions. After completing her PhD in Applied Social Sciences at the French-language Université de Montréal, she briefly was a sessional lecturer in its Geography department. Her doctoral thesis and subsequent research has explored the experience of leisure and tourism of people with reduced physical abilities. Beth is based in Montreal (Quebec), Canada, but travels extensively overseas.

Simone Fullagar is an Associate Professor and Deputy Head of Department in the Department of Tourism, Leisure, Hotel and Sport Management at Griffith University, Australia. She is an interdisciplinary sociologist with research interests in social equity related to leisure, sport and tourism participation, and links to well-being. Simone is also the President of the Australian and New Zealand Association for Leisure Studies and has a long standing interest in the disability field.

Elina Michopoulou is a Lecturer in Tourism at the University of Derby and a researcher at the University of Surrey, UK. She is about to complete her Doctorate on the user requirements of tourism information systems for people with disabilities and she is active in several research fields including tourism, technology and disability. She holds a BSc in Tourism

Management from the Technological Institute of Patras, Greece, and a Masters degree (MSc) in eTourism, from the University of Surrey, UK. Previously she worked for two-and-a-half years as a Research Officer in eTourism Research Development and Evaluation at the University of Surrey for the European Commission-funded eContent Project OSSATE (One-Stop-Shop for Accessible Tourism in Europe). Elina also worked for the Olympic and Paralympic Games 2004 in Athens, Greece.

Gerhard Nussbaum (Dipl.-Ing.) is project manager and technical engineer at the Competence Network Information Technology to Support the Integration of People with Disabilities (KI-I). He studied computer science at the Johannes Kepler University Linz and graduated with distinction in 2003. During his work at the KI-I he is and was involved in numerous national and international founded projects in the area of e-inclusion. His current research work is related to the use of ICT to enable the integration of people with disabilities that concerns the field of assistive technology as well as accessibility and usability of modern ICT including the internet. His special fields of research are smart environments, environmental control and mobile computing.

Ian Patterson is Associate Professor in the School of Tourism at the University of Queensland, Australia. He teaches courses in leisure, tourism and sport management and has published over 70 scholarly publications. His most recent book is *Growing Older: Tourism and Leisure Behaviour of Older Adults* (CABI Publishing, 2006). He is currently an editor of the journal *Annals of Leisure Research*.

Michael C. Pearn has cerebral palsy and throughout his life, both academically and socially, he has strived to maintain an ordinary and fulfilled lifestyle. He places immense importance on the fair and just treatment of all people with disabilities and is a committed advocate of societal inclusion. He completed his PhD in the spring of 2009 in which he researched the quandary over introducing improvements to disabled access within heritage sites without encroaching upon traditional and historically authentic environments. As well as studying the ideological clash between disability issues and heritage preservation, this research involved investigating the differing attitudes of disabled and able-bodied visitors.

Shane Pegg is a Senior Lecturer with the School of Tourism and Leisure Management in the Faculty of Business, Economics and Law at The University of Queensland, Australia. Shane is a past recipient of the Future Scholars Award from the Academy of Leisure Sciences and is a current member of the World Leisure Commission on Access and Inclusion. His research interests include therapeutic recreation, tourism access and inclusion issues, and the tourism and leisure behaviour of people with disabilities.

Yaniv Poria is a Senior Lecturer at the Department of Hotel and Tourism Management, Guilford Glazer School of Business and Management, Ben-Gurion University of the Negev, Israel. His main research interest is people's experiences at heritage settings.

Franz Pühretmair (Dipl.-Ing. Dr.) is scientific and managing director of the Competence Network Information Technology to Support the Integration of People with Disabilities (KI-I). He studied computer science and data engineering. In 2003 he finished his PhD at the Johannes Kepler University Linz. During his work he was involved in numerous projects directly with industrial and business partners as well as EC-funded projects in the areas of e-inclusion, medicine and tourism applications. His current research work is related to the use of information and communication technology for people with disabilities that concerns the field of assistive technology as well as accessibility and usability of modern IT and the internet.

Arie Reichel is a Professor and the Dean of the Guilford Glazer School of Business and Management, Ben-Gurion University of the Negev, Israel. His main research interests are service marketing and tourism management.

Stephen Schweinsberg is a Lecturer in the School of Leisure, Sport and Tourism at the University of Technology, Sydney. His recently completed PhD considered the development of frameworks to assess the role of nature tourism as an agent of economic and social change in Australian rural communities. His PhD study was supported through a Sustainable Tourism Cooperative Research Centre (STCRC) Industry Scholarship, jointly funded by TTF Australia: Tourism and Transport Forum and the Australian Sport and Tourism Youth Foundation. Stephen has published in a range of academic forums including *Australian Planner*, the *Finnish Journal of Tourism Research*, *Australasian Parks and Leisure* and *Geographical Research*. He has completed technical reports for the Australian Commonwealth Government and the STCRC and has graduate and undergraduate teaching experience in the School of Leisure, Sport and Tourism (UTS), the Graduate School of the Environment (Macquarie University) and the School of Geosciences (University of Sydney).

Gareth Shaw is Professor of Retail and Tourism Management at the University of Exeter Business School and also currently an Innovation Fellow at the Advanced Institute of Management. He was formerly Professor of Human Geography at Exeter and has a BA and PhD in Human Geography. He has worked on numerous research projects related to retail development, all of which have been funded by major grant awarding bodies. He has written widely within tourism and produced key texts on tourism studies. He has also acted as a consultant for many local, national and international organizations, including UNESCO, The National Trust, American Express, The European Union and Amoco Oil. He is an elected member of the International Academy for the Study of Tourism.

Jennifer Small is a Senior Lecturer in the School of Leisure, Sport and Tourism at the University of Technology, Sydney, having joined the School in 1994. She has a background in environmental psychology, urban planning and tourism management. She commenced her academic career as a tutor at the ANU and then worked as an academic researcher in the UK and Australia in environmental psychology, urban planning and tourism. Her specific research interest is tourist behaviour from a Critical Tourism approach, focusing on equity and social justice issues in tourism. She is a registered psychologist and a Co-ordinator of the Council for Australian University Tourism and Hospitality Education (CAUTHE) Special Interest Group, Critical Approaches in Tourism and Hospitality.

Chris Veitch is an independent consultant with an interest in accessible tourism. After gaining a First Class degree in Tourism Management at London South Bank University, he was a policy executive in the English Tourism Council (ETC) managing projects to improve the accessibility of tourism in England. In 2003 he set up his own practice and has been involved in significant European projects to improve accessible information for consumers as well as helping to produce online toolkits with a number of regions in England encouraging tourism businesses to improve their accessibility.

Yawei Wang is currently an Assistant Professor of Marketing in the School of Business at Montclair State University in the US. She develops an interest and expertise in the areas of leisure, tourism and marketing with specialisation in the mature travel market. Besides her research focus on mature tourism, she also expands her interest in other areas such as consumer behaviour and sports marketing. She teaches both tourism and marketing courses. Prior to joining Montclair State University, she worked with the Gerontology Research Interdisciplinary Team in the College of Health Education and Human Development at Clemson University in South Carolina.

Foreword

It is my great pleasure to recommend *Accessible Tourism: Concepts and Issues* as a fine addition to academic writing and industry practice.

While the economic importance of tourism is undeniable within developing and developed nations, tourism is also an agent for social change by promoting human rights and sustainability. Accessible Tourism provides a wonderful link between human rights, sustainability and tourism, affirming that one cannot exist without the other.

This important book connects the economic growth potential of tourism with a very important area of social change, an ageing population and increasing rates of disability. For tourism to be a true social agent of change, equal opportunities for all society groups to participate independently and with dignity in tourism activities must be assured.

The World Tourism Organization (UNWTO) works to promote 'responsible, sustainable and universally accessible tourism'. In particular, Article 7 of the UNWTO Global Code of Ethics for Tourism approved by the UN on the 'Right to Tourism' states that 'family, youth, student and senior tourism and tourism for people with disabilities, should be encouraged and facilitated'. *Accessible Tourism: Concepts and Issues* progresses our knowledge and understanding in this important area and supports both tourism destinations and organizations as they work towards total tourism accessibility.

Dr Taleb Rifai
Secretary General
United Nations World Tourism Organization

Chapter 1

Introduction: From Disabled Tourists to Accessible Tourism

S. DARCY and D. BUHALIS

Accessible Tourism Concepts/Issues

Inclusion, disability, the ageing population and tourism are increasingly important areas of study due to their implications for both tourism demand and supply. This book therefore sets out to explore and document the current theoretical approaches, foundations and issues in the study of accessible tourism. Accessible tourism is an evolving area of academic study and industry practice. As with other areas of tourism, the field is multidisciplinary, with influences from geography, disability studies, economics, public policy, psychology, social psychology, organisational management, postmodern cultural studies, marketing, architecture and medicine, to name a few.

In drawing together the 19 chapters and 25 contributors to this volume the editors have woven a broader social constructionist approach to understanding the dimensions of the accessible tourism phenomena. The rationale for this is a belief that disability is a social construct, which is characterised by varying cultural responses over different time periods. Within the tourism field, tourists with disabilities have a variety of motivations, desired experiences and support requirements. The heterogeneous nature of tourists with disabilities means that if managers are to pursue an enabling, inclusive approach to the provision of tourism products and services, they must approach tourists with disabilities in the same way that they would approach any other consumer group. They should be aware of the group characteristics through understanding the socially constructed nature of the accessible tourism phenomena, but tailor the individual's experiences by discussing their needs directly with them.

This chapter therefore presents an introduction to the book by examining the key concepts underlying the chapters to be presented. These concepts include:

- Defining tourism and the tourism system.
- Human rights.
- Social model, disability and embodiment.

1

- Disability/ageing nexus.
- Market segment.
- Enabling environments.
- Universal design.
- Defining accessible tourism.

Defining Tourism and the Tourism System

This book is focused on synthesizing a number of theoretical approaches to enrich our understanding of accessible tourism. Given this, it is essential to understand the parameters of the tourism phenomena before subsequently focusing discussion on the accessible tourism sector. The United Nations World Tourism Organisation (UNWTO) has defined tourism as a diverse industry, which is a central economic driver for socio-economic development in a number of areas/destinations throughout the world:

> Today, the business volume of tourism equals or even surpasses that of oil exports, food products or automobiles in many regions around the world. Tourism has become one of the major players in international commerce, and represents at the same time one of the main income sources for many developing countries. This global spread of tourism, especially in industrialising and developing states has produced economic and employment benefits in many related sectors – from construction to agriculture or telecommunications. (United Nations World Tourism Organisation, ND)

The sheer range of industries that are represented under the banner of 'tourism', as well as the number of tentacles which exist between tourism and other sectors of the economy, has made tourism a difficult subject for stakeholders to achieve definitional consensus on. Weaver and Lawton (2010) note that it was only in the 1980s that the UNWTO managed to align the majority of countries to a standardised set of tourism definitions. Despite this, debate persists on a number of central issues relating to the study of tourism, including whether or not there is such a thing as a single identifiable tourism industry.

The presence of complex inter-relationships between a diverse range of stakeholders and industry sectors has led some commentators to pursue a systems approach to the study of tourism management (Chan & Huang, 2004; Holden, 2008; Inskeep, 1991; Jamal *et al.*, 2004; Jamal & Getz, 1995; Laws, 1991; Leiper, 1990; Page, 1995). Tourism system theories recognise that 'all development sectors and support facilities and services are inter-related with one another and with the natural environment and society of the area' (Inskeep, 1991: 27). One of the most commonly cited approaches to tourism systems study was proposed by Leiper (1990) who identified that they are composed of five interdependent elements:

(1) At least one tourist.
(2) At least one tourist-generating region.
(3) At least one transit region.
(4) At least one tourist destination.
(5) A travel and tourism industry that facilitates movement within the system.

Leiper's systems model is often held up as the starting point for understanding how system philosophies can be applied to the study of tourism. Within Leiper's model tourists are identified as being influenced by the human, socio-cultural, economic, technological, physical, political and legal environments in which they are operating (Weaver & Lawton, 2010). As accessibility is a social construct, the exact nature of the relationship between the tourist with disability and the rest of the tourism system is not constant. This issue will be explored in this volume in the context of the changing experience expectations amongst tourists with disabilities, as well as an increased level of acceptance of disabled people by other stakeholders in a tourism systems environment.

Human Rights Approaches

As Hurst (2004) suggests, international human rights conventions supported by nationally-based legislation can bring about substantial material change in accessible tourism when vigorously implemented. The most recent addition to the United Nations' conventions is the *Convention on the Rights of People with Disabilities* (United Nations, 2006, 2008). An unprecedented number of nations signed this convention. However, the relative success of the convention must be supported by nationally based legislation, not just in the areas of disability discrimination but also in the areas of national building codes, standards for access and mobility, and across administrator procedures. Even when these are in place, there still needs to be a political will to implement and enforce the legislation. While a number of countries have a significant history of having nationally based disability discrimination legislation, building codes and standards for access, there are significant institutional problems with their implementation (Handley, 2001).

In the tourism context, a number of US, UK and Australian papers have identified the introduction of the human rights legislation as an important event for improving the tourism conditions for people with disabilities (Darcy, 2002b; Gallagher & Hull, 1996; Goodall, 2002; Goodall *et al.*, 2004; Griffin Dolon, 2000; Miller & Kirk, 2002; Peniston, 1996;

Upchurch & Seo, 1996). Yet, the number of disability discrimination complaints has continued to rise (Darcy & Taylor, 2009). While the reasons for this are not clear, there is no doubt that disability discrimination legislation, as an evolving set of benchmarks, means that interpreting the law is dynamic and ongoing. For example, there has been a greater number of complaints made against the providers of websites by people who are vision-impaired or blind and this has become one of the areas for research focus in tourism (Foggin *et al.*, 2003; Oertel, 2004; Shi, 2006; Williams & Rattray, 2005; Williams *et al.*, 2006; Williams *et al.*, 2004). Lastly, there is recognition that there is a very different level of compliance between developed and developing world, East and West, and matters of cultural difference when it comes to defining disability, adopting and implementing human rights and associated legislation. Reports by the European Union and UN ESCAP (United Nations Economic and Social Commission for Asia and the Pacific) have outlined the significant differences between countries within Europe and the Asia-Pacific respectively (Eurostat, 2005; Toegankelijkheidsbureau v.z.w Hasselt & LIVING Research and Development s.p.r.l. Brussels, 2001; UN ESCAP, 2008; USAID, 2009).

Social Model, Disability and Embodiment

As outlined in Chapter 2, this book takes a social approach to disability, which challenges the underlying discourse of identifying disability as medical problem. The medical model views the person's impairment – their embodiment – as their disability, their 'personal' problem, which directly causes their deficit through disease, trauma or health conditions (Oliver, 1996). This requires medical intervention in the form of individual treatment to normalise their disabled body. Management of their disability is aimed at 'normalising' the person's bodily functions. Health care is viewed as the main issue and at the political level, it is health care policy that is the focus of intervention.

The social model of disability in contrast sees the issue mainly as the 'socially constructed' environment that excludes people with disabilities from participation. In this case, it is not the person's impairment that disables them but the complex collection of social environments, practices and attitudes, which are imposed on top of a person's impairment. Hence, the disability is created through the disabling social environment that requires social action to change and it is the collective responsibility of society to make the environmental and attitudinal modifications necessary for the full participation of people with disabilities into all areas of citizenship. The issue is, therefore, placed on the political, economic, social and attitudinal agendas and is primarily ideological. Social change is sought by people with disabilities through individual empowerment, collective advocacy and is supported at the political level through the United Nations' *Convention of the Rights of People with Disabilities* (2006) and national human rights legislation.

Yet, this ideological transformation of a person's impairment into their disability has further layers of complexity. Rather than being a one-dimensional construct, disability is multidimensional with an understanding of a person's embodiment central to developing enabling practices to provide accessible environments and attitudes. Most human rights and legislative approaches enshrine a multidimensional construct of disability within their approaches. However, rather than focusing on a person's deficits, as has historically been done within medical approaches (World Health Organization, 2002), the United Nations' (2006) Convention focuses far more on the dimensions of disability as an outcome of their access needs. These dimensions of disability and their resultant access needs have been identified as:

- Mobility.
- Vision.
- Hearing.
- Intellectual/cognitive/learning.
- Mental health.
- Sensitivities – including respiratory, food and chemical.
- Other.

The advantage of the above conceptualisation is that the focus is on the provision of the broad dimensions for access to create enabling environments, as advocated by social approaches to disability (Oliver, 1990, 1996; Swain *et al.*, 2004; Thomas, 1999, 2007; Thomson, 1997).

Disability and Ageing

The US National Institute on Ageing identifies that in 2006 500 million people worldwide were 65 and older. However, by 2030 this is estimated to increase to 1 billion or one in every eight people, with the most rapid increase in the 65+ cohort in developing countries. This is an increase of 140% (Dobriansky *et al.*, 2007). This situation is largely reflected in all Western developed nations with a noticeable difference in Asian countries where ageing is occurring at a faster rate (Altman, 1975; World Health Organization, 2007a). These trends have considerable implications for global tourism (Dwyer, 2005).

What is often not as clearly understood is that there is a significant relationship between ageing and rates of disability (Uhlenberg, 2009). For example, the Australian data shows a person is 14 times more likely to have a disability at age 65 than they are as a four-year-old (Australian Bureau of Statistics, 2004). The best estimates suggest that about 10% of the world's population has some form of disability and this equates to an estimated 650 million people worldwide (Sharma, 2008). The World Health Organization (WHO) has reflected concerns of ageing with the recent release of *Global Age-friendly Cities: A Global Guide* (2007a). The guide offers directions for urban planners, but also instils accountability through providing a checklist that older citizens can use to 'monitor progress towards more age-friendly cities' (WHO, 2007b). This is timely in that the approach taken mirrors a great deal of what disabled activists have been lobbying for over many years – accessible environments for ease of access. When the WHO document is read in conjunction with the United Nations *Millennium Development Goals* (2009) it is clear that no city can be planning for a sustainable future unless it incorporates all elements of accessibility into city planning (see section on universal design later).

Market Segment

Accessible tourism, like other niche areas of tourism, has been described most commonly through an estimation of the market size (Keroul, 1995; Touche Ross, 1993) and, more lately, the estimation of the economic contribution of the group (Buhalis *et al.*, 2005; Darcy, 1998; HarrisInteractive Market Research, 2005b; Neumann & Reuber, 2004). While providing a useful way for outsiders to understand the size of the group, it does little to assist in understanding the complexity of the market segment (Dolnicar, 2002). Quite simply, what are the characteristics of the accessible tourism market that may make it a distinctive market segment as opposed to a consideration across market segments in tourism? (Wedel & Kamakura, 2000).

No papers have explicitly reviewed the market segmentation of accessible tourism – a rich area for further research. However, many papers have started to provide insight into the different aspects of the accessible tourism market through predominantly focusing on one dimension of disability or access – mainly mobility (Avis *et al.*, 2005; Bi *et al.*, 2007; Burnett, 1996; Burnett & Bender-Baker, 2001; Darcy, 2002a; Gallagher & Hull, 1996; Lovelock, 2010; Ray & Ryder, 2003; Woodside & Etzel, 1980). Within mobility or physical disability related research, the most notable areas of market segmentation occur due to the level of support needs of the individuals.

Fewer studies or papers have looked at cross disability research due to the complexity of employing methodology across different dimensions of embodiment (Darcy, 2010; HarrisInteractive Market Research, 2005a). A number of chapters in this book will address embodiments not previously presented in the research literature. The book itself also opens discussion about whether accessible tourism is a specific market segment, contemplates the nature of the market segment, discusses the characteristics that may contribute towards the development of market segmentation for the group that may be pertinent and examines how industry has engaged with these groups.

Enabling Environments

Following from social model and social constructionist approaches came the seminal work that looked at articulating what disabling barriers are socially constructed and, most importantly, how to move beyond the negative to positive and create enabling environments (Swain *et al.*, 2004). In attempting to outline and then operationalise the social change elements of the developing disability studies theory, Swain *et al.* (2004) use their collective experience across welfare, education, employment, built environment, the media, housing, technology, communication, leisure, independent living, organisational politics and others to show a way forward to enable environments, attitudes and society. Others in each of these fields have sought to move forward, empirically measure, challenge dominant institutional constraints and provide strategies for change within each context (Steinfeld & Danford, 1999). For example, there has been a great deal of work done on the creation of enabling practices to ensure accessibility of buildings and around cities (Imrie, 1996, 2000, 2005; Sawyer & Bright, 2006).

In a tourism context, the most directly relevant work has come from the inclusion of leisure constraints theory, which is a distinct area of research within the field of leisure studies. Leisure constraints is concerned '... about barriers, non-participation in recreation activities and lack of leisure opportunities has always been an important progenitor of [public sector] park, recreation, and leisure' (Goodale & Witt, 1989: 422). This non-participant focus has a rich resonance with disability studies where tourism studies has traditionally been predicated on the idea of the tourist as consumer and factors that stimulate or facilitate demand (see Darcy, 2004: 77–84). Smith (1987) works from leisure constraints theory in the first examination and categorisation of barriers to leisure-travel for people with disabilities – intrinsic, environmental and interactive barriers. Once constraints are identified the field then focuses on a relative hierarchy of the constraints and how constraints are negotiated for those that still want to participate (Jackson & Scott, 1999).

Leisure constraints theory became established through a series of studies focusing on the specific nature of tourism constraints (Darcy, 1998; Turco *et al.*, 1998). However, many other studies by their nature identify barriers or constraints to the tourism experiences of people with disabilities without applying a leisure constraints framework (e.g. Burnett & Bender-Baker, 2001; Darcy, 2002a; Israeli, 2002; Ray & Ryder, 2003). The approach can also be garnered in an interpretive approach to provide a deeper understanding of the constraints faced and the way that they are negotiated in tourism. For example, Daniels *et al.* (2005) use leisure constraints theory to examine consumer travel stories from a disability travel website, concluding an interactive rather than a hierarchical relationship between constraint categorizations. The combination of Swain *et al.*'s (2004) disability studies approach to creating enabling environments and leisure and tourism constraints theory provides a rich foundation for better understanding accessible tourism. As we will see, a number of the chapters develop these ideas.

Universal Design

In bringing together some excellent work by a team of researchers from Hong Kong, disability is more than an access issue and there is a complex interplay between the individual, the environment and the tourism industry (Packer *et al.*, 2007; Yau *et al.*, 2004). Yet, an emerging concept within the disability, design and architecture literature is universal design (Preiser & Ostroff, 2001). Universal design moves beyond access and inclusion to incorporate:

> ... the design of products and environments to be usable by all people, to the greatest extent possible, without the need for adaptation or specialised design ... The intent of the universal design concept is to simplify life for everyone by making products, communications and the built environment more usable by more people at little or no extra cost. The universal design concept targets all people of all ages, sizes and abilities. (Center for Universal Design, 2009)

This universal design philosophy was an important component of the Australian national research agenda for accessible tourism, which called for the industry to 'operationalise universal design and easy living principles within tourism product development' (Darcy, 2006: ix). To date, however, the application of universal design principles to accessible tourism has remained conceptual (Rains, 2004; Walsh, 2004) or applied specifically to the accommodation sector (Rossetti, 2009). Yet, the foundation of the concept is eminently applicable and sensible to a service industry like tourism. Universal design is based on seven principles to facilitate equitable access across the lifespan (Center for Universal Design, 2009; Preiser & Ostroff, 2001). They are:

- Principle 1: Equitable Use.
- Principle 2: Flexibility in Use.
- Principle 3: Simple and Intuitive Use.
- Principle 4: Perceptible Information.
- Principle 5: Tolerance for Error.

- Principle 6: Low Physical Effort.
- Principle 7: Size and Space for Approach and Use (Center for Universal Design, 2009).

The implication of this design approach is that access would become central to design, rather than an add-on for compliance reasons. As indicated in Figure 1.1, by Darcy and Dickson (2009), it is not only those with access needs who benefit but all users as a universally designed environment considers occupational and safety issues, making it a safer environment for all as well as supporting more efficient operational management of facilities. There has been a call for the tourism industry to adopt universal design principles as a foundation to achieving greater social sustainability (Rains, 2004; Walsh, 2004). This foresight not only places the industry in a more appropriate, effective and efficient position to benefit from triple bottom line accountability but aligns the industry with the United Nations *Millennium Development Goals* (United Nations, 2009).

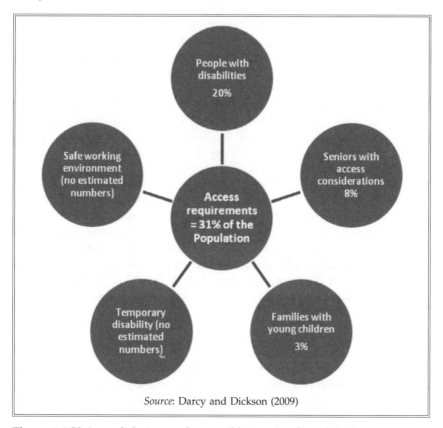

Source: Darcy and Dickson (2009)

Figure 1.1 Universal design and accessible tourism beneficiaries

Accessible Tourism: Towards a Definition

It is interesting that while accessible tourism has been developing as an area of academic study and industry practice, there has been relatively little discussion defining the field. Most study has focused on the experiences of people with disabilities while travelling without an articulation of the defining elements of the field. The field has been variously described as disabled/disability tourism (Buhalis, 2005; Burnett & Bender-Baker, 2001; Daniels *et al.*, 2005; Darcy, 2002a; O'Neill & Ali Knight, 2000; Shaw & Coles, 2004; Yau *et al.*, 2004), easy access tourism (Cameron, 2000; Tourism New South Wales, 2005), barrier-free tourism (Cameron *et al.*, 2003; Community Based Rehabilitation Development and Training Centre, 2000; ESCAP, 2000; Foggin *et al.*, 2003; Vignuda, 2001), inclusive tourism (Buhalis *et al.*, 2005; Shaw, 2007; Yates, 2007), universal tourism (Darcy, 2006) and, more recently, accessible tourism (Buhalis *et al.*, 2006; Darcy, 2006, 2010; Darcy *et al.*, 2008; Darcy & Dickson, 2009; Shaw, 2007; Wu & Cheng, 2008). For the purposes of this book, we are adopting the term accessible tourism and will briefly discuss the adopted definition.

Definitions are dynamic and evolving and, hence, there is no real agreement as to one definition. Most definitions focus on the functional elements of tourism being accessible to all people. Darcy and Dickson (2009) provided an extension to this definition through the Whole of Life Approach to disability – the beneficiaries are identified in Figure 1.1. This approach has a nexus to universal design where access is not isolated to disability but is more broadly linked to people's embodiment over their lifespan (United Nations, 2009; World Health Organization, 2007). This provided the opportunity to be far more inclusive of a broader group of people who benefit from access provisions. Yet, there needs to be recognition that for accessible tourism to occur, a process needs to be in place that is firmly based on values guiding the direction of development, products and services. In this context, the principles of universal design outlined above, together with the values of independence, equity and dignity provide a sound foundation on which to establish the functional elements required for individuals tourism experiences through the framework provided by the tourism system (Leiper, 2003) and its stakeholders (Weaver & Opperman, 2000). As such, the following definition is used for this book:

> Accessible tourism is a form of tourism that involves collaborative processes between stakeholders that enables people with access requirements, including mobility, vision, hearing and cognitive dimensions of access, to function independently and with equity and dignity through the delivery of universally designed tourism products, services and environments. This definition adopts a whole of life approach where people through their lifespan benefit from accessible tourism

provision. These include people with permanent and temporary disabilities, seniors, obese, families with young children and those working in safer and more socially sustainably designed environments. (Adapted from Darcy & Dickson, 2009: 34)

Book Structure and Chapter Summaries

To begin the process of understanding the socially constructed nature of accessible tourism, Chapters 2 and 3 begin by defining the core terms of disability and accessibility. In Chapter 2, Darcy and Buhalis review the contemporary models and discourses of disability to provide a theoretical base on which to understand tourism from a disability perspective and, hence, the development of accessible tourism. An important aspect of this chapter is the canvassing of the different aspects of the medical and social conceptualizations of disability. The authors also provide a detailed breakdown of the dimensions of disability. Understanding the different dimensions of disability is a necessary precursor to understanding the ways in which disability may act as a barrier to participation. In Chapter 3, Eichhorn and Buhalis further characterise the various physical access, attitudinal and information barriers that govern disabled participation in tourism. The prevalence of barriers will vary throughout the world due to a number of external forces including situational disability legislation. In Chapter 4, Shaw and Veitch provide a case study analysis of the evolution of disability discrimination legislation in the United Kingdom, focusing on the recent uptake of the Disability Discrimination Act. In addition to focusing on the legislative context of their operations, operators must also be mindful of the benefits of using assistive technologies to ensure equitable access to information within a tourism marketing context

With a generic understanding of some of the constraints and barriers that may govern disabled peoples' participation in tourism, the next section of this volume fleshes out our understanding of the various experiences of tourists with disabilities. In Chapter 5, Small and Darcy consider the tourists with disabilities experience through the lens of critical theory in tourism studies and critical disability studies theory. Focusing on the lived experiences of tourists with disabilities the authors have sought to create a direct link between experience and needs, documenting their personal experiences of people moving through different stages of the tourism system. Further developing this idea of a personal relationship between experience and tourism participation, Foggin in Chapter 6 presents the results of research which has sought to examine the relationship between the inner (attitudes, feelings, etc.) and outer worlds (natural, built, political environment) of tourists with disabilities through the lens of Paul Ricoeur's concept of life and narrative

A core facet of much of the existing tourist experience research relates to the phenomenology of the tourist experience (Cohen, 1979; Mannell & Iso-Ahola, 1987) where it is proposed that tourists are heterogeneous with respect to how they engage with host cultures and landscapes. With this in mind Fullagar in Chapter 7 considers the experiences of people with mental health needs in the accessible tourism market. By seeking to consider the relationship between emotional distress and tourism experiences of 11 women suffering postnatal depression, the chapter contributes a feminist perspective to the growing body of research into wellness tourism. Understanding the experiences of distinct sections of the accessible tourism market is a necessary precursor to understanding the ways in which they relate to other actors within a tourism encounter.

An important characteristic of Fullagar's work is the notion that becoming travellers involves a transition from fear to freedom. This transition, for Fullagar, involves women taking 'a number of emotional risks and confront[ing] fears such as risking upsetting their husbands and the assumed gender order of the household'. The lessons that can be learned from this discussion of how women travellers can become assertive and challenge traditional gender relations resonates with a broader debate of how stakeholders interact in an accessible tourism setting. In Chapter 8, Arola, Cooper and Cooper explore the experiences of people with disabilities on the tourism stage as they react to the presence of other actors. This study is undertaken in the context of the Goffmanian Approach. The ways in which tourists with disabilities interact with other actors is similarly canvassed by Poria, Reichel and Brandt in Chapter 9. In the course of a detailed study of blind people's tourism experiences the authors identify that the relationship with tourism staff can serve as one of the core difficulties for blind people seeking to participate in tourism activities. The managerial implications of this study stress Darcy's (2002a) reference to the social model of disability, which emphasises that attention should be given to addressing the way society approaches people with impairments rather than viewing a disability as a person's shortcoming. The notion that the tourism industry should develop in a manner which encourages access for all is explored by Shaw and Veitch in Chapter 10. Through a discussion of the demographics of the accessible tourism market, the authors identify that constraints and barriers to disabled participation in tourism often have both physical and social (service and experience offerings) dimensions. The challenges for industry therefore become to provide inclusive tourism products, which emphasise links to mainstream tourism markets and play down the existence of contrived differences between disabled and mainstream travellers.

The notion that tourists with disabilities seek an experience, as opposed to stylised and contrived access to a destination, is taken up by Patterson in Chapter 11 and Wang in Chapter 12. Both these chapters focus on the aged traveller's participation in tourism activities. Through a discussion of aged traveller demographics, the tourism constraints of an ageing population, the aged traveller's accessibility requirements and their desired experiences, the chapters draw attention to the need of the industry to understand the unique experience preferences of aged tourists. It is through such understanding that the industry can move to install appropriately trained staff and other facilities/infrastructure to allow mature travellers to fulfil their desired tourism experiences.

The provision of access infrastructure is one of the most obvious visual features of any accessible tourism enterprise. Whilst disabled access points are necessary foundations for the provision of tourism experiences, they are not always practical in tourism environments, which are characterised by strict planning regulations. In Chapter 13, Pearn explores the uneasy relationship between heritage area conservation and the provision of accessible tourism environments. The impetus for this study was the notion that architectural constraints barriers to access for the disabled can have the effect of confining visitors with disabilities to back regions, a situation which is contrary to the principles of access for all.

The final section of this volume concerns the tourism industry itself and the development of an economically profitable accessible tourism sector. In Chapter 14, Darcy and Dwyer present the results of national visitor data research, which considered the economic contribution of tourists with a disability to the Australian economy. Drawing together secondary data from sources including the Disability and Ageing and Carers Survey and the National Visitors Survey, the authors have provided information on the level of support needs, market segment comparison between disabled and non-disabled travellers, and the purchasing patterns of tourists with disabilities. Darcy and Dwyer note that a number of supply-side constraints, including accommodation requirements, visitor support needs and desired experiences, may underpin the performance of the disability tourism sector.

Ensuring the sustainability of such a complex and diverse sector as tourism requires that industry actively engages with sustainability doctrines such as the triple bottom line and stakeholder analysis. By breaking down the often hazy notion of sustainability into more manageable economic, social and environmental components of development, the triple bottom line can be a means of both defining and operationalising sustainability. John Elkington formalised discussion of the triple bottom line in 1994. The early framing of the triple bottom line was with respect to business and sustainable capitalism, a product of Elkington's work since late 1987 with the firm SustainAbility (see http://www.sustainability.com/). The triple bottom line gained widespread exposure with the 1997 publication of Elkington's *Cannibals with Forks: The Triple Bottom Line of 21st Century Business* (Elkington, 1999). Many of the principles behind the term had, however, already been canvassed in the 1975 *Corporate Report* (Gray & Milne, 2002) and *The Green Consumer Guide* (Elkington, 1989). The close relationship between business sustainability and the triple bottom line has perpetuated the notion of triple bottom line reporting (Sustain-Ability & United Nations Environment Programme, 2000). The triple bottom line is the focus of Darcy, Cameron and Pegg in Chapter 15 where they consider the business case for adopting universal design principles in the disability sector as a foundation to achieving triple bottom line sustainability. Core aspects of this work include the development of financial, as well as environmental and social, report cards for business. Understanding the range of stakeholders who may have a perspective on the composition of such sustainability instruments is the subject of Chapter 16. In this chapter Michopoulou and Buhalis elaborate on the possible range of accessible tourism stakeholders making reference to possible constraints on their participation, as well as developing a classification for mainstream, mixed and specialist service providers.

The service providers identified in Chapter 16 include a number of well known businesses such as the Marriott Hotel, Lonely Planet and Thomas Cook Travel. In order for these and other organisations to provide appropriate services to the disabled there must be recognition of the changing nature of assistive technologies. An explanation of assistive technologies is provided in Chapter 17 by Pühretmair and Nussbaum. The volume then concludes with a chapter by Michopoulou and Buhalis, who consider some of the challenges inherent in ensuring inclusive/assistive technologies are embraced by the tourism sector. Several challenges were identified, including interoperability, content integration, personalisation and accessible design.

Conclusion/Welcome

Rather than concluding the chapter, we, the editors, would like to welcome you to an examination of an area that we are passionate about and we hope that you will engage in. Together we can contribute to the development of an emerging area of academic study and contribute to expanding upon some of the innovative industry practice that is already occurring around the world. While this book focuses on concepts and issues, a second book is published in parallel to present a series of best practice international case studies that highlight innovative industry practice, government policy approaches, national tourist office coordination strategies and provocative third sector advocacy of accessible tourism. The combination of the supply, demand and coordination/regulation perspectives creates an exciting environment for the mixed economy of accessible tourism. We strongly suggest that this book is used in conjunction with the international case studies to highlight the very practical implementation of complex concepts and issues. Let the accessible tourism journey begin ...

References

Altman, I. (1975) *The Environment and Social Behavior*. Monterey, CA: Brooks-Cole Publishing Co.

Australian Bureau of Statistics. (2004) *Disability, Ageing and Carers – Summary Of Findings, 2003 (Cat No. 4430.0)*. Canberra: Australian Bureau of Statistics.

Avis, A.H., Card, J.A. and Cole, S.T. (2005) Accessibility and attitudinal barriers encountered by travelers with physical disabilities. *Tourism Review International* 8, 239–248.

Bi, Y., Card, J.A. and Cole, S.T. (2007) Accessibility and attitudinal barriers encountered by Chinese travellers with physical disabilities. *International Journal of Tourism Research* 9, 205–216.

Buhalis, D. (2005) Disability Tourism – OSSATE Links. On WWW at http://www.ossate.org/. Accessed 18.9.2005.

Buhalis, D., Michopoulou, E., Eichhorn, V. and Miller, G. (2005) *Accessibility market and stakeholder analysis – One-Stop-Shop for Accessible Tourism in Europe (OSSATE)*. Surrey: University of Surrey.

Buhalis, D., Michopoulou, E., Michailidis, S. and Ambrose, I. (2006, 6–9 February) *An eTourism Portal for the Disabled Tourism Market in Europe: The OSSATE Portal Design (One-Stop-Shop for Accessible Tourism)*. Paper presented at the Council for Australian University Tourism and Hospitality Education Incorporated 16th annual conference – To the City and Beyond, Melbourne.

Burnett, J.J. (1996) What services marketers need to know about the mobility-disabled consumer. *Journal of Services Marketing* 10 (3), 3–20.

Burnett, J.J. and Bender-Baker, H. (2001) Assessing the travel–related behaviors of the mobility–disabled consumer. *Journal of Travel Research* 40 (1), 4–11.

Cameron, B. (2000) *Easy Access Australia* (2nd edn). Kew, Vic: Kew Publishing.

Cameron, B., Darcy, S., and Foggin, S.E.A. (eds) (2003) *Barrier-Free Tourism for People with Disabilities in the Asian and Pacific Region*. New York: UN ESCAP.

Center for Universal Design. (2009) Universal Design Principles. On WWW at http://www.design.ncsu.edu/cud/about_ud/about_ud.htm. Accessed 20.5.2009.

Chan, S-L. and Huang, S-L. (2004) A systems approach for the development of a sustainable community – the application of the sensitivity model (SM). *Journal of Environmental Management* 72 (3), 133–147.

Cohen, E. (1979) A phenomenology of tourist experiences. *Sociology* 13 (2), 179.

Community Based Rehabilitation Development and Training Centre. (2000) *The Bali Declaration on Barrier-free Tourism for People with Disabilities*. Bali: CBRDTC/ESCAP.

Daniels, M.J., Drogin Rodgers, E.B. and Wiggins, B.P. (2005) 'Travel Tales': An interpretive analysis of constraints and negotiations to pleasure travel as experienced by persons with physical disabilities. *Tourism Management* 26 (6), 919–930.

Darcy, S. (1998) *Anxiety to Access: Tourism Patterns and Experiences of New South Wales People with a Physical Disability*. Sydney: Tourism New South Wales.

Darcy, S. (2002a) Marginalised participation: Physical disability, high support needs and tourism. *Journal of Hospitality and Tourism Management* 9 (1), 61–72.

Darcy, S. (2002b, 16–18 May) People with disabilities and tourism in Australia: A human rights analysis. Paper presented at the Tourism and Well Being – 2nd Tourism Industry and Education Symposium, Jyvaskyla, Finland.

Darcy, S. (2004) Disabling journeys: the social relations of tourism for people with impairments in Australia – an analysis of government tourism authorities and accommodation sector practices and discourses. At http://epress.lib.uts.edu.au/dspace/handle/2100/260.

Darcy, S. (2006) Setting a research agenda for accessible tourism. In C. Cooper, T.D. Lacy and L. Jago (eds) *STCRC Technical Report Series* (p. 48). At http://www.crctourism.com.au/BookShop/BookDetail.aspx?d=473.

Darcy, S. (2010) Inherent complexity: Disability, accessible tourism and accommodation information preferences. *Tourism Management* 31 (6), 816–826.

Darcy, S., Cameron, B., Pegg, S. and Packer, T. (2008) Technical Report 90042: Developing Business Cases for Accessible Tourism, STCRC technical report. At http://www.crctourism.com.au/default.aspxg.

Darcy, S. and Dickson, T. (2009) A whole-of-life approach to tourism: The case for accessible tourism experiences. *Journal of Hospitality and Tourism Management* 16 (1), 32–44.

Darcy, S. and Taylor, T. (2009) Disability citizenship: An Australian human rights analysis of the cultural industries. *Leisure Studies* 28 (4), 419–441.

Dobriansky, P., Suzman, R. and Hodes, R. (2007) Why population aging matters: A global perspective. National Institute on Aging, National Institutes of Health, US Department of Health and Human Services, US Department of State. On WWW at news.thomasnet.com/IMT/archives/2007/03. Accessed 31.7.2010.

Dolnicar, S. (2002) A review of data-driven market segmentation in tourism. *Journal of Travel & Tourism Marketing* 12 (1), 1–22.

Dwyer, L. (2005) Trends underpinning global tourism in the coming decade. In W. Theobald (ed.) *Global Tourism* (pp. 529–545). Burlington, MA: Butterworth Heinemann.

Elkington, J. (1989) *The Green Consumer Guide*. Ringwood, Victoria: Penguin.

Elkington, J. (1999) *Cannibals with Forks: The Triple Bottom Line of 21st Century Business*. Oxford: Capstone.

ESCAP (2000) *Promotion of Barrier-free Tourism for People with Disabilities in the Asia and Pacific Region* (No. ctctid3_7e). Bangkok: Economic and Social Commission for Asia Pacific.

Eurostat (2005) Population and social conditions: Percentual distribution of types of disability by sex and age group. At http://epp.eurostat.cec.eu.int.

Foggin, S. E. A., Darcy, S. and Cameron, B. (2003) Vers un tourisme sans barrières: Initiatives dans la région Asie-Pacifique. *TÉOROS: Revue de recherche en tourisme* 22 (3), 16–19.

Gallagher, J.M. and Hull, A.H. (1996) Cruise ship accommodations for passengers with physical limitations due to disability or age. *American Journal of Occupational Therapy* 50 (8), 685–687.

Goodale, T.L. and Witt, P.A. (1989) Recreation Non-participation and barriers to leisure. In E.L. Jackson and T.L. Burton (eds) *Understanding Leisure and Recreation: Mapping the Past, Charting the Future*. State College, PA: Venture Publishing.

Goodall, B. (2002, 16–18 May) Disability discrimination legislation and tourism: The case of the United Kingdom. Paper presented at the Tourism and Well Being – 2nd Tourism Industry and Education Symposium, Jyvaskyla, Finland.

Goodall, B., Pottinger, G., Dixon, T. and Russell, H. (2004) Heritage property, tourism and the UK Disability Discrimination Act. *Property Management* 22 (5), 345–357.

Gray, R. and Milne, M. (2002) Sustainability reporting: Who's kidding whom? On WWW at http://www.accaglobal.com/pdfs/environment/newsletter/gray_milne.pdf. Accessed 20.7.2006.

Griffin Dolon, J. (2000) Accessibility, the Americans with Disabilities Act, and the natural environment as a tourist resource. *anatolia: International Journal of Tourism and Hospitality Research* 11 (2), 101–110.

Handley, P. (2001) 'Caught Between a Rock and a Hard Place': Anti-discrimination legislation in the liberal state and the fate of the Australian Disability Discrimination Act. *Australian Journal of Political Science* 36 (3), 515–528.

HarrisInteractive Market Research (2005a, January) Research among adults with disabilities – travel and hospitality. At http://www.opendoorsnfp.org/page3.html.

HarrisInteractive Market Research (2005b) *Research Among Adults with Disabilities – Travel and Hospitality*. Chicago: Open Doors Organization.

Holden, A. (2008) *Environment and Tourism* (2nd edn). London: Routledge.

Hurst, R. (2004) Legislation and human rights. In J. Swain, V. Finkelstein, S. French and M. Oliver (eds) *Disabling Barriers – Enabling Environments* (3rd edn) (pp. 297–302). London: Sage Publications Ltd.

Imrie, R. (1996) *Disability and the City: International Perspectives*. London: Paul Chapman.

Imrie, R. (2000) Disabling environments and the geography of access policies and practices. *Disability & Society* 15 (1), 5–24.

Imrie, R. (2005) *Accessible Housing: Quality, Disability and Design*. Routledge.

Inskeep, E. (1991) *Tourism Planning: An Integrated Sustainable Development Approach*. New York: Van Nostrand Reinhold.

Israeli, A. (2002) A preliminary investigation of the importance of site accessibility factors for disabled tourists. [Swetswise]. *Journal of Travel Research* 41 (1), 101–104.

Jackson, E.L. and Scott, D. (1999) Constraints to leisure. In E.L. Jackson and T.L. Burton (eds) *Leisure Studies: Prospects for the Twenty-first Century* (pp. 299–332). State College, PA: Venture Publishing, Inc.

Jamal, T., Borges, M., Peterson, M., Peterson, T. and Figueiredo, R. (2004) A systems tool for sustainability-based planning: Modelling socio-cultural impacts in rural Texas. *Journal of Tourism Studies* 15 (1), 18–33.

Jamal, T. and Getz, D. (1995) Collaboration theory and community tourism planning. *Annals of Tourism Research* 22 (1), 186–204.

Keroul (1995) *Tourism for People with Restricted Physical Ability*. Quebec: Keroul.

Laws, E. (1991) *Tourism Marketing*. Cheltenham: Stanley Thomas.

Leiper, N. (1990) *Tourism Systems: An Interdisciplinary Perspective, Occasional Paper No. 2*. Massey University: Department of Management Systems/Business Studies Faculty.

Leiper, N. (2003) *Tourism Management* (3rd edn). Sydney: Hospitality Press.

Lovelock, B.A. (2010) Planes, trains and wheelchairs in the bush: Attitudes of people with mobility-disabilities to enhanced motorised access in remote natural settings. *Tourism Management* 31 (3), 357–366.

Mannell, R. and Iso-Ahola, S. (1987) Psychological nature of leisure and tourism experience. *Annals of Tourism Research* 14 (3), 314–331.

Miller, G.A. and Kirk, E. (2002) The Disability Discrimination Act: Time for the stick? *Journal of Sustainable Tourism* 10 (1), 82–88.

Neumann, P. and Reuber, P. (2004) *Economic Impulses of Accessible Tourism for All* (Vol. 526). Berlin: Study commissioned by the Federal Ministry of Economics and Technology & Federal Ministry of Economic and Labour (BMWA).

Oertel, B., Hasse, C., Scheermesser, M., Thio, S.L. and Feil, T. (2004) Accessibility of Tourism Web Sites Within the European Union. Proceedings of the *11th International Conference on Information and Communication Technologies in Tourism (ENTER 2004)*. ISBN 3-211-20669-8, Springer Verlag, pp. 358–368, Cairo, Egypt.

Oliver, M. (1990) *The Politics of Disablement*. Basingstoke, Houndmills: Macmillan.

Oliver, M. (1996) *Understanding Disability: From Theory to Practice*. Basingstoke, Houndmills: Macmillan.

O'Neill, M. and Ali Knight, J. (2000, 2–5 February 2000) *Accessing the Disability Tourism Dollar – Implications for Hotel Enterprises in Western Australia*. Paper presented at the Peak performance in tourism and hospitality research, Mt Buller, Victoria, Australia.

Packer, T.L., McKercher, B. and Yau, M. (2007) Understanding the complex interplay between tourism, disability and environmental contexts. *Disability & Rehabilitation* 29 (4), 281–292.

Page, S. (1995) *Urban Tourism*. London: Routledge.

Peniston, L.C. (1996) Hotel accessibility and accommodations for people with disabilities. *Parks & Recreation* 31 (12), 24–29.

Preiser, W.F.E. and Ostroff, E. (2001) *Universal Design Handbook*. New York: McGraw-Hill.

Rains, S. (2004) *Universal Design and the International Travel & Hospitality Industry*. Paper presented at the Designing for the 21st Century III, Rio de Janeiro, Brazil: 7th – 12th December, 2004.

Ray, N.M. and Ryder, M.E. (2003) 'Ebilities' tourism: An exploratory discussion of the travel needs and motivations of the mobility-disabled. *Tourism Management* 24 (1), 57–72.

Rossetti, R. (2009) *A Universal Design Approach for the Hospitality Industry*. Paper presented at the Hospitality Design 2009 Expo & Conference.

Sawyer, A. and Bright, K. (2006) *The Access Manual: Auditing and Managing Inclusive Built Environments* (2nd edn). Boston: Blackwell Pub.

Sharma, S. (2008) Public policy for people with disabilities: The UN and WHO perspectives. *Health Policy* 21 (4), 1–4.

Shaw, G. (2007) Disability legislation and empowerment of tourists with disability in the United Kingdom. In A. Church and T. Coles (eds) *Tourism, Power and Space* (pp. 83–100). London: Routledge.

Shaw, G. and Coles, T. (2004) Disability, holiday making and the tourism industry in the UK: A preliminary survey. [Science Direct]. *Tourism Management* 25, 397–403.

Shi, Y. (2006) The accessibility of Queensland visitor information centres' websites. *Tourism Management* 27 (5), 829–841.

Smith, R. (1987) Leisure of disabled tourists: Barriers to participation. *Annals of Tourism Research* 14 (3), 376–389.

Steinfeld, E. and Danford, G.S. (1999) *Enabling Environments: Measuring the Impact of Environment on Disability and Rehabilation*. New York; London: Kluwer Academic/Plenum Publishers.

SustainAbility and United Nations Environment Programme (2000) The Global Reporters. On WWW at http://www.sustainability.com/downloads_public/insight_reports/global_reporters.pdf. Accessed 20.7.2006.

Swain, J., Finkelstein, V., French, S. and Oliver, M. (2004) *Disabling Barriers – Enabling Environments* (2nd edn). London: Sage Publications Ltd.

Thomas, C. (1999) *Female Forms: Experiencing and Understanding Disability*. Buckingham: Open University Press.

Thomas, C. (2007) *Sociologies of Disability and Illness: Contested Ideas in Disability Studies and Medical Sociology*. Houndmills, Hants: Palgrave Macmillan.

Thomson, R. G. (1997) *Extraordinary Bodies: Figuring Physical Disability in American Culture and Literature*. New York: Columbia University Press.

Toegankelijkheidsbureau v.z.w Hasselt and LIVING Research and Development s.p.r.l. Brussels (2001) *Accessibility Legislation in Europe Status Report on building regulations, standards, design guidelines and other measures for ensuring access to the built environment for persons with disabilities*: Toerisme Vlaanderen – Meeting of EU Ministers of Tourism.

Touche Ross (1993) *Profiting from Opportunities – A New Market for Tourism*. London: Touche Ross & Co.

Tourism New South Wales (2005) Easy Access Markets. On WWW at http://corporate.tourism.nsw.gov.au/scripts/runisa.dll?CORPORATELIVE.65632:2COLUMN:933237702:pc=EASYACCESS. Accessed 10.5.2005.

Turco, D.M., Stumbo, N. and Garncarz, J. (1998) Tourism constraints – People with disabilities. *Parks and Recreation Journal* 33 (9), 78–84.

Uhlenberg, P. (2009) *International Handbook of Population Aging*. Springer Verlag.

UN ESCAP (2008) Disability at a glance: a Profile of 28 Countries and Areas in Asia and the Pacific (Vol. 2002, At http://www.unescap.org/esid/psis/disability

United Nations (2006) *Convention on the Rights of Persons with Disabilities*. New York http://www.un.org/esa/socdev/enable/rights/convtexte.htm: United Nations General Assembly A/61/611 – 6 December 2006.

United Nations (2008, 3 May) Landmark UN treaty on rights of persons with disabilities enters into force. On WWW at http://www.un.org/esa/socdev/enable/rights/convtexte.htm; http://www.un.org/apps/news/story.asp?NewsID=26554&Cr=disab&Cr1=. Accessed 12.5.2008.

United Nations (2009, 2 June 2009) Millennium Development Goals. On WWW at http://www.un.org/millenniumgoals/. Accessed 14.2.2010.

United Nations World Tourism Organisation (ND) About UNWTO: Why tourism. At http://www.unwto.org/aboutwto/why/en/why.php?op=1

Upchurch, R.S. and Seo, J. W. (1996) Civic responsibility and market positioning: complying with the Americans with Disabilities Act. *Facilities* 14 (5/6).

USAID (2009) *The Prevalence of Disability in Europe and Eurasia – Final Report*: prepared by Creative Associates International, Inc. & Aguirre Division of JBS International, Inc.

Vignuda, J-L. (2001) *Promotion of Barrier-Free Tourism for People with Disabilities in the Asian and Pacific Region*. Tokyo: Economic and Social Commission for Asia and the Pacific (ESCAP).

Walsh, C.J. (2004) Rio de Janeiro Declaration on Sustainable Social Development, Disability & Ageing. Paper presented at the *Designing for the 21st Century III* – an international conference on universal design, Rio de Janeiro, Brazil: 7th – 12th December, 2004.

Weaver, D. and Lawton, L. (2010) *Tourism Management* (4th edn). Milton: John Wiley and Sons.

Weaver, D. and Opperman, M. (2000) *Tourism Management*. Milton Park, Queensland: John Wiley and Sons Australia Pty Ltd.

Wedel, M. and Kamakura, W. (2000) *Market Segmentation: Conceptual and Methodological Foundations*. Kluwer Academic Pub.

Williams, R. and Rattray, R. (2005) UK hotel web page accessibility for disabled and challenged users. *Tourism & Hospitality Research* 5 (3), 255–267.

Williams, R., Rattray, R. and Grimes, A. (2006) Meeting the on-line needs of disabled tourists: An assessment of UK-based hotel websites. *International Journal of Tourism Research* 8 (1), 59.

Williams, R., Rattray, R. and Stork, A. (2004) Website accessibility of German and UK tourism information sites. *European Business Review* 16 (6), 577–589.

Woodside, A.G. and Etzel, M.J. (1980) Impact of physical and mental handicaps on vacation travel behaviour. *Journal of Travel Research* 18 (3), 9–11.

World Health Organization (2002) *Towards a Common Language for Functioning, Disability and Health – ICF*. Geneva: World Health Organization.

World Health Organization (2007) Global age-friendly cities guide. At http://www.who.int/ageing/age_friendly_cities/en/index.html.

World Health Organization (2007a) Global age-friendly cities: A guide. At http://www.who.int/ageing/publications/Global_age_friendly_cities_Guide_English.pdf.

World Health Organization (2007b) Media Release: New guide on building age-friendly cities. On WWW at http://www.who.int/mediacentre/news/releases/2007/pr53/en/index.html. Accessed 26.10.2007.

Wu, Y. and Cheng, M. (2008) Accessible tourism for the disabled: Long tail theory. *Emerging Technologies and Information Systems for the Knowledge Society* (p. 572). Heidelberg: Springer.

Yates, K. (2007) Understanding the experiences of mobility-disabled tourists. *International Journal of Tourism Policy* 1 (2), 153–166.

Yau, M. K-s., McKercher, B. and Packer, T.L. (2004) Traveling with a disability: More than an access issue. *Annals of Tourism Research* 31 (4), 946–960.

Chapter 2

Conceptualising Disability

S. DARCY and D. BUHALIS

Introduction

Disability is a social construct with approaches to and concepts of disability changing over history, between societies within historical periods and having cultural contexts (Gleeson, 1999). At different times and places, the dominant worldview affects the position of disability within the social context. It is important to understand these conceptual approaches and the implications they have for the treatment of people with disabilities in a tourism context. This chapter reviews the contemporary models and discourses of disability to provide a theoretical base on which to understand tourism from a disability perspective and, hence, the development of accessible tourism. Firstly, it reviews the most influential models of disability and their contribution to conceptualising disability. Secondly, it provides a detailed examination of the medical model of disability through the World Health Organization (WHO) definitions on which national disability statistics are collected. This serves as a precursor to understanding the polemic surrounding the medical model from a disability perspective. Thirdly, the chapter discusses two social approaches to disability and extends this discussion by examining the importance of the organisation of space in a tourism context.

Impairment and Disability: What is the Difference?

Definitions of disability often vary according to the purpose of the data collection or according to different classifications used (Australian Bureau of Statistics, 2000; Eurostat, 2002; WHO, 1980, 1997). The most commonly cited definitions are by the WHO (1980) and the United Nations Enable (2009), which draw the distinction between impairment and disability:

- 'Impairment is any loss or abnormality of psychological, physiological or anatomical structure or function.' (WHO, 1980; United Nations Enable, 2009)

- 'A disability is any restriction or lack (resulting from an impairment) of ability to perform an activity in the manner or within the range considered normal for a human being.' (WHO, 1980; United Nations Enable, 2009)

According to Oliver (1990) and operationalised by the disability advocacy movement, these definitions of the WHO create an individual or medical approach to 'disability' and 'impairment'. This is because of the definitions' focus on the 'loss' of the individual by referring to the physical or cognitive limitations that an individual may have (e.g. the inability to walk or speak). Similarly, disability in this definition also focuses on the 'lack of ability' and, hence, places the emphasis on the individual's loss or their 'tragedy'.

From the 1970s a number of social approaches to disability theory developed that have become known as disability studies. Pfieffer (2001) offers a definition of disability studies as, '... the field which examines the experience of being disabled and the lives of people with disabilities'. The models, paradigms and conceptualisations of disability have been reviewed by a number of writers. Table 2.1 provides a summary of these seminal reviews and the basic features they attribute to the various models.

These reviews chart the overwhelming dominance of the medical model in influencing domain assumptions about disability held by society. The social approaches described in the reviews are critiques of the individualised medical model that permeates institutional practices and, in particular, informs government legislation and policy. The emergence of social approaches to disability emanates from the experience of people with disabilities themselves and provides a framework to understand these experiences from the disability perspective. Several of these social approaches offer a framework for developing explanations for the tourism constraints of people with disabilities.

The main social approaches to disability can be summarised as individual idealist, social model and cultural representation. While the individual idealist and cultural representations of disability are of major interest to many academics, and clearly affect public perceptions, attitudes and priorities, in the case of this chapter a more specific focus has been made on the tension between medical and social models of disability. Throughout the book, recognition of the core discourses of the tourism environment points to the critical role played by these two discourses. While they may be further illuminated by examinations from social psychology and cultural representation, such an investigation in this chapter would divert the focus needed to effectively examine the medical and social modalities. As will become evident, it is these competing modalities that influence and structure the majority of the

Table 2.1 Reviews of models of disability

Source	*Models*	*Basic Understanding*
Hahn (1986)	• Medical • Economic • Minority	• Disability as functional loss • Disability as a socioeconomic issue (work) • Disability as oppressed minority
Oliver (1990, 1996)	• Individual (medical) • Social	• Disability as functional loss • Disability as product of disabling environment
Bickenbach (1993)	• Biomedical • Economic • Minority	• Disability as functional loss • Disability as a socioeconomic issue (work) • Disability as oppressed minority
Priestley (1998)	• Individual materialist (medical) • Individual idealist • Social materialist • Social idealist (constructionist)	• Disability as functional loss • Disability as stigma (disabled/non-disabled) • Disability as product of disabling environment • Disability as cultural representation

decision-making frameworks for government and industry. However, these examinations are the focus of other chapters and may provide fertile ground for further research that may take direction from these other social approaches to disability (Albrecht, 2006; Albrecht *et al.*, 2001; Corker & French, 1999; Davis, 2006; DePoy & Gilson, 2004; Shakespeare, 2006; Shakespeare & Corker, 2001; Siebers, 2008; Thomas, 1999, 2007).

From this basic understanding of definitional approaches a variety of models for defining disability have emerged of which the medical model and social model are discussed in the next section.

Models of Disability: Medical and Social Model

In general, disability scholars describe two main modes of disability: firstly, the medical or individual model; and secondly, the social model. This section will briefly outline the models before providing a comparative summary stating how this may provide a direction for the book. Lastly, the WHO's Disability Classification Systems are discussed in context to the medical and social models.

The medical model

The medicalisation of disability accelerated post World War II with the advancement in medical technology, where more people with traumatic injuries and congenital impairments were able to live with what were once fatal conditions. The subsequent growth of other therapies surrounding the rehabilitation process brought a new group of professionals who sought to normalise these people (Longmore & Umansky, 2001). Yet a permanent impairment is unlike an illness and the medical professions were unprepared for impairments that could not be normalised. Over time these medicalised groups' intervention in disabled people's lives disempowered, marginalised and created dependency. Central to this was the paternalistic attitude of these groups towards disabled people. This paternalism manifested itself in the disabled person as 'subject', not worthy of consultation or at times even communication. The 'professions' knew best and were able to 'prescribe treatment' accordingly (Barnes, 1996). Recreation workers first became involved in this process as an extension of physical therapies.

The predominant model of disability in Western countries has its origins in a medical approach. The basis of this can be found in the WHO (1980, 1997) classification system for impairment, disability and core activity restriction (previously handicap). A simplified examination of these terms is an important starting point to understand this approach, and hence, how member nations define disability and collect statistics. Impairment is any loss or abnormality of psychological, physiological or anatomical structure or function. For instance, damage to the spinal cord of someone with a spinal cord injury is an impairment. A disability is any restriction or lack (resulting from an impairment) of ability to perform an action in a manner, or within the range, considered normal for a human being. WHO stipulates a list of actions that are 'considered normal', and hence, constitute disability if they cannot be performed. For example, a person with spinal cord impairment is defined as having a disability because of the effects of the resulting spinal cord injury on the use of legs, feet, other muscles and bodily functioning.

To recap, impairment is the resulting loss of anatomical, psychological or physiological function (e.g. spinal cord injury). Disability is any identified restriction or lack of ability to perform an action resulting from the impairment (e.g. use of legs). A core activity restriction is a limitation to perform certain tasks associated with everyday life (e.g. mobility/walking). Time has been taken to explain these definitions because it is these definitions that are the basis of the contention between the medical and social models of disability.

The approach adopted by WHO is based on a range of normative assumptions. These normative assumptions influence every sphere of social organisation for disabled people. It is these definitions that create the dichotomy of normal/abnormal and, hence, are the origin for considering disability as other. This issue is at the heart of debate in disability studies. As Oliver (1996: 31) notes, there are two components to the medical approach to disability. The first component locates the problem of disability within the individual as a 'personal tragedy'. The second, sees the cause of disability as the product of the abnormal body brought about by the disease, illness or trauma. It is this premise that sees medical intervention through treatment and rehabilitation that attempts to normalise disabled people.

The definition given by the WHO (1997) characterises disability as being the 'problem' of the individual. This medical approach to disability focuses on the loss or dysfunction and assumes that it is both permanent and encompasses every aspect of the individual's life (Aitchison, 2003; Darcy, 2002). The medical orientation positions individuals with disabilities as less able than those who are non-disabled. In this view, the individual, who cannot be modified or changed by professional intervention, remains deficient (Gilson & Depoy, 2000). The individual with a disability is in the sick role or the victim under the medical model. When people are sick, they are excused from the normal obligations and are excluded from social participation and the rights of citizenship. Figure 2.1

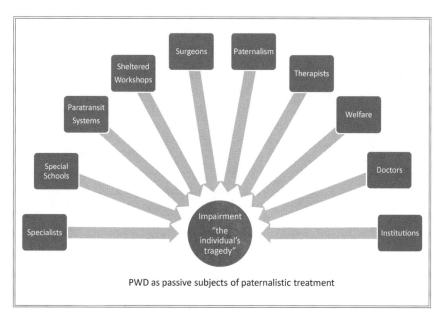

Figure 2.1 Medical model
Source: Modified from http://www.diseed.org.uk/Medical_Social_Model.htm

provides an understanding of the underlying position people with disabilities are subjected.

There is no doubt that the medical model serves as the basis for many negative and limiting attitudes, policies and outcomes (Ells, 2001; Vash, 2001). Disabled people have been very critical of this model. While medical intervention can be required by the individual at times, it is simplistic to regard the medical system as the appropriate focus for disability-related policy matters. Many disabilities and chronic medical conditions cannot be cured. Instead of being seen as inseparable or purely defined by their illness, disease and disability, the majority of disabled people want to acknowledge their state of health alongside any physical or mental conditions that may be present (Odette *et al.*, 2003; Putnam *et al.*, 2003). In fact disabled people often develop different skills and abilities that people without disabilities may not possess. For example a blind person may be using smell or hearing to perform specific activities and may have a much better understanding and appreciation of space.

Health is a multifaceted phenomenon, encompassing physical health, emotional well-being and social cohesion (Jamner & Stokols, 2001). This alternative approach is often called the social model. It looks at human health from a broad perspective and challenges society and service providers to look not only at the indications of disease, illness and disability, but also examine the individual's overall level of well-being and quality of life (Odette *et al.*, 2003). Within this approach the focus is placed on providing necessary services and supports in order to remove or minimise social and environmental barriers to full social, physical and leisure participation (Aitchison, 2003; Darcy, 2002; Gilson & Depoy, 2000; McKercher *et al.*, 2003; Shaw *et al.*, 2005; Shelton & Tucker, 2005). Therefore the problem of disability is revised and it is defined as inadequate support services with regard to the particular needs of people with disabilities when compared with the whole of society. Attitudinal, architectural, sensory, cognitive, and economic barriers, and the strong tendency for people to generalise about all persons with disabilities, overlooking the large variations within the disability community, also play a major role within this model (Aitchison, 2003; Shelton & Tucker, 2005).

The social model

The emergence of the disability political movements of the 1970s in Britain re-conceptualised disability from a 'personal tragedy' to a complex form of social oppression (Abberley, 1987). This has seen the emphasis move from the individual's impairment, their 'personal tragedy' as the 'victim' (Oliver, 1990, 1996), to the disabling social environment and prevailing 'hostile social attitudes' (Barnes, 1996: 43). As such, the social model of disability was developed as a direct challenge to the medical model through the essential difference in definitions between impairment and disability.

The earliest articulation of this social construction of disability was through the Union of the Physically Impaired Against Segregation (1975), which defined impairment and disability as follows:

> An impairment is lacking part of or all of a limb, or having a defective limb, organism or mechanism of the body. (Union of the Physically Impaired Against Segregation, 1975)

> Disability is the disadvantage or restriction of activity caused by contemporary organisation which takes no or little account of people who have physical impairments and thus excludes them from the mainstream of social activities. (Union of the Physically Impaired Against Segregation, 1975)

This definition of disability reflects the socially constructed nature of disability and the resultant exclusion. The degree of exclusion becomes dependent on the type of impairment and the level of support the person requires for social participation in all areas of citizenship. These further layers of complexity will be discussed later in the chapter as part of the disability statistical framework.

The social model defines disability as a product of the socially constructed disabling environment and prevailing hostile social attitudes that oppress, exclude and marginalise disabled people from social participation (Oliver, 1990, 1996). The defining element of the social model lies in the transformation of an impaired person to a disabled person as a product of the ways in which society is organised (economic, social, cultural, transport, built environment, leisure services etc.). This social organisation is discriminatory because it is based on a non-disabled interpretation of what is 'normal'. The social model views disability as having a social dimension and regards impairment as part of human diversity. These socially constructed barriers affect an individual's social participation, create disability on top of a person's impairment and discriminate against a person because of their impairment.

Central to this is the recognition that the 'normal activities and roles' of the medical model take place within the material world, and that the socially constructed environment affects an impaired person's ability to undertake these socially constructed activities and roles. Consequently, the social model stresses that disability should not be regarded as a deviance from the normal but celebrated as part of the spectrum of human diversity. In doing so, the social model rejects the notion that people with disabilities are in some inherent way 'defective' from the benchmarked yet elusive norm. In places where universal design is practiced and disability legislation followed, such as in the Scandinavian countries, even people with severe disabilities can participate in most economic and socio-cultural activities. Over their lifespan most people will experience some form of disability, either permanent or temporary, from the beginning of their lives or acquiring it during their life course through traumatic injury or the side-effects of illness. For example, broken limbs or some outcomes of difficult pregnancies may be good examples of such temporary disabilities. There is a well defined correlation between ageing and disability, with disability rates significantly higher as people age. Given this reality, if disability was more commonly recognised and accepted in the way that society designs environments or systems, it would be regarded as normal and it would enable a more inclusive way of life for people with disabilities.

The cultural habit of regarding the condition of the person, not the built environment or the social organisation of activities, as the source of the problem, is the most prevailing issue within the discussion of the social model of disability. 'Disabled people' are a result of the way that society has socially constructed the environment that they confront every day. The social model of disability does not deny an individual's impairment but strongly states that the resultant disabilities are a product of socially constructed barriers that exclude or segregate people with impairments from participation in mainstream social activities. It firmly places disability in the social, economic and political agendas rather than locating disability as the fault of an individual's body. As Barton (1998: 56–57) states:

> To be a disabled person means to be discriminated against. It involves social isolation and restriction. This is because of an essentially inaccessible socio-economic and physical world (Finkelstein, 1994). Disability is thus a significant means of social differentiation: the level of esteem and social standing of disabled people are derived from their position in relation to the wider social conditions and relations of a given society. Particular institutions have a crucial influence on social status including the level and nature of employment, education and economic well-being.

Disability advocates argue that disability is imposed on top of their impairment not because of their impairment but due to socially constructed barriers and attitudes (Barnes *et al.*, 1999). A person with an impairment need not acquire a disability if enabling environments are developed through the incorporation of economic, political and social structures (Swain *et al.*, 2004). Instead of the 'fault' residing in the individual, the disability becomes part of the social constraints imposed on those with impairments through the lack of inclusive, accessible built environments, transport, service attitudes and employment practices. A number of studies have shown where these discriminatory environments constrain the citizenship of people with disabilities generally and in a tourism context (Darcy & Taylor, 2009; Goodall *et al.*, 2004).

The social model informs an understanding of tourism by suggesting that the socially constructed relationships developed from three elements:

(1)   experiences of disabled people;
(2)   identifying disability as the combination of impairment and socially constructed barriers; and
(3)   part of a conceptual clarification designed to facilitate a scientific attack on the constraints and barriers that oppress disabled people and therefore lead to their impoverishment and social dysfunction.

The important change in orientation of the third point is that it directs scientific attention toward the *disabling barriers* (Swain *et al.*, 2004) that are the sites of oppression that actively produce *disabled* people. It changes the focus from the individual's 'problem' or 'personal tragedy' to that of the socially constructed barriers that produce disability. These *disabling barriers* have physical, social, economic and political contexts. The social structures are a product of historical development and cannot be divorced from their cultural context. The cultural context involves both a material and ideological transformation of the way people with impairments are treated by society. As Gleeson (1999: 13) comments, society has in the past changed its attitude towards institutional oppression of other groups in society, such as women and indigenous groups, 'whilst continuing to ignore the material hardships and injustices to which they are subjected'.

Therefore, the overall aim of this model is to move the whole society to a more positive understanding of what it means to live with a disability and to adapt the environment accordingly. Further, since disability is regarded as socially constructed then there has to be a social solution. As Figure 2.2 suggests, by creating more accessible social structures people with disabilities are not only able to participate in their rights of citizenship but become active agents in affecting social change. In Western nations many non-disabled people support these notions as evidenced by the Eurobarometer study (Europeia, 2001) where 97% of Europeans state that something should be done to ensure better integration of people with disabilities into society. In a tourism context, disability awareness training has proven to be an effective practice of tourism related organisations (Daruwalla & Darcy, 2005).

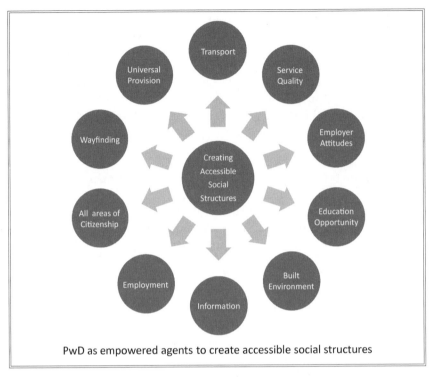

Figure 2.2 Social model
Source: Modified from http://www.diseed.org.uk/Medical_Social_Model.htm

Comparative Summary and Underlying Approach Taken in the Book

Table 2.2 presents a comparative summary of the differences between the medical and social models. The medical model views the disablement phenomenon as a 'personal' problem, directly caused by disease, trauma or health conditions, which requires medical care provided in the form of individual treatment by professionals. Management of disablement is aimed at the person's better adjustment and behaviour change. Health care is viewed as the main issue and at the political level it is health care policy that needs to be modified. The social model of disablement, on the other hand, sees the issue mainly as a 'social construct' from the viewpoint of integration of persons with disabilities into society. Disablement is not an attribute of a person, but a complex collection of conditions many of which are created by the social environment, which is imposed on top of a person's impairment. Hence, the disability created by the disabling social environment requires social action and it is the collective responsibility of society to make the environmental modifications necessary

Table 2.2 Medical v Social Model

Medical	*Social*
PERSONAL problem	SOCIAL issue
Medical care	Social integration
Individual treatment	Social action
Professional help	Individual and collective responsibility
Personal adjustment	Environmental manipulation
Behaviour	Attitude
Care	Human rights
Health care policy	Politics
Individual adaptation	Social change

Source: Adapted (World Health Organization, 2002)

for the full participation of people with disabilities into all areas of citizenship. The issue is, therefore, placed on the political, economic, social and attitudinal agendas and is ideological. Social change is sought by people with disabilities through individual empowerment, collective advocacy and supported by at the political level through the United Nations' *Convention of the Rights of People with Disabilities* (2006) and national human rights legislation.

For the purposes of this book, a broad social approach to disability is adopted. In doing so, it is recognised that many tourism environments are disabling by nature. A starting point is to acknowledge the disabling barriers and that the tourism industry, government authorities, disability service and advocacy organisations, and tourists need to work towards a more enabling tourism environment. The outcome of such an approach would remove attitudinal, social, physical and informational barriers that currently prevent or reduce the travel options for people with disabilities.

World Health Organization ICIDH and ICF

At this point it needs to be acknowledged that the WHO revised the classification system over the 1990s to bridge the gap between the medical and social models (WHO, 1980, 1997, 2001). Through the development of a universal biopsychosocial classification system they seek to establish a common language for the area, provide a scientific basis for comparative data collection and provide a systematic coding scheme for health information systems (Bickenbach *et al.*, 1999). Referred to as ICIDH-2 or the ICF, Figure 2.3 shows the revised approach related to health domains and health-related domains (WHO, 2001: 1) with the classifications changed to 'Body Function/Structure, Activities and Participation'. While the definition and understanding of body function/structure remains the same as for impairment in ICIDH (WHO, 1980, 1997) the addition of 'Activities and Participation' includes personal and environmental contextual factors (WHO, 2001: 9). Health conditions then serve as an umbrella term for body function/structure, activity limitations or participation restrictions, and hence, replace disability conditions. WHO hopes that this new classification system will provide unified, standard language and a framework to be inclusive of the personal and environmental perspectives of health conditions. Importantly, the ICF recognises the importance of cultural context that has been identified as a significant polemic in the conceptualisation, social approaches and comparison of disability statistics between Eastern and Western countries (Miles, 2000).

However, this approach remains controversial amongst disability studies theorists as the basis of the system is still founded upon medical conceptualisations of health conditions, disorders and diseases (Anderberg, 2005; Andersson, 2006; Hammell, 2004; Imrie, 2004; Pfeiffer, 2000). As Table 2.3 outlines, it is argued that it does not classify people but describes the situation of each individual within the spectrum of health and health-related domains. The health and health-related status associated with all health conditions is therefore not only about people with disabilities but about all people. The universal application of this approach is

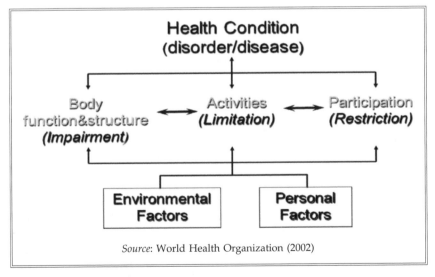

Figure 2.3 ICF Classification

Table 2.3 The International Classification of Functioning, Disability and Health

	Part 1: Functioning and Disability		Part 2: Contextual Factors	
Components	Body Functions and Structures	Activities and Participation	Environmental Factors	Personal Factors
Domains	Body functions Body structures	Life areas (tasks/ actions)	External influences on functioning and disability	Internal influences on functioning and disability
Constructs	Change in body functions (physiological) Change in body functions (anatomical)	Capacity Executing tasks in a standard environment Performance Executing tasks in a current environment	Facilitating or hindering impact of features of the physical, social and attitudinal world	Impact of attributes of the person
Positive aspects	Functional and structural integrity	Activities Participation	Facilitators	*Not applicable*
	Functioning			
Negative aspects	Impairment	Activity limitation	Barriers/hindrances	*Not applicable*
	Disability			

Source: World Health Organization (2001)

that it identifies components that either act as facilitators or hindrances for individuals in the physical, social or attitudinal world (WHO, 2001).

Classifying disability using ICF

In taking a pragmatic approach, the authors of this chapter recognise that the majority of disability statistics are collected using this system as a foundation for understanding the scope and dimensions of disability on a national and international basis. With this caveat, the next section of the chapter looks at the dimensions of disability through definitional and statistical approaches. Table 2.4 and the following section briefly describe the main categories of impairment and resultant areas of 'difficulties' identified by the classification list and resultant statistics.

Mobility impairments refer to a wide range of physical mobility restrictions, e.g. reach, stretch, dexterity and locomotion. In this case, the physical capacity to move, coordinate actions, or perform physical activities can be significantly limited, impaired, or delayed. People with mobility impairments have difficulties in one or more of the following areas: physical and motor tasks, independent movements or performing basic life functions (DEO, 2005; Householder, 2001).

The category of sensory and communication impairments include vision, hearing and also speech impairments. When visually impaired,

Table 2.4 Dimensions of disability

Type of impairment	Description	Difficulties in one of more of the following areas:
Mobility	Varying levels of physical mobility restrictions, affecting legs, feet, back, neck, arms or hands	– physical and motor tasks – independent movements – performing basic life functions
Sensory	Capacity to see is limited or absent Completely deaf or are hard of hearing	– reduced performance in tasks requiring clear vision – difficulties with written communication – difficulties with understanding information presented visually – reduced performance in tasks requiring sharp hearing – difficulties with oral communication – difficulties in understanding auditorily-presented information
Communication	Limited, impaired, or delayed capacities to use expressive and/or receptive language	– general speech capabilities, such as articulation – problems with conveying, understanding, or using spoken, written, or symbolic language
Intellectual/ mental health	Lifelong illnesses with multiple aetiologies that result in a behavioural disorder	– slower rate of learning – disorganised patterns of learning – difficulties with adaptive behaviour – difficulties understanding abstract concepts – limited control of cognitive functioning – problems with sensory, motor and speech skills – restricted basic life functions
Hidden	Variety of illnesses	– heart problems – blood pressure or circulation problems – breathing difficulties – problems with stomach, liver or kidneys – problems in controlling the level of sugar in the blood (diabetes) – disorder of the central nervous systems (epilepsy)

the capacity to see is limited or absent. Blindness or partial sightedness results in a reduced performance in tasks requiring clear vision, difficulties with written communication and/or difficulties with understanding information presented visually (American Foundation for the Blind, 2005; DEO, 2005).

The second subcategory of sensory impairments refers to people that are completely deaf or are hard of hearing. Hard of hearing is defined as having partial hearing capabilities in one or both ears, requiring the use of a hearing aid. Hearing impairments result in a reduced performance in tasks requiring sharp hearing, difficulties with oral communication and/or difficulties in understanding auditorily-presented information (DEO, 2005)

Communication or speech impairments refer to limited, impaired or delayed capacities to use expressive and/or receptive language. People with speech impairments have difficulties with general speech capabilities, such as articulation. Further they might have problems with conveying, understanding or using spoken, written or symbolic language (DEO, 2005).

Intellectual/mental impairments are lifelong illnesses with multiple aetiologies (Pomona, 2004a, 2004b) and result in a behavioural disorder. These are apparent if the capacity of the nervous system is limited or permanently impaired or if the capacity for performing cognitive tasks, functions, or problem solving is significantly limited or impaired. Intellectual/mental impairments are exhibited by a slower rate of learning, disorganised patterns of learning, difficulties with adaptive behaviour and/or difficulties understanding abstract concepts. Further, they can result in limited control of cognitive functioning, problems with sensory, motor and speech skills or restricted basic life functions (DEO, 2005).

The WHO (1992) classifies four groups of intellectual disability, ranging from mild to profound intellectual disability. Within these four categories varying degrees of communication, sensory, motor and behavioural factors can be found. In addition, there is an increased level of care and supervision required, from mild to profound intellectual disability. People with intellectual disability also have a strong need for accessibility depending on the level of mobility to immobility.

Hidden impairments comprise a wide range of illnesses that are sometimes not obvious or not seen at all times but require special attention. These health problems might result in limited strength, vitality or alertness, attention deficit disorders or hyperactivity disorders among many others (DEO, 2005). Examples of hidden impairments are diabetes, epilepsy, heart problems, blood pressure or circulation problems, breathing difficulties and problems with stomach, liver or kidneys. People are either born with some of these illnesses or they develop over time. Further, some of the illnesses included in this category, such as Parkinson's or a stroke, are the cause of mobility impairments.

Dimensions of Disability: Focusing on Access Needs

While Table 2.4 may be useful from a medical perspective, it does little to assist us with increasing social participation as identified. There are literally thousands of disabling conditions that can arise from a variety of impairments. Yet, as the social model suggests, it is not the impairment that should be the focus but the identification of disabling environments and the creation of enabling strategies to increase social participation. One way of conceptualising a social approach to the dimensions of impairment is to focus attention on the access needs of those identified. The *dimensions of disability* provides a basis on which to create more enabling environments for people with impairments to participate in all social activities.

Table 2.5 identifies examples of inclusive and universal practice that provide an enabling environment for six of these groups. Table 2.5 is presented as a foundation for understanding what promotes independent, dignified and equitable access that is at the core of the definition of accessible tourism (Darcy, 2006).

Access requirements are needed in all parts of the tourism system (generating region 1 ↔ transit 1 ↔ destination region) and all sectors of the industry (for a description of both the tourism system and the sectors of the industry see Leiper, 2003). Figure 2.4 illustrates the interaction of accessibility with the physical access (transit and destination) and the access to information (customers' information need chain) within the

Table 2.5 Dimensions of access and examples of inclusive practice in tourism

Mobility	*Hearing*	*Vision*	*Cognitive*	*Hidden/ Sensitivities*	*Ageing/Health*
Continuous pathway	Telephone typewriters (TTYs)	Tactile ground surface indicators; Audio signals	Plain English text	Chemical free environments	Medical support
Circulation space	Hearing loops	Alternative formats e.g. large text, Braille; audio	Attendant support	Dietary considerations	Supportive environment
Specialist equipment	Captioning	Areas for guide dogs	Opportunities for group travel for those in communal supported accommodation	Non-smoking areas	Opportunities for group travel
Low-floor buses	Sign language interpreters	Sensory trails	Activity programming	Organisational promotion	Advocacy and philanthropy programs
Customer service attitude	Customer service attitude	Customer service attitude	Customer service attitude	Customer service attitude	Customer service attitude
Wayfinding systems	Wayfinding systems	Wayfinding systems	Wayfinding systems	Clearly labelled areas	Specialist equipment
Information systems	Information systems	Information systems	Information systems	Information systems	Information systems

Source: Constructed for the chapter

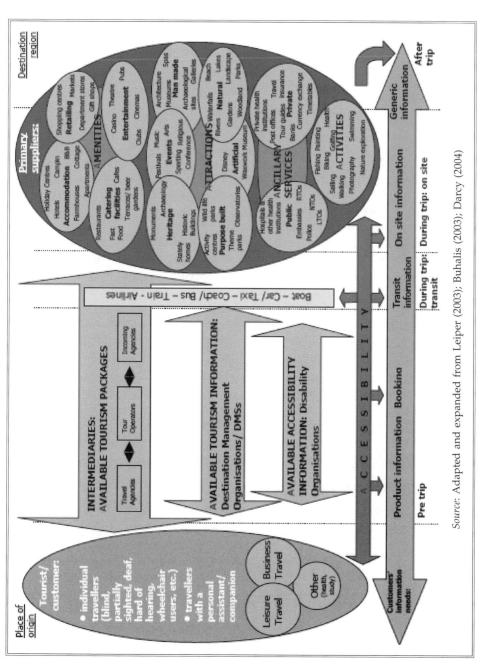

Source: Adapted and expanded from Leiper (2003); Buhalis (2003); Darcy (2004)

Figure 2.4 The tourism system and accessibility

tourism system. Therefore, accessible information is used to describe facilities or amenities to assist people with disabilities to make informed decisions on the suitability of these facilities. Accessibility requirements vary depending on the dimensions of access, level of support needs and the adaptive/assistive equipment used. Many of the chapters in this book go into a great deal of detail regarding the accessibility requirements of the dimensions of access.

Inclusive design and information provision does not only improve the accessibility and usability for people with disabilities but makes tourism in general more approachable for elderly people and a wider range of the population (Pühretmair, 2004). Beneficiaries of a service providing information on accessibility include all citizens and in particular people with different types of impairments (impairment sub-markets) and the elderly population. A service offering reliable information on accessibility supports thereby a variety of target customers. Some people might acquire a greater level of accessibility needs for a limited period of time (pregnancy, broken limbs, etc.), whereas others have accessibility requirements during their whole life. Everyone has specific individual requirements due to different abilities. Thus, it is a heterogeneous market, which entails a series of different sub-markets.

By looking specifically at people with impairments as well as the elderly population, seven main clusters can be identified:

(1) Mobility.
(2) Blind or vision impaired.
(3) Deaf or hearing impaired.
(4) Speech.
(5) Cognitive (mental health/intellectually/learning).
(6) Hidden.
(7) Elderly/Seniors/Boomers.

Level of independence

The dimensions of access provide a focus for enabling facilities and social participation. The complexity of understanding the market includes recognising that the individual's impairment may mean that an individual has multiple dimensions of access, which require multiple levels of accessibility for social participation. For example, a person with an impairment like cerebral palsy may have a mobility restriction and use a wheelchair or crutches, whilst they may also have a communication restriction through an associated speech impairment for which they use a communication board. Depending on their level of independence with personal care, they may also travel with an attendant. This person requires an accessible physical environment as well as assistant technologies and social policy inclusions (Darcy, 2002). This person's access

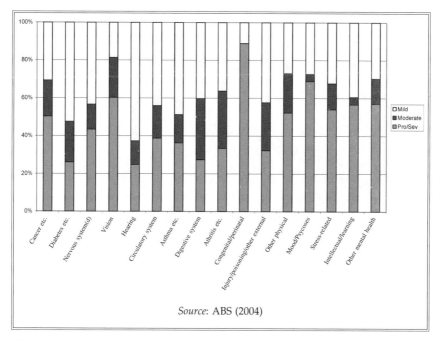

Source: ABS (2004)

Figure 2.5 Level of support needs by impairment

requirements are different to a person with arthritis who has a basic requirement for a continuous pathway that includes handrails to assist in weight bearing, seats to provide a resting area, universal handles on door-ways and taps to assist with reduced dexterity. From Dwyer and Darcy's (2008) study using the Australian Bureau of Statistics *Disability, Ageing and Carers Survey* (2004) this is demonstrated in Figure 2.5, where those identified as having a disability had differing levels of independence and support needs as shown below:

- None (independent).
- Mild.
- Moderate.
- Severe.
- Profound (requiring 24hr assistance).

The Continuum of Ability: Understanding the Market

Prospective customers might travel alone or in the company of able-bodied assistants, friends or family members. This illustrates the real market size for accessibility, which is addressed by a number of chapters. Figure 2.6 presents a pyramid that demonstrates key variations of demand types for the disabled and the elderly population that require accessibility.

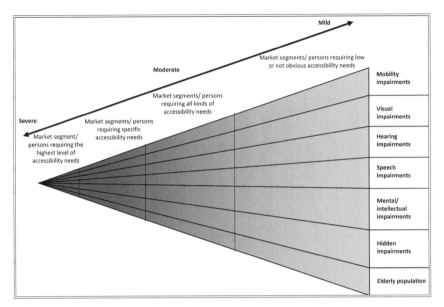

Figure 2.6 Pyramid of demand types: the continuum of abilities

The elderly, who have low to moderate access needs, make up the majority of the whole range of those with any sort of access need. All accessibility requirements represent a continuum. The demand types identified and illustrated have different levels of requirements ranging from profound, severe to low or mild. It is the understanding of the type and level of requirements that needs to drive the development of products and services that can satisfy this particular type of demand. Although inclusive design can address the vast majority of the specific needs, appreciation of requirements is critical for the development of the right attitudes and services.

People with all kinds of access requirements represent a combination of challenges and opportunities for the travel and tourism industry. Serving these market segments requires considerable efforts due to the very different requirements and information needs. Therefore, the need for inclusive design on the one hand and good market segmentation on the other can support organisations to deliver adequate tourism products and services to these groups. Dividing the market into distinct groups of people with similar needs and wants allows tourism planners and managers to understand what really matters for consumers and to create unique product offers. By targeting these groups, they have the chance to achieve competitive advantages through differentiation.

Further, the establishment of well-defined demand types has profound implications in the marketing and positioning of destinations and organisations. The higher the access requirements, the more attention has to be paid to certain accessibility criteria. Individuals with the highest accessibility requirement might therefore be better served by specialised providers that have a profound knowledge of their high needs. People with more moderate needs should be served by mainstream providers who have utilised inclusive design in their facilities.

This is mainly due to two reasons. First, many people who suffer from a temporary disability like a broken limb do not often see themselves in need of special services and hence purchase tourism products from mainstream providers. Secondly, disabled people with moderate or low access needs do not feel that they should be using specialised facilities that may stigmatise them and argue for an inclusive design and service. Increasing legislative and social responsibility will enable mainstream players to adapt their services to all types and grades of disability.

Conclusion

In an attempt to conceptualise disability this chapter explores the two dominant models of disability: the medical and the social model. By highlighting the major existing types of impairments, it becomes obvious that disability is not a homogeneous concept and depending on the types of impairments, people have varying levels of accessibility requirements. The elderly population has been identified as an important group that shares many of the same access barriers as people with impairments. Further, it has been emphasised that all citizens benefit from the accessible design of facilities. In summary the chapter has presented the following concepts:

- Definitions and discourses of disability depend on the distinction between impairment and disability.
- The medical model reduces disability to impairment, thereby positioning the disability as being the 'problem' of the individual.
- The crucial separation of these two terms by the social model approach stressed the notion that disability is a social construct. Impairment refers to biological characteristics of the body and mind; these are physical or cognitive limitations that an individual may have. In contrast, disability refers to socially imposed restrictions, that is, the system of social constraints that are imposed on those with impairments by the discriminatory practices of society.
- This chapter adopts the social approach to disability as it is regarded as essential for the travel and tourism industry to create and implement strategies to remove attitudinal, social, cultural, physical and informational barriers that currently prevent or reduce travel options for disabled people.

- Disabling conditions arise from a variety of impairments. The most common types range from mobility, sensory and communication impairments to intellectual impairments and mental health disorders as well as hidden impairments in the form of health problems.
- Given the strong and positive correlation between age and disability, it is acknowledged that the elderly population faces similar access barriers as people with impairments – this is alongside the population as a whole which also requires accessibility as a means for general comfort and quality in life.
- Understanding the types and levels of disability is critical for the development of an enabling environment, as well as for ensuring that facilities, attitudes and services are all aligned to ensure an inclusive experience for travellers.
- It is of tremendous importance to consider the diversity of all citizens, who have varying levels of accessibility requirements, and strive towards universal design.

References

Abberley, P. (1987) The concept of oppression and the development of a social theory of disability. *Disability, Handicap & Society* 2 (1), 5–19.

Aitchison, C. (2003) From leisure and disability to disability leisure: Developing data, definitions and discourses. *Disability & Society* 18 (7), 955–969.

Albrecht, G.L. (2006) *Encyclopedia of Disability*. Thousand Oaks, CA: Sage Publications.

Albrecht, G.L., Bury, M. and Seelman, K.D. (2001) *Handbook of Disability Studies*. Thousand Oaks, CA: Sage Publications.

American Foundation for the Blind (2005) Key definitions of statistical terms. On WWW at http://www.afb.org/section.asp?SectionID=15&DocumentID=1280. Accessed 15.6.2010.

Anderberg, P. (2005) Making both ends meet. *Disability Studies Quarterly* 25 (3).

Andersson, Y. (2006) Reflections on disability language and the ICIDH/ICF. *International Views on Disability Measures: Moving Toward Comparative Measurement*, 55.

Australian Bureau of Statistics (2000) Disability, ageing and carers: Change over time for disability surveys. On WWW at www.abs.gov.au/CA25670D007E9EA1/0/5F41D2ECF62F1219CA2569440005E3B1?Open&Highlight=0,disability,1993. Accessed 11.2001.

Australian Bureau of Statistics (2004) *Disability, Ageing and Carers – Summary of Findings, 2003 (Cat. No. 4430.0)*. Canberra: Australian Bureau of Statistics.

Barnes, C. (1996) Theories of disability and the origins of the oppression of disabled people in western society. In L. Barton (ed.) *Disability and Society: Emerging Issues and Insights* (pp. 40–59). New York: Longman.

Barnes, C., Mercer, G. and Shakespeare, T. (1999) *Exploring Disability: A Sociological Introduction*. Malden, MA: Polity Press.

Barton, L. (1998) Sociology, disability and education. In T. Shakespeare (ed.) *The Disability Reader: Social Science Perspectives* (pp. 53–64). London: Cassell.

Bickenbach, J. E. (1993) *Physical Disability and Social policy*. Toronto: University of Toronto Press.

Bickenbach, J.E., Chatterji, S., Badley, E.M. and Ustun, T.B. (1999) Models of disablement, universalism and the international classification of impairments, disabilities and handicaps. *Social Science & Medicine* 48 (9), 1173–1187.

Buhalis, D. (2003) *e-Tourism: Information Technology for Strategic Tourism Management*. UK: Prentice Hall.

Corker, M. and French, S. (1999) *Disability Discourse*. Buckingham: Open University Press.

Darcy, S. (2002) Marginalised participation: Physical disability, high support needs and tourism. *Journal of Hospitality and Tourism Management* 9 (1), 61–72.

Darcy, S. (2004) Disabling journeys: The social relations of tourism for people with impairments in Australia – An analysis of government tourism authorities and accommodation sector practices and discourses. At http://epress.lib.uts.edu.au/dSpace/handle/2100/260.

Darcy, S. (2006) Setting a research agenda for accessible tourism (pp. 48). At http://www.crctourism.com.au/BookShop/BookDetail.aspx?d=473.

Darcy, S. and Taylor, T. (2009) Disability citizenship: An Australian human rights analysis of the cultural industries. *Leisure Studies* 28 (4), 419–441.

Daruwalla, P.S. and Darcy, S. (2005) Personal and societal attitudes to disability. *Annals of Tourism Research* 32 (3), 549–570.

Davis, L.J. (2006) *The Disability Studies Reader* (2nd edn). London; New York, NY: Routledge.

DEO (Department of Education, Massachusetts) (2005) Disability definitions and related links. On WWW at http://www.doe.mass.edu/sped/definitions.html. Accessed 30.5.2005.

DePoy, E. and Gilson, S.F. (2004) *Rethinking Disability: Principles for Professional and Social Change*. Belmont, CA: Thomson/Brooks/Cole.

Dwyer, L. and Darcy, S. (2008) Economic contribution of disability to tourism in Australia. In S. Darcy, B. Cameron, L. Dwyer, T. Taylor, E. Wong and A. Thomson (eds) *Technical Report 90040: Visitor Accessibility in Urban Centres* (pp. 15–21). Gold Coast: Sustainable Tourism Cooperative Research Centre.

Ells, C. (2001) Lessons about autonomy from the experience of disability. *Social theory and practice* 27 (4), 599–615.

Europeia, C. (2001) Attitudes of Europeans to Disability: Eurobarometer.

Eurostat (2002) *Health Statistics: Key Data on Health*. Luxembourg: European Communities.

Gilson, S.F. and Depoy, E. (2000) Multiculturalism and disability: A critical perspective. *Disability & Society* 15 (2), 207–218.

Gleeson, B. (1999) *Geographies of Disability*. London: Routledge.

Goodall, B., Pottinger, G., Dixon, T. and Russell, H. (2004) Heritage property, tourism and the UK Disability Discrimination Act. *Property Management* 22 (5), 345–357.

Hahn, H. (1986) Disability and the urban environment: A perspective on Los Angeles. *Environment and Planning D: Society and Space* 4, 273–288.

Hammell, K.W. (2004) Deviating from the norm: A sceptical interrogation of the classificatory practices of the ICF. *The British Journal of Occupational Therapy* 67 (9), 408–411.

Householder, J. (2001) Mobility impairment. On WWW at http://atoz.iqhealth.com/HealthAnswers/encyclopedia/HTMLfiles/3246.html. Accessed 17.5.2005.

Imrie, R. (2004) Demystifying disability: A review of the International Classification of Functioning, Disability and Health. *Sociology of Health and Illness* 26 (3), 287–305.

Jamner, M.S. and Stokols, D. (2001). *Promoting Human Wellness: New Frontiers for Research, Practice, and Policy*: CA: University of California Press.

Leiper, N. (2003) *Tourism Management* (3rd edn). Sydney: Hospitality Press.

Longmore, P. and Umansky, L. (eds) (2001) *The New Disability History*. New York: New York University Press.

McKercher, B., Packer, T., Yau, M. and Lam, P. (2003) Travel agents as facilitators or inhibitors of travel: perceptions of people with disabilities. *Tourism Management* 24 (4), 465–474.

Miles, M. (2000) Disability on a different model: Glimpses of an Asian heritage. *Disability & Society* 15 (4), 603–618.

Odette, F., Israel, P., Li, A., Ullman, D., Colontonio, A., Maclean, H. and Locke, D. (2003). Barriers to wellness activities for Canadian women with physical disabilities. *Health Care for Women International* 24 (2), 125–134.

Oliver, M. (1990) *The Politics of Disablement*. Basingstoke, Houndmills: Macmillan.

Oliver, M. (1996) *Understanding Disability: From Theory to Practice*. Basingstoke, Houndmills: Macmillan.

Pfeiffer, D. (2000) The devils are in the details: The ICIDH2 and the disability movement. *Disability & Society* 15 (7), 1079–1082.

Pfieffer, D. (2001) The conceptualization of disability. In S.N. Barnartt and B. Mandell Altman (eds) *Exploring Theories and Expanding Methodologies* (Vol. 2, pp. 29–52). Stamford: JAI Press.

Pomona (2004a) Health indicators for people with intellectual disability. On WWW at http://www.pomonaproject.org/3_health_indicators.pdf. Accessed 25.8.2010.

Pomona (2004b) People with intellectual disability in the member states. On WWW at http://www.pomonaproject.org/1_people_member_states.pdf. Accessed 25.8.2010.

Priestley, M. (1998) Constructions and creations: Idealism, materialism and disability theory. *Disability & Society* 13 (1), 75–94.

Pühretmair, F. (2004) It's time to make etourism accessible. In K. Miesenberger, J. Klaus, W. Zagler and D. Burger (eds) *Computers Helping People with Special Needs* (pp. 272–279). Berlin: Springer.

Putnam, M., Geenen, S., Powers, L., Saxton, M., Finney, S. and Dautel, P. (2003) Health and wellness: People with disabilities discuss barriers and facilitators to well being. *The Journal of Rehabilitation* 69 (1), 37–46.

Shakespeare, T. (2006) *Disability Rights and Wrongs*. London; New York: Routledge.

Shakespeare, T. and Corker, M. (2001) *Disability/Postmodernity: Embodying Disability Theory*. New York: Continuum.

Shaw, G., Veitch, C. and Coles, T.I.M. (2005) Access, disability, and tourism: Changing responses in the United Kingdom. *Tourism Review International* 8 (3), 167–176.

Shelton, E.J. and Tucker, H. (2005) Tourism and disability: Issues beyond access. *Tourism Review International* 8 (3), 211–219.

Siebers, T. (2008) *Disability Theory*. Ann Arbor: University of Michigan Press.

Swain, J., Finkelstein, V., French, S. and Oliver, M. (2004) *Disabling Barriers – Enabling Environments* (2nd edn). London: Sage Publications Ltd.

Thomas, C. (1999) *Female Forms: Experiencing and Understanding Disability*. Buckingham: Open University Press.

Thomas, C. (2007) *Sociologies of Disability and Illness: Contested Ideas in Disability Studies and Medical Sociology*. Houndmills, Hants.: Palgrave Macmillan.

Union of Physically Impaired Against Segregation (1975) *Fundamental Principles of Disability*. London: Union of Physically Impaired Against Segregation and The Disability Alliance.

United Nations (2006) *Convention on the Rights of Persons with Disabilities*. New York. At http://www.un.org/esa/socdev/enable/rights/convtexte.htm: United Nations General Assembly A/61/611 – 6 December 2006.

United Nations (2009, 2 June 2009) Enable. At http://www.un.org/disabilities/.

Vash, C.L. (2001) Disability attitudes for all latitudes. *The Journal of Rehabilitation* 67 (1).

World Health Organization (1980) *International Classification of Impairments, Disabilities and Handicaps (ICIDH)*. Geneva: World Health Organization.

World Health Organization (1992) *International Classification of Diseases* (10th revision). Geneva: World Health Organization.

World Health Organization (1997) *International Classification of Impairments, Disabilities and Handicaps (ICIDH)*. Geneva: World Health Organization.

World Health Organization (2001) *International Classification of Functioning, Disability and Health (ICIDH-2)*. Geneva: World Health Organization.

World Health Organization (2002) *Towards a Common Language for Functioning, Disability and Health – ICF*. Geneva: World Health Organization.

Chapter 3

Accessibility: A Key Objective for the Tourism Industry

V. EICHHORN and D. BUHALIS

Introduction

Ensuring access to travel and tourism opportunities for people living with a disability as well as for the entire population requires knowledge and design structures that are inclusive for all citizens. 'Tourism For All' is an often stated target, and existing research emphasises that people with disabilities are not adequately served by the tourism industry due to the existence of a variety of barriers (Burnett & Bender Baker, 2001; Daniels *et al.*, 2005; Darcy, 1998; Darcy & Daruwalla, 1999; Daruwalla & Darcy, 2005; Israeli, 2002; McKercher *et al.*, 2003; Packer *et al.*, 2007; Ray & Ryder, 2003; Shaw & Coles, 2004, Smith, 1987; Yau *et al.*, 2004). By drawing on the social model of disability, all disabling barriers and constraints that impact upon tourism participation need to be dismantled or reduced to allow for travel opportunities for all individuals (Stumbo & Pegg, 2005).

Preceding the elimination of impediments is the actual identification of existing barriers, which this chapter aims to address. As barriers to participation 'need to be addressed in the widest sense of access, if the ultimate goal of eliminating social injustice for people with disabilities is to become a reality' (Darcy & Daruwalla, 1999: 45), the chapter commences by clarifying key concepts with regards to access and accessibility. Due to limitations in terms of word limit and scope of this chapter, a holistic account of the debate cannot be provided. Instead, a framework is established on how to describe accessibility within the tourism system. The chapter proceeds by investigating the foundational literature on barriers to tourism faced by people with different types of impairments. The main aim is to provide a comprehensive review and in-depth understanding of access barriers that can be addressed by the tourism industry, which in turn assists in creating a conceptual framework. This corresponds to claims made by a number of authors (Card *et al.*, 2006; Darcy, 2002; Takeda & Card, 2002) stressing that the 'plethora of barriers' faced by disabled people has to be identified (Smith, 1987). The final part of the chapter highlights key aspects with regard to the future of accessible tourism development.

Accessibility: Towards Conceptual Clarification

Although often taken for granted, the words 'access' and 'accessibility' are complex concepts and have different meanings to different individuals in different contexts (Iwarsson & Ståhl, 2003; Jensen et al., 2002; Veitch & Shaw, 2004a). Hence, accessibility is not consistently defined across all sectors, which makes the enforcement of standards difficult. Further, standards for accessibility vary across European states (European Disability Forum, 2001). Iwarsson and Ståhl (2003) argue that a common language is needed not only to increase marketing efficiency but also to create the primary base for theory development.

By looking at tourism, transport and disability, Cavinato and Cuckovich (1992) refer to access in terms of dealing with and addressing a wide range of constraints. Iwarsson and Ståhl (2003) discuss different dimensions of accessibility based on different geographical levels, such as micro, meso and macro levels. At each level, a distinction can be made in terms of physical access, access to information or to social activities and services. While the latter two are often neglected, the former represents the most common dimension when debating accessibility (Iwarsson & Ståhl, 2003). Darcy (1998) divides the term 'access' into three dimensions: physical access, sensory access and communication access. Within all three categories, the provision of access should not be regarded as a problem area. Instead, access provision needs to be viewed as an inclusive marketing process, which allows tourism players to realise the potential of 'accessibility' for the marketing of tourism products and services to the widest possible client base (Darcy, 1998).

To enhance the theoretical understanding of the concept of accessibility, Jensen et al. (2002) argue that accessibility is one facet of the person-environment relationship. As such, accessibility is a highly relative concept (Iwarsson & Ståhl, 2003) and a comprehension of environmental elements is only possible by relating environmental factors to the person component, as individual interpretations influence the perceptions on what counts as accessible (Jensen et al., 2002). Expanding the conceptual framework of the person-environment relationship, Iwarsson and Ståhl (2003) argue that a clarification is needed by looking at the differences between accessibility, usability and universal design. While accessibility and usability are usually used to determine the observed performance, with usability being more centred on individual interpretations, universal design is highlighted as a more process-oriented approach instead of a focus on results. At its core, universal design addresses the inclusion of the entire population, incorporates aspects of accessibility and usability from the beginning and represents a less stigmatising concept (Iwarsson & Ståhl, 2003).

Related to the accessibility debate is the International Symbol of Access (ISA). While the symbol is widely recognised as representing the interaction between accessibility and disability, it does not remain uncontested. It is often criticised for its exclusivity, inaccuracy and incompleteness in terms of its universal application. Further, the use of the symbol as signifier is highly complex. While it can act as negative signifier in terms of stigmatisation, the symbol can also signify liberation and independence (Ben-Moche & Powell, 2007).

The above debate does, by no means, provide an exhaustive account on the concepts of accessibility and access. However, it serves as a preliminary basis to highlight the complexity inherent in this debate. Discussing the term accessibility, Iwarsson and Ståhl (2003) assert that whether or not a concept is useful depends on the way it is being used. The authors propose a three-tier procedure for using the concept of accessibility. First, individual components involve a description of the functional capacity of individuals or groups. Second, a comprehensive account on the barriers in the environment faced by the target audience has to be provided. Within the third step, personal and environmental components are brought together (Iwarsson & Ståhl, 2003).

Given the current lack of a comprehensive description of barriers faced by people with a disability in tourism, this chapter focuses on the second step of Iwarsson and Ståhl's schemata for accessibility and reviews those barriers that can be actively targeted and altered by the tourism industry.

Accessibility and the tourism system

The tourism industry is a complex system of independent providers which aim to serve the consumer. A variety of stakeholders are involved which often have conflicting needs, wants and interests in the industry (Buhalis, 2003). The entire tourism system is defined by five elements: a traveller-generating region, a destination region, a transit region, a travel and tourism industry as well as the external environment (for a detailed explanation, see Leiper, 1995). Figure 3.1 develops the framework of the tourism system developed by Leiper (1995) and Buhalis (2003) further by adding customers' information needs. These are spread alongside the system, ranging from the pre-travel stage via the actual travel phase (transit and at the destination) to the after-trip period. Throughout all travel stages, customers have particular information needs that have to be fulfilled in order to deliver tourism products and services (Eichhorn et al., 2008).

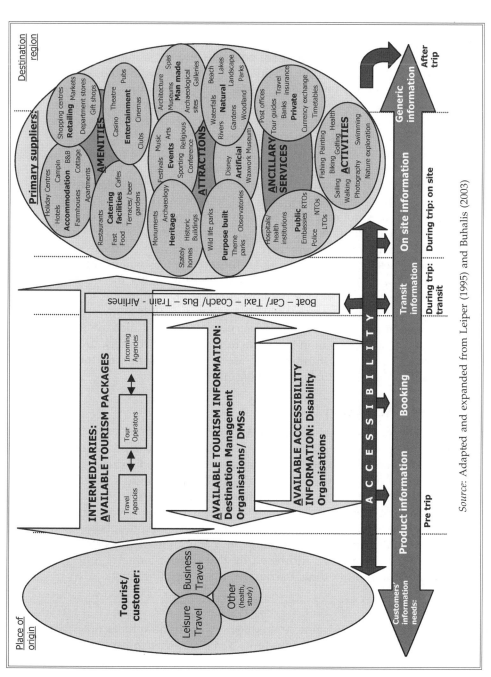

Figure 3.1 The Tourism system and accessibility

By focusing on tourism products and services, the expanded framework also incorporates the six 'As', which are regarded as essential for analysing tourism destinations. These are amenities, attractions, ancillary services, activities, available tourism packages and accessibility (Buhalis, 2000). These 'As' represent the destination's amalgam within the destination region, including amenities (e.g. hotels, restaurants, etc.), attractions (e.g. museums), ancillary services (e.g. health care) and activities. Available tourism packages are offered by travel agencies, tour operators or other intermediaries. Tourism information is offered by all active stakeholders in the system and often brought together and promoted by Destination Marketing Organisations (DMOs). A number of disability organisations also provide tourist information in terms of accessible destinations, sites and venues, which is incorporated into this model. Accessibility does not only refer to the transport part of the system, but interacts with all components of the customers' information need chain. Figure 3.1 illustrates the interaction of accessibility with physical access (transit and destination) and access to information (customers' information need chain). While the above illustration highlights the need for physical access as well as access to information within the tourism industry, barriers to access are complex and not reducible to the physical environmental and information constructs. Important hereby is the recognition that all sectors in the tourism system need to work towards dismantling negative attitudes that are a major barrier to tourism participation for individuals with a disability.

Barriers to Accessing Tourism

A variety of authors have endeavoured to group barriers and constraints to tourism opportunities into categories. The use of categorisations is regarded as beneficial to understanding the nature of individual barriers and to show their interrelation (Smith, 1987). Although it is argued that research should move beyond the restricted focus on barriers to participation and employ the broader conceptualisation of 'constraints' (Daniels *et al.*, 2005; Arab-Moghaddam *et al.*, 2007), both concepts are used interchangeably throughout the following paragraphs. Three categories are employed that can be addressed by the tourism industry: physical access constraints, attitudinal barriers and lack of information.

Physical access

By considering physical access issues, a variety of authors note that an inaccessible environment represents a major barrier to people with a disability (Daniels *et al.*, 2005; Darcy, 1998; Darcy & Daruwalla, 1999; Ernawati & Sugiarti, 2005; Goodall, 2006; Goodall *et al.*, 2005; Horgan-Jones & Ringaert, 2001; Imrie & Kumar, 1998; Israeli, 2002; Packer *et al.*,

2007, Shaw & Coles, 2004; Smith, 1987; Takeda & Card, 2002; Turco *et al.*, 1998; Veitch & Shaw, 2004b; Yates, 2007). Darcy (1998) points out that physical access is one of the most important supply-side issues in tourism. In addition, Burnett and Bender Baker (2001) found that the more severe a mobility impairment, the greater are individuals' needs in terms of an accessible tourism infrastructure.

Aspects of limited physical access include inaccessible transportation, accommodation facilities and attractions (Turco *et al.*, 1998), which leads to oppression in the built environment (Imrie, 2001), with transport being of special concern for disabled people (Shaw & Coles, 2004). Yau *et al.* (2004) argue that over the last two decades, progress has been made in removing obstacles in the physical environment. Also, with regard to transportation for people with impairments, Cavinato and Cuckovich (1992) claim that the transport sector has reduced barriers, whereas Darcy (1998) and Stumbo and Pegg (2005) show that inaccessible public transport is still a major constraint. In general, access to transport embraces two components: arriving and leaving the destination as well as travelling whilst at the destination (Darcy, 1998). By looking at airline practices in Australia, Darcy (2007) emphasises that air travel generates a disembodied experience which is socially constructed. This is due to airline staff not being aware of the needs of disabled people, general regulatory mechanisms in the airline industry and airline procedures. Airline experiences could potentially be improved by incorporating a social approach to disability to airline management (Darcy, 2007). In addition, Stumbo and Pegg (2005) stress the need to develop joint cooperation between airports and airlines to ensure access for people with a disability.

As outlined earlier, together with transportation, inaccessible accommodation and attraction establishments represent further obstacles in the physical environment. Israeli (2002) investigates the relative importance of accessibility features for mobility-impaired travellers in tourist attraction settings in Israel and compares those to non-disabled counterparts. Findings include that among seven accessibility attributes (staircase, elevators, parking, sidewalks, access ramps, paths and restrooms), elevators are identified as the most critical access issue. However, with more travel experience, the relative importance of these factors changes and more weight is given to paths, parking and staircases. While able-bodied tourists can make a trade-off between different features of a site, travellers with a disability are unable to make these trade-offs, especially in the case when attributes support accessibility (Israeli, 2002). Particularly with regard to the accommodation sector, individuals with a disability cannot easily choose an alternative accommodation establishment if they are not satisfied due to the limited number of accessible rooms available (Darcy, 1998; Darcy & Daruwalla, 1999). Thus, regardless of the attractiveness of a destination, accessibility components are non-compensatory (Israeli,

2002; Yates, 2007) and as a result, people with a disability often need to abandon their plans (Darcy, 1998).

Further, often neglected aspects are accessible pathways from the hotel to attractions, amenities and events (Stumbo & Pegg, 2005; Darcy & Harris, 2003). An accessible path of travel, or alternatively labelled a 'continuous pathway', is an uninterrupted path to or within a building(s), which allows disabled people to access all required facilities (Darcy, 1998). The absence of accessible pathways prevents people with a disability having an independent and complete travel experience (Darcy, 1998) and the importance given to paths tends to increase as people with disabilities gain more travel experiences (Israeli, 2002).

Some countries have introduced legislation designed to make it compulsory for tourism suppliers to create an environment that is accessible to people with impairments. Three examples of national legislation are the United Kingdom (DDA), the USA (ADA) and Australia (Commonwealth DDA). Even though legislative acts are in place, with accessibility standards offering insights into minimum acceptable levels of accessibility, a number of obstacles hinder the development of a fully accessible tourism environment.

First, private ownership structures of most of the tourism infrastructure represent a major impediment to the removal of barriers (Rains, 2008). Private owners usually regard the laws protecting the rights of people with a disability as centring around an additional cost category (Imrie & Kumar, 1998) or as legal risks of law suits to be managed (Rains, 2008). In this respect, legal acts generate resistance with the result that private businesses do not regard individuals with disabilities as lucrative customers (Rains, 2008). Thus, the needs of impaired individuals are often perceived as marginal (Imrie & Kumar, 1998).

Second, and as a result of the first argument, minimum standards set by legal acts are often poorly implemented (Stumbo & Pegg, 2005). All this adds up to the political exclusion of people with a disability (Gleeson, 2001). Apart from ensuring that standards are put into action, Dattilo (2002) argues that society should aim towards implementing criteria of universal design instead of designing facilities *for* disabled people.

Third, an additional obstacle refers to the likely incompatibility between access objectives, as laid down in legal acts and conservation policies for historic environments. Within a tourism heritage context, individuals with a disability and heritage service providers are identified as key stakeholders. However, other stakeholders act as 'gatekeepers', using their power to prevent providers making improvements to their heritage sites (Goodall, 2006; Goodall *et al.*, 2005). Primary gatekeepers are conservation planning authorities, leading to conservation issues precluding improvements in physical accessibility. In this context, Goodall *et al.* (2005) state that 'when irreconcilable differences arise between conservation and physical access improvements, the former prevails' (p. 189). As a result, as no heritage tourism provider has been successful in achieving an equitable balance between conservation issues and access needs, a possible solution for overcoming physical inaccessibility is the creation of intellectual access through Information Communication Technologies (ICTs), based on which people with disabilities would potentially be able to 'access' the heritage site in an alternative manner (Goodall, 2006). However, the success of such an 'alternative' access strategy should be evaluated by people with disabilities (Goodall *et al.*, 2005).

Incompatibility between access and conservation objectives is not the only obstacle that impedes the development of a fully accessible tourism environment. The majority of natural or wilderness settings also offer limited accessibility for people with a disability (Brown *et al.*, 1999). Using the example of natural areas can serve as an analogy to heritage sites. Here, the area of conflict focuses on making natural areas accessible for people with impairments while at the same time following principles of preservation (Muloin, 1992). The controversy arises as access to natural areas such as natural parks or nature reserves for leisure purposes is regarded as a key right. However, people with a disability cannot access these areas due to physical barriers, hence being denied of this right. Further, it is argued that physical adaptations to natural areas result in a diminishing experience, a loss of the 'true wilderness' experience (Muloin, 1992). While more access to natural environments is aspired, for people with a disability, these desires exist alongside goals of environmental protection (Nisbett & Hinton, 2005). Natural areas should only be modified when it does not eliminate the reason for visiting the place in the first instance (Muloin, 1992). In cases, where modifications would alter the ecological system, alternative access should be provided (Muloin, 1992), similar to the ongoing debate on heritage sites. Shelton and Tucker (2005), claim that ecotourism is a line of thought that runs parallel to providing access to tourism for people with a disability, emphasising the need to ensure that social and conservation goals operate alongside the need for economic viability. However, by letting tourism providers decide what is economically feasible for achieving socially inclusive tourism settings ignores the requirements and needs of people with impairments.

According to Imrie and Kumar (1998), the origins of structural barriers in the built environment are grounded in the domination of able-bodied values which excludes people with disabilities from key decisions concerning land use and building design. By using the example of building access into special event planning, Darcy and Harris (2003) show that direct involvement of disabled people in the planning process leads to more inclusive approaches. The lack of opportunities to influence building constructions is coupled with wider negative perceptions of disability by the able-bodied population, which stresses the interrelationship between physical access and attitudinal barriers. One respondent of Imrie and Kumar's (1998) focus groups stressed this point by saying: 'It is important to not only change the shape and size of buildings but we've got to change the attitudes too' (Imrie & Kumar, 1998: 367).

Attitudinal barriers

While some authors argue that there has been a change in public awareness, which led to more positive attitudes towards people with a disability over the last decades (Cavinato & Cuckovich, 1992), others argue that negative attitudes still represent a major barrier to tourism participation (Horgan-Jones & Ringaert, 2001; Muloin, 1992; Murray, 2002; Murray & Sproats, 1990; Shaw *et al.*, 2005; Smith, 1987). For example, McKercher *et al.* (2003) report that some travel agents held the extreme belief that a disability per se effectively excluded people from travelling and Muloin (1992) goes as far as stating that barriers in terms of negative attributes are at the 'roof of all barriers to outdoor participation for persons with a disability' (p. 23).

By investigating young disabled teenagers' experiences of access to inclusive leisure, Murray (2002) states that despite the fact that an inaccessible environment was often stated as a barrier to participation, people's attitudes represent the focal constraint for accessing leisure opportunities. By overcoming attitudinal barriers, a real difference could be made to outdoor recreation experiences (Muloin, 1992), which subsequently leads to an easier management of physical access barriers (Packer *et al.*, 2007). In relation to this, it is claimed that any barrier in the physical environment can only be reduced or eliminated through a profound change in attitudes (Murray & Sproats, 1990). Opposing this view, Darcy (2003) argues that it is easier to change the physical environment than people's attitudes. By examining whether the Sydney 2000 Games have assisted in improving the accessibility infrastructure of the region as well as raising the level of disability awareness, Darcy (2003) concludes by affirming the former and questioning the latter. While the Games have probably accelerated changes for improving the physical accessible infrastructure, social change in terms of more favourable attitudes or increased awareness remains deficient. For example, the Official Olympic Games Ticket Book, which included in its 'Frequently Asked Questions' section the question: 'I am confined to a wheelchair. Will I miss out on the Games?' (cited by Darcy, 2003: 744), reinforces rather than dismantles existing stereotypes (Darcy, 2003).

Despite the fact that many scholars have investigated attitudinal barriers, only a few examine the subject at a deeper level. A notable exception is Daruwalla and Darcy (2005), who make a distinction between personal and societal attitudes. While the former refers to beliefs and opinions that individuals possess with regard to certain objects, the latter relates to widespread attitudes held by society at large. Societal attitudes are influenced by, for example, legal rights, and are generally more remote to the individual and are also not necessarily compatible with personal attitudes. Findings of Daruwalla and Darcy's study indicate that both types of attitudes can be altered through training programmes. However, it was found easier to change societal attitudes. In contrast, more challenging is the (re)formation of peoples' personal attitudes, which should receive precedence over societal attitudes. It is not sufficient to emphasise the need to move from a medical model perspective to a social dimension, but instead, personal contact with a disabled person is required which needs to be reinforced on a regular basis. The use of contact should then be placed within the social model perspective to avoid the 'personal tragedy' perception (Daruwalla & Darcy, 2005). Thus, the need to provide sensitivity staff training is crucial (Card *et al.*, 2006; Gladwell & Bedini, 2004; McKercher *et al.*, 2003), particular with regard to increased consultation and interaction with people with a disability in everyday situations (Stumbo & Pegg, 2005).

Lack of information

By looking at barriers with regard to tourism staff, negative and condescending attitudes are usually coupled with the inability to provide people with a disability with correct and reliable information (Stumbo & Pegg, 2005). This leads to questioning whether travel agencies act as facilitators or barriers for people with impairments in terms of representing a reliable information source. Often, it is shown that travel agencies act as inhibitors to travel due to a number of reasons (McKercher *et al.*, 2003; Stumbo & Pegg, 2005). First, travel agencies were perceived to hold negative attitudes and the overall perception of certain service providers was that disability and taking holidays was incompatible (McKercher *et al.*, 2003). Given the limited experience in catering for travellers with a disability, the second obstacle relates to the over-emphasis on selling package tours, which do not meet the needs of disabled people (Cavinato & Cuckovich, 1992; McKercher *et al.*, 2003). Third, the quality of information provided was perceived as inaccurate and incomplete due to difficulties in obtaining all disability-related information crucial for trip planning (Cavinato & Cuckovich, 1992; McKercher *et al.*, 2003). Resulting from these obstacles, travel agencies are often not trusted by people with a disability (Ray & Ryder, 2003). Hence, the travel trade largely promotes a myth by presenting travel agencies as experts for all travel-related issues. What is needed is a shift from selling inflexible packages, designed to meet the industry's needs, to offerings that correspond to consumer needs and information requirements (McKercher *et al.*, 2003).

The lack of accurate information is often stated as a major barrier (Darcy, 2002; Darcy & Daruwalla, 1999; Eichhorn *et al.*, 2008; Horgan-Jones & Ringaert, 2001; McKercher *et al.*, 2003; Miller & Kirk, 2002; Packer *et al.*, 2007; Stumbo & Pegg, 2005; Turco *et al.*, 1998; Veitch & Shaw, 2004b; Yates, 2007). Darcy (1998) outlines deficiencies in information provision in terms of the general availability of the information, lack of accuracy and detail in the information provided as well as the format of the presented information. Expanding Darcy's (1998) account, Eichhorn *et al.* (2008) stress the need for reliable and rich information, appropriate travel information sources as well as customer-oriented and communication services.

While an accessible infrastructure is clearly the basis for tourism participation (Pühretmair, 2004), a fully accessible environment is unlikely to be achieved in the short to medium term. In contrast, the provision of accurate and reliable information can be dealt with in the short term (Darcy & Daruwalla, 1999) and is regarded as the most effective means for opening tourism opportunities for disabled people (Cavinato & Cuckovich, 1992). As individuals with a disability have to undertake a high degree of pre-planning to ensure that their needs are met (Darcy, 1998; Pühretmair, 2004), detailed information is required for reaching the destination, returning home, moving around at the destination as well as for checking the availability of accessible accommodation, attractions and other amenities (Veitch & Shaw, 2004b). For a successful marketing of accessible facilities it is important to communicate this information to all potential customers, since the strategic planning of tourism-related products and services does not start at the destination. Thus, the provision of accessibility information influences the tourist decision making, travel planning and booking process (Pühretmair, 2004). In contrast, the lack of accurate and reliable information can lead to abandoning the holiday intention (Darcy, 1998). Therefore, the provision of accurate accessibility information represents an important step in overcoming barriers (Darcy, 2002). But what is the ideal travel information source to overcome existing constraints?

Given the lack of systemic approaches for accessing the required information, Cavinato and Cuckovich (1992) suggest that special support groups and public agencies should be responsible for providing information. In contrast, Ray and Ryder (2003) stress the value of word of mouth communications, followed by the internet and travel guides. While the internet is regarded as a unique opportunity for providing reliable and up-to-date information, the inaccessibility of websites represents a major obstacle (Pühretmair, 2004). Additionally, part of the population might not have access and/or the skills to deal with information and communication technology (Sen & Mayfield, 2004). A synthesis of the discussion on informational constraints and travel information sources is provided by Eichhorn *et al.* (2008). By reviewing access schemes as a potential information communication source, different types of informational requirements need to be considered. Further, the fulfilment of informational needs would potentially assist in eliminating physical barriers by highlighting where environmental barriers have been removed or contrarily are still in existence (Eichhorn *et al.*, 2008).

Identification of Access Barriers – What Next?

The review of access barriers in terms of physical access, attitudinal barriers as well as lack of information has highlighted that the tourism industry has to support all travellers at all travel stages in the planning process as well as during the holiday. All stages are essential for the improvement of service quality as well as for complying with customers' needs (Pühretmair, 2004), with tourism providers having control over reducing these barriers.

Within the travel planning process, an inclusive marketing approach is necessary to provide adequate and reliable information as well as adequate booking channels. Travel planning of people with disabilities is normally characterised by a more detailed information enquiry and the higher the accessibility requirements, the more detailed information is needed. However in reality, the supply of detailed information tends to be smaller the higher the level of accessibility requirements, which often leads to abandoning the idea of taking holidays in the planning phase (Waschke, 2004). To avoid this situation, accessibility and sensitivity training procedures are regarded as crucial to ensure not only high knowledge levels with regard to accessible facilities, but also to work towards dismantling negative attitudes. During the trip, information and positive attitudes remain decisive elements for enjoyable, barrier-free holiday experiences, which have to be supported by an accessible physical environment. Particularly important when considering physical access issues are 'accessible pathways' as accessible hotels and venues alone do not add to genuine holiday experiences.

Depending on the type of impairment, physical access barriers do not affect individuals in the same way, whereas, information needs are equally important to all. As a result, it is advocated that it is of tremendous importance to actively remove informational barriers that currently reduce travel options. While the collection and dissemination of comprehensive information about the entire accessible sub-system is a very difficult and challenging task, given the amount of tourist destinations and tourism suppliers in Europe and worldwide, it is essential to recall that accessibility is not only critical for people with impairments. The possibility to receive information about accessible destinations is a key quality criterion that influences all tourists and their decision-making process. Creative marketing strategies should focus on criteria that are important to all individuals and should be developed by investigating information search characteristics of all market segments.

While norms and recommendations represent a good starting point for the tourism industry, equally important is a rethinking of what access means for the entire population. This requires shifting the focus from removing barriers to embracing an inclusive design approach (Iwarsson & Ståhl, 2003) as a way to opening the market (Veitch & Shaw, 2004a). Hence, accessibility and tourism should be reconciled by stressing the need for inclusive design as a fundamental aim and target for the tourism industry. This requires a horizontal approach through the incorporation of a number of interrelated policy areas, such as regional, environmental and social policy (European Disability Forum, 2001), in addition to user groups, architects, health care professionals, politicians and researchers (Iwarsson & Stahl, 2003).

Conclusion

Tourism is a complex system where accessibility is an important component interacting with the customers' need chain, ranging from the travel planning process via the transit stage to the destination with its heterogeneous attributes. As the participation in travel and tourism opportunities is regarded as a key social right (European Disability Forum, 2001), the tourism industry has to play a major role in the implementation and execution process of this right.

The chapter has provided a comprehensive account on barriers faced by people with a disability, which can be altered by the tourism industry. It has highlighted the need to remove barriers in terms of physical access, attitudes and information provision with the overall aim of moving towards a full incorporation of universal design criteria. Whereas inclusive design approaches are crucial supply-side issues, in the short-term, access to information is regarded as the determining factor for deciding whether tourism remains an abstract concept or individuals become active travellers. The provision of access to information is hence a key success factor for tourism destination marketing and represents a quality criterion for all citizens.

While this chapter focused on accessibility from a supply-side perspective, future research will have to work towards providing a comprehensive framework of demand-side factors. As structural and interpersonal constraints are interrelated with intrapersonal aspects (Crawford & Godbey, 1987), a deeper examination of personal and collective experiences and contexts is needed (Mactavish *et al.*, 2007, Yau *et al.*, 2004). Little is yet known about the complex interplay of barriers, examining how individual dimensions interact with the social environment (Bickenbach *et al.*, 1999; Packer *et al.*, 2007). A holistic framework, providing improved insights into the ongoing interaction between individuals and the environment, would mean that tourism comes one step closer to understanding the dialectic relationship between the social and the physical.

References

Arab-Moghaddam, N., Henderson, K.A. and Sheikholeslami, R. (2007) Women's leisure and constraints to participation: Iranian perspectives. *Journal of Leisure Research* 39, 109–126.

Ben-Moche, L. and Powell, J.J.W. (2007) Sign of our times? Revis(it)ing the international symbol of access. *Disability & Society* 22, 489–505.

Bickenbach, J.E., Chatterji, S., Badley, E.M. and Üstün, T.B. (1999) Models of disablement, universalism and the international classification of impairments, disabilities and handicaps. *Social Science & Medicine* 48, 1173–1187.

Brown, T.J., Kaplan, R. and Quaderer, G. (1999) Beyond accessibility: Preferences for natural areas. *Therapeutic Recreation Journal* 33, 209–221.

Buhalis, D. (2000) Marketing the competitive destination of the future. *Tourism Management* 21, 97–116.

Buhalis, D. (2003) *eTourism: Information Technology for Strategic Tourism Management*. Harlow: Prentice Hall.

Burnett, J.J. and Bender Baker, H. (2001) Assessing the travel-related behaviors of the mobility-disabled consumer. *Journal of Travel Research* 40, 4–11.

Card, J.A., Cole, S.T. and Humphrey, A.H. (2006) A comparison of the accessibility and attitudinal barriers model: Travel providers and travelers with physical disabilities. *Asia Pacific Journal of Tourism Research* 11, 161–175.

Cavinato, J. and Cuckovich, M. (1992) Transportation and tourism for the disabled: An assessment. *Transportation Journal* 31, 46–53.

Crawford, D.W. and Godbey, G. (1987) Reconceptualising barriers to family pleasure. *Leisure Sciences* 9, 119–127.

Daniels, M.J., Drogin, E.B. and Wiggins, B.P. (2005) 'Travel Tales': An interpretive analysis of constraints and negotiations to pleasure travel as experienced by persons with physical disabilities. *Tourism Management* 26, 919–930.

Darcy, S. (1998) *Anxiety to Access: Tourism Patterns and Experiences of New South Wales People With a Physical Disability*. Sydney: Tourism New South Wales.

Darcy, S. (2002) Marginalised participation: Physical disability, high support needs and tourism. *Journal of Hospitality and Tourism Management* 9, 61–72.

Darcy, S. (2003) The politics of disability and access: The Sydney 2000 Games experience. *Disability & Society* 18, 737–757.

Darcy, S. (2007) *Improving Airline Practices by Understanding the Experiences of People with Disabilities*. Travel and Tourism Research Association – TTRA. Charlottetown: Canada.

Darcy, S. and Daruwalla, P.S. (1999) The trouble with travel: People with disabilities and tourism. *Social Alternatives* 18, 41–46.

Darcy, S. and Harris, R. (2003) Inclusive and accessible special event planning: An Australian perspective. *Event Management* 8, 39–47.

Daruwalla, P. and Darcy, S. (2005) Personal and societal attitudes to disability. *Annals of Tourism Research* 32, 549–134.

Dattilo, J. (2002) *Inclusive Leisure Services: Responding to the Rights of People with Disabilities.* State College, PA: Venture Publishing.

Eichhorn, V., Miller, G., Michopoulou, E. and Buhalis, D. (2008) Enabling access to tourism through information schemes. *Annals of Tourism Research* 35, 189–210.

Ernawati, D.B. and Sugiarti, R. (2005) Developing an accessible tourist destination model for people with disability in Indonesia. *Tourism Recreation Research* 30, 103–106.

European Disability Forum (2001) *EDF Position Paper on Tourism: Framing the Future of European Tourism.* Doc. EDF 01/13 EN, Brussels: Belgium.

Gladwell, N.J. and Bedini, L.A. (2004) In search of lost leisure: The impact of caregiving on leisure travel. *Tourism Management* 25, 685–693.

Gleeson, B.J. (2001) Disability and the open city. *Urban Studies* 38, 251–265.

Goodall, B. (2006) Disabled access and heritage attractions. *Tourism, Culture and Communication* 7, 57–78.

Goodall, B., Pottinger, G., Dixon, T. and Russell, H. (2005) Access to historic environments for tourists with disabilities: A compromise? *Tourism Review International* 8, 177–194.

Horgan-Jones, M. and Ringaert, L. (2001) *Accessible Tourism in Manitoba.* TTRA – Travel and Tourism Research Association. Niagara Falls: Canada.

Imrie, R. (2001) Barriered and bounded places and the spatialities of disability. *Urban Studies* 38, 231–237.

Imrie, R. and Kumar, M. (1998) Focusing on disability and access in the built environment. *Disability & Society* 13, 357–374.

Israeli, A.A. (2002) A preliminary investigation of the importance of site accessibility factors for disabled tourists. *Journal of Travel Research* 41, 101–104.

Iwarsson, S. and Ståhl, A. (2003) Accessibility, usability and universal design – positioning and definition describing person-environment relationships. *Disability and Rehabilitation* 25, 57–66.

Jensen, G., Iwarsson, S. and Ståhl, A. (2002) Theoretical understanding and methodological challenges in accessibility assessments, focusing the environmental component: An example from travel chains in urban public bus transport. *Disability and Rehabilitation* 24, 231–242.

Leiper, N. (1995) *Tourism Management.* RMIT Press: Melbourne.

Mactavish, J.B., MacKay, K.J., Iwasaki, Y. and Betteridge, D. (2007) Family caregivers of individuals with intellectual disability: Perspectives on life quality and the role of vacations. *Journal of Leisure Research* 39, 127–155.

McKercher, B., Packer, T., Yau, M.K. and Lam, P. (2003) Travel agents as facilitators or inhibitors of travel: Perceptions of people with disabilities. *Tourism Management* 24, 465–474.

Miller, G. and Kirk, E. (2002) The Disability Discrimination Act: Time for the stick? *Journal of Sustainable Tourism* 10, 82–88.

Muloin, S. (1992) Wilderness access for persons with a disability. In G. Harper and B. Weiler (eds) *Ecotourism* (pp. 20–25). Canberra: Australian Bureau of Research.

Murray, M. and Sproats, J. (1990) The disabled traveller: Tourism and disability in Australia. *Journal of Tourism Studies* 1, 9–14.

Murray, P. (2002) Hello! Are you listening? Disabled teenagers' experience of access to inclusive leisure. York: Joseph Rowntree Foundation.

Nisbett, N. and Hinton, J. (2005) On and off the trail: Experiences of individuals with specialised needs on the Appalachian Trail. *Tourism Review International* 8, 221–237.

Packer, T.L., McKercher, B. and Yau, M.K. (2007) Understanding the complex interplay between tourism, disability and environmental context. *Disability and Rehabilitation* 29, 281–292.

Pühretmair, F. (2004) It's time to make etourism accessible. In K. Miesenberger, J. Klaus, W. Zagler and D. Burger (eds) *Computers Helping People with Special Needs*. (pp. 272–279). Berlin: Springer.

Rains, S. (2008) Culture in the further development of universal design. *Design for All* 3, 18–34.

Ray, N.M. and Ryder, M.E. (2003) 'Ebilities' tourism. An exploratory discussion of the travel needs and motivations of the mobility disabled. *Tourism Management* 24, 57–72.

Sen, L. and Mayfield, S. (2004) Accessible tourism: Transportation to and accessibility of historic buildings and other recreational areas in the city of Galveston, Texas. *Public Works Management & Policy* 8, 223–234.

Shaw, G. and Coles, T. (2004) Disability, holiday making and the tourism industry in the UK: A preliminary survey. *Tourism Management* 25, 397–404.

Shaw, G., Veitch, C. and Coles, T. (2005) Access, disability, and tourism: Changing responses in the United Kingdom. *Tourism Review International* 8, 167–176.

Shelton, E.J. and Tucker, H. (2005) Tourism and disability: Issues beyond access. *Tourism Review International* 8, 211–219.

Smith, R.W. (1987) Leisure of disabled tourists – Barriers to participation. *Annals of Tourism Research* 14, 376–389.

Stumbo, N.J. and Pegg, S. (2005) Travelers and tourists with disabilities: A matter of priorities and loyalties. *Tourism Review International* 8, 195–209.

Takeda, K. and Card, J.A. (2002) U.S. tour operators and travel agencies: Barriers encountered when providing package tours to people who have difficulty walking. *Journal of Travel and Tourism Marketing* 12, 47–61.

Turco, D.M., Stumbo, N.J. and Garncarz, J. (1998) Tourism constraints for people with disabilities. *Parks and Recreations* 33, 78–84.

Veitch, C. and Shaw, G. (2004a) *Access and Tourism: A Widening Agenda*. Insights – Tourism Intelligence Papers, British Tourist Authority, January 2004: A-121.

Veitch, C. and Shaw, G. (2004b) *Understanding Barriers to Tourism in the UK*. Insights – Tourism Intelligence Papers, British Tourist Authority, May 2004: A-185.

Waschke, S. (2004) Labeling im barrierefreien tourismus in Deutschland – Vergleichende analyse auf basis Europäischer beispiele. Unpublished thesis, University of Lüneburg.

Yates, K. (2007) Understanding the experiences of mobility-disabled tourists. *International Journal of Tourism Policy* 1, 153–166.

Yau, M.K., McKercher, B. and Packer, T.L. (2004) Travelling with a disability – More than an access issue. *Annals of Tourism Research* 31, 946–960.

Chapter 4

Disability Legislation and Empowerment of Tourists with Disability: The UK Case

C. VEITCH and G. SHAW

Introduction: Changing Views

The latter part of the 20th century saw a dramatic change in the way people with disabilities were viewed within society. The United Nations 1 (2008) has in part summarised these changes in its recognition that people with disabilities have become increasingly proactive in asserting strength and confidence in their abilities to lead self-reliant and independent lives. This assertion of the right to lead an independent life is slowly being translated within some countries into legislation which ensures people with disabilities are not subject to discrimination. However such legislation has not been universally embraced. This potentially reduces the opportunities for global travel for those with disabilities. Equally where there is legislation across continents, such as Europe. However, this can be different and patchy for visitors with implications for seamless travel across the different countries within the European Community. Whilst the legislation empowers disabled people, it does not necessarily enable them, as wider government and social policies impact on the lives of the disabled whereby they are unable to travel because of the lack of means, possibly living on low incomes and therefore excluded from such societal norms as taking a holiday. The only opportunities to enjoy a break or a holiday this group is likely to have is through policies of social tourism, whereby those on low incomes are helped to take holidays.

Anti-discrimination legislation does not automatically mean that change is necessarily brought about, at least quickly. It cannot therefore be seen as a panacea to bring about change in the short term for the benefit of people with disabilities. As the UK experience shows, despite legislation being introduced in 1995 many people with disabilities still encounter difficulties planning and taking a domestic holiday or short break.

The aim of this chapter is to review the impact of disability legislation on the holiday process particularly in the context of experiences within the UK.

Legislation and the Implications for People with Disabilities

The United Nations have identified that comparative studies show however that at present those countries which have enacted such legislation are relatively few with only 45 countries having anti-discrimination and other disability-specific laws. Amongst these are included some significant tourist destinations such as: the USA – Americans with Disabilities Act (1990); Australia – Disability Discrimination Act (1992) and the UK – Disability Discrimination Act (1995).

The implications of so few countries having such legislation is that the opportunities for people with disabilities to be able to enjoy barrier-free tourism and be truly global travellers remains rather limited. This patchy approach has implications on a practical level as well sometimes within the same country. For example a person with disabilities visiting or resident in Canada will benefit whilst in the state of Ontario with the Ontarians with Disabilities Act (2005). This is the first act of its kind in Canada and means that businesses and organisations who provide goods and services to people in Ontario will have to meet certain accessibility standards in five key areas (Ontario – Ministry of Community and Social Services, 2008):

- customer service;
- transportation;
- information and communications;
- built environment;
- employment.

However, should they wish to travel to the rest of Canada, at present they would not enjoy the assured accessibility which the provision of such legislation offers them. Similarly for visitors and people with disabilities living in Europe, there is not a universal harmonised approach to disability legislation. The goal of the European Union Disability Strategy is 'A society open and accessible to all' (EC1, undated), however there is much variation in the progress made towards removing barriers at tourist destinations. A report examining standardising accessible tourism information in Europe identified that, 'This is due to several factors, including *different access requirements* in the prevailing legislation, varying *levels of technical know-how* and development, and even different *cultural norms, geographical* and *climatic* factors' (Vos & Michopoulou, 2005). The report also identified that:

The situation today is that a variety of different laws, access standards and guidelines are applied to building design throughout Europe. Besides this, there is also a diverse collection of guidelines issued by standards organisations, sectoral interest groups and disability organisations. Some of these standards being mandatory in certain countries and others being voluntary. (Toegankelijkheidsbureau vzw & LIVING Research and Development s.p.r.l., 2001: 6)

In large part this legislation reflects the changing societal views of people with disabilities. Within the literature this is reflected in two differing models, namely:

- The medical model – which focused attention on the physical aspects of disability.
- The social model – this argues that the way in which the experience of disability is structured is conditioned through the context of society and social organisation (Oliver, 1990: 2).

Within the UK the social model emerged following the activities of the Union of the Physically Impaired Against Segregation (Oliver, 1996). The model has become an important, if recently contested, paradigm, and argues that people with impairments are excluded by a society not organised to cope with their needs (Shaw, 2007). Massie (1994: 1) argues that such failures set-up barriers to the full participation of the disabled in society. He identifies two forms that discrimination takes: personal discrimination – experienced by individuals when using services; and structural or institutional discrimination – rooted in the way structures are designed. Whether intended or not the results are the same in limiting opportunities for those with disabilities.

Other emerging views, such as the 'affirmation model' also contribute to our understanding of the disabled and their relationships with society. This particular model rejects earlier views of the medical model and develops ideas from the social model. As Swain and French (2000: 578) observe, 'the affirmative model directly challenges the notion that the problem lies within the individual or impairment, recognising disabled people's experiences as valid individuals, determining their own lifestyles, culture and identity'.

Thus legislation in some parts of the world has been used to counter discrimination against the disabled. With roots often founded in civil rights, legislation attempts to give equal opportunities to people with disabilities and promote greater social inclusion. This chapter explores the impact of such legislation on access to tourism within the UK. We start with a discussion of the evolution of disability discrimination legislation before going on to examine its impact on tourism.

The Evolution of Disability Discrimination Legislation in the UK

In the United Kingdom the Disability Discrimination Act (DDA) 1995 is a significant piece of legislation as it impacts on all economic sectors of the UK, including those businesses involved in the tourism industry. Whilst the act was passed in 1995 it has been brought into effect in phases in order to give service providers time to make the changes which are required of them.

The DDA uses a broad definition of disability, which is defined in part one of the act, which states that a disabled person is someone with 'a physical or mental impairment which has a substantial and long-term adverse effect on his ability to carry out normal day-to-day activities' (Equality and Human Rights Commission (a), undated). This embraces people with a range of impairments. (See Table 4.1).

Disability is not however one dimensional and as can be seen from Table 4.1 there are a range of different disabilities which can affect people in different ways, and for each of these disabilities people will feel the effects of impairment. The implications are that their needs or requirements when taking a short break or a holiday can range from being low and cause no real difficulties for them, to being high, which for these people can mean that taking a holiday has the potential to be far more complicated to plan.

The law expects people with disabilities to be treated fairly. Since 1995, it has been illegal to refuse to serve somebody on the grounds that they have a disability. Therefore, it is illegal for example, to refuse to take

Table 4.1 Identifying those with disabilities

• people who are blind or partially sighted
• people who are deaf or hard of hearing
• people who have heart conditions
• people who have epilepsy
• people who have problems with continence
• people who have insulin dependent diabetes
• people who have Down's syndrome
• people who have dyslexia
• people who have arthritis
• people who are wheelchair users
• people who have experienced mental health problems
• people who have learning disabilities
• people who have multiple sclerosis (MS)
• people who have cancer
• people who have HIV

Source: Disability Rights Commission (undated)

a booking from a guest simply because they have a disability. This is covered in part three of the act that covers goods, facilities and services. The act also covers deliberately providing a poorer quality of service to disabled people by, for example, taking longer to serve a disabled person breakfast, or applying terms that are unreasonable. Other examples may be asking for a higher deposit from a customer because they have a disability or charging a disabled guest more than a non-disabled guest. (Disabled Rights Commission, undated).

Since 1999, service providers have been expected to amend their policies, practices and procedures so that disabled people can better access their services, and to provide auxiliary aids, such as an induction loop system, and auxiliary services, for example serving a guest breakfast in their room if they are unable to access the dining room due to a physical barrier such as steps. (Disabled Rights Commission, undated).

In 2004 a further part of the DDA known as the physical features duties of the DDA became law. This expects service providers to remove, alter or provide a reasonable means of avoiding any physical barriers to accessing and using their premises. There is no absolute level of compliance that can be achieved, working as the DDA does on the basis of reasonable adjustments. Many factors are taken into account when considering what is reasonable, such as the fact that some changes may be beyond a service provider's resources or are totally impracticable. Other technical constraints such as fire regulation, health and safety factors may also be taken into account. However providers must be able to clearly demonstrate that changes have been considered and where these are not possible provide evidence in support of their decisions (Disability Rights Commission, undated). Policing of the act is dependent on individuals who, if they believe they have been discriminated against by a service provider because of their disability, have the right, under the DDA, to challenge this discrimination and they may be able to make a claim against the person or organisation responsible. They may also be able to go to court and be paid compensation.

Legislation and the Empowerment of Tourists with Disabilities

The DDA affects therefore all parts of the tourist system where there is a service element involved such as; transport, accommodation, attractions, restaurants, pubs, bars, retail, etc.

Whilst people with disabilities, both living in the UK and visiting, have been empowered by law, making it illegal for service providers to discriminate against them on grounds of disability, the law does not reach into other areas which affect them. The first of these concerns the spirit of the law, which at its heart aims to give equal rights and opportunities by removing barriers for people with disabilities and to offer them the same quality of service provided to people without disabilities. Therefore some service providers, such as hoteliers, may well execute their physical features duties under the DDA and make the reasonable changes expected of them based around the built environment. However, they may not have necessarily gone further with their services to help make the visitor experience for people with disabilities an easy and pleasant one. The second area centres around issues of social exclusion where people with disabilities may find themselves on low income and on the margins of society and unable financially to be able to afford a short break or a holiday.

Despite the DDA being introduced in 1995, which gave notice to service providers of the intent of the law and set out what was required of them, over a decade after its introduction and many disabled people still find taking a short break or a holiday a very stressful experience. Research by VisitBritain (2007), the National Tourist Board for the UK, examining the holidaying experiences of people with disabilities highlighted a number of threats to the perfect holiday, including insensitive, uncaring and poorly trained staff. This is where the spirit of the act is not engaged to ensure a positive experience for people with disabilities. This could however be seen as part of an overall quality issue that is sometimes seen within British tourism in that many non-disabled people come across poor service, however, for those people with disabilities this is far too critical and has the potential to be a major barrier.

Other findings from this research were that planning and booking holidays can be particularly problematic for consumers with a disability (VisitBritain, 2007). This took the form of:

- Advance planning and extensive research being needed before booking suitable accommodation, often using a variety of sources and asking around for word of mouth experiences.
- According to the respondents there is currently no comprehensive source of information relating to accessible accommodation in England. If there was this would remove significant barriers when planning a holiday, including psychological barriers such as 'worry', 'fear' and 'anxiety'. When considering motivation, the research also found that it was evident that informal information sources, in terms of word of mouth recommendations from friends and relatives and previous visits, were most influential in encouraging respondents to book accommodation based on its accessibility.

Another key finding was that booking a holiday was quite stressful and worrying for all groups, particularly:

- Deciding where to go – it was clear that the destination needs to be accessible as well as accommodation.

- The need to plan well in advance of the break/holiday to ensure all needs were accommodated.
- There was a feeling of 'making do' with what was there – where provision was lacking consumers were 'making do' which detracted from the whole holiday experience.
- There was a lack or incomplete description of accommodation available.
- Travel operators and booking offices often didn't have the relevant information, although when a particular agent was found to be helpful and understood the needs of an individual all holidays were booked through this one agent (the individual never went anywhere else).
- Call centres were cited as a problem and often did not carry the relevant accessible information about individual properties. They were a particular worry for hearing-impaired guests trying to communicate their needs.

These difficulties have been confirmed by other studies, most notably by the charity Leonard Cheshire who have reported on UK hotels (Leonard Cheshire, 2005a), the travel industry (Leonard Cheshire, 2004), and holiday experiences (Leonard Cheshire, 2005b). In terms of the latter survey, barriers to holiday-taking were significant and covered both physical and financial access through to poorly informed staff. The report concluded that: 'Too often successful trips were the product of an individual's sheer determination as opposed to genuine accessibility on the part of the travel industry'.

The results of all of this research suggests that despite the DDA having been in operation for sometime, the positive effect which the act aims to achieve, that is an inclusive experience for people with disabilities, does not yet appear to have been fully realised. Thus, whilst the legislation might have put in place critical changes to physical features and services it has not been effective in addressing two key areas which are critical to tourism and of interest to everyone. The first is that tourism is disparate and relies on the sum of parts, e.g. transport, accommodation, attractions, hospitality etc., working together to achieve a positive experience. This has impacts on people without disabilities; however it becomes far more critical for people with disabilities. If these are not all developed to a point of synergy where there is the ability to reach a destination and it is itself fully accessible, this can create potential barriers (see Table 4.2). Secondly, reliable, accurate information needs to be available to help the decision-making process, so that people are aware of and fully understand potential barriers as these could influence their choices.

In addition to the spirit of the act not being universally in place, there is the issue of social exclusion which many people with disabilities face.

Palmer *et al.* (2005) found that 30% of working-age disabled adults have incomes that leave them below the poverty line. This rate was found to be higher than ten years previously and fully double the rate for working-age adults without a disability (Palmer *et al.* 2005: 13). The implications of this are that people with disabilities who fall into this low income group are unlikely to be able to afford to take a short break or holiday, a feature confirmed in Table 4.2. Howard (1999) observes that what makes exclusion so pernicious is the way many problems interact with each other. Therefore, the issue of poor access to education means that people with disabilities are less likely to have formal qualifications and therefore limited employment opportunities which limit access to decent income and standard of living. In this wider context the notion of empowerment is an issue that falls in large part outside the function of the DDA (Shaw, 2007).

This raises the issue of social tourism which has its roots in the notion of human rights which has been expressed by the United Nations in several statements since the first in 1948 when their 'Universal Declaration of Human Rights' stated that 'everyone has the right to rest and leisure, including reasonable limitations of working hours and periodic holidays with pay' (United Nations, 1948: Article 24). The Disability Rights Commission (DRC), which was set up to promote disability equality in the UK, merged on the 1st October 2007 with the Commission for Racial Equality (CRE), and the Equal Opportunities Commission (EOC) to become the Equality and Human Rights Commission. Unfortunately, this organisation does not promote or openly support the concept of social tourism whereby those who are disadvantaged can afford to take part in tourism activities which are supported in some form.

Therefore, whilst people with disabilities living in the UK have been empowered by legislation, namely the DDA, some of them, those who do

Table 4.2 Key issues of people with disabilities and holiday-taking

Key Issues	% reporting
1. Problems with accessibility on last holiday	57
2. Travel agents/tour operators lacked basic awareness of disability problems	43
3. Problems of access to holiday accommodation	29
4. Unable to afford a holiday in 2004	27
5. Problems of transporting mobility aids	22
6. Difficulties in obtaining travel insurance	22
7. Unable to take a holiday due to access problems	25

Source: Leonard Cheshire (2004)

not have access to the means or resources, have not necessarily been enabled because of the impact of low incomes. The implication of this is that the DDA does not support what has been established internationally as a human right to have a holiday and therefore the legislation has a limited effect for them.

Conclusions

Major worldwide events, such as the Paralympics, have shown globally, how people with disabilities can lead independent, successful lives and play a full role in society. This comes after having fought hard for rights for themselves which in some countries are enshrined in laws and recognised around the world. However, these laws are by no means universal and a comparatively small number of countries have enshrined rights for people with disabilities in legislation. In the UK these rights have been manifested in the DDA of 1995, which gives disabled people access to activities such as tourism so that they are not discriminated against in any way and can enjoy the same level of service as everyone else. However, whilst the legal framework is in place there is evidence to suggest that 15 years after its introduction that, whilst the DDA has achieved some changes with service providers changing and adapting their businesses to meet the requirements of the disabled, it has not necessarily achieved what it set out to. The spirit of the act has not been universally applied and the evidence suggests that for some people with disabilities they still find planning and taking a holiday an extremely difficult and stressful activity because of issues such as the lack of good, reliable accurate information provision or knowing how truly accessible a destination as a whole is. For some these may make no difference whilst for others they will make do and the holiday experience is diminished and for other individuals it may prove to be a real barrier preventing them from taking a holiday. As the Leonard Cheshire report (2005b: 3) concluded, 'there is still much to be done to make holidays truly accessible'.

Equally, whilst the law has empowered disabled people and many will be enjoying the benefits of that position it has not necessarily enabled all disabled people to be able to take a short break or a holiday. This applies to those people who are disabled and find themselves socially excluded on the margins of society and unable to participate due to low incomes.

Legislation has shown therefore that it can make a difference, but it does not necessarily bring about the changes that many would seek. The moral issues of inclusion, access to work and better incomes, as well as service providers responding to the spirit of the act, are key factors. We would argue that change comes therefore as a package and no one single thing, such as legislation, can enact this.

References

Accessibility for Ontarians with disabilities. At www.mcss.gov.on.ca/mcss/english/pillars/accessibilityOntario.

Americans with Disabilities Act. At www.ada.gov/.

Australian Human Rights Commission. At www.hreoc.gov.au/disability_rights/index.html.

BITS – Social Tourism. At www.bits-int.org/en/index.php?menu=1.

Department for Work and Pensions [DWP] – Case Studies. At www.dwp.gov.uk/employers/dda/case_tourism.asp.

Disability Discrimination Act (Australia) (1992). At http://www.Comlaw.gov.au/Comlaw/management.nsf/lookupindexpagesbyid/IP200401406?OpenDocument.

Disability Discrimination Act (UK) (1995). At http://www.opsi.gov.uk/acts/acts1995/ukpga_19950050_en_1.

Disability Rights Commission (undated) *What do guest accommodation owners need to know? What you should know about the law and disability?* (for Disability Rights Commission reference): At http://www.dwp.gov.uk/docs/guest-accomm.pdf.

Drake, R. F. (1999) *Understanding Disability Politics*. Basingstoke: Macmillan Press Ltd.

EC1 (undated – online document). At http://ec.europa.eu/employment_social/disability/strategy_en.html.

EC2 (2008 – online document) The magazine of enterprise policy – Supporting social tourism. At http://ec.europa.eu/enterprise/e_i/news/article_7041_en.htm.

Equality and Human Rights Commission (a) (undated). At www.equalityhumanrights.com/en/yourrights/equalityanddiscrimination/disability/pages/introduction.aspx.

Equality and Human Rights Commission (UK). At www.equalityhumanrights.com/.

Howard, M. (1999, July 28) Social Exclusion Zone. *The Guardian*.

Massie, B. (1994) *The Commission on Social Justice, Disabled People and Social Justice*. London: Institute For Public Policy Research.

Leonard Cheshire (2004) Disability and the travel industry: Attracting disabled travellers. London: Leonard Cheshire.

Leonard Cheshire (2005a) No room at the inn: a report on UK hotels and accessibility.

Leonard Cheshire (2005b) Wish you were here? Disabled people's holiday experiences.

Oliver, M. (1990) *The Politics of Disablement*. Basingstoke: Macmillan Press Ltd.

Oliver, M. (1996) *Understanding Disability from Theory to Practice*. Basingstoke: Macmillan Press Ltd.

Ontarians with Disabilities Act (2005). At http://www.e-laws.gov.on.ca/html/statutes/english/elaws_statutes_05a11_e.htm.

Ontario – Ministry of Community and Social Services (2008) (Online document) Accessibility for Ontarians with disabilities. At www.mcss.gov.on.ca/mcss/english/pillars/accessibilityOntario.

Palmer, G., Carr, J. and Kenway, P. (2005) *Monitoring poverty and social exclusion in the UK, 2005*. York: Joseph Rowntree Foundation.

Shaw, G. (2007) Disability, legislation and the empowerment of tourists with disabilities in the UK. In A. Church and T. Coles (eds) *Tourism, Power and Space*. Abingdon: Routledge.

Swain, J. and French, S. (2000) Towards an affirmation model of disability. *Disability & Society* 15 (4), 569–582.

Toegankelijkheidsbureau v.z.w Hasselt and LIVING Research and Development s.p.r.l. Brussels (2001) *Accessibility Legislation in Europe Status Report on building regulations, standards, design guidelines and other measures for ensuring access to the built environment for persons with disabilities*: Toerisme Vlaanderen – Meeting of EU Ministers of Tourism.

United Nations (1948) The universal declaration of human rights (Article 24). NY: United Nations.

United Nations 1 (2008) History of United Nations and persons with disabilities – Introduction. At www.un.org/disabilities/default.asp?id=122.

United Nations 2 (2008) Convention on the rights of persons with disabilities – Some facts about persons with disabilities. At www.un.org/disabilities/convention/facts.shtml.

United Nations Enable – Promoting the rights of persons with disabilities. At www.un.org/disabilities/.

VisitBritain (2007) *Access Consumer Research*. London: VisitBritain.

Vos, S. and Michopoulou, E. (2005) Inventory of accessibility schemes and data sets within the EU-tourism sector. Unpublished.

Chapter 5

Understanding Tourist Experience Through Embodiment: The Contribution of Critical Tourism and Disability Studies

J. SMALL and S. DARCY

Introduction

This chapter seeks to understand the tourist experiences of people with disabilities, including the seniors who also constitute the accessible tourism market. Tourism experiences can be viewed through many approaches. The following discussion is situated within the framework of critical theory in tourism studies and critical disability studies theory, both of which focus on ends rather than means, examining social power structures with a commitment to emancipation. The lived experience of the person is the subject matter and within the approaches of critical tourism and critical disability studies, the lived experience is a bodily experience. This chapter examines the embodied experience of those with disabilities within the tourism context. For the purposes of this chapter, the authors take Osborne's (2000: 51) definition of embodiment where ' "embodiment" is used to describe the way in which the bodily bases of individuals' actions and interactions are socially structured: that is, embodiment is a social as well as natural process'. In this case, embodiment as it relates to disabilities includes mobility, hearing, vision, cognitive/ learning, sensitivity and mental health but, in the developing field of critical disability and tourism studies, the areas most researched are mobility and vision. While it is recognised that disabled/non-disabled subjectivity intersects with other subjectivities such as gender, age, culture, ethnicity, sexuality, economic position etc., a dearth of research in tourism and disability studies (and the word length of this chapter) prevent a discussion of these intersections.

Boorstin (1987) in *The Lost Art of Travel* distinguished between travellers of the past and today's tourists, noting that 'until almost the present century, travel abroad was uncomfortable, difficult and expensive' (p. 80). Indeed, the word travel comes from *travail* – 'meaning "trouble", "work"

73

or "torment"' (Boorstin, 1987: 85). He viewed the *traveller* of the past as someone who worked at the experience, whereas the *tourist* of today waits for things to happen to them. Boorstin (1987) claimed: 'Nowadays it costs more and takes greater ingenuity, imagination and enterprise to fabricate travel risks than it once required to avoid them' (p. 117). Today's travel might be seen as easier than travel of the past. Today, air travel allows us to cross the globe within a day. Travel companies now have organised tours to places unimaginable even since Boorstin wrote his chapter – computers allow us to seek travel information, purchase the holiday and check-in without leaving home and, for some, have virtual tourism experiences (Turner *et al.*, 2005: 43). We don't need 'real' money to travel – we have credit cards. Mobile phones and email allow us to stay in constant touch with home while away. And so on. The commonplace of travel today and the ease with which many non-disabled people engage can conceal the socially constructed barriers and constraints encountered in travel by those with access needs. Developments in travel technology can be a blessing for some but those who are restricted in their access to a computer, ATM, mobile phone or other technology remain segregated. In many ways, services and facilities for people with disability have increased but in other ways service personnel are scant and travel has become a DIY venture. Where are the porters of yore at travel termini – not everyone can carry a suitcase! Travel is still geared for bodies and minds that conform to a very narrow definition of embodiment.

A Critical Approach to the Tourist Experience of People with Disabilities

Critical theory in tourism is an approach to research that has developed in the last 20 years. As explained below, the criteria of critical theory are that:

> It must be explanatory, practical, and normative, all at the same time. That is, it must explain what is wrong with current social reality, identify the actors to change it, and provide both clear norms for criticism and achievable practical goals for social transformation. Any truly critical theory of society, as Horkheimer further defined it in his writings as Director of the Frankfurt School's Institute for Social Research, 'has as its object human beings as producers of their own historical form of life'. (Horkheimer, 1993: 21, in Bohman, 2005)

Wilson *et al.* (2008: 16) explained that critical theory is not simply a criticism of past grand tourism theories but one that challenges enquiry to seek a solution for inequalities where they exist:

> While ontological, epistemological and methodological differences may exist, those employing a critical approach would generally be

concerned with resisting positivist modes of enquiry, unmasking power relations, seeking emancipation, addressing inequalities, or calling for change or action within the field they are exploring. (Brookfield, 2005; Hooks, 2003)

While sharing some traditions with critical theory, *critical disability studies*[1] is a challenge to a dominant medical discourse that pervades all social structures for people with disabilities. In disability studies, the critical approach challenges the traditional medical model which is founded on the 'personal tragedy theory of disability' (Oliver, 1996: 31). The medical model locates the problem of disability within the individual as their 'fault', and sees the cause of the problem as emanating from the functional/psychological losses (their impairment/embodiment) arising from the disability. This medical discourse views able-bodiness as the social norm and, hence, excludes the 'abnormal' (people with impairments) from citizenship. Critical, or social approaches to disability, on the other hand, place the lived experiences of people with disabilities at the centre of understanding, focus attention on the disabling environment and hostile social attitudes, and seek solutions through the creation of enabling environments (Barnes, 1996: 43).

The fundamental distinction between the medical and social models lies in the difference between *impairment* and *disability* (UPIAS, 1975). The social model changes the focus of disability from the agency of the individual to the social structure of society. It is the disabling social practices that transform the individual's *impairment* (embodiment) into a disability. Social model analysis focuses on disabling barriers, hostile social attitudes and the material relations of power (see Figure 5.1).

While the social model is more emancipatory than the medical model, Shakespeare and Watson's (2001: 22–23) critique of social model approaches identifies three central criticisms of the social model that focus on: impairment; the impairment/disability dualism; and the issue of individual identity. It is suggested that an *embodied ontology* would contribute towards developing a complexity and richness to the social model by creating a space and place for embodiment within the paradigm. Shakespeare and Watson conclude that an embodied ontology offers a starting point for disability studies to begin to develop a more adequate social theory of disability. As they suggest, developing an embodied ontology of disability needs to consider that impairment and disability are not dichotomous but are different places and times on a continuum. They suggest that disability should not be reduced to just a medical condition or to just social barriers alone as it is more complex. In effect, the embodied ontology challenges the dichotomies of impairment/disability and illness/health and offers a model that intertwines structure

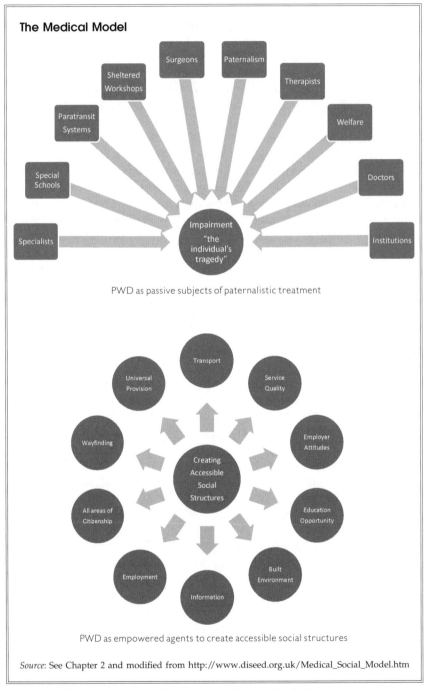

Figure 5.1 Social versus medical approaches to disability

and agency. To summarise, Figure 5.1 presents a representation of the differences between the models.

Critical approaches in tourism studies also recognise that the lived tourist experience is a bodily experience. Firstly, it is a corporeal experience of the senses, organs and emotions. The tourist body sleeps, eats, aches, sunburns, relaxes, cries, laughs, smells, hears, sees and so on. Secondly, it is a body that is socially constructed. Different bodies have different social images, meanings, value and worth. The body is gendered and aged and disabled/non-disabled etc. Thus the tourist experience is an embodied experience. For some postmodernists the body is solely discourse but as Bordo (1989: 13) says, the body is more than 'a *text* of culture'. It is also 'a *practical*, direct locus of social control'. Harper (1997: 161) refers to 'the ongoing tension between the body as constructed and the body as experienced, the body as an inscribed exterior and the body as a lived interior'. Grosz (1993: 196) deals with this tension by connecting the 'two' bodies and explains the body 'as a kind of *hinge* or threshold: it is placed between a psychic or lived interiority and a more socio-political exteriority that produces interiority through the *inscription* of the body's outer surface'. To avoid the dichotomous, mutually exclusive categories of mind and body, new terminology is required. Grosz (1994: 22) suggests that 'some kind of understanding of *embodied subjectivity*, of *psychical corporeality*, needs to be developed'. The body is matter but it is not a fixed essence on which the social is inscribed. As Holland *et al.* (1994: 22) say, 'The material body and its social construction are entwined in complex and contradictory ways which are extremely difficult to disentangle in practice'.

Representation

Hargreaves (1986: 14) comments that, 'The body is clearly an object of crucial importance in consumer culture and its supply industries'. Tourism is an industry in which the body is central to its purpose and consumption. How the body is represented in tourism can provide some context for how a person might experience tourism. Analyses of tourism images of the body indicate that Western tourism discourse constructs the tourist body in a particular way: young, non-disabled, slim, tanned, Caucasian and what would generally be considered 'attractive'. Underlying the discourse are power relations that posit youth and the idealised body as the focus of the 'tourist gaze' (Urry, 1990). While tourism managers may present a *politically correct* public attitude by recognising the importance of employing people with disabilities (e.g. valued social roles) they still choose to exclude people based on their 'abnormal' appearance (Ross, 1994). This attitude of managers extends to the context of tourist to tourist interaction, where people with disabilities are considered *inappropriate other* for social consumption by non-disabled tourists (Urry, 1990: 141).

Attitudes of non-disabled managers become evident through decisions made on marketing of how tourism product is represented. One example of representation research focused on the production of images in Qantas brochures. Edelheim (2007) in a study of Qantas brochures for Australian domestic destinations found that only 10% of the people pictured in the brochures were aged 45 and over although at the time 35% of the population was over 45 years of age. In addition to age discrimination, 'not one photograph in any of the twelve brochures portrayed people with any types of visual signs of disabilities'. He added, 'Although the accommodation providers in the brochures have indicated if there are facilities suited to people with disabilities, the invisibility of disabilities tends to further highlight the hegemonic norm these brochures are focusing on' (Edelheim, 2006: 104). A study of Air New Zealand and Qantas in-flight magazines similarly revealed that, of the people pictured in the advertisements, there was no evidence of a person with a disability (with one exception being a Qantas advertisement for the packaging and assembly service of Disability Services Australia). The finding that representations of people in tourism material privilege the hegemonic gaze is continually reported in the tourism literature.

Travel Patterns and Embodiment

Woodside and Etzel (1980) established that on a regional level, households with people with disabilities travelled less than non-disabled households did. Darcy (1998) noted that of those who did not travel, a proportion of people with a disability would *like* to travel but did not due to socially constructed constraints rather than their impairment. Only Australia has collected data at a national level to provide an insight into the comparative travel patterns of people with disabilities and the non-disabled at a national level (BTR 1998; 2003). This work was recently reinforced through a more extensive analysis that estimated the economic contribution of accessible tourism to the economy (Dwyer & Darcy, 2008). As Figure 5.2 shows, people with disabilities travel at lower levels than the non-disabled for overnight stays and outbound travel. Interestingly, they travel at the same rate for day trips where the complication of overnight/outbound travel includes the provision of accessible accommodation. The significance of the research by these authors was that it clearly established the significantly lower travel rates of people with disabilities when compared to the non-disabled population.

What becomes apparent in interrogating the constraints-related research is that the difference in travel patterns can be explained by a series of socially constructed constraints by people with disabilities (Daniels *et al.*,

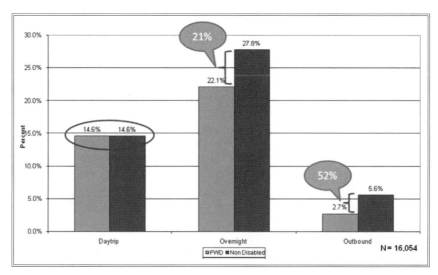

Figure 5.2 Comparative travel patterns between PWD and the non-disabled

2005; Darcy, 2004; Turco *et al.*, 1998). This work clearly establishes that people with disabilities travel at a lower rate to the general public, have different embodied experiences at different levels of disadvantage and for the most part this is not the outcome of their embodiment. Further, as shown in Figure 5.3, there are significant differences in the travel patterns of disability groups (Darcy, 2003). While constraints theory has provided insights into the relative disadvantage that people with disabilities experience, critics of positivist approaches and constraints-related research have called for a greater understanding of the disability experience through listening to the voices of those with disability (Samdahl & Jekubovich, 1997a, 1997b).

Embodied Tourist Experiences

The major conceptualisations of embodiment have drawn on medicalised discourses where social approaches focus on the creation of enabling environments through inclusive and universal practices (Preiser & Ostroff, 2001; Swain *et al.*, 1997). This changes the medicalised discourse to one of social inclusion where the emphasis is on changing the disabling environment and hostile social attitudes to one that empowers people with disabilities. Rather than focusing on the individual's impairment (their embodiment), the attention is directed towards creating an enabling environment for their dimension of access. The major dimensions discussed under human rights legislation include: Mobility; hearing; vision; cognitive/learning; sensitivities; health related (cancer/HIV); mental

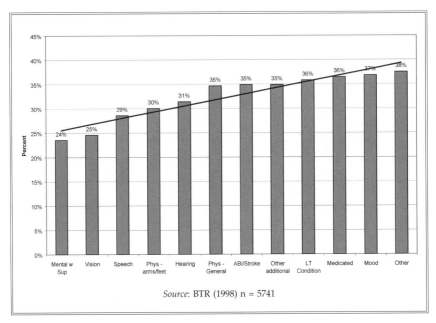

Figure 5.3 Impairment by traveller

health; and others. The way that the United Nations (2006) *Convention on the Rights of Persons with Disabilities* and, hence, national disability discrimination legislation is framed, disability is an evolving construct. What was acceptable 20 years ago is no longer acceptable as the material position of people with access needs continues to develop. For example, online environments that were not conceived of 20 years ago have now evolved through browser development, PC-based software for interpreting web-based communication to people with vision impairments (e.g. Jaws software) and organisational commitment to accessible information. These developments have been reinforced through common law precedent (e.g. 'Maguire v SOCOG [HREOCA H 99/115]', 2000).

A great deal of the tourism research and practice is focused on people with mobility disabilities. There has been some limited research on people with vision, hearing, children with cancer and sensitivities. More recently there have been significant discussions about embodiment, obesity and air travel (Vedelago, 2009) with legal arguments as to whether obesity could be regarded as a disability and the consequent implications for air carriers. Table 5.1 identifies examples of inclusive and universal practice that provide an enabling environment for six of these groups. The table is presented as a foundation for understanding what promotes independent, dignified and equitable access that is at the core of the definition of accessible tourism (Darcy, 2006).

Table 5.1 Examples of inclusive practice in tourism for the dimensions of access

Mobility	Hearing	Vision	Cognitive	Sensitivities	Health
Continuous pathway	Telephone typewriters (TTYs)	Tactile ground surface indicators; Audio signals	Plain English text	Chemical free environments	Medical support
Circulation space	Hearing loops	Alternative formats e.g. large text, Braille; audio	Attendant support	Dietary considerations	Supportive environment
Specialist Equipment	Captioning	Areas for guide dogs	Opportunities for group travel for those in communal supported accommodation	Non-smoking areas	Opportunities for group travel
Low-floor buses	Sign language interpreters	Sensory trails	Activity programming	Organisational promotion	Advocacy and philanthropy programs
Customer service attitude	Customer service attitude	Customer service attitude	Customer service attitude	Customer service attitude	Customer service attitude
Wayfinding systems	Wayfinding systems	Wayfinding systems	Wayfinding systems	Clearly labelled areas	Specialist equipment
Information systems	Information systems	Information systems	Information systems	Information systems	Information systems

Source: Constructed for the chapter

Research Design

The rest of this chapter seeks to explore the embodied experiences of people with mobility and vision impairments that emerged from three studies of the authors based on modified grounded or phenomenological approaches. Elsewhere in the book, other embodiments are specifically explored including people with mental health issues, vision impairment, seniors and children with cancer. The research design of each of these studies has been comprehensively outlined in the original sources (Darcy, 1998, 2004; Packer *et al.*, 2008). The remainder of the chapter takes the lived experience of people with disabilities from these studies and seeks to understand their journey through their own words. It does so by firstly presenting an overview of the journey through presenting key stages with quotes identifying the experiences of people with mobility impairments

(MI) and people with vision impairments (VI). The chapter then seeks to present an understanding of the action between people with disabilities and the tourism environment using the accommodation sector as a focal point. For this last section, only people with mobility impairments experiences will be presented.

Embodied Tourist Experiences – Understanding the Journey

> 'I have not had a holiday for 35 years. I have not had a day trip for over eight years.' (MI)
>
> 'I think if people have very little sight, they don't bother about travelling . . .' (VI)
>
> 'Well I've given it up. Yeah, well, it's too hard.' (VI)

The reasons for non travel can be simply a consequence of the person's impairment. However, a great deal of the research suggests that for most, impairment collides with social circumstances

> Being a quadriplegic, on a full pension and with three children it is very hard to travel great distances and find suitable accommodation at a reasonable price – almost impossible. That's why we do not travel very much at all. (MI)

Depending upon their embodiment and dimension of access, the experiences of those who do travel can differ dramatically. Tourism can bring joys when all the travel plans come to fruition but those with disabilities carry with them an anxiety and trepidation through each stage of the journey. Countless experiences tell us that people with disabilities are expecting their plans to go wrong, not because the travel agent has not booked the flights but because their access needs have been overlooked by the socially constructed environment. Those with disabilities need to place a great deal of trust in others including strangers.

The quotations in Table 5.2 highlight the elation, the nightmares and the frustrations of travel. Tourism is a journey with many components, beginning before one leaves home. Satisfaction or dissatisfaction can occur at any of the stages of the journey and with any of the industry sectors or non-industry relationships experienced at any of the stages. How one experiences any of these 'moments' of travel can affect the pleasure or displeasure of the whole trip.

The remainder of the chapter documents experiences that emerged from the journeys undertaken. The headings that emanated from the grounded approach reflect the sequential process of undertaking a journey.

Table 5.2 The elation, the nightmares and the frustrations of travel

> ... regardless of whether I have a disability or not, I still like to live and I enjoy travelling and on that general principal I don't feel I'm much different to anyone else. I just like to be able to see the world or see the country and just get out there and live, whether it involves travelling and making friends or just going up the road or to a different country. I think it's all exciting, just the same as anyone else that would enjoy it. To find somewhere near and the sense of adventure isn't lost on someone vision impaired. (VI)
>
> Travelling with a disability is a never-ending nightmare, hell on Earth, indescribable, nerve-wracking, stomach churning, unbelievably expensive experience. (MI)
>
> [Travel] can be very, very, very, scary and I think more so for those people who are blind or have low vision than those who are sighted. And I think [a] daunting thing for a person with no disability, let alone one that has one. And it's not being recognised, because if it were then it'd be a lot more accessible. (VI)

Table 5.3 presents examples of embodied quotations from tourists with mobility (MI) and vision impairment (VI) at each of the key stages identified. Following the overview, is a detailed examination of the inter-action between impairment, and accommodation provision in the lived experiences of people with mobility disabilities. The reason for examining accommodation is that people with mobility disability cannot undertake an overnight stay without being certain of an accessible place to stay. This section concludes with a discussion of the *essence* of the embodied tourism experiences of people with impairments.

Access, Embodiment and Accommodation

For tourists with mobility disabilities, physical access into and within accommodation can be critical to having a tourist experience. This section draws on two studies to examine specifically the accommodation experiences of people with mobility disabilities (Darcy, 1998, 2004). Kristy (below), whose impairment affects her mobility, stipulates her access requirements as *ground floor* accommodation:

> We've been stuffed around quite a few times and we've been really aware of making sure that what they [providers] say is in fact actually going to eventuate ... even though you think you already have [made sure]. It's amazing what goes wrong nevertheless ... we've gone

Table 5.3 Tourist voices: Examples of embodied experiences

Stage/system	Experience
Travel planning	(1) ... the frustration I guess of having to put so much planning into a travelling trip which almost exhausts you before you start. (MI)
	(2) Access to information I think is the biggest barrier, even before you go overseas. It's non-existent. So you can't research that country because you don't have access to information such as the 'Lonely Planets' or brochures from tourist agencies [*these are only in printed format*]. The internet is inaccessible for people who use adapted technology. So you're very much relying on word of mouth, somebody else reading it to you. (VI)
Travel agents	(3) I tried to explain to a senior staff member at Harvey World Travel my need to take up two place seats because of my stiffened legs. This travel agent told me that if the plane was not full, then I would be able to have two seats, but unless I wanted to pay for the extra seat, he could not assure me of the two seats. He curtly told me that he did not think this was discriminatory because other people often bought two plane seats – fat people for instance, and people who travel with large musical instruments. (MI)
	(4) I was talking [to the travel agent] about wanting to go on the European tour for a holiday five-day trip. He made a phone call and basically said to the operator, 'I have this person here who is legally blind and he uses a cane and do you think you could possibly get him on the tour?' The person on the other end of the phone said, 'That sounds a bit risky, I am not so sure'. So I went to another travel agent because I was not happy about his approach, you know, every phone call was becoming harder to book things. The second travel agent called exactly the same place and said, 'Oh, I am just booking this European tour for a guy here: he has a vision impairment but he is very capable, he has no night vision, and may need to hang onto someone's arm from time to time, otherwise he is completely mobile and totally independent. That is not a problem is it?' 'No of course not!' It's the way you sell yourself! It was true, all I needed was to hold onto someone else's arm from time to time and it was fine. (VI)
Transportation to and from destination	**Air travel** (5) You get the odd one who is quite rough, and they pick you up like a sack of potatoes. They do not really have any idea of safe lifting and positioning, they just dump you and walk off. I have had that happen before, that was terrible ... As soon as you get out of your motorised chair, you often feel very vulnerable. You can't move anywhere. (MI)

	(6) I found the airline was really quite rude, in that June and I went to get on the plane and he yelled down the corridor, 'I've got a couple of carry ons here' ... That whole bad attitude to the customers' rights ... not realising that people with disabilities know what they're talking about and deserve respect. (MI)
	(7) If I choose to inform them that I am visually impaired, the meet and greet service with the airlines is great. They escort me onto the plane, find my seat. Also then they will give me an aisle seat if that is possible. (VI)
	(8) This lady [flight attendant] said, 'Ok you just walk down the aisle and past first class, blahblahblah'. And I went, 'Right did you just comprehend ... I'm vision impaired'. And it was almost as if I was this really insecure young adult that was fibbing a disability to get additional assistance. Because I really had to justify how much I could and couldn't see. Almost to the extent where I had to say, 'I can see these many fingers'. You know, really get down to their level. Really insulting, really unnecessary, particularly when you've got all the additional anxieties. So that was a horrible, horrible experience. (VI)
	(9) I have had some airlines coming out with wheelchairs to take me on the plane. I go, 'Oh no, I don't think so. I can adequately walk, thank you'. (VI)
Other transportation	(10) ... we phoned up Sydney Railway Station to ask for information about catching a train to the Blue Mountains. And he said it is tricky ... we could arrange to get you into a carriage, at this end, but I'm not sure whether you can get out of Katoomba Station. I said, that's not terribly helpful. (MI)
	(11) And one couple that was on that [Italian coach] tour ... he had just had a hip replacement and she had just had a triple by-pass ... and had no idea that the buses wouldn't drive them up to the Baptistery in Florence ... all the brochures have these silences. They don't tell you things ... (Older tourist)
Accommodation	(12) On our last trip away, we rang and checked with the place about wheelchair accessibility and were assured it was fully accessible. However, upon arrival there we discovered the door was not wide enough to fit my wheelchair, the step which I was told was only four inches high was in fact closer to 14 inches high. My wife checked inside and discovered there was no way possible to get to the bed or even move inside with the wheelchair. When this was mentioned to the manager, their response was they had nothing else and the information in the NRMA directory was incorrect. They suggested we travel 40km back and try there. However, we were lucky and found accommodation at a motel just down the road. They were only too pleased to help

us and informed us that they had heard many
complaints about the other place. (MI)

(13) When I stayed in London, they took me up and the
gentleman was brilliant. He was like, 'You've got ...
the light switches ... here. The remote control is here.
Do you want me to describe the room?' ... And he was
great. He was great. And he said, 'Ok, in the morning,
just give me a yell, I'll come down, and take you down
to the restaurant, and I'll make sure that I tell the other
receptionist downstairs' ... so they were good. They
were good. (VI)

(14) Certainly being able to get a shower commode chair
over the toilet, so that you can actually use the loo ...
A roll-in shower, a hand held hose, I need a sink that I
can actually get my knees under, rather than having
facia boards underneath the sink and vanity so you
can't wheel under the sink. Otherwise if I try and clean
my teeth, have a wash, do whatever, I finish up getting
my shirt and my trousers very wet ... And I need the
razor plug to be in an accessible position rather than
over behind the sink or up too high. (MI)

(15) I don't know of a hotel access room I've been in other
than the Crown Plaza, Terrigal, that you actually got a
view of the water, if you're near water that is. The one
in the Novotel in Woolongong looks out over the air-
conditioning plant; the one in the Park Royal in Darling
Harbour looks straight on to the office building next
door ... (MI)

(16) Well my ideal hotel would have a simple layout, I
suppose it's unlikely that it would not have a large
open space for its foyer, because they all do, but ideally
it would have some identifiable path from the entrance
doors to the reception and that might be that the floor
of the hotel foyer was marble, but there was a carpet
that took you from the entrance doors to the reception
desk. I don't really care what it is, just that it is
identifiable. That the street entrance was not too
complicated or had too many stairs (I mean stairs are
ok, but you know, not a huge flight of stairs), not
revolving glass doors that are always very difficult to
negotiate as a vision impairment person. (VI)

(17) Hotels are set up visually not 'auditorily' ... I travel
with a guide dog and most hotels are not really set up
for guide dog travel. Unfortunately it's still the case
that a lot of accommodation providers don't realise that
they have to take the dog. It tends to be the smaller
single operators, not the big ones. And I don't think
that has ever happened to me personally, but I'm
aware of the fact that it's quite a frequent occurrence. I
have certainly experienced [it] in relation to hospitality
mainly ... restaurants and cafes. (VI)

	(18) I couldn't even get in to the top of the bath, into the bathtub, the wall was so high on it ... If I'd been twenty years younger I could have. (Older tourist)
	(19) The bedroom had a double bed in it, but the bed was so low I knew I'd never get out of it, with my arthritic knee ... (Older tourist)
Destination experience	(20) Byron's great because you do not feel like a freak; everybody is feral with whatever goes hairstyle, tatts, piercings, drugs ... nobody stares. It's like you're normal. (MI)
	(21) Get on a bus ... the best time that I had has been with other tourists that just happened to be there, you know, have a chat with somebody and talk about normal, touristy type things. And rather than being segregated, going in special purpose taxis or in a van by yourself where you do not get that social interaction. (MI)
	(22) I found that ... because it is a small town, at night when I brought out my cane, it was almost like an alien film ... I suddenly got looks and people just couldn't comprehend ... I had people ask, well if you've got the cane, how can you still see my face? You know, just didn't quite fathom or well, rather comprehend that you can have low vision, use a cane. You don't have to be completely blind. So I thought that was really interesting in terms of the education there, [it] was a lot more dated ... their knowledge and awareness of people who are blind and vision impaired ... (VI)
	(23) [I] think Melbourne, in many ways [is] a lot more accommodating [than Sydney] for people who are blind/vision impaired. Their Tactile Ground Surface Indicators are placed correctly, for starters, and they use them a lot more than we do. And the fact that they are placed correctly, it plays a very important role when you've got low vision, like myself. (VI)
	(24) I started to wheeze and produce mucus. This doesn't happen these days unless there is environmental tobacco smoke ... I felt pain and discomfort ... When I started struggling to breathe I looked around and saw some women smoking. I went to the women's toilets fairly quickly because I hoped that it would be a safer place. I was feeling pretty distressed physically (Francey & Meeuwissen v Hilton Hotels, 1997). (S)
Restaurants	(25) Restaurants are badly lit and dim and I really cannot see ... suddenly I am confronted by a meal I don't know how to eat. I often don't know what's on my plate. (VI)
	(26) Menu is not in large print or Braille. You have to listen to someone read out the whole menu. That is very frustrating. It would be great if I could do it on my own ... It's frustrating going through a menu that

	seems to have 400 items on it. You suddenly think 'now which one did I like again?' You don't want to ask the person to go through it again so you have to quickly make up your mind and get on with it, without making too much of a fuss about it. (VI)
Tourist attractions	(27) It is frustrating that many places of historical interest etc. are not accessible but that is a penalty of being in a wheelchair and sometimes can't be helped. One thing you have to pack first is a sense of humour, the fact that you may not be able to see everything you would like and that sometimes others have to be your eyes through description and pictures. (MI)
	(28) ... I have gone to get into it, and they tip my chair back. I have got my front wheels on, I'm driving forward and, being a narrow doorway, it actually caught the control function (on the power wheelchair), and I've tipped back on a steep 25 degree angle. I couldn't control the control button and the gondola is still moving! So I've got the front wheels up on top of the gondola floor and it's moving, and I am stuck, and couldn't control the chair. Ohhh, like panic stations ... What got me was, that won an award for tourism. (MI)
	(29) For me, I need to touch it; if I can I'll walk on it, sit on it whatever. But I need to touch it, I need to do the activity to be able to get that experience. (VI)
	(30) I am not one for art galleries and museums, because that is a lot of visual stuff so I will avoid them ... But we had a great time in the Vatican City because there was a lot of tactile stuff. You could feel, carvings and ... because I could feel it ... I was blown away by it ... Commentary is good, but sometimes it is too much. In Europe, they have lots of audio tours, but they are in such detail that I would *just say, 'Let's move on, I have had enough now'. (VI)*
Desire & solutions	(31) I have learned now not to think of possible problems, but to confront problems as they arise which seems to be a lot less than the problems you imagine before you leave. 'Get out there and do it'; these problems are not as frequent or difficult as you may think. (MI)
	(32) Just because you can't see the Eiffel Tower, or you can't see the Silk Road, it doesn't necessarily mean that you can't experience the ambience, the culture, the food, the language. And I think that that's the underlying issue there in itself, and hence the reason why there are no accommodations out there for people who are blind and vision impaired, because people's ignorance [is] ... because you're blind, or you've got low vision, why would you want to travel anyway? (VI)

Note: MI = Mobility Impairment; VI = Vision Impairment; S = Sensitivities places where the unit was on the ground floor and then it was actually booked out or something and you have to go upstairs ... we've stood our ground and refused to move our bags ... (Kristy).

The experience of being 'stuffed around' when requesting accessible accommodation is a common one. Kristy's experience is disconcerting in that a request for ground floor accommodation would be the most basic of access requirements but even this request could not be relied upon within the booking process. As Tim (below) suggests, what people with impairments may regard as an information issue has a much broader organisational context:

... You go to the owner or the manager and they have no idea, they have had one woman arrive in a wheelchair who can actually walk and they say, 'oh yeah, we've had somebody in a wheelchair' (Tim).

As Tim suggests, if the owner or manager is unsure of the level of access of their property then this cannot be communicated with any degree of reliability. Many people with impairments said that staff reported that they had disabled facilities that had been successfully used by 'the disabled'. However, many staff may have had limited experience with people with impairments, generalising from a single experience. This generalisation becomes compounded where staff, managers and owners may not understand the function of the inclusions in an accessible room. People with impairments consistently mentioned this lack of knowledge of disability and access as a reason for their experiences. It is not surprising that many of the general public hold the belief that all wheelchair users can walk if they need to. To develop an explanation of these issues, the perceptions held by accommodation managers about people with impairments are examined in Chapter 9.

The next accommodation requirement is *level* access of ground floor accommodation. As one person states, 'The percentage of ground floor accommodation with no steps is very small'. Ideally, all rooms have threshold-free entry as physical access is also a social issue.

... I think too few resorts provide good access. They may provide one or two rooms but that doesn't allow you to get around the resort all that well. Why can't all rooms within a resort be adaptable and at least visitable (Don).

The next criterion after level access involves *ingress and egress* from the room. The method of access to rooms requires little consideration for the non-disabled person but can offer insurmountable issues of dependence for people with impairments. Don's experience highlights some of these issues for people with limited hand function:

Door heights or door handles are a real pain. As a person who has very limited hand function, I find it difficult to operate those mini-card entry door locks ... I have had to punch a hole in the top of the card and put a little bit of string through it so I can hook my finger in and whip it out. If they have got a lever handle door knob on the outside, I can get in ... that's if the door closer isn't too heavy but even with the Crown Plaza Canberra, the inside door knob is round so I can't get out. Very smooth, satin finish and I've got to ring the porter to come and open the door when I want to get out of my room! That's just bloody nonsense, even then getting them to remove the door-closer. The hotels won't do it. They insist on fire regulations and that makes it very hard (Don).

Don's point also raises issues of conflicts between access and fire regulations. Once inside the room the next criterion is the *organisation of space* to maximise circulation. Many people related that they physically change the configuration of the room for their needs. This may involve removing furniture excess to their needs or changing the position of the bed. It is not just the size of the room that is critical but the furniture provided must also meet the needs of his travel companions. '... I might want two single beds or a double' (Tim). Access is an issue of spatial use which involves an understanding of designing rooms that accommodate use by people of all abilities. In Don's case, this involves a multitude of considerations to promote independent access:

Light switches at a reasonable height, wardrobes with hangers actually down at a reasonable level rather than six foot in the air, with long detachable coat hangers. I take my own coat hangers away because I can never get a coat hanger on, and a table within the room that you can actually get to. I was delighted to see the Crown Plaza had taken out their previously low desk, a fixed desk, and put in a table that has 700mm clearance underneath so I was able to wheel in. That was a perfect height for me to access my meal or writing or doing whatever I needed to do there ... I usually try and get a telephone with a longer cord so that I put that on the bed when I'm there on my own (Don).

With these design issues incorporated, Don was able to independently use the room. For others, it involves modifying the height of the bed to allow transfer from a wheelchair or easier access for people with arthritis or back problems. As Andrew (below) suggests, this can involve make-shift modifications:

... we went to the Western Plains Zoo just before Christmas because I am a keen photographer, went with a couple of others from the camera club and I just said when we got there, 'Well the bed's a bit low. Can we pack it up on a few bricks?' Next thing the girl was out finding bricks and we packed it up. It wasn't any problem ... (Andrew).

This was a simple example of finding a solution to create an enabling environment for the individual using the room. However, once this has been identified by an individual, the organisation should respond by noting the adaption, seeking more than a makeshift solution that can be easily found – in this case by providing bed raisers.

Room and bathroom accessibility is critical not only for ease of manoeuvrability but because of personal care issues, the interaction with an attendant (if needed) and the equipment required for personal care. If personal care tasks cannot be carried out successfully and reliably then the tourism experience will not be possible. This level of accessibility then requires a greater level of communication with the intermediary or accommodation provider:

My needs aren't that great but ... I went to a friend's wedding up in Alice Springs at Lasseter's Casino, asked for a disabled room ... but when I got there the door to the bathroom opened inward and it opened straight in onto the toilet. Once you got in there with a wheelchair, you couldn't shut it behind you because there wasn't enough room. You couldn't get onto the toilet so I had to get them to take the door off the bathroom just so I could use the bathroom and the shower ... It was meant to be a disabled room. They were more than helpful and in the end it didn't wind up being a problem, but ... if you ask for a disabled room you expect to be able to go in and do your thing (Justin).

An Explanation of Their Lived Experiences

The above quotations come from two studies focusing on constraints for people with mobility disabilities (Darcy, 1998, 2004) where thousands of individual accessible inclusions were identified. The question arises: How can people with impairments and providers of accommodation have such different understandings of *access*? What emerged from these experiences was a greater understanding of what contributes to the discourses of access to accommodation. The most important access criteria, and, hence, information requirements involve detailed dimensions and organisation of space at the premises.

The socially constructed understanding emerging from these experiences and other studies focusing on experience is both simple and complex. Disability can be deconstructed into an understanding of access needs that can service discrete group cohorts of disability outlined at the beginning of chapter. When seen in conjunction with the guidelines for the built environment, standards for access, universal design principles and the voices of people with disabilities – the core set of access considerations can be constructed. Investigation into human rights disability discrimination complaints regarding accommodation has identified the complexity of the issues and recommended that they should not be reduced to simplified ratings or icons (Eichhorn *et al.*, 2008).

The complexity is that the embodiment of each individual will interact with the accommodation environment depending on their particular needs. This interaction is a product of their impairment, the level of independence, mobility aid used, cultural background, equipment needs, and sociodemographic circumstances. The resulting discourse of access comes down to the individual involved and their needs. For example, two wheelchair users may have totally different set-ups when it comes to using toilets and showers. One may transfer onto the toilet or the shower bench and another may use a commode within that same space. The accommodation can cater for hundreds of individuals if the information is documented in a way that allows informed decisions to be made. Table 5.4 presents a summary of other considerations within premises, rooms and bathrooms outlined by the legislative requirements, which are remarkably similar across nations with building codes that include access and mobility.

Research has consistently shown that information about tourism accommodation was not available, was not provided accurately when requested or was misunderstood by the managers and staff interacting with guests (Daniels *et al.*, 2005; Darcy, 1998, 2002; Gallagher & Hull, 1996; Murray & Sproats, 1990; Ray & Ryder, 2003; Turco *et al.*, 1998; Upchurch & Seo, 1996). The general accessibility of properties, the associated facilities and the specific criteria of rooms and bathrooms require detailed and accurate information provision, communication and marketing. Otherwise, as one person notes, the essence of the tourist experience for people with disabilities can be, 'soul-destroying, exhausting and you are left with the feeling "why did I bother?"'. The experiences create a cynicism about the accommodation sector practices. A great deal of these experiences is because, 'just so many do not know what is required as far as access'. Yet, where good customer service exists people with impairments acknowledge the benefits with repeat patronage.

The authors posit that people with disabilities understand access from their individual needs and they communicate this to providers. Specific providers have a limited understanding of access based on their experiences of customers with disabilities. A communication disconnection occurs where the lived experience of one person with a disability is significantly different to another person with a disability. Hence, the provider's past customers may not match the needs of future customers. The communication of access information for accommodation needs to

Table 5.4 Accommodation access needs – general, room-specific and bathroom-specific

Accommodation General	Room-specific
• Parking	• Uncluttered furniture layout
• Drop off points at reception	• Window position
• Continuous pathways – from parking or drop off throughout all hotel facilities and to the room	• Location of cupboards, fridge, TV, clock radio, microwave, telephone, ironing equipment, air cons etc.
• Kerb ramps throughout grounds	• Access to balconies
• Door widths	• Table heights
• Door stops weight	• Bed heights, circulation space
• D type door handles	• Clearance under beds
• Reception counter height	• Access to room controls from bed
• Assistance with luggage if required	**Bathroom-specific**
• Table height in restaurants	• Hobless roll-in showers
• Circulation space in corridor	• Lever taps
• Circulation space in all rooms	• Mirror location
• Access signage	• Hand basin positioning and bench space for toiletries
• Directional signage	• Space under the hand basin
• High contrast surfaces	• Adequate shower chair or bench
• Good lighting levels	• Location of handrails
• Appropriate hand rails	• Toilet height and positioning (distance from walls and front clearance from obstructions)
• Slip resistant surfaces	• Hand held shower hose and length of hose
• No steps into rooms (< 5mm)	• Non-slip floor surface

Sources: Australian Council for Rehabilitation of Disabled (ACROD) Ltd. (1999); Darcy (2004); Europe for All (2007); Standards Australia (2001)

brokered through the different understandings or discourses of access from:

(1) the technical considerations (planning, architecture, design and construction industries);
(2) how individuals express their needs (demand); and
(3) how the operations of the accommodation sector represent their properties.

Some of these issues have been fully explored in the European situation and provide a way forward to having better information provision of information based on accessibility schemes documents (Eichhorn *et al.*, 2008).

Conclusion

In this chapter, we have listened to the voices of people with a disability – their joys, disappointments and frustrations. The above discussion not only details how the tourist body experiences the holiday trip but how society understands and responds to impairment. The above discussion is critical in that it tells us what is right and wrong with current social reality, it identifies the actors to change the reality – the tourism industry, community and people with impairments themselves who are agentic. Exclusionary practices identified in this chapter involve considerations of whether the tourism industry is being *politically correct* in their treatment of people with impairments by superficially addressing the requirements of the disability discrimination legislation without treating this group as it does other market segments. As the following quotation suggests, the tourism environment is changing and the nature of disability and access evolves as time goes on. Watershed shifts have occurred in the past and will continue in the future. While people with disabilities empower themselves through human rights legislation it is up to all other tourism stakeholders to assist in bringing about change for the inclusion of all. The voices also inform us how tourism has already been transformed for the benefit of all.

> Having travelled a fair amount before a vehicle accident in 1978, I have 'battled' to enjoy further travel, but have many experiences and disappointments because of so many places of interest and accommodation not being accessible. Much is being accomplished and attitudes of management and staff has improved enormously since 1981 – 'The International Year of the Disabled'.

Note

1. The term critical disability studies is used to differentiate social approaches to disability from medicalised discourses.

References

Australian Council for Rehabilitation of Disabled (ACROD) Ltd. (1999) Room 206 – Accommodating travellers with disabilities. On WWW at www.acrod.org. au/access/room206.htm. Accessed 17.5.2002.

Barnes, C. (1996) Theories of disability and the origins of the oppression of disabled people in western society. In L. Barton (ed.) *Disability and Society: Emerging Issues and Insights* (pp. 40–59). New York: Longman.

Bohman, J. (2005) Critical Theory. *Stamford Encyclopaedia of Philosophy*. On WWW at http://plato.stanford.edu/entries/critical-theory/. Accessed 21.1.2009.

Boorstin, D.J. (1987) *The Image, A Guide to Pseudo-Events in America*. New York: Atheneum.

Bordo, S. (1989) The body and the repoduction of femininity: A feminist appropriation of Foucault. In A. Jaggar and S. Bordo (eds) *Gender/Body/Knowledge: Feminist Reconstructions of Being and Knowing* (pp. 13–33). New Brunswick NJ: Rutgers University Press.

Brookfield, S. (2005) *The Power of Critical Theory for Adult Learning and Teaching.* Berkshire, England: Open University.

Bureau of Tourism Research (1998) *National Visitor Survey: Travel by Australians.* Canberra: Bureau of Tourism Research.

Bureau of Tourism Research (2003) *National Visitor Survey: Travel by Australians.* Canberra: Bureau of Tourism Research.

Daniels, M.J., Drogin Rodgers, E.B. and Wiggins, B.P. (2005) 'Travel Tales': An interpretive analysis of constraints and negotiations to pleasure travel as experienced by persons with physical disabilities. *Tourism Management* 26 (6), 919–930.

Darcy, S. (1998) *Anxiety to Access: Tourism Patterns and Experiences of New South Wales People with a Physical Disability.* Sydney: Tourism New South Wales.

Darcy, S. (2002) Marginalised participation: Physical disability, high support needs and tourism. *Journal of Hospitality and Tourism Management* 9 (1), 61–72.

Darcy, S. (2003, 5–8 February) Disabling journeys: The tourism patterns of people with impairments in Australia. Paper presented at the Riding the Wave of Tourism and Hospitality Research, CAUTHE – Southern Cross University, Lismore.

Darcy, S. (2004) Disabling journeys: The social relations of tourism for people with impairments in Australia – An analysis of government tourism authorities and accommodation sector practices and discourses. Unpublished PhD, University of Technology, Sydney, Sydney.

Darcy, S. (2006) *Setting a Research Agenda for Accessible Tourism.* Gold Coast: Sustainable Tourism Cooperative Research Centre.

Dwyer, L., and Darcy, S. (2008) Chapter 4 – Economic contribution of disability to tourism in Australia. In S. Darcy, B. Cameron, L. Dwyer, T. Taylor, E. Wong and A. Thomson (eds) *Technical Report 90040: Visitor Accessibility in Urban Centres* (pp. 15–21). Gold Coast: Sustainable Tourism Cooperative Research Centre.

Edelheim, J.R. (2006) *Analysis of HEgmonic Messages that Tourist Brochures Sell.* Paper presented at the 16th Annual CAUTHE 2006 Conference 'to the city and beyond …'

Edelheim, J.R. (2007) Hidden messages: A polysemic reading of tourist brochures. *Journal of Vacation Marketing* 13 (1), 5–17.

Eichhorn, V., Miller, G., Michopoulou, E., and Buhalis, D. (2008) Enabling access to tourism through information schemes? *Annals of Tourism Research* 35 (1), 189–210.

Europe for All (2007) *Tourism Providers reports on The Europe for all Self-Assessment Questionnaire: For owners/managers of Hotels and Self-Catering Establishments & The Europe for all Photo and Measurement Guide.* Europe for All – Better information for discerning travellers, EU. At http://www.europeforall.com/tourismProviders.seam?conversationPropagation=end&conversationId=162076

Francey and Meeuwissen v Hilton Hotels Of Australia Pty Ltd (1997) (Human Rights and Equal Opportunity Commission H97/50 & H97/51 1997).

Gallagher, J.M. and Hull, A.H. (1996) Cruise ship accommodations for passengers with physical limitations due to disability or age. *American Journal of Occupational Therapy* 50 (8), 685–687.

Grosz, E. (1993) Bodies and knowledge: Feminism and the crisis of reason. In L. Alcoff and E. Potter (eds) *Feminist Epistemologies* (pp. 187–215). New York: Routledge.

Grosz, E. (1994) *Volatile Bodies: Toward a Corporeal Feminism*. St Leonards NSW Allen and Unwin.

Hargreaves, J. (1986) *Sport, Power and Culture: A Social and Historical Analysis of Popular Sports in Britain*. Cambridge: Polity Press.

Harper, S. (1997) Constructing later life/constructing the body: Some thoughts from feminist theory. In A. Jamieson, S. Harper and C. Victor (eds) *Critical Approaches to Aeging and Later Life* (pp. 160–172). Buckingham: Open University Press.

Holland, J.C.R., Sharpe, S. and Thomson, R. (1994) Power and desire: The embodiement of female sexuality. *Feminist Review* (46), 21–38.

Hooks, B. (2003) *Teaching Community: A Pedagogy of Hope*. New York: Routledge.

Maguire v Sydney Organising Committee for the Olympic Games (Internet) (2000) (Human Rights and Equal Opportunity Commission No H 99/115 2000).

Murray, M., and Sproats, J. (1990) The disabled traveller: Tourism and disability in Australia. *Journal of Tourism Studies* 1 (1), 9–14.

Oliver, M. (1996) *Understanding Disability: From Theory to Practice*. Basingstoke, Houndmills: Macmillan.

Osborne, P. (2000) *Travelling Light: Photography, Travel and Visual Culture*. Manchester: Manchester University Press.

Packer, T., Small, J. and Darcy, S. (2008) *Technical Report 90044: Tourist Experiences of Individuals with Vision Impairment* Sustainable Tourism Cooperative Research Centre, Gold Coast. At http://www.crctourism.com.au/default.aspxg.

Preiser, W.F.E. and Ostroff, E. (2001) *Universal Design Handbook*. New York: McGraw-Hill.

Ray, N.M. and Ryder, M.E. (2003) 'Ebilities' tourism: an exploratory discussion of the travel needs and motivations of the mobility-disabled. *Tourism Management* 24 (1), 57–72.

Ross, G.A. (1994) Attitudes towards the disabled in destination marketing organizations (marketing organizations). Unpublished PhD thesis, Virginia Polytechnic Institute and State University.

Samdahl, D.M. and Jekubovich, N.J. (1997a) A critique of leisure constraints: Comparative analyses. *Journal of Leisure Research* 29 (4), 430.

Samdahl, D.M. and Jekubovich, N.J. (1997b) A rejoinder to Henderson's and Jackson's commentaries on 'A critique of leisure constraints'. *Journal of Leisure Research* 29 (4), 469–471.

Shakespeare, T. and Watson, N. (2001) The social model of disability: An outdated ideology? In S.N. Barnartt and B. Mandell Altman (eds) *Exploring Theories and Expanding Methodologies* (Vol. 2, pp. 9–28). Stamford: JAI Press.

Standards Australia (2001) *AS 1428.1 Design for access and mobility – General requirements for access – New building work*. Homebush, NSW: Standards Australia.

Swain, J., Finkelstein, V., French, S. and Oliver, M. (1997) *Disabling Barriers – Enabling Environments*. London: Sage Publications Ltd.

Turco, D.M., Stumbo, N. and Garncarz, J. (1998) Tourism constraints – People with disabilities. *Parks and Recreation Journal* 33 (9), 78–84.

Turner, P., Turner, S. and Carroll, F. (2005) The tourist gaze: Towards contextualised virtual environments. *Spaces, Spatiality and Technology*. Dordrecht: Kluwer.

United Nations (2006) *Convention on the Rights of Persons with Disabilities.* New York http://www.un.org/esa/socdev/enable/rights/convtexte.htm: United Nations General Assembly A/61/611 – 6 December 2006.

Upchurch, R.S. and Seo, J.W. (1996) Civic responsibility and market positioning: complying with the Americans with Disabilities Act. *Facilities* 14 (5/6).

UPIAS (1975) *Fundamental Principles of Disability.* London: Union of Physically Impaired Against Segregation and The Disability Alliance.

Urry, J. (1990) *The Tourist Gaze: Leisure and Travel in Contemporary Societies.* London: Sage.

Vedelago, C. (2009, 18 January) When size matters: obese passengers and economy seating. *Sydney Morning Herald. At* http://www.smh.com.au/travel/when-size-matters-obese-passengers-and-economy-seating-20090114-7gm7.html.

Wilson, E., Harris, C. and Small, J. (2008) Furthering critical approaches in tourism and hospitality studies: Perspectives from Australia and New Zealand. *Journal of Hospitality and Tourism Management* 15 (1), 15–18.

Woodside, A.G. and Etzel, M.J. (1980) Impact of physical and mental handicaps on vacation travel behaviour. *Journal of Travel Research* 18 (3), 9–11.

Chapter 6

Tourism in the Leisure Lives of People with Disability

B. FOGGIN

Introduction

More than just a modern-day burgeoning industry, tourism has, through the ages, remained an important social and cultural phenomenon. Generally, tourism is seen as involving temporary displacement from one's normal environment, usually for leisure purposes and has a capacity to impact or influence the character of all those involved (Leiper, 2003). While the range of motivations for and the potential benefits of leaving one's normal environment to experience tourism may be the same for tourists with or without disabilities, such a voluntary 'displacement' from their normal environment for those with reduced mobility might be quite different from the experience of non-disabled tourists, with potential constraints or barriers to participation affecting them disproportionately. As outlined in the introduction to the book, it is the socially constructed tourism environment that can turn a person's impairment into a disabling environment and hostile social attitudes. People with reduced mobility often encounter architectural, transportation, attitudinal or other kinds of constraints or barriers (Daniels *et al.*, 2005; Darcy, 1998; Smith, 1987; Turco *et al.*, 1998). As such, it is not surprising that the impact of any displacement within the tourism experiences may be amplified in relation to the type and degree of reduced mobility.

During a programme of doctoral research, the tourism experiences of 16 people with reduced mobility were examined. The primary focus was on the significance or meaning that they attached to their personal experience of leisure tourism with its potential benefits and constraints, real or perceived, and whether physical, psychological, cognitive, economic, social or structural in nature. Although this research revolved around the experiences of residents of Quebec, Canada it should be possible to apply the findings to other provinces or countries as well as to sectors of the population with other types of disabilities. It would also become applicable for an ever-increasing number of people who might experience reduced abilities as the general population continues to age.

This chapter first provides an overview of the fields of study that the research traversed. Paul Ricoeur's concept of life and narrative as related to the biographical method is presented as the lens through which the data was examined and interpreted. Next, the research design is presented. Although it includes biographic sketches of all 16 participants, it is three distinct case studies that best illustrate the findings about the role of tourism within the leisure lives of people with disabilities. Finally, there is a discussion of the implications of the research in the context of the individuals' lives, the tourism industry and the potential of accessible tourism.

Fields of Study and Theoretical Foundation

Four conceptual traditions of leisure are briefly noted. A humanistic model would be similar to the Greek concept, which saw leisure as a form of schooling or cultivation of the self (Lynch & Veal, 2006). Other models were identified as therapeutic (Stumbo, 2001), time-oriented (De Grazia, 1994) and socio-descriptive (Haworth & Veal, 2004). Definitions, interpretations and meanings associated with leisure are as value-laden and subjective as they are numerous. Yet certain features or dimensions seem to be consistently present including physical, cognitive, material and social well-being (Driver *et al.*, 1991). Tourism, a preferred form of leisure for many, offers a similar range of meanings and benefits. In *The Holiday Makers: Understanding the Impact of Leisure and Travel*, Josh Krippendorf (1999) shows how its meaning or significance might be experienced. Even as the benefits that can be reaped through tourism are numerous, so too are barriers or constraints that can negatively affect the experience.

While no one is completely unfettered from some form or other of constraints, members of the population with disabilities are affected disproportionately. This may be due to their particular life situation or to the lack of 'tools' needed to explore new leisure horizons. Leisure constraints research as outlined by Smith (1987), suggest that these are intrapersonal, interpersonal and structural. Proponents of the social model of disability would say that it is due mainly to the disabling nature of society where not enough has been done to create enabling environments and welcoming social attitudes (Barnes, 1999; Swain *et al.*, 1997).

The Office of the United Nations High Commissioner for Human Rights (OHCHR) emphasizes in various documents (OHCHR, 2010) that persons with disabilities are entitled to the enjoyment of the full range of civil, cultural, economic, political and social rights embodied in international human rights instruments on an equal basis with other persons. It acknowledges, however, that in all societies of the world, including countries which have a relatively high standard of living, the reality is different. Persons with disabilities often encounter discriminatory practices and impediments which prevent them from exercising their rights and freedoms and make it difficult for them to participate fully in the activities of their societies.

Certainly leisure and tourism are key aspects of many societies in which people with or without disabilities should have the freedom to participate.

Theoretical approach

Leisure, tourism and disability studies are interdisciplinary, each with their own particular theoretical foundations. Even though all three fields were an integral part of this multidisciplinary research project that involved a highly 'experiential' approach, the two basic theoretical frameworks used were both related to how life stories are experienced and told. Paul Ricoeur's (1984) treatise on life and narrative helps elucidate the process by which people experience and recount their lives and stories. According to Ricoeur (1984), once events and human action or activities in a person's life are shaped or configured into a comprehensible plot or narrative, the person is then able to refigure 'his or her own world in light of the possibilities offered by experiencing the world of the text' (Kerby, 1991: 43). As Kerby goes on to say, the person is able to 'change his or her ideas and behaviour as a result of discovering new dimensions of life.' Other 'readers of the text' or the resultant narrative are also provided the opportunity to discover 'new dimensions of life', to experience the 'creative moment that fosters new insights' leading to possible changes in ideas and behaviour (Joy, 1997: xxviii). According to Ricoeur, any such 'possible activity' is a natural and even necessary flow of the narrative character of life.

If, as Ricoeur proposes, life is 'in quest of narrative' or 'a story in search of a narrator' (Joy, 1997: xxviii), then certainly the qualitative research interview with its inherent narrative quality and its 'phenomenological and hermeneutic mode of understanding' (Kvale, 1983) is an important way of capturing these stories. The biographical essays – developed from the material expressed in the interviews – offer a complementary framework through which the 'experience of tourism of people with disabilities' was examined. They join and record in a single personal document the 'inner world of thought and experience' and 'an outer world of events and experience' (Denzin, 1989: 28). Clearly it is not only environmental factors or the person's impairment that affect the experience. Attitudes, senses and feelings are intangible factors that nevertheless can have a tangible influence or significant role in the constant interplay between the inner and outer world of the tourist. (See Figure 6.1).

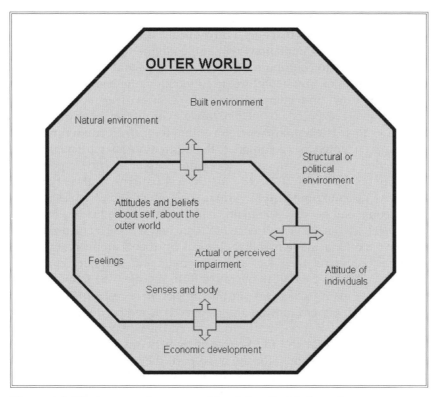

Figure 6.1 The inner and outer worlds of the disabled tourist

Research Design

The working definition of a mobility-disabled tourist was one who, according to Kéroul (1994: 4), had 'difficulty in moving about either temporarily or permanently because of, for example, their stature, their physical condition or an impairment ... and must, therefore, move around in a wheelchair or with the help of crutches or a cane.' The definition currently used by Statistics Canada (2006) for the most recent Participation and Activity Limitation Survey (PALS) (NWT Bureau of Statistics, 2007) incorporates a broader range of people. A person with a mobility disability is said to be one who has 'difficulty walking half a kilometre or up and down a flight of stairs, about 12 steps without resting, moving from one room to another, carrying an object of 5 kg (10 pounds) for 10 metres (30 feet) or standing for long periods.' The results of this 2006 PALS survey show that mobility, along with agility and pain, continue to be the three most prevalent forms of disability reported. Like those related to hearing and seeing, the degree increases with age. Indeed, the overall rates of disability or activity limitations increase with age, reaching 43% of the population aged 65 and over. Thus, as the baby boomer cohort reaches that age, it might be expected that the numbers of people with activity limitations will also continue to grow.

In an attempt to contribute to a broader understanding of the experience of tourism of people with reduced mobility, the researcher listened to 16 people tell and interpret their own stories. They spoke of their motivations and expectations, of their travel styles, of their happy memories as well as their frustrations when travelling to or in an environment not adequately adapted to accommodate their differences or particular needs.

Selection of the participants was made to assure a certain degree of diversity not only with respect to their travel patterns, to their type and degree of disability but also to various socio-economic variables such as age, income and gender. The main characteristics to be held in common were that each one had experienced tourism and that each one used some technical aid to facilitate mobility. Table 6.1 presents an overview of the 16 participants and their key socio-economic and disability characteristics. A collective portrait in narrative form revealed the following:

All of the main participants in this project were residents of Quebec province, with either French or English as their mother tongue. Nine of the 16 individuals interviewed were women. The youngest and the oldest of the group were 24 and 61, the rest being between 32 and 46, with the mean age being 40. Thus, for the most part, they could be classified as baby boomers. They had experienced reduced mobility from seven to 43 years, the mean number of years being 20. The cause was most often due to vehicle-related accidents. Quadra- or tetraplegia was given as the type of disability for ten, paraplegia for five and one spoke of the effects of arthritis and spina bifida that had begun to manifest themselves at age 17. A few were able to use simpler mobility aids such as canes or braces but most used either manual or electric wheelchairs.

All were living independently in a house or apartment on their own, with family or with a partner. One was temporarily staying at his parent's place for financial reasons. Three had young children. Several mentioned parents or other family members living nearby. Some had an assistant come to their home for morning and evening personal care. For several, it was their partner who also was their personal assistant.

Formal education ranged from some secondary school to Master's level education. Professions or occupations included social worker, businessman, technician, public relations officer, student, volunteer worker and unemployed. For income, some earned a salary or a pension from previous employment while others had income from insurance or disability benefits. Some had, in addition, occasional financial help from family or various disability organisations. Apart from the salaried workers, those whose accidents were vehicle-related had been covered by the *Société de*

Table 6.1 Response group characteristics

Name	Socio Economic Data					Disability Data			
	Sex	Age	Education Level Attained	Income Source	Living Arrangement	Years with Disability	Type of Disability	Disability Aids Used	Personal Assistant Used
André	Male	46	High school	Salary	Live alone	26	Paraplegia	Wheelchair (manual) and walking cane or braces	No
Barbara	Female	42	University Undergraduate	Salary	Live alone	23	Spina bifida/ arthritis	Wheelchair (manual) and walking cane or braces	No
Cherie	Female	34	High school	Société de l'assurance automobile du Québec	Partner and children	20	Quadriplegia	Wheelchair (electric/ manual)	Yes
Daniel	Male	37	College	Disability Pension	Live alone	14	Quadriplegia	Wheelchair (electric/ manual)	Yes
David	Male	44	University Undergraduate	Société de l'assurance automobile du Québec	Partner	18	Paraplegia	Wheelchair (manual)	No
Denise	Female	41	University Undergraduate	Société de l'assurance automobile du Québec	Partner	20	Quadriplegia	Wheelchair (electric/ manual)	Yes
France	Female	24	University Undergraduate	Insurance	Live alone	7	Quadriplegia	Wheelchair (electric/ manual)	Yes
Hélène	Female	44	University Undergraduate	Salary	Partner and children	43	Paraplegia	Wheelchair (manual)	No
Isabelle	Female	32	University Undergraduate	Société de l'assurance automobile du Québec	Live alone	10	Quadriplegia	Wheelchair (electric/ manual)	Yes

Table 6.1 *Continued*

Name	Socio Economic Data						Disability Data			
	Sex	Age	Education Level Attained	Income Source	Living Arrangement	Years with Disability	Type of Disability	Disability Aids Used	Personal Assistant Used
Janet	Female	40	Masters	Various	Partner and other family members	26	Quadriplegia	Wheelchair (manual)	Yes
Madeleine	Female	32	Masters	Société de l'assurance automobile du Québec	Partner and children	14	Quadriplegia	Wheelchair (manual)	Yes
Monika	Female	35	College	Société de l'assurance automobile du Québec	Live alone	10	Quadriplegia	Wheelchair (electric/manual)	Yes
Nissim	Male	39	Masters	Salary	Live alone	21	Paraplegia	Wheelchair (manual)	No
Normand	Male	40	University Undergraduate	Société de l'assurance automobile du Québec	Live alone	18	Quadriplegia	Wheelchair (manual)	Yes
René	Male	61	College	Société de l'assurance automobile du Québec	Live alone	30	Paraplegia	Wheelchair (manual)	No
Serge	Male	40	High school	Salary	With other family members	22	Quadriplegia	Wheelchair (manual)	Yes

l'assurance automobile du Québec (SAAQ) and generally had more disposable income than those whose accidents were not.

Following the qualitative or life-oriented interviews, the information gleaned from each person was not only formed into biographical essays about how each one lived and expressed her or his experience of tourism but also was analysed thematically, each theme echoing the voices of many. Brief biographical sketches for each person (see Table 6.2) were provided to facilitate the reading of the resultant text.

Table 6.2 Narrative sketches for each of the 16 interviewees:

André, with his relative ease of mobility refers to himself as a 'deluxe disabled person'. Being a busy owner of a store offering service and products for clients with various disabilities does not stop André from enjoying time away for outdoor activities such as skiing or diving. Earlier travel had been closely related to Olympic and other sports competitions, in which he competed very successfully.

Barbara, 42, uses a wheelchair but could also move about with a cane to help her balance for short distances and a short time. The effects of spina bifida began to limit her activities around the age of 17. Since then, arthritis has continued to reduce her mobility. She is a salaried technical manual writer in the electrical engineering field. Travel for business or pleasure is mostly in North America with a dream of going to Australia specifically for diving on the Great Barrier Reef.

Cherie, living with her husband and young son, finds that family travel and vacations must now fit around the school calendar and her child's capacity for sitting through long journeys. Any current constraints to tourism are more related to William's needs than to her own disability (quadriplegia) incurred 20 years earlier at the age of 14. In the summertime, the form of travel for various types of excursions or holidays will be mostly by car around the province of Quebec. She likes to have one sun destination holiday each winter if at all possible.

Daniel's travel style even after becoming quadriplegic in a non-vehicle related accident at age 23 revealed the adventurous spirit he had had even before, as experiences in the Caribbean or Costa Rica revealed. Whether for health or financial reasons, he no longer travels as much as he would like. However, Daniel keeps occupied with the many leisure activities available around Montreal especially in the summertime.

David and his partner, Maria, have a special interest in art which has taken them travelling in Europe or to exhibitions in North America. Sun destinations, too, are particularly appealing, especially in the winter months. Although able to travel on his own, David prefers travelling with a partner with whom to enjoy the experience. Since a car accident at age 26, some 18 years earlier, David has been using a manual wheelchair for mobility.

Denise, as soon as possible after a car accident at age 21, set out with a friend for five months in Europe, determined to do what any young person might like to do. But it was much harder than she had anticipated. Now, 20 years older, she is happy to stay closer to home and practice some of her favourite activities of skiing, sailing, cycling and, more recently, painting. Having been frustrated too many times, she prefers not to have to spend a night away from home since she no longer trusts any claims made about the availability of, for example, accessible hotel rooms.

France, at 24, was the youngest of those interviewed and the one that had experienced disability (quadriplegia) for the least length of time (seven years). She had just come back from time spent in England where she had been involved in an internship in line with the Bachelor of Arts degree she is pursuing in the history of dance. Currently living alone, she nevertheless travels with others. Despite difficulties encountered, she finds that on every trip something magical happens. If one can have a house and travel each year, then, one has, 'in spite of everything, a good life. That's enough for me.'

Hélène, having become paraplegic as a small child, said she had never learned to depend on 'gadgets' or rehabilitation techniques for mobility – since hardly any existed at the time. She believes that having to figure out things while growing up at home has made it easier for her when she travels on her own, being used to figuring out a way to 'make do.' While describing a recent trip to Europe with her husband, eight-year old daughter and another couple it was evident that bureaucracy related to disabilities might bother her more than does lack of physical accessibility to a place.

Isabelle, 32, became quadriplegic ten years previously in a car accident and now uses an electric wheelchair for mobility. Living independently with an assistant coming mornings and evenings, she remains active in disability-oriented associations as well as with university studies at Hautes Etudes Commerciales in view of becoming better equipped for active participation in the tourism industry with respect to people with disabilities. Frequent winter vacations in the Caribbean have earned her the reputation as a reference source for others wishing to travel. Her long time dream to visit Australia came true shortly after the first interview.

Janet has been using a wheelchair for 26 years. She works as a counsellor or chaplain for various organisations. Shortly after the interview, she began working towards a Master's degree in counselling. Janet's experience of train travel has been less than satisfactory and so she does not even want to take a chance with air travel. Short day or weekend excursions by car, in the company of her 'significant other', are her preferred form of tourism – and will almost always include shopping as an activity.

Madeleine, a mother of three and pregnant with the fourth, delights in sharing her love of learning through travel with her family – just as her parents did with their children. The easiest way for them to travel is with an adapted trailer, in light of her disability as well as of the children. Her studies and training in social work correspond not only with her current home situation but also with her interests in travel i.e. trying to find out in greater depth about the people and situations they encounter, fully experiencing the journey as well as the destination.

Monika lives alone, requiring assistance only in the morning and evening and, when travelling to unfamiliar places, in the daytime as well. Heading to the eastern Townships or New England states for rolling along cycling trails using her electric wheelchair alongside a friend on a bike is a favourite day or weekend activity. For even longer trips she prefers travelling with her own van (rather than going to destinations involving air transportation) in order to have all the necessary equipment and supplies with her. She says the income from the SAAQ insurance coverage following an accident some ten years earlier allows her the possibility to have her own van, and to be able to travel and live as she does.

Nissim has a salaried position since recently completing a Master's degree in Social Work. Shortly after becoming paraplegic at the age of 18 some 21 years earlier, he began travelling mostly for wheelchair sports competitions, tennis in particular. He can travel on his own but may appreciate the presence of a companion especially for long-distance air travel. Just the previous year, he had enjoyed a touring holiday combined with visiting relatives in Israel.

Normand lives on his own in a Montreal suburban house, an assistant coming for personal care as necessary. Actively involved with the Paraplegic Association, Normand makes good use of his training in Public Relations. A year before his accident at age 22, Normand had cycled from Vancouver right to the Mexican border. He has continued to travel, but, of necessity, with a different style. His most frequent overseas destination has been the Dominican Republic where he has spent several winters enjoying not only the warm weather but also the warm welcome by the local people.

René, the oldest of those interviewed, has been travelling for many years having started through wheelchair sports competitions shortly after his accident. With his wife and friends (*cf.* Hélène), he recently spent holidays in France – visiting with family members, savouring food and wine, touring the countryside and exploring the cities. Wherever he goes, René also likes to visit rehabilitation centres to compare with the centre where he works in Montreal.

Serge and I talked as he was being fitted with custom-made gloves for cycling competitions. Even apart from competition, Serge cycles not only for the pleasure of being in nature but also for work. He was just starting a contract to evaluate the accessibility of the cycle paths of Quebec for wheelchair users. During time recently spent in Europe, Serge discovered that, although certain difficulties were encountered, some cities like Lyon and Barcelona were relatively accessible to him – even on public transit.

Throughout the process, the author attempted to respect Norman Denzin's (1989: 83) advice to 'remember that our primary obligation is always to the people we study, not to our project or to a larger discipline ... [since the] lives and stories that we hear and study are given to us under a promise.' Although various disciplines contributed to the understanding of the issues, it was the participants who were on 'centre stage' and whose stories or discourses formed the heart of the research project.

By the time the 16th person had been interviewed, saturation had been reached with all major themes having already being raised by several others. As pointed out by Bibeau and Perreault (1995), between the requirements of a representative sample and the clinical method of in-depth analysis of a single case, researchers are unanimous around the idea of saturation, signifying that the information about a social phenomenon, even the most complex, can become saturated. After a certain number of interviews, any complementary or additional interviews bring only nuances or non-essential particularities to the understanding of the phenomenon being studied. In practice, it is up to the researcher to determine when there is saturation.

Themes that emerged from the 16 interviews dealt with the numerous elements of the entire tourism experience – from the initial 'dreaming' or planning stages, through the actual tourism event and to the recollection of it after returning home. They concerned concrete elements such as transportation, accommodation, choice of companions, climate, built and natural environments, availability of essential goods and services as well as more intangible ones such as motivations, feelings, attitudes, dependency, coping strategies, dreams, travel style preferences and expectations. A portrait of the collective travel experiences of the 16 follows:

Travel experienced after the onset of a reduction in mobility often involved sun destinations like Florida or the Caribbean, destinations chosen not only for the sun and warmth but also because of their affordable cost. Travel destinations also included further afield in North America, Central America, Europe, Israel, Asia and Australia. Florida and Vancouver were mentioned as being hospitable destinations for wheelchair users. Countries with old historic building and environments were often considered to be more difficult to get around because of limited architectural access.

A wide range of transportation modes was used – private adapted vans, local taxis, train, bus, boat, and plane. Accommodation varied from camping vans, private homes, youth hostels, motels, hotels, and resorts to cruise ships, the price range extending from budget to five-star category.

Reasons given for a trip or travel included visiting friends and relatives, sports competition, family vacation, recreation and relaxation.

Activities included 'just visiting', dining out, attending theatre perform-ances or cultural manifestations, city or country tours, as well as outdoor and more adventurous types of activities. Travel, except for team sports competitions, occurred mostly in the company of one to four other people, of which one would possibly be an attendant for personal care.

Information for effective planning and decision-making most often came by word of mouth from other people who had experienced and subsequently recommended the proposed destination and facilities. If accessible accommodation was requested through a travel agent, the traveller might then personally contact the hotel to ensure that it indeed was adapted for his or her needs. Often an adapted room would have been requested but was not always available. Most often accommodation was booked directly by the tourist to ensure that it was.

Planning was sometimes very carefully done, especially for verifying the accessibility of the accommodation at the destination, but some trips were more spontaneous, with arrangements being made while on the way. It was said by several that they could 'make do' with whatever was available but that it was 'little things', little adaptations by the owners or managers, that could make a big difference to the client.

'Bad' experiences or concerns existed but only a few said that, because of them, they no longer wanted to travel except for local day trips around Montreal. While a few had had unfortunate dealings with uninformed travel industry personnel, several acknowledged that the staff and people had been willing to help as needed. The general although not unanimous consensus was that there was almost always 'a way to make do' (*Système D*, débrouillard), albeit inconvenient, difficult and sometimes nearly impossible to get around obstacles. They found a way to make do with a less than ideal situation. In that way, they were able to experience many of the pleasures and benefits of leisure tourism that they sought.

From among the 16, the voices of three key actors were then chosen to be heard above the rest. They were chosen as being representative or 'typical' of three general types or situations of tourists with disabilities. The determining criteria for this choice involved family or life stage, type and degree of disability and type of travel patterns. The reason for the choice of each is briefly examined.

The story of Madeleine was chosen primarily to show the impact of the family or life stage that, in conjunction with her disability, had a significant impact on her experience of tourism. She usually travelled with family members that included young children. Her story might also have been chosen in light of the emphasis she places on cultural or educational tourism or it might be considered representative of those who must travel with a personal assistance as well as technical aids.

André was more oriented to tourism that involved sports or outdoors activities. It was friends rather than family with whom he usually travelled. His story was selected as being representative of those whose type and degree of disability allows for a good deal of independence. In his own words, he was, therefore, 'a deluxe disabled person'.

While the majority of those interviewed travelled as often as they could, Denise's story was chosen to represent those who had decided to restrict travelling because of the difficulties so often involved in it. Nevertheless, she enjoyed participating in several outdoor leisure activities within a day's drive of her home. Travel for Denise necessitates having a partner or personal assistant.

A more complete version of these three stories follows in the following biographical narratives. They illustrate many of the themes that emerged from many or all of the interviews.

Biographical Narratives

Madeleine

When we first met, Madeleine had three boys (13-year-old twin sons and four-year-old Gabriel) and was pregnant with the daughter who was born a few months later. The family lived in an old country house that her husband had skilfully and beautifully renovated to be wheelchair accessible. With her husband also being her professional caregiver, it allowed the family to travel together, the only limitation being the school year. 'We've got the summer. We can take time whenever we really want to.' One of her greatest pleasures was 'being a mother. I just love it, just all the teaching part of it'. Travelling together as a family offers Madeleine ample opportunity to do just that.

Raised in a family where her parents sought to expand their children's mind and horizons through activities during travel and vacations, family holidays for Madeleine were always 'a really big deal. My parents had taught me to learn as much as you could from wherever you were'. She developed 'a desire to learn about people, to learn about places. So wherever I go I've got my eyes wide open'. She seeks to pass on this heritage to her own growing family.

Madeleine was 18 years old and in college when she was hit by a car. Formal education remained a priority for Madeleine. So, while still in rehabilitation, she continued taking courses. 'It was so physically demanding. I just needed a little something more but I couldn't do a whole lot more.' But she persisted. By the time she was a graduate student in Social Work, she herself had married, become a stepmother and had her own first child, with a second on the way.

Studies took up much of her spare time and energy. But there was still time for holidays and travel. At first, after the accident, 'my parents still tried to get me around'. With brothers and sisters spread across the country, travel on a regular basis becomes a 'necessity. We're very close although we are very far. Yeah, getting together. We've got to do it at least once a year'.

Once married, Madeleine and her husband knew that they would 'have to really think this travel thing through. Because it was tough. We saw the problems right away' of travelling with his two small children and a mom in a wheelchair who needed adapted facilities. During their first trips, they developed a better idea of what were minimal necessities. 'We needed to have an accessible bathroom and a shower and a bed. That's really all we needed. And everything else was the bumping up stairs, taking off wheels if I couldn't get through the door. So, for a while, what we were doing was to find a suitable place and just go there.' And stay there.

That was fine. It was convenient. But, said Madeleine, 'it wasn't satisfying my travel need. Sure it's nice to go to a nice place. But my argument against cottages is that you're always in the same place and you can only go so far on little out-trips. So what I like to do is go and take everything I need and get to (further) places. Or take the back roads, taking an extra day if you had to'. To see what treasures can be found off the beaten track.

For Madeleine, the process or journey and not just the destination, was a crucial part of the tourist or travel experience. She realises there may be extenuating circumstances affecting just how much time can be taken for exploring while *en route*. Like having a two-year-old on board! 'So then, you just have to get there.'

Besides, stopping overnight on the way meant thinking about where they were going to be able to stay that night. 'You spend a lot of time, looking, wondering "Am I going to get through the door? Am I going get into the bathroom?" Then you finally get settled. We wouldn't get very far in a day.'

'So we thought, "A Winnebago. That's the best thing." If you don't have to worry about your toilet and where you can have a shower, all the other things fall into place and are less irritating.' Besides, 'it was economically more agreeable for us to camp and go for longer periods of time'.

They bought a used Winnebago and had good holidays but realised they still needed an adapted van to get around once they had arrived somewhere. So the Winnebago was replaced by a trailer to be towed with their adapted van. But the trailer also needed to be adapted – enlarging the door, making a ramp, putting in a bed and a bathroom with shower and toilet for Madeleine. It was a good solution for the family and 'it gives us privacy that we need … while getting me ready (in the morning)'.

It is clear that Madeleine loves to travel with her family. Her experience of travel has been generally a positive one. Considering what it has been like in the past, she reckons it is 'pretty good'. But there still are 'issues', such as when she has gone to local restaurants or attractions. She has to decide what place to go, what chair to use. 'Well, it's always an issue. You find that you've got to pick your place. And it depends what kind of chair you're in. Often I'll go with my lightweight chair because I can assume that wherever we're going to be, there will be a few steps. Or else we just have to avoid some things.' There still are times when she needs to be lifted over or around some obstacle. So she could never be able to travel alone in the same way, to the same places. Madeleine recognises that lifting her in her chair is not always going to be an option. Although her husband was only 40, 'he's not picking me up and lifting me here and there like he was ten years ago when I was a little lighter. We have to think about him, too. We're not as young as we were when we first started out'.

Madeleine appreciates when others offer to help and yet, she says, 'It's all very wonderful to pick me up and get people to help but it is *so* much easier when people are aware and the buildings are accessible and you can get in', independently, by yourself without this extra lifting and manipulation. 'And when you can get (your chair) under the table in the restaurant, it just makes it so much easier, so much more agreeable. Otherwise it's too hard. I love a challenge and I love to make it work. But when it is too hard sometimes it takes a lot of the pleasure out of it. It happens that it often works out and we make it work out. But sometimes it doesn't.'

Not having an activity happen as planned puts a damper on the enjoyment of the day. It is especially hard when there are children 'that have had a disappointing afternoon or we haven't gone somewhere just because of the wicked old stepmother in a wheelchair'. It puts an additional pressure on Madeleine to make sure things work out. 'I leave on holiday and I feel totally responsible for how it's going to turn out. So I do the research. I plan a lot ahead. You can't have too many disappointing days in a holiday that might last three weeks. It's got to work.'

Madeleine plans in a way so that not only are they all learning things as they go but also so that 'all the silly little details of life like access to bathrooms and those things, those little basics, are not even an issue. Let's not even have to talk about them. If I found that the place is accessible and I found that I've got a bathroom, then that's great'. She'll make do with the rest. But she wants to be sure of the basics. 'Planning,' she concludes, 'is a big thing.'

Planning, yes. Even for the future, when the children are older, to be able to go further afield. But meanwhile, Madeleine continues to enjoy the travels that they are already doing and uses every opportunity to learn. It is the social even more than the physical environment than captures her attention. 'I'm always asking, "Why?" I talk with people if I can. Love watching people go by. I like to ask questions. My kids think I'm crazy but I try to open their eyes to see things.'

Madeleine hopes that as the children get older they will have acquired a taste not only for travel in itself but also for 'learning as they go' – something that they will cherish even when they have grown up and, with their own kids, joined in the family tradition, handing down from one generation to the next, the love of exploring the world around them, of learning 'on the road'.

André

Over a 20 year period, after a spinal cord injury through a car accident, André had done a lot of travelling almost exclusively for sports competitions. Never having travelled before his accident, he talks about his 'baptism by air in a wheelchair'. His first victory in a local marathon in 1979 was followed by participation in five Paralympics, two Olympic Games, 12 Boston Marathons as well as countless other marathons, competitions and conferences around the world – earning him not only numerous medals but also related honors (including his investiture as an Officer of the Order of Canada in 1990.) It necessarily afforded him innumerable opportunities for travel. It was only more recently that he had really begun travelling as a 'regular tourist'.

Upper body strength gave the advantage of making it easier while travelling – to transfer into and out of a vehicle or to the washroom on a plane, for example. 'I am able to do it and get there on my own. [It] doesn't worry me. Doesn't stress me out.' Although not strictly necessary, André will nevertheless take an adapted hotel room if one is available. But, he says, 'I've got a small wheelchair. So it's always gone through wherever I've gone. I can get through even standard-width doors.'

One time, however, when he went to Asia, he felt concerned. 'Asia is another world. Another culture. And you run into problems that you don't have in North America. Their plumbing system, the bathrooms, put me off. We're spoiled in North America. We've got beautiful washrooms. You can get in them easily. You can turn in them. In some countries the support bar on the wall doesn't even exist.'

André has had to resign himself to the effects of getting older. 'It takes a lot of energy to be able to continue to train. It's really quite demanding.' But his sense of adventure and pushing himself to the limits is still evident in his choice of leisure activities and tourism experiences.

Several trips have been for scuba diving. 'Ahhh. Diving. It's magnificent. Just so beautiful.' One feels so free in the water. Tandem skydiving as well as bungy-jumping while still attached in his wheelchair have been added to André's list of adventurous experiences.

Winter, for André, signifies the possibility to ski, using a style known as mono- or sit-skiing. Day trips to the nearby ski slopes were frequent. During longer ski vacations, it was not so much the room accommodation but other facilities at the resort that posed a problem. For example, 'There was a bar joined to (the condo). Now, when you went to the bar, there was an adapted washroom. But there were about six steps to climb to get to the adapted washroom. But that's nothing new,' he remarked, shaking his head.

Despite such cases of obvious inaccessibility, he felt that over the 20 or more years he had been travelling, there had been general improvement in the tourism infrastructure. 'For sure it must have evolved. There are several places that now take into consideration the clientele that uses wheelchairs. I think that it is an appreciable enough percentage (of the market) that businesses or companies shouldn't neglect. In the long run, on the bottom line, everything is tied to money.' It seems that the attitude is, 'If it pays, let's do something about it. If it doesn't pay, let's not get involved or do anything about it. It's too much of a problem otherwise.' But, says André, that's 'just not right. Not at all.' So sometimes action has to be taken.

André himself, however, says that he has 'not had any particularly bad experience. My philosophy has always been not to try to change anybody but to try to adapt to it myself. That way I've never had the feeling of needing or wanting to go on the warpath against the infrastructure or society'.

After his accident, instead of militating for 'rights', André put his 'emphasis on learning how to walk again to combat all those problems. So my philosophy is different from that of the person who is always in a wheelchair and who lives a certain frustration that I myself have never had to live. I've never had to face any really bad experience, and I've not had to live with frustrations that I might have if I had a more severe disability. In the final analysis,' concludes André, 'I'd call myself a deluxe disabled person'.

Addendum: When inducted into the Canadian Paralympics Hall of Fame in 2005 it was written that 'André's successes are not limited to sports. His determination has set the example for all Canadian emerging athletes ... André has never done anything halfway. He has always given his all, good days or bad'. On October 1, 2006, a few days after his 54th birthday, André Viger died of cancer. During the 2008 Paralympics in Beijing, he was posthumously inducted into the International Paralympics Hall of Fame.

Denise

Denise has been using a wheelchair for over 20 years. Because the accident was motor-vehicle related, she receives regular income from the government's automobile insurance plan. This income has allowed her to go back to school to eventually complete a Bachelor's degree in Psychology, to have an apartment, to get involved in certain leisure activities and to have an adapted vehicle. And her vehicle, says Denise, 'is really what's almost the most important thing in my life'. It has allowed her to begin to enjoy even winter!

For many years she had 'just stayed at home and done nothing'. Especially in winter. 'I feel the cold terribly. I spent several winters without ever going out, or almost never. But since I've started to ski, the cold doesn't bother me now. Just the sheer pleasure that you have is really motivating. That's a really great thing for the morale, for the spirit. So now I participate in wintertime life just like everyone else. I just take off'. With her own van she can go in the morning and come back to sleep in her own bed at night!

In the summer, Denise meets up with friends at 'someplace nice along the water front where we can roll! Like along bike paths. You bring a lunch. It's fun. And besides, it's good physical exercise. I like it a lot. It's better even than sailing. Easier. More accessible, too. It's really great'.

Although she had only recently started doing adapted sailing, her initiation to sailboats had happened further afield. It was when she joined Michel, with whom she now lives in Montreal, on his sailboat in Martinique. It wasn't at all adapted. But, as Michel says, 'If the captain is adapted' then you can usually make do. Denise reflects: 'The first day, I relax. It's sheer luxury. Like a princess. But after a few days it's – hmmmm. It's really hard. Because after two weeks, *he*'s tired and, as for me, I can't move around like I'd like so I get a little frustrated. I am completely dependent. But still it was a great experience. I'm happy to have experienced it. But there's a price to pay.'

Before the accident, Denise had travelled a lot with friends. 'Our life was just that – always wanting to travel. So after my accident I kept trying to do things. I went to California to celebrate the first anniversary of the chair. Then after that, I spent five months in Europe. We moved around a lot. We wanted to be adventurous, be free – but was it ever complicated! It was really difficult. Well, it took away my taste for travel. Five months!' she reiterated. 'I was young. In my early twenties. I wanted to do it. I had the same tastes as any girl (my age). But I sure found it hard.' It was hard to have to ask (for help) and for the travel partner 'to always have to do it. It's hard on the character. Maybe I wanted to do too much. I got burnt somewhere in the process'.

A few years later she and a friend went to Venezuela. To soak up some sun. The travel agent sold them a package holiday in which the hotel, she assured them, was wheelchair-friendly. 'We get there and, yes, there was an elevator in the hotel but there were five steps to get to it! So for two weeks that's how it was. Then, when we see the bathroom, there was a step there as well. So the other girl always had to be with me to help out. That changes everything – roles, relationships. It just wasn't planned on. I really need every possible adaptation in order to be autonomous. Now I don't have any more confidence. I don't trust anything.' When things are never quite what you need or expect, the enthusiasm is dampened. 'You lose the taste. A lot! For me, now, trips are like problems that always have to be resolved. It's no longer pleasurable. I've had my fill of travel.'

Perhaps, as Denise suggested, she had 'overdosed' on her early European trip and then become 'allergic' to travel. She readily acknowledges that she does not regret the sights she's seen, the places she has been. But enough is enough. So rather than travelling away from home, she instead does sailing, cycling and skiing. 'I'm like a tourist around Montreal.'

Denise recognises that environment has become more accessible over the years. But she still has little confidence in counting on even what is promoted as being accessible. For the situation to really improve in accommodation or other such elements of a tourism experience, she figures that it will have to start with willingness on the part of the owners or managers of those places. 'Perhaps if people like hoteliers could see for themselves that there is some advantage in it for them then maybe then they might do something.'

People, whether in the tourism business or not, get wrapped up in the present, Denise suggested. They don't stop to think about how maybe something accessible might be needed not too far in the future. Maybe even for themselves or others they know. 'You never know when something might happen to you. But life takes on such a rapid pace and people don't have the time and aren't always aware of that fact. It's hard. There are so many things to think about in life. Those who aren't disabled don't ever imagine that someday they might be. Someone might imagine that they will become the prime minister some day, but disabled? Never or hardly ever.'

Discussion and Conclusion

Stories provide us with an opportunity to understand both the storyteller and reader, and the environment in which they operate. It is only after stories have been told and interpreted in the description-interpretation-action continuum associated with qualitative interviews that one can seek to actively engage with the world (Kvale, 1983). Using Ricoeur's approach to life and narrative and the biographical method the author has charted the stories of individual tourists, focusing on significance or meaning that they attached to their personal experience of leisure tourism.

While this paper presented several case studies of disabled tourists from Canada, they may well have come from other countries, with the possible number of such life stories increasing over the coming years as the world's ageing population grows in number.

In the report, World Population Ageing: 1950–2050, prepared for the United Nations' Second World Assembly on Ageing in 2002 (United Nations, 2002), it was noted that, worldwide, the proportion of persons 60 and older is projected to reach 21% in 2050, a figure nearly reached in the more developed nations already by 2000. In these nations the proportion is expected to reach one third by 2050. Similar figures are found in OECD statistics (OECD, 2007).

The UN report concludes that population ageing is unprecedented, pervasive, enduring and has profound implications for many facets of human life. Among those many facets would be those related to health and well-being, including the experience of leisure activities.

Statistics demonstrate that, on a global scale and for most population groups, there is a strong and positive correlation between ageing and disability. In the United States alone, according to the American Community Survey of 2006, 15.1% or 41.3 million people aged five years and over of the civilian, non-institutionalised population reported a physical disability. Of that number, the prevalence (41%) was highest among the population 65 years and older (Brault, 2008).

It is also among the developed economies that comes not only the major 'supply' of tourism products and services (with their developed infrastructures) but also the greatest 'demand' (with their growing, ageing populations' increasing discretionary time and income) (United Nations, 1997: 181–197).

By looking at the various aspects in conjunction with each other, it might, therefore, be logically concluded that there will be growing numbers of tourists with reduced abilities. Buhalis *et al.* (2005) estimated that 25% of the 1.56 billion worldwide arrivals estimated in WTO's Tourism 2020 Vision forecasts for 2020 will have some sort of disability or impairment.

In light of such figures, the number of potential stories of disabled tourists worldwide multiplies radically from the comparatively small Quebec-based sample. Variations on the themes would depend, for example, on the physical environment (cold, snowy climates versus temperate or tropical ones), the existence and effective application of human rights legislation or societal attitudes towards disability within the various countries

Even within the sample of just 16 people, the personal circumstances of the disabled tourists that shared their stories during this study were varied. Some of those realities were permanent and would not likely change. Other realities, such as certain socio-economic factors, might be changed in the future (see Table 6.1). In their physical and social environment as well, some elements were less amenable to possible change (i.e. sand or other natural terrain) than others (i.e. built environment or attitudes). Just as there were variations in their outer experiences because of such personal and contextual factors, so too were there variations in their inner experiences of tourism. Among the wide range and variations of experiences represented by people like Madeleine, André and Denise there was, however, a common ground of agreement, not necessarily verbalised as such but evident nonetheless. Participation in some form or degree of leisure tourism which takes into account one's personal and environmental situation can and does contribute in a beneficial way to one's life story, influencing both the inner and outer worlds.

Based on what was expressed or implied in the stories, conclusions in the form of suggestions were made for 'possible activity' that might be undertaken by tourists themselves as well as in concerted action with others. As Ricoeur infers, there is 'life in quest of a narrative' all around us. As we and other people in the various sectors of society including the tourism industry begin to listen and hear how the plot unfolds, then perhaps we might 'discover through our understanding of narrative new possibilities for our own action in that this world is one that potentially we might inhabit' (Pellauer, 1997: 16).

Various media can contribute to this understanding as they, through informed, creative thinking, help deconstruct rather than propagate some of the commonly held beliefs or misconceptions about disability. There needs to be a change in attitudes before society at large, government organisations and offices or the various public and private segments of the tourism industry will act in a way that will benefit this market segment. Indeed, a first, even necessary 'possible activity' is, as suggested by Gadacz's (1994) creative title, to 'reThink disAbility'.

Educators at whatever level can have significant influence on individuals and on society. They, too, can act either as guardians of the *status quo* or as agents of change with regard to attitudes about disabilities. They can stimulate concrete changes. Linton (1998) strongly advocates that the academic milieu through its various fields of study or departments, institutes and schools can play a major role in helping change these conceptual errors and lead to changes in the environment. She proposes concrete suggestions as to how various fields of study might incorporate disability issues. Then, when through stories like those told in this study, professors and students in Schools of Architecture, for example, consider the implications of the still numerous architectural barriers that effectively exclude a significant number of people both physically and psychologically, they might begin to look for more innovative building and landscape design (Linton, 1998: 167).

Tourism and hospitality institutes or schools have an important role to play as they train management and front line staff for work in the travel industry. Tourism boards, associations or suppliers associated in any capacity with the provision of tourism products and services can actively contribute to enhancing the tourism experience of people with reduced abilities. Several concrete examples are discussed in *Different Ways of Seeing Things: Some Food for Thought* (Foggin, 1999).

Tourism boards and suppliers might consider more carefully the content of promotional materials, choosing to use images and representations that include those potential tourists whose bodies or capacities do not conform to those of the picture-perfect 'young and beautiful'. Or they might offer alternate formats for the visually or hearing impaired. Fortunately, with the advent of specialised computer technology, their web pages can be modified to allow easier access to information by any user who functions with reduced physical capacity. Feeling a sense of exclusion or inclusion even in the planning stages can affect the whole of a tourism experience.

The culinary aspect of the travel and tourism experience is important for most tourists – not only for the food and wine but also for the social interaction. It is possible that through accident, disease or simply the process of ageing, some form of impairment might make it more difficult to relish the experience. Perhaps it is vision and the client cannot read the fine print of the menus. Or arthritic fingers that are unable to cut into a steak, digestive systems that have become more 'fussy' with the passing of time. Those with impaired hearing could perhaps benefit from an environment with acoustics that reduces ambient noise as they share a meal with friends. There is a need for innovative planning to meet the growing demand for alternatives to standard or gourmet fare in a welcoming ambiance by a discerning clientele with dietary or other physical restrictions.

The most commonly encountered barriers or constraints in the tourism experience of the 16 were those related to the inaccessibility or inadequacy of transportation, accommodation and other buildings or sites. Such elements are an integral part of travel and tourism as well as of day-to-day living.

With regard to accommodation, several architectural barriers might require just simple adjustments: door-frames that contrast in colour to the walls so as to allow people with low vision to move more easily and safely about the room, flat door handles, flexible shower heads, ramps to negotiate around steps. Other adaptations require more work to respect building codes that accommodate clients with certain impairments.

Even though many ways have already been devised, there is still a lot of scope for finding and implementing creative ways to enhance the tourism experience of people with reduced ability. It is not just a question of a small group in the marketplace, a so-called 'special population' to be served by a specialised few. It is a large and growing clientele within the general population.

Listening to the multiple voices of professionals and of discipline-oriented specialists is important. But placing the people with disabilities and their voiced concerns on centre stage, listening and learning directly from them and their experiences, is critical. In order to 'get it right', it would be beneficial, indeed necessary, to get input and feedback directly from the 'users' or clients most concerned.

Like Ulysses, the renowned, albeit fictional, world traveller, the participants in this study experienced far more in their travels than just the 'manners, climates and councils'. Although 'time and fate' meant that some might not travel as much as they once did or wanted to, they nevertheless found that, although 'much is taken, much abides'. There are always ways to expand leisure horizons. They have a story to tell.

When a person's destination becomes more than just a place but rather 'a new way of looking at things' then all that one experiences in life can become, as it did for Ulysses, an arch through which gleams all the potential of a yet 'untravelled world'.

I cannot rest from travel ...
For always roaming with a hungry heart
Much have I seen and known; cities of men
And manners, climates, councils
Myself not least ...

I am a part of all that I have met;
Yet all experience is an arch wherethrough
Gleams that untravelled world, whose margin fades
For ever and for ever when I move
... yearning in desire
To follow knowledge like a sinking star,
Beyond the utmost bound of human thought.
. . . .
Though much is taken, much abides; and though
We are not now that strength which in old days
Moved earth and heaven; that which we are, we are;
One equal temper of heroic hearts,
Made weak by time and fate, but strong in will
To strive, to seek, to find and not to yield.

excerpt from *Ulysses* (1842) Alfred, Lord Tennyson, 1809–1892

References

Barnes, C. (1999) Disability studies: New or not so new directions? *Disability & Society* 14 (4), 577–580.

Bibeau, G. and Perreault, M. (1995) *Dérives montréalaises*. Montréal: Les Éditions du Boréal.

Brault, M. (2008) Disability status and the characteristics of people in group quarters: A brief analysis of disability prevalence among the civilian non-institutionalized and total populations in the American Community Survey, based on 2006 American Community Survey, US Census Bureau. On WWW at http://www.census.gov/hhes/www/disability/GQdisability.pdf. Accessed 20.8.2010.

Buhalis, D., Michopoulou, E., Eichhorn, V. and Miller, G. (2005) *Accessibility Market and Stakeholder Analysis – One-Stop-Shop for Accessible Tourism in Europe (OSSATE)*. Surrey, UK: University of Surrey.

Daniels, M.J., Drogin Rodgers, E.B. and Wiggins, B.P. (2005) 'Travel Tales': An interpretive analysis of constraints and negotiations to pleasure travel as experienced by persons with physical disabilities. *Tourism Management* 26 (6), 919–930.

Darcy, S. (1998) *Anxiety to Access: Tourism Patterns and Experiences of New South Wales People with a Physical Disability*. Sydney: Tourism New South Wales. Document Number)

De Grazia, S. (1994) *Of Time, Work, and Leisure* (1st Vintage Books edn). New York: Vintage Books.

Denzin, N. (1989) Interpretive Biography. *Series Qualitative Research Methods 17*. Newbury Park CA: SAGE Publications.

Driver, B.L., Brown, P.J., and Peterson, G.L. (1991) *Benefits of Leisure*. State College, PA: Venture Pub.

Foggin, E. (1999) Different ways of seeing things: Some food for thought. Conference proceedings, CAUTHE (Council for Australian University Tourism and Hospitality Education). Bureau of Tourism Research, Canberra (February 1999).

Gadacz, R. (1994) *ReThinking DisAbility: New Structures, New Relationships*. Edmonton: The University of Alberta Press.

Haworth, J.T. and Veal, A.J. (2004) *Work and Leisure*. London: Routledge.

Joy, M. (ed.) (1997) *Paul Ricoeur and Narrative: Context and Contestation*. Calgary: University of Calgary.

Kerby, A. (1991) *Narrative and the Self*. Bloomington: Indiana University Press.

Kéroul. (1994) Etude du marché touristique des personnes à capacité physique restreinte. Rapport Final, Montréal.

Krippendorf, J. (1999) *The Holiday Makers: Understanding the Impact of Leisure and Travel*. Oxford: Butterworth-Heinemann.

Kvale, S. (1983) The qualitative research interview: A phenomenological and hermeneutical mode of understanding. *Journal of Phenomenological Psychology* 14 (2), 171–196.

Leiper, N. (2003) *Tourism Management* (3rd edn). Sydney: Hospitality Press.

Linton, S. (1998) *Claiming Disability: Knowledge and Identity*. New York: New York University Press.

Lynch, R. and Veal, A.J. (2006) *Australian Leisure* (3rd edn). Sydney: Pearson Education.

NWT Bureau of Statistics (2007) Participation and Activity Limitation Survey: 2006. At http://www.stats.gov.nt.ca/Statinfo/Health/PALS/PALS_2006_Newstat.pdf

OECD (2007) OECD Demographic and labour force database. Society at a glance: OECD Social indicators 2006 (www.oecd.org/els/social/indicators/SAG > See indicators GE2 age dependency ratio). At http://www.oecd.org/dataoecd/52/31/38123085.xls.

Pellauer, D. (1997) Foreward: Recounting narrative. In J. Morny (ed.) *Paul Ricoeur and Narrative: Context and Contestation* (pp. ix-xxiii).

Ricoeur, P. (1984) *Time and Narrative*. Chicago: University of Chicago Press.

Smith, R. W. (1987) Leisure of disabled tourists: Barriers to participation. *Annals of Tourism Research* 14 (3), 376–389.

Statistics Canada (2006) Participation and Activity Limitation Survey. On WWW at http://www.statcan.ca/english/freepub/89-628-XIE/2007002/profileadults-en.htm and http://www.statcan.ca/english/freepub/89-628-XIE/89-628-XIE 2007002.htm. Accessed 22.1.2009.

Stumbo, N. (2001) *Professional Issues in Therapeutic Recreation: On Competence and Outcomes*. Champaign, Ill: Sagamore.

Swain, J., Finkelstein, V., French, S. and Oliver, M. (1997) *Disabling Barriers – Enabling Environments*. London: Sage Publications Ltd.

The Office of the United Nations High Commissioner for Human Rights (OHCHR) (2010). See websites: http://www2.ohchr.org/english/issues/disability/intro.htm#human; http://www.ohchr.org/Documents/Publications/training14.en.pdf; http://www.ohchr.org/Documents/Publications/HRDisabilityen.pdf.

Turco, D., Stumbo, N., and Garncarz, J. (1998) Tourism constraints for people with disabilities. *Parks and Recreation* 33 (9), 78–83.

United Nations (1997) International travel: A vital dimension of global integration. In *World Economic and Social Survey 1997*. New York: United Nations.

United Nations (2002) World Population Ageing: 1950–2050, United Nations' Second World Assembly on Ageing, Population Division, DESA, United Nations. At http://www. un.org/esa/population/publications/worldageing19502050/.

Chapter 7

Travelling with and Beyond Depression: Women's Narratives of Recovery and Identity

S. FULLAGAR

Introduction

Despite the growing prevalence and variety of mental health 'problems' within contemporary societies there has been surprisingly little exploration of the relationship between emotional distress/well-being and tourism experiences. This chapter aims to contribute a feminist perspective to the growing body of research into 'wellness tourism' (Smith & Kelly, 2006) through a focus on travel within Australian women's narratives of recovery from depression. Hence, it builds upon the expanding literature on women travellers (Small, 1999; Tiyce, 2008; Wearing & Wearing, 1996; Wilson & Harris, 2006) by developing closer connections with work in disability studies, leisure studies and mental health (Fullagar, 2008; Fullagar & Brown, 2003; Kleiber *et al.*, 2002; Stoppard, 2000). In particular I consider how meaningful travel experiences figured within women's stories of moving through depression and renegotiating their sense of self in recovery (Wilson & Harris, 2006). In this way I explore a tension shaping the travel experience between understanding the 'disabling effects' of being diagnosed as mentally 'ill' as well as the transformative possibilities travel affords women.

In this chapter I argue that the liminal space of travel affords us another way of understanding the relational and multiple nature of women's identity. Travel involves the movement away from home with its gendered responsibilities and expectations, as well as the movement towards other worlds and possible selves experienced within a relation to difference. In particular I focus on 11 narratives that identified the significance of travel within an Australian Research Council funded qualitative study involving 80 Australian women aged 20–75 who self-identified as recovering from depression. Ten women who identified themselves as travellers or tourists spoke of the embodied longing to move through places that gave them hope, desire and the vitality to escape the weight of depression. In contrast one woman spoke of how travel actually contributed to her depression rather than recovery. My analysis considers how women draw upon gendered discourses to articulate their recovering identity and identified three interrelated themes about travel experiences. These themes include; travel as a narrative of escape from gendered expectations of home, travel as a pleasurable form of risk taking and travel as a quest for a purposeful identity beyond deficit and depression.

Mental health and illness are also 'liminal' categories of human experience that have been culturally produced through the oppositional relations of the mind and body, reason and emotion, healthy and sick, normal and abnormal, self and other (Ussher, 1991; Wiener, 2005). In this context I explore how travel and tourism figure in the stories of those who are living with and moving through an identity formed around depression and gender. I conclude with a reflection upon the implications of the study for the fields of tourism and mental health with respect to ways of thinking about well-being.

Discourses of Depression and Recovery

Depression has been identified as the most common 'mental disorder' in Australia, and the single largest 'cause of disability' accounting for over $3 billion annually in direct and indirect costs (Commonwealth of Australia, 2006). It is the third largest cause of disease burden for women and the eighth for men. Depression is also responsible for 9.8% of all years 'lived with disability' for women and 6.2% for men (Noble, 2005). Depression is a complex mental health condition in terms of its effects on an individual's life – chronicity and often lifelong recurrence, periods of instability and loss of employment/income, relationships and social connection, as well as the profound loss of self-identity and social worth that is calculated through the crude measure of 'years lost to disability'. The experience of depression varies in relation to its severity and treatment from hospitalisation in psychiatric care to the use of long term anti-depressants designed to maintain 'normal' functioning and alleviate distress. The ongoing embodied effects on individual lives are also highly temporal ranging from severe periods of incapacitation, emotional ups and downs, periods of 'normal' functioning, and these effects can be highly visible to others or largely invisible with distress unrecognised. Despite greater awareness depression is still stigmatised as a mental health disorder that is seen to reflect an individual's weakness, inability to cope with modern life or a biochemical imbalance in the brain (Crosbie & Rosenberg, 2007). Drawing upon insights from the social approach to disability it can be argued that the discourse and experience of depression has 'disabling effects' in that discrimination, stigma and devaluing of difference derives from socio-cultural norms that privilege a limited model of humanness (Mulvany, 2000).

In contrast to biomedical and individualised models of depression that explain the cause of disability in terms of biochemical or psychological deficits, a growing body of research identifies depression as a deeply gendered, social phenomenon (Fullagar, 2008; Schreiber, 2001; Stoppard, 2000). Depression has been linked to a sense of loss of self experienced in relation to childhood abuse, family and domestic violence and other inequities that women experience in relationships, work and leisure (Stoppard & McMullen, 2003). In addition, depression is also linked to women's experience of marginalisation in relation to class, cultural, sexuality and age differences as well as cultural expectations that women 'be all things to all people'. There is a growing literature on women's experience of depression that identifies how recovery is connected to the negotiation of gendered identity beyond the normalised 'good woman' (as wife, mother, daughter) articulated through the heterosexual matrix (Stoppard, 2000). Hence, further exploration of what women identify as significant in their experience of recovery can help to shift popular and medical-therapeutic understandings from the pharmacological treatment paradigm towards a focus on meaningful experiences (such as travel).

Recognition of leisure and travel practices that enable the transformation of self through recovery refocuses attention on the social processes that can enable change in different life domains (O'Brien & Fullagar, 2008). The recovery orientation in mental health policy and research has also called for new ways of supporting people who continue to experience severe emotional distress that emphasises their capacities, potential capabilities and renewed life purpose beyond a simplistic notion of cure (Pilgrim, 2009). The capabilities approach advocated by Hopper (2007) draws insights from the social model of disability to acknowledge and challenge the social forces shaping the experience, conceptualisation and stigmatising response to 'mental illness'. Although the emphasis on individual capabilities is important in understanding the personal meaning of recovery there is also the need for a more critical understanding of the assumptions informing recovery discourses (Keane, 2000). The recovery of one's life and identity 'from' or 'within' mental illness (and social exclusion) still ties the self to a powerful narrative about disorder, dysfunction and disease (Davidson & Roe, 2007). Investigating the discursive repertoires that women use to talk about their travel experiences in the context of recovering from depression can help to identify other practices that support emotional well-being as well as other ways of experiencing humanness. For women travel narratives co-exist with a range of other narratives of gendered selfhood that give rise to particular discursive tensions within and across these identities. There is an emerging literature that explores this connection between narrative and identity transformation in both the leisure and tourism fields (Fullagar, 2002; Hood, 2003; Kleiber *et al.*, 2002; Wearing & Wearing, 2001) as well as recovery focused research (Frank, 1998; McIntosh & McKeganey, 2000; Ridgway, 2001; Wirtz & Harari, 2000). The social model of disability that has informed research on leisure, sport and tourism identifies the socio-cultural and physical barriers to participation and full citizenship (Darcy, 2004; Kwai-sang Yau *et al.*, 2004). While the focus has largely been on the experiences of sensory, physical and learning disability, the links to the rather more slippery conceptualisation of mental heath/illness requires further examination. There are commonalities that arise out of the recognition of diverse ways of experiencing humanness and con-structions of capability that bring into question normalised assumptions underpinning the exclusion of difference.

Women's Depression and Recovery Project

If travel enables women to mobilise a different experience of self-identity then how do we understand the gendered relation of freedom from, and freedom to, within the specific context of recovery from depression? How does travel as a relation with the 'otherness' of the world, cultural difference and even oneself, effect a transformation of women's identity in the process of recovery? And in particular what is the embodied significance of travel as a (non-medical) mode of healing? Travel offers a distinct spatio-temporal practice through which the recovering self is literally and metaphorically moved beyond the identity-related pressures that create the social conditions for depression to flourish. In this chapter I draw upon the narratives of travel that appeared in 11 stories out of the 80 that were gathered as part of an Australian Research Council funded project on women's recovery from depression. The project aimed to identify what women did and how they created meaning about their recovery in the gendered context of everyday life. In-depth interviews with a semi-structured format were conducted and fully transcribed by myself and research assistants within women's homes or preferred locations. Ethical approval for the study was granted by Griffith University. Women were asked a range of questions about their experience of moving through depression, in particular, what helped and hindered their recovery. A diagnosis of depression was not required of participants (although the majority were diagnosed) and women responded to notices in community newspapers, fliers in health centres, email lists and radio interviews. Participants came from middle and working class backgrounds, were predominantly Anglo-Celtic, hetero-sexual, with a mix of mothers and non-mothers.

The sample included women with a range of diagnoses including mild, moderate, major, bipolar and post-natal depression. Often there were other issues such as anxiety, panic attacks and sometimes psychosis. The participants had extensive depression-related experience with 60%

experiencing depression three times or more, 21% experienced two to three episodes and 14% had depression once in their lives (5% unknown). This highlights the complex issue of recurrence or relapse that has been identified in health policy and mental health promotion initiatives for depression. The majority of participants identified themselves as 'recovering' from depression with only a few identifying as fully 'recovered'. In addition to, or instead of, medication the majority of participants in the study employed a wide range of everyday practices such as seeking social support, counselling, greater work-life balance as well as changing relationships and involvement in active leisure, travel and creative pursuits.

In terms of the 11 interviews in which travel was identified, ten women talked of how travel helped their recovery while one spoke of how it contributed to her depression. For Nora (56 years) travelling non-stop across Canada with her sister and nieces left her feeling unstimulated, lonely and disconnected from her family. Travel in this instance was not an experience of freedom but served to reinforce Nora's self-blame as she attributed her depression to 'her nature and bad mental habits'. The other ten women aged from 30 to 69 years (most were over 50 years) spoke to varying degrees about how travel figured in their recovery with some speaking in much greater detail than others. In the analysis I identified the themes across the range of participants and also considered how discourses of gender and risk played out in the way participants created a narrative of the travelling self in their own story of recovery from depression (Alvesson & Skoldberg, 2000). I acknowledge that writing this chapter is also a research process through which I reproduce what participants said at a particular point in time. Hence, I do not claim to provide a representative account or generalisable findings, but rather offer an interpretative glimpse into the narrative accounts of a particular group of Australian women.

Getting Away – Ambivalent Relationships with Home and Work

Of the ten participants who felt travel was a positive force in their recovery from depression, seven women talked about the importance of getting away from pressures at home or work to have time and space to be themselves. The other three women talked about their desire to travel in terms of a strong life interest or identity project (two were retired). Whether it was getting away for a short time or travelling over a longer period many women identified powerful experiences articulated through embodied and emotional metaphors that had changed them in some way. With respect to the gendered context of such experiences travel figured as a site of identity formation that enabled women to perform a different feminine self – a self that was not primarily defined by relations of care for others nor by depression. In particular women who were mothers valued travel as a time-space for reflection on their own desires and a positive emotional experience. For women without children who had high pressured jobs travel also provided a freer emotional space as Harriet (30 years) said, 'that three weeks of being completely away from it (workplace issues) ... the change of scenery, sharing a room with a very dear friend who didn't mind if I burst into tears at the dinner table ... those sorts of things really did make a difference, it was very healing to have that complete psychic break'.

In everyday life the multiplicity of women's desires (for their own lives, and in relation to others) tended to be submerged by the feeling of emotional overload related to maintaining family relationships, a lack of support from husbands, multiple care and/or work responsibilities and the loss of an autonomous sense of identity. For example, Delia (49 years) as a mother with young adults at home was able to enjoy a novel week away by herself on the coast (paid by a friend) to reflect, rest and breathe. The independence she experienced during that week away stayed with Delia as a positive source of hope that a sense of emotional wellbeing was possible amidst the ongoing struggles. Meredith (41 years) talked about how a holiday away from family enabled her to feel differently about herself, 'when I'm away from my home situation... I feel free and strong. Like I'm my own person. I can do things I want to do. When I get caught up in the domestic situation (two children and husband), I just get weighed down again. I have so many responsibilities I don't feel free to be what I want to be...'. Juanita (56 years) echoed this sentiment when she talked about saving hard and travelling 'on the smell of an oily rag' to go overnight to a music festival or to undertake longer trips overseas with her daughter, friends or by herself as her husband was reluctant to go. She said 'I guess what the travel represents is my younger self... not being burdened, being unencumbered and meeting people... when I am with those people I am not burdened by the hard work of the children and the husband... we only have one life'. Juanita also drew upon the metaphoric travel relation between home and away when describing depression as 'being paralysed, not wanting to go out the front door'. In contrast she described recovery as 'closing the door of my house and being out there'. Travel in this sense involves taking an emotional risk as women cross a gender threshold and step beyond normalised gender expectations that others hold (children, husbands, ageing parents) and that they often hold of themselves (pleasing others first). Getting away figures as a powerful metaphor in these narratives of recovery as it signifies a key moment in which women refuse to accept the gendered conditions that produce emotional distress and it mobilises their desire for other emotionally satisfying experiences.

Travel as Ethical Relation of Care for Self

Beyond the desire to get away from home many women identified the importance of travel as the freedom to create an ethical relation to self that involves caring for themselves (O'Grady, 2005). Allie (69 years) talked about how she had developed purposeful practices (meditation, exercise, writing, music, volunteering, social connection and travel) that prevented depression dominating her life. These leisure practices enabled her to perform a different relation to self, 'I self nurture, I've got a number of strategies for caring for me and putting myself first, it's really easy now I'm retired!'. As an extension of these everyday activities travel offered a kind of hopefulness and purpose, 'Travelling is my big thing ... I've travelled a fair bit in Australia, even when the kids were little, I'd cart them along and we'd go camping and so on, and I only started travelling overseas in 1990. I'm just back from China'. In contrast to the sacrificing, other pleasing and responsible self who often lacks a sense of entitlement to leisure of her own, the travelling self that women identify actively engages in seeking pleasurable, enjoyable and at times challenging experiences.

Phyllis (62 years) had a long history of hospitalisation and therapy for depression, abuse and had received different mental illness diagnoses, yet she found travel to be a new kind of freedom that enabled her to care for herself differently. She started travelling independently after a breakdown: 'I had to learn that it wasn't selfish to consider yourself ... it was a big revelation about human rights, to be able to say "no" without explanation ... Travel was the thing I was free to do ... I go really frugally, cheap places all on my own ... I've got to be free ... I walk everywhere and I absorb cultures ... you learn to just get about in other cultures, with no language and to me that was such a challenge and so rewarding ... the thing (in my life) that thrills is travel'. Travel offered Phyllis a means of experiencing her emotions as positive aspects of identity and her sense of capability as an independent woman. To further illustrate the significance of travel in facilitating relations of self care and self knowledge within a complex process of recovery from depression I provide a more detailed account of one participant's narrative. This biographical context can provide a more nuanced understanding of different kinds of meaningful travel experiences – in this case it was a one week stay at a health retreat.

Phoebe's story

At the time of the interview Phoebe was 43 years old, married a second time with one child and worked as a teacher. She had experienced depression since childhood but had been 'diagnosed' four years ago after a traumatic incident at work when she was threatened with violence by a male student. At this time Phoebe miscarried her second child which resulted in anxiety, panic attacks and severe sleep deprivation and led her to admit herself into a private psychiatric hospital for several months to rest and recuperate. Phoebe's treatment before hospitalisation had primarily involved anti-depressants, hormones and sleeping tablets. She felt that this treatment did not really help the recovery process, 'that 12 months really messed me up'. The realisation that drug treatments and therapy sessions were not going to 'fix' her depression 'was a turning point I think in my recovery, when I realised it was never going to be any one thing; there was a lot of work to do here. A lot of stuff to deal with ... And I needed to do many things, in many ways, in order to heal'. Phoebe talked about how her experience of recovery over the past five years had been very up and down as depression was a very 'intangible' condition that was not recognised as legitimate in society. Her experience of recovery was one of moving forward and sliding back as she shifted out of her 'comfort zone' to try new things in her leisure time, relationships or take on more responsibility in her work as a teacher.

Phoebe began to change the gendered expectations about being a 'good woman' at work and home that had contributed to her emotional overload, 'I sort of still realise that I struggle with that wanting to do a good job, and wanting it to be wonderful and great at my own expense'. She also made changes in her relationships at home by 'facing the reality of what was going on in my marriage' (lack of emotional support). She sought out individual and couple therapy to deal with childhood issues of abuse, domestic violence in her first marriage and the effects on her sense of self, 'I was a survivor. You know, I sort of took on that role quite a bit ... now I think I've got a bit of a goddess/warrior-ess thing happening ... I've had a very dysfunctional family'.

Phoebe identified the gendered conditions that contributed to her depression, 'For women in particular, I think we bury ourselves and we lose ourselves in pleasing and we think it's not okay to be who we are.' Recovery involved developing greater self-awareness about 'speaking her truth', 'asking for help' (at school and from her husband) and enacting a range of recovery practices to maintain her well-being, 'I'm starting to learn the things that work for me, the things that I need to do in order to stay well'. These embodied practices (exercise, yoga retreats, meditation and journal writing) helped her control negative thoughts and moved her into a different ethical relation to self that generated affirming emotions. Yet, acting on her desire for change when she was not feeling well was the most difficult part of recovery 'because you've got to be your own advocate at a time when you're probably least able to do it'. At one of her yoga classes Phoebe recalled being struck by a comment someone made about the importance of addressing mind-body disconnection, 'She said "We forget that we have a body, a lot of us see ourselves as a head walking around in space." And it hit me that I had been so removed from my body for so long ... women who've been sexually abused; that's often their experience ... I knew that I needed to start doing some things to get back into my body'. Phoebe decided to go away to a health retreat for a week to experience her self differently and engage in adventure activities that she would normally find terrifying. She describes the week away as 'very eye opening in that I was amazed at what my body could do. I did things that I had never done before and I did things that I was terrified to do. I climbed this pamper pole ... why they call it a pamper pole has got me beat, there's nothing pamper about it at all; it's this bloody great telegraph pole ... (you) actually pull your whole body weight ... it's got these things in it. And you climb up and you stand on the top ... and you're in a harness, and you jump off ... absolutely terrified ... but it was good terrifying and I'd forgotten there's a good terrifying; I'd spent so many years (as a single parent) with my heart in my throat ... those years were tough ... And I had forgotten there are good ways to be ... stressed and afraid ... And the other thing I did was the flying fox. Once again; jumping off a cliff ... And learning to trust ... trust in support systems and that sort of thing ... you have a choice ... you can do the 'sloth for a week' thing, where you lay by the pool. You can do the middle of the road, which I did, which was sort of quite a lot of exercise and ... there's yoga, there's weights ... there's the tribal dance which I loved, and circus sort of things'. Phoebe likened these intensely embodied experiences to learning cognitive techniques that changed not only her thinking but, 'it's challenging your emotions, it's getting to your core self'.

The liminal space of the health retreat opened up a very different experience of self that was produced through the embodied pleasure in risk taking and the feeling of trust in her capabilities. Phoebe spoke about this different feeling of aliveness in an intense momentary sense of wonder, 'There was something else that happened there ... I was walking back down this hill and I had this really weird experience where I was just overcome with peace, and I saw myself clearly for the first time in my life. And it was all good ... I was a thing of beauty, and grace ... and I understood for the very first time, my connectedness to everything; to every blade of grass, to everything. And I saw my place, and I saw my insignificance, and my significance ... I get shivers when I think about it ... when I journal about it; I cry ... it wasn't a high ... it was just a deep understanding of my place ... And a deep love for myself and for everything around me ... like I haven't had that experience to that degree since. It was very brief ... but I just got it, I just understood... And I knew that I would be okay, and I knew that I had a purpose here on earth ... I was able to really let go of that victim role; I knew that I would never see myself as a victim anymore'. This powerful memory was central in Phoebe's story about the process of recovery as one of ongoing learning about 'what I need to keep doing in order to take care of myself, and still learning those boundaries and those limits, and learning when I'm overwhelmed and when I'm taking on too much'. The health retreat experience as a site of learning or self-knowledge offered Phoebe a very powerful sense of capable feminine embodiment. Although she was not experiencing chronic depression at the time Phoebe attended the nurturing space of the retreat her story stands in stark contrast to many women's comments about the limitations of 'medicated rest' offered by the psychiatric hospital. The public mental health system provides very limited forms of in and out patient 'treatment' for depression and the private system is often too costly for many women. This means that there is little publicly funded intervention support for women who really need to get away to rest, reflect and experience a different sense of identity beyond the emotional spiral of depression.

Becoming Travellers – From Fear to Freedom

The theme of overcoming fears that kept women trapped in feelings of depression and helplessness was evident in women's narratives about the freedom of travel. In order to act on the desire to travel women had to take a number of emotional risks and confront fears such as risking upsetting their husbands and the assumed gender order of the household, speaking up assertively about their own wishes and venturing into the unknown. Allie (69 years) made the connection between her desire to travel and risk extending herself (and her limited finances) and the desire to overcome the gendered fears that often fed her depression. When asked about her metaphor for recovery Allie said it is 'freedom from fear ... freedom to be who you are ... I have no fear now ... I think it's fear that keeps us locked into depression ... [it] might be fear of what other people will think of you, or not living up to expectations'. Allie identified how as an older woman she was able to more easily question and let go of the gendered expectations to be the perfect wife, worker or mother. The metaphor of letting go also literally freed her up to experience different cultures and places through her emerging identity as a traveller.

This desire to overcome fear was also echoed in Anya's (36 years) metaphor of the journey of depression that she had struggled with since adolescence. She said, 'You may be travelling alone ... [there are] certain dangers that you experience. And the worst of which, of course, is being alone and having to travel alone in quite a seriously dark space ... And each year there are times when you actually have to hike quite solidly through thick forest, but you might find yourself in an open field for a little while. And then, at some point, you're going to have to climb up the other side of the valley to get to the next valley, and you have to work your arse off to do that. But at some point you come to a peak and then following that peak, you're going to have to descend again into the next valley'. When asked about her metaphor for recovery Anya spoke through a different, enlivened tone of voice about feeling 'Surprised – perpetually surprised. Surprised at myself, at my capacity. Like, I can push myself so much further than I do, and I'm capable of so much more. And I think ... and I'm not necessarily talking about work or productivity or employment or money, it's actually more about capability ... like, just not being afraid'.

For Anya travel was one of the most important experiences in her recovery and could be described as a life project through which she created memories via photographs and stories that were shared with others at home. She spoke of enjoying her independence and not needing others, 'So travel is a key, it always makes me feel better ... I had a counsellor once who told me that I had to learn how to be happy without being on a bus, or a train, or moving with a back pack on'. Anya's travelling self was produced in complete contrast to her depressed and anxious self that was governed by fears and expectations she could never quite meet. The pleasure of travel was about 'arriving ... or just exploration, it's sort of inspiration – the capacity to adapt to something new, as well. Like, I've travelled to some really challenging places, where a lot of people wouldn't feel very comfortable. And dealt with a lot of kinda strange situations and everything is invigorating'. In the context of independent travel fear and risk were a source of embodied pleasure through which Anya performed a strong sense of capable womanhood. As she says, 'Without any stress whatsoever, I can pack a bag and be on the other side of the world tomorrow. I have no worries about that. I don't feel there's any risk. I have complete confidence and control ... and if something is not working, it's okay I can cope with it somehow. I know how to cope with it ... I spend a lot of my spare money on travel, take photographs, I love photography ... it's actually a creative thing ... I don't buy much. I just take photographs. And I experience culture, it's enough for me.'

Anya invoked a family narrative of travel as she identified with her father who was a great traveller (he did not live with her as a child) and encouraged her interest through National Geographic magazines. She described travel as 'fun' and recognised this was something often missing in the seriousness of her everyday life, feelings of pressure to succeed and sense of over responsibility. Anya contrasts her travel pleasures with the neo-liberal demand that she be productive at work and occupied in her leisure at the expense of her emotional wellbeing, 'I mean being productive is all very well and good of course. It's sort of like "I've got a spare three hours, what can I do now?" Instead of "what do I need?" at this moment'. She contrasts this with 'the whole travel thing is like... if I know I've got the ticket to go overseas, I'm happy. I don't even have to be overseas. There's the ticket okay ... I went to India in December. I bought the ticket in July, I was happy for months'. Travel affords Anya a sense of hope that counters the weight of depression that is intertwined with her everyday life and the competitive, success oriented and status seeking characteristics of the social world. Central to her recovery was an embodied sense of experiencing herself differently, 'I'm having fun, well you don't intellectualise it, you're actually experiencing it. And then later you realise "oh cool" and it was good. Like, only recently have I really been having fun'. For Anya travel was also a space for reflection on her ethical relation to self and world, 'And I have to monitor my behaviour at work sometimes ... to make sure I don't overdo it ... a lot of that work stuff is daily satisfaction and that's why I like it. What did change though recently, spending a month in India really made me realise how much I have, how ambitious I am – without any reason really, how much small things matter – being a genuine honest person'. As a liminal space travel invoked reflection on the different places and people in the present as a relation to women's reflection on their past and future selves. The compelling question about who they desired to be in life was more easily addressed away from the gendered pressures of home that had become embodied in the form of paralysing fears. Travel generated disturbing pleasures that invoked different emotions and it was the embodied nature of such experiences that women identified as vital in moving their sense of self beyond the narrow confines of depression. These travel narratives offer an important insight that much 'mental health' literature ignores – the importance of recognising experiences that invoke connections between mind-body-emotion as the material base of women's identities beyond illness categories (Phillips, 2006).

Discussion and Conclusion

Travel as a metaphor for the journey of self knowledge also resonates with the metaphor of recovery as a journey of experiencing healing that moves the self beyond the stasis of depression. In this study women draw upon gendered discourses to articulate their recovering identity in relation to travel experiences in three major ways. These themes include; travel as a narrative of escape from gendered expectations of home, travel as a pleasurable form of risk taking and travel as a quest for a purposeful identity beyond deficit and depression. These findings resonate with recent work on the meaning of women's travel experiences identified in relation to the healing of loss and grief, the significance of independent risk taking and the transformative movement of identity (Tiyce, 2008). Feminist research identifies how the meaning of travel for western women is highly gendered in relation to the demands of home, expectations of paid work and the desire for 'freedom from' such norms or 'freedom to' experience oneself differently in the world. In this study women's travel embodied an emotional experience of risk taking that was connected to the gendered norms of home that regulate women's identities as 'good' mothers, wives, daughters, workers etc. as well as the dangers, pleasures and surprises generated through new experiences. The gendered risk discourses that shaped how women ascribed particular significance to travel differed from masculine notions of risk implied in activities aimed at overcoming and conquering physical or emotional limits. Risking one's safety through travel may indeed inform women's desire to overcome or resist limits, but this played out in a different way for women who have been positioned as 'risky identities' due to their mental illness diagnosis, feelings of emotional turmoil, shame and stigma (their mental health difference).

For women who have experienced marginalisation because of their mental health-illness identity travel involved taking substantial emotion risks in terms of how others may have judged their 'coping abilities' in challenging situations. The pleasure of risky travel (enjoying the emotional challenge) can be seen in contrast to the 'safe' expectation that women will do the emotion work of caring for others at home, family and in paid work as their primary source of identity. Travel, like leisure and sport, has been theorised as a site of women's resistance to gender discourses that inferiorise the feminine, the body and emotions in relation to privileging the masculine, mind and rationality as defining aspects of humanness (Wearing & Wearing, 1996). The findings from this study suggest that travel is not only a site of resistance against gender norms but importantly is a site for the positive performance of different identities for women that emphasise capability, mind-body connection and ethical reflexivity.

Within women's narratives of recovery travel figured as a means of transforming the ethical relation to self and hence emotional well-being. Hence, the travel narratives through which women retell and reconstruct their sense of self are a powerful cultural medium that is sustained beyond the immediacy of experience through photos, memories and the discourses of mobility. From a post-structuralist perspective the identity of women travellers can be characterised by multiplicity and this stands in stark contrast to the singularity of the depressed, immobile self who feels little desire to engage with the world (as a participant said, a state of 'un-wanting' that is barely living). In this way travel narratives throw into relief the normalising discourses and moral codes of selfhood that govern women's subjectivities as good/immoral, worthy/shameful, successful/ failures, useful to others/self-determining purposeful life. Depression is tied up with self-limiting practices of femininity and in contrast these narratives of travel invoked desires to discover unknown aspects of self and world – competence, capability, autonomy, self reliance. This ethical relation involved taking risks, thus overcoming some of the self-limiting feminine practices of risk avoidance and fears about the likelihood of relapse in recovery. Travel was a means of addressing the risk of depression returning by embracing risk – generating a range of emotions (joy, surprise, wonder, fear) that countered the fearful stance embodied in depression. The risks and pleasures experienced through travel practices can open up a liminal space through which women travellers engage in the process of restorying their identities, desires and modes of becoming feminine subjects.

The insights generated through understanding women's recovery from depression can inform a more critical appreciation of the social forces that shape how emotional distress and well-being are experienced. There are also practical implications for tourism services in relation to understanding the different meanings and motivations for travel, questioning assumptions made about people experiencing mental health issues and a more critical appreciation of how gender issues shape women's identities. In addition, there are broader issues of work-life balance that arise for employers who regulate access to annual leave entitlements and hence can promote or impede women's opportunities for travel and time out. Important questions for governments arise in relation to the funding of mental health services through the rhetoric of rehabilitation, community inclusion and recovery, that exists in tension with individualised treatment-focused regimes. In Australia public funding is available to support women's recovery via individualised therapy and medical treatment. Yet, many women in this study identified how the process of recovering their sense of identity beyond depression was very much connected to the pursuit of meaningful experiences such as leisure and travel. In this sense recovery is about supporting individual capabilities while recognising collective issues of exclusion and hence it requires much more than expert driven treatment. Women's recovery is practiced and performed through experiences that produce a sense of emotional well-being, challenge gender norms through the exercise of human rights and require an active engagement with the world.

References

Alvesson, M. and Skoldberg, K. (2000) *Reflexive Methodology: New Vistas for Qualitative Research*. London: Sage.

Commonwealth of Australia (2006) *Select Committee on Mental Health: A National Approach to Mental Health – From Crisis to Community*. Canberra: Senate Select Committee.

Crosbie, D. and Rosenberg, S. (2007) *COAG Mental Health Reform. Mental Health and the New Medicare Services: An Analysis of the First Six Months*. Canberra: Mental Health Council of Australia.

Darcy, S. (2004) *Disabling Journeys: The Social Relations of Tourism for People with Impairments in Australia – An Analysis of Government Tourism Authorities and Accommodation Sector Practice and Discourses.* University of Technology, Sydney, Sydney.

Davidson, L. and Roe, D. (2007) 'Recovery from' and 'recovery in' serious mental illnesses: One strategy for lessening the confusion plaguing recovery. *Journal of Mental Health* 16 (4), 459–470.

Frank, A. (1998) Stories of illness as care of the self: A Foucauldian dialogue. *Health* 2 (3), 329–348.

Fullagar, S. (2002) Narratives of travel: Desire and the movement of feminine subjectivity. *Leisure Studies* 21, 57–74.

Fullagar, S. (2008) Leisure practices as counter-depressants. *Leisure Sciences* (1) 1–18.

Fullagar, S. and Brown, P. (2003) Everyday temporalities: Leisure, ethics and young women's emotional well-being. *Annals of Leisure Research* 6 (3), 193–208.

Hood, C. (2003) Women in recovery from alcoholism: The place of leisure. *Leisure Sciences* 25 (1), 51– 79.

Hopper, K. (2007) Rethinking social recovery in schizophrenia: What a capabilities approach might offer. *Social Science and Medicine* 65 (5), 868–879.

Keane, H. (2000) Setting yourself free: Techniques of recovery. *Health* 4 (3), 324–346.

Kleiber, D., Hutchinson, S. and Williams, R. (2002) Leisure as a resource in transcending negative life events: Self-protection, self-restoration and personal transformation. *Leisure Sciences* 24 (2), 219–235.

Kwai-sang Yau, M., McKercher, B. and Packer, T. (2004) Traveling with a disability more than an access issue. *Annals of Leisure Research* 31 (4), 946–960.

McIntosh, J. and McKeganey, N. (2000) Addicts' narratives of recovery from drug use: Constructing a non-addict identity. *Social Science and Medicine* 50, 1501–1510.

Mulvany, J. (2000) Disability, impairment or illness? The relevance of the social model of disability to the study of mental disorder. *Sociology of Health and Illness* 22 (5), 582–601.

Noble, R. (2005) Depression in women. *Metabolism: Clinical & Experimental* 54 (5 Suppl 1), 49–52.

O'Brien, W. and Fullagar, S. (2008) Rethinking the Relapse Cycle of Depression and Recovery: A qualitative investigation of women's experiences. *Social Alternatives* 27 (4), 6–13.

O'Grady, H. (2005) *Woman's Relationship with Herself.* London: Routledge.

Phillips, L. (2006) *Mental illness and the Body: Beyond Diagnosis.* London: Routledge.

Pilgrim, D. (2008) 'Recovery' and current mental health policy. *Chronic Illness* 4 (4), 295–304.

Ridgway, P. (2001) Restorying psychiatric disability: Learning from first person recovery narratives. *Psychiatric Rehabilitation Journal* 24 (4), 335–343.

Schreiber, R. (2001) Wandering in the dark: Women's experiences with depression. *Health Care for Women International* 22 (1), 85–98.

Small, J. (1999) Memory-work: A method for researching women's tourist experiences. *Tourism Management* 20, 25–35.

Smith, M. and Kelly, C. (2006) Wellness tourism. *Tourism Recreation Research* 31 (1), 1–4.

Stoppard, J. (2000) *Understanding Depression: Feminist Social Constructionist Approaches.* London: Routledge.

Stoppard, J. and McMullen, L. (eds) (2003) *Situating Sadness: Women and Depression in Social Context*. New York: New York University Press.

Tiyce, M. (2008) Healing through travel: Two women's experiences of loss and adaptation. Paper presented at the Where the bloody hell are we? conference. Cauthe, Gold Coast.

Ussher, J. (1991) *Women's Madness: Misogyny or Mental Illness?* New York: Havester Wheatsheaf.

Wearing, B. and Wearing, S. (1996) Refocussing the tourist experience: The flaneur and the choraster. *Leisure Studies* 15 (4), 229–243.

Wearing, S. and Wearing, B. (2001) Conceptualizing the selves of tourism. *Leisure Studies* 20 (2), 143–159.

Wiener, D. (2005) Antipsychiatric activism and feminism: The use of film and text to question biomedicine. *Journal of Public Mental Health* 4 (3), 42–47.

Wilson, E. and Harris, C. (2006) Meaningful travel: Women, independent travel and the search for self and meaning. *Tourism* 54 (2), 161–172.

Wirtz, H. and Harari, R. (2000) Deconstructing depression: A narrative groupwork approach. *Journal of Narrative Therapy and Community Work* 1 & 2, 42–51.

Chapter 8

Encounters of Disabled Customers on the Tourism Stage

E. AROLA, C. COOPER and R. COOPER

Introduction

The subject of this paper is tourism for the disabled, a topic that often leads to heated discussion amongst tourism businesses and those with disabilities. Unfortunately this phenomenon has not yet been surveyed, defined or recognised by those delivering commercial leisure and recreation services within the tourism industry. Consequently, tourism businesses do not recognise people with disabilities as potential customers and vice versa.

Goffman's *The Presentation of Self in Everyday Life* (1959) and Pine and Gilmore's (1999) *The Experience Economy: Work is Theatre and Every Business a Stage* both use the concept of a theatrical performance as a metaphor for life. This theory has been applied to a functioning tourism system and following the ideas of Goffman, Pine and Gilmore, this chapter draws out new ideas examining tourism as a staged business. This is done using a model which conceptualises any tourism enterprise, facility or service process as a region, divided into front and back stage on which all encounters and interactions, or performances, take place (Arola, 2003, 2005), and where the actors are:

- management and front-line staff; and
- where members of the audience are customers – disabled or non-disabled.

The general objective of this research is to examine the role of disabled people as consumers in the contexts of inclusion, legislation, and commercial tourism (Arola, 2003). The research also aims to:

- define the term disability in the context of tourism;
- examine the experiences of disabled customers on the tourism stage;
- examine and clarify the interrelated attitudes and behavioural patterns between four different groups involved in service processes within the hotel restaurant setting (management, front-line staff, customers with disabilities and able-bodied customers); and

- an overall objective of the research is to assess and examine the encounters of disabled customers on the tourism stage.

Following the identification of disabled tourists as an unrecognised segment of the tourism market, the crucial research questions that arise are:

- In modern society, is there a growing demand for the provision of tourism services generated by the needs of the disabled?
- Does the infrastructure of the tourism industry (as represented by tourism companies in the research destination area) know or recognise the potential market well enough to effectively serve the disabled as customers?
- Do staff and managers of tourism companies have particular attitudes towards the disabled as customers?
- Are disabled customers satisfied with the way they are treated as customers in commercial tourism businesses?

The Disabled Consumer

According to Burnett and Bender-Baker (2001: 4–11):

> Few consumer groups have greater potential and are more ignored than the disabled. Consisting of 50 million individuals in the United States, with discretionary income of over $200 billion, this largest of all minority groups has been viewed by many tourist businesses as a source of confusion, requiring extra expenditures on ramps, specially fitted rooms, and the loss of prime parking.

Despite the critical need to understand the disabled as consumers, the general focus has been on satisfying a set of costly rules for a customer group that is often not even desired. Building ramps, giving up prime parking spaces, constructing disability-friendly rooms and installing expensive technology reflect some of the more common requirements that have soured the perceptions of travel-related businesses towards the disabled. This is a serious mistake. While traditional marketing researchers frequently employ segmentation studies on ethnicity, age, and socio-economic sub-groups, the potential of the disabled market segment in terms of size, access and responsiveness is largely ignored. Research needs to address the particular problems, needs, behavioural patterns and choice models used by consumers who are physically or emotionally challenged (Burnett & Bender-Baker, 2001: 4).

Attempting to describe and understand disabled people as consumers is a very recent phenomenon. Partly, it is due to the work of the ADA.

However, another possible reason is the changing attitudes that non-disabled people have towards the disabled. Simply, there are more people with a disability in the community, and with familiarity comes a higher level of acceptance. Familiarity of the disabled in the workplace is especially important. Another reason for the greater acceptance of the disabled is the improved portrayal of the disabled in the media, where an increased number of television programmes, advertisements, movies, and news programmes no longer stigmatise the disabled. Instead, current portrayals depict inspiration, not limitation. However, negative portrayals are still prevalent and our knowledge of the disabled is still somewhat superficial and distorted (Burnett & Bender-Baker, 2001: 5).

The Theatrical Nature of Services

The Goffmanian approach (the theatre metaphor) was chosen as the theoretical frame of reference largely due to its social, psychological and sociological nature. Goffman also used the hotel restaurant as the frame of reference to visualise everyday interactions. The tourism industry can therefore be seen as a network of stages, for example, hotel restaurants, airliners and theme parks. Programme service products create experiences on these stages with theatrical action where the actors (i.e. staff and customers) co-create the experience.

In his book, Goffman (1959) examined the structure of social interaction between people in the presence of others, and how a definition of the behavioural situation is created and maintained, even in the face of potential disruptions. Goffman (1959: 32) explains his use of a theatrical performance as follows:

> I have been using the term performance to refer to all the activity of an individual, which occurs during a period marked by his continuous presence before a particular set of observers. It will be convenient to label as front that part of the individual's performance, which regularly functions in a general and fixed fashion to define the situation for those who observe the performance.

A correctly staged and performed scene leads the audience take on a performed character as themselves. The self, then, as a performed character, is not an organic thing that has a specific location, whose fundamental fate is to be born, to mature, and to die; rather, it is a dramatic effect arising diffusely from a scene that is presented, and the characteristic issue, that crucial concern, is whether it will be credited or discredited.

> There will be a back region with its tools for shaping the body, and a front region with its fixed props. There will be a team of persons

whose activity on stage in conjunction with available props will constitute the scene, from which the performed character's self will emerge, and another team, the audience, whose interpretive activity will be necessary for this to emerge. The self is a product of all these arrangements, and in all of its parts bears the marks of this genesis. (Goffman, 1959: 249–255).

It is obvious that service organisations can use Goffman's social interaction theory. Even in his simple examples, Goffman used expressions and examples such as restaurant milieu as theatre. These are highly relevant to framing services as theatre performance (performance teams, re: front-stage, back-stage) and region behaviour and impression management. According to Fisk and Grove (2001), 'service theatre' is an analytical framework for services marketing:

> A service experience occurs whenever a customer and a service organization interact, for instance a meal or a social meeting in a restaurant are examples of service experiences taking place in an organization's not only physical but also social environments and surroundings. Most services are the result of numerous workers performing various tasks. Overall, the physical setting, the service-workers and their tasks and the other customers combine to influence the nature of the service experience. Due to the intangibility and simultaneity of production and consumption of services, customers often have difficulty with the quality of the service they receive. Hence, the social milieu (i.e. interaction with the workers and other customers) and the service's physical environment (i.e. the nature of the facilities and equipment) provide important cues to the excellence of the service rendered. Based on this observation, astute service organizations are wise to 'tangibilise' their service offering by managing these aspects of the customer's experience. Because the staging of a theatrical performance involves many of the same considerations important to fashioning a successful service experience, the authors suggest that it is plausible to approach service similar to a theatre. (Fisk & Grove, 2001: 83)

In this chapter, hotel restaurants are seen as theatres where the actors (front-line staff and management) and the audience (customers with disabilities and able-bodied customers) are observed and interviewed about their recent experiences of behaviour and performance on this particular tourism stage. By viewing the hotel restaurant as a service theatre, the groups of people acting as participants are given their own status, those of actors and audience. The hotel restaurant also represents the necessary commercial organisation being managed and making profit in order to be competitive. Furthermore, the physical and social environments and their complexity can closely be viewed in the context of the research. Thus it is possible to concretely discuss the notable physical and attitudinal barriers encountered by customers with disability.

Empirical Survey

A pilot survey was carried out to investigate the scale of demand and supply of travellers with disabilities in Finland. The survey established any differences between disabled customers and the tourism businesses. Questionnaires were sent to disabled customers (using the Union for People with Disability) and to tourism businesses in Central Finland. The pilot survey acted as the foundation for the main survey and posed the important question: How can we examine and crystallise different attitudes and behaviours of the four groups interviewed (management, front-line staff, customers with disabilities, able-bodied customers)? It also underlined the importance of a wide literature review based on sociological and business literature for a better understanding of the research area. To summarise, the core findings of the pilot survey were:

- Commercial tourism enterprises are unable to offer a sufficient number of services to satisfy the needs of customers with disabilities.
- Customers with disabilities are unhappy with the service of commercial tourism enterprises.
- Commercial tourism enterprises and/or entrepreneurs are unaware of consumer behaviour of customers with disabilities.
- Commercial tourism for people with disabilities is still a hazy phenomenon, and there are many myths and beliefs with a severe lack of basic research in the field.

Interviews were carried out in a hotel restaurant as it provided both an experimental setting of action as well as a scene suitable for carrying out the interviews. A questionnaire based upon 20 statements was based upon the pilot survey. The statements were grouped as introductory; the suitability of the facilities available to disabled customers, and potential differences in consumer behaviour between disabled and non-disabled customers. Most statements, tended to visualise the interactions and related attitudes between disabled customers and hotel restaurant staff. The groups interviewed were as follows:

(1) *Restaurant customers with disabilities.* The interviewees were chosen at random, and most were physically handicapped, but people with other disabilities were also included in this group. However, the nature of the disability was not relevant and disabled customers were viewed as a distinctive group.

(2) *Front-line staff serving customers at hotel restaurants.* This group was also selected at random. Those interviewed were waiters and waitresses, bar tenders or receptionists aged 25 to 37 years working at the same restaurants as the managers interviewed.
(3) *Managers at five hotel restaurants.* They included restaurant and duty managers aged between 35 and 52 years.
(4) *Able-bodied customers* interviewed at the same restaurants.

Findings

In the discussions with the interviewees from the management group the standard statement emerged: 'We are running the business according to the law but that is all'. Apparent distinctions and tensions were evident between the attitudes of management and their front-line staff towards their disabled customers. Further discussions with the staff members revealed that they had neither been told nor trained how to encounter disabled customers in service situations, which had led to staff members trying to avoid meeting disabled customers due to the lack of training and proper instruction. Comments given by the interviewees also proved that the staff had more realistic conceptions than the management of how to serve disabled customers. This is a natural consequence of having a more frequent and direct contact with these customers. On the other hand, the management interviewees said that they did understand the disabled as customers, which made it more difficult to manage the quality of the service company as a whole.

The attitudes of the disabled were evenly divided into positive and negative throughout the entire data collection phase. Approximately 50% of all the interviewees thought that there was nothing dramatic or discriminating in these 'encounters' and generally attitudes had been improving. Conversely, the other 50% of the answers demonstrated a negative attitude with customers feeling they had experienced discrimination. Similarly, this group did not like being customers of commercial enterprises due to 'the lack of top quality and equal service'. Both the groups, however, wanted to express their own opinions, which in many cases was quite difficult depending on the degree of disability in question.

Almost all the disabled customers interviewed shared the opinion of not wanting to take any risks when choosing the environment where the service encounters would take place. They seemed, without exception, to return to the hotels and restaurants where the service at the first visit had been good. The companies surveyed should realise the importance of customer satisfaction when providing for customers with disabilities: once a satisfied customer, now a regular customer. The purpose of including non-disabled customers in the survey was for them to act as a parallel group to the disabled customers, which, for some reason, did not give the desired results due to the strong 'this is how it should be' character of the attitudes measured. Furthermore, the sample of the non-disabled interviewees seemed to avoid expressing their personal opinions, instead, quoting legislation in their answers and comments. Generally speaking, the results of this group were similar to those of the disabled group rather than the management and staff. It might be that the professional status of the groups representing the tourism industry strongly affected their answers and comments in comparison to those of the non-disabled, whose position is much more personal. As far as the disabled customers are concerned, the status and roles are extremely personal making their positions in the encounters much more dramatic in comparison with those of the non-disabled customers.

The most noticeable differences in attitude were found between the management and front-line staff and between the management and disabled customers. The results clearly prove that the groups interviewed had different views of how well or badly the disabled were felt to adapt themselves to the frame of reference used – the hotel restaurant on the tourism stage. The results from the interviews of disabled customers are naturally realistic, and somewhat more subjective than those of the other groups. It seems evident that the attitudes of the enterprises, and those of the management are prejudiced and this calls for further research.

Conclusion

The original frame of reference for this chapter is the Goffmanian theatre metaphor. This was applied to the empirical material, in which all the interviewees were seen as actors in a service play on the tourism stage, in this case the hotel restaurant. For the sake of authenticity, the principle of the theatre metaphor was explained to the interviewees at the beginning of every session. For the same reason, all the interviews took place on authentic stages in the hotel restaurants. This made it possible for both the interviewers and interviewees alike to observe the environment at the moment of the interviews, which helped them to better understand the statements put to them.

The responses to the research questions which were presented at the beginning of the paper are summarised below.

(1) In modern society, is there a growing demand for the provision of tourism services generated by the needs of the disabled?

Examination of the social discourse during the research process, for example published international and national reports and the resolutions of the Year of the Disabled 2003, strongly supports the first question. The pilot study already showed the potential demand and this was also unanimously confirmed by the disabled and the tourism industry. As the results of this paper show, people with disabilities would travel considerably more, if they had the opportunity and information on accessible resorts. This is also supported by the numerous examples of successful domestic and overseas trips given by the interviewees. On the other hand, tourism companies do not, to a great extent, recognise the disabled as a real segment of the market. Neither are they willing 'to mix segments' – as a well-known marketing slogan goes. This results in the disabled being discouraged to travel to new destinations. They remain, accordingly, regular visitors to familiar destinations.

(2) Does the infrastructure of the tourism industry (as represented by tourism companies in the research destination area) know or recognise the segment of the disabled well enough to be able to serve the disabled as customers?

This relates to the previous comment. The survey conducted among tourism companies (n=24) unfortunately revealed that less than 15% of the companies in the same role had ever met their disabled customers. Therefore, they did not believe that they understood the special features and requirements inherent in serving people with disabilities. On the other hand, the responses given by the majority of the companies showed that they regarded special investments, marketing efforts or other product innovations as 'emphatically' unrealistic.

(3) Do staff and managers of tourism companies have particular attitudes towards the disabled as customers?

According to the results the staff took a realistic attitude towards the disabled, while the management was more or less seeking shelter in legislation, which effectively hid their real attitudes. However, the answers of the management may seem more prejudiced than they really were due to their lack of direct contact with disabled customers.

(4) Are disabled customers satisfied with the way they are treated as customers in commercial tourism businesses?

Even though the experiences of the disabled as customers were 'true stories', it should be underlined that the disabled were, to a certain extent, subjective in their opinions. Furthermore, it is worth noting that a few disabled interviewees had never experienced negative attitudes within the service industry. On the contrary they thought that things were (slowly) improving. Even though the research results themselves had few traces of attitudinal barriers, the between the lines interpretations of the interviews often revealed that these barriers did exist, which also referred to a gap between staff and management. Staff are willing to admit that they sometimes have negative attitudes to disabled people as customers, often due to a lack of training. However, almost all the front-line employees were eager to have additional training, which, in their opinion, would certainly diminish their fears of how to encounter customers with disabilities. As mentioned earlier, the management were unaware of what was really going on in front-line service situations and most often sought shelter behind legislation. This leads us to ask the question of the feasibility of 'gap management': the first gap is already so fuzzy that those belonging to the management do not know their customers, whether disabled or non-disabled. With the longish research process now completed, many things have gradually been changing for the better. The media is more willing than ever before to deal with the special issues of tourism and service for the disabled. We are constantly making schools and colleges and even villages and cities accessible for all. Similarly, service providers on the tourism stage could try to pay closer attention to providing for disabled customers, consequently adding value to the competitiveness required within national and global markets. The research has challenged a number of conclusions but also myths and beliefs concerning the market segment of people with disability, including their tourism experiences. The data has also challenged a number of thoughts about the situation when disabled customers enter commercial and entrepreneurial recreation units in the tourism industry.

References

Arola, E. (2003) Encounters of disabled customers on the tourism stage. PhD thesis, The University of Queensland.

Arola, E. (2005) Encounters of disabled customers on the tourism stage. In E. Arola, P. Blinnika and M.L. Sitari (eds) *Tourism as a Contributor to Well-Being and Social Capital* (pp. 103–117). Jyvaskyla: Jyvaskyla Polytechnic.

Bullock, C. and Mahon, J. (1997) *Introduction to Recreation Services for People with Disabilities: A Person-Centred Approach.* USA: Sagamore Publishing.

Burnett, J. and Bender-Baker, H. (2001) Assessing the travel-related behaviours of the mobility-disabled consumer. *Journal of Travel Research* 40 (August), 4–11.

Cooper, C., Shepherd, R. and Westlake, J. (1994) *Tourism and Hospitality Education.* Guildford: The University of Surrey.

Cooper, C.P., Fletcher, J., Gilbert, D., Shepherd, R. and Wanhill, S. (1998) *Tourism Principles and Practice.* Longman Harlow.

Crossley, J.K. and Jamieson, L.M (1993) *Introduction to Commercial and Entrepreneurial Recreation.* USA: Sagamore Publishing Inc.

Dattilo, J. (1999) *Inclusive Leisure Services: Responding to the Rights of People with Disabilities.* PA: Venture Publishing Inc.

Department for Work and Pensions (UK) Tourism for everyone – Adjusting to the needs of disabled people in the tourism industry (Example: Muncaster Castle). At http://www.dwp.gov.uk/employers/dda/real-tourism.asp.

Directgov (UK) Tourism and the Disability Discrimination Act. At http://www.direct.gov.uk/en/DisabledPeople/TravelHolidaysAndBreaks/TravelAndHolidaysInTheUk/DG_4019030.

Fisk, R. and Grove, S. (2001) Service theatre: An analytical framework for services marketing. In C. Lovelock, *Services Marketing: People, Technology, Strategy*. NJ: Prentice Hall.

Goffman, E. (1959) *The Presentation of Self in Everyday Life*. Harmondsworth: Penguin.

Helander, E., Mendis, P. and Nelson, G. (1989) *Training Disabled People in the Community (RHB/84)*. Geneva: World Health Organization.

Holden, A. (2000) *Environment and Tourism*. London: Routledge.

Iso-Ahola, S.E. (1980) *The Social Psychology of Leisure and Recreation*. Dubuque: W.C. Brown Co. Publishers.

Lett, J. (1989) Epilogue to tourist studies in anthropological perspective. In V. Smith (ed.) *Host and Guests: The Anthropology of Tourism* (pp. 275–279). Philadelphia: University of Pennsylvania Press.

Lockwood, R. and Lockwood, A. (eds) (1999) *Recreation and Disability in Australia*. University of Western Australia: DUIT Multimedia, Uniprint.

Mathieson, A. and Wall, G. (1982) *Tourism: Economic, Physical and Social Impacts*. Harlow: Longman.

Pine, B.J. and Gilmore J.H. (1999) *The Experience Economy: Work is Theatre and Every Business a Stage*. Boston: Harvard Business School Press.

Poon, A. (1993) *Tourism, Technology and Competitive Strategies*. Wallingford: CABI.

United Nations (2009) Enable – Rights and Dignity of People with Dignity. At http://www.un.org/disabilities/.

Urry, J. (1990) *The Tourist Gaze*. London: Sage.

US Government (1990) *Americans with Disabilities Act*. Washington: US Government Publishing Service. At http://www.ada.gov/.

World Health Organization – Disabilities. At http://www.who.int/topics/disabilities/en/.

Chapter 9

Blind People's Tourism Experiences: An Exploratory Study

Y. PORIA, A. REICHEL and Y. BRANDT

Research concerning blind people's tourism experiences is limited. This study explores blind people's experiences with respect to four travel components: hotel accommodations, restaurants, flights and museums. The study employed a qualitative approach and data were subject to thematic content analysis. The findings indicate that blind tourists contend with diverse physical and social difficulties. The behavior of tourist staff, an issue that has received minimal attention in the literature about service provision for people with disabilities, was found to be a crucial element in blind people's tourist experiences. The paper concludes with implications for research and practice, based on the methods implemented by the participants to cope with the reported challenges.

Introduction

The tourism literature is increasingly turning its attention to tourists with diverse physical disabilities (Chou & Chao, 2007; Eichhorn et al., 2008; Yates, 2007). However, there is a dearth of studies about disabled people's perceptions of the tourism experiences. Furthermore, most existing studies focus on wheelchair users, ignoring other segments of the disabled population such as blind or deaf people. This study, centring on blind people's perceptions of the tourism experiences, is aimed at minimising this gap.

This chapter is part of a series of studies documenting the tourism experiences of Israelis with diverse disabilities. The chapter addresses elements which play an important role in blind people's tourism experiences including flights, hotels, hotel restaurants and museums.

Conceptualising blindness, disability and tourism experiences

The current study adopts Nicolle and Peters's approach to disability (1999: 122) which asserts that being handicapped is a result of 'a mismatch' between the individual's needs and abilities, and the environment. The importance of the link between the individual and the environment was used in the present study with regard to the term 'disability'. This approach considers the human environment affecting the process through which things are done.

This study is also in line with World Health Organization (2007) eco- logical conceptualisations of disability and concurs with the social model of disability. The latter presents issues such as the social construction of disability as a state of marginalisation and highlights social issues as potential barriers, rather than mere physical aspects of the environment (Shaw & Coles, 2004). This conceptualisation was also adopted in recent studies on the tourism experience of people with disabilities (Daruwalla & Darcy, 2005; Yates, 2007).

Existing studies have devoted little, if any, attention to the experiences of blind people. This lack of attention is surprising, first, because of the considerable size of the blind population; second, blind people often travel accompanied by others; third, during group travels, the presence of blind people may affect the travel patterns and itineraries of their fellow travellers; fourth, legislation requiring organisations and companies to offer accessibility to all members of society, particularly to people with disabilities, should also be taken into account. Such accessibility legislation is also reflected in rules (e.g. the ADA and the DDA) relevant to the tourism experience of disabled people. In addition, prevailing western social norms recognise travel as a social right of all members of society (Hazel, 2005; Yates, 2007). Finally, travel's contribution to the quality of life of people with disabilities and their well-being is well recognised (Kinney & Kinney, 1992; Yau *et al.*, 2004). Therefore, both researchers and practitioners need to investigate blind people's tourism experience in terms of theory and practice.

This chapter focuses on blind people's experiences of flights, hotels and art museums. With regard to the flight experience, there are virtually no empirical studies focusing on blind people. A limited number of studies contain some implicit reference to this topic, while focusing on wheelchair users (Takeda & Card, 2002; Turco *et al.*, 1998; Yates, 2007). Abeyratne (1995), for example, focuses on the flight and airport experience, referring to issues such as accessibility to the aircraft and flight safety.

With respect to museums, hotels and their restaurants, to the best of our knowledge, no studies exist which refer to the blind. Perhaps, the assumption is that if you cannot see, there is no point being involved in tourist activities. Traditional understandings equating travel with a visual experience may further explain the limited scholarly interest in blind people's tourism experiences (Small, 2008).

Methodology

Research objectives

Given the very limited attention paid to blind travellers in tourism studies, the overall objective of this study was to shed light on the specific elements of blind people's tourism experiences. In essence, this study aspires to provide an unheard population with a voice, to capture their feelings, and to learn about their suggested solutions to barriers, hurdles and impediments to a fully gratifying tourist experience.

As noted earlier this study is part of a series of studies focusing on the tourism experiences of people with disabilities (Poria, *et al.*, 2009, 2010). The exploratory nature of this study, and the aspiration to hear the 'voice of the customer' (Pakdil & Aydin, 2007), required a qualitative research approach. Such a research approach is often recommended for studying people with disabilities, particularly in tourism (Riley & Love, 2000).

The study population was exclusively Israeli. Respondents represent a cross-section of the blind population. Participants were recruited through the researchers' personal contacts, through organisations for people with disabilities in Israel, and through Israeli community centres serving this population and their families. Fifteen participants were interviewed, the youngest of whom was 23 years of age and the oldest 70 years of age ($m = 37$). Data were collected from both men and women in an attempt to reduce the likelihood of gender bias.

The main study interview was comprised of several sections, with questions based on information derived from the literature review and the preliminary interviews. The interviews lasted an average of 75 minutes, and, in accordance with the interviewee's preference, were either recorded or transcribed.

Subsequent to data collection, the notes were then subjected to thematic content analysis to illuminate underlying themes. A differentiation was made between *difficulties* and *barriers*. This distinction prescribed by the informants is uncommon in the literature. *Difficulties* and *barriers* were coded into two distinct categories: (a) *difficulties* and *barriers* linked to types of environment (human or physical) and (b) *difficulties* and *barriers* linked to emotions (pain, shame, frustration or all of the aforementioned). An attempt was made to employ assessment procedures that will assure credibility, trustworthiness and dependability.

Findings: Blind travellers in different contexts

The findings centred on four main themes: the flight, the hotel and restaurants, museums, and staff behaviour.

The flight experience

Blind people nearly always fly with a companion who is familiar with the disability and the means of assistance. From the study's outset, the integral role of pre and post flight arrangements became clear. All the participants reported that they board the airplane first and leave last, and highlighted the advantages of this procedure. They indicated that this policy provides them with extra time to settle down and organise themselves once on board, without people queuing behind them and pressuring them. Participants praised the procedure whereby a special vehicle is available to transport them to the passport control and baggage claim areas, and also spoke of the importance of provided baggage assistance. Participants related to this service as crucial for creating a positive flight experience. Participants also referred to the need for reliable information and the importance of accurate and immediate notification of changes in flight schedules. Blind people tend to fear missing information dealing with a change of gate or flight schedule – especially in the case of connecting flights – as they cannot read the electronic signs. Participants reported feeling insecure about hearing or understanding messages relayed on the public announcement system due to airport noise or lack of familiarity with local accents. They specifically mentioned a preference for quiet spaces where they can more easily hear airport staff announcements.

Few difficulties were reported with regard to the actual flight. Participants noted that their flight companion and the attendant adequately meet their in-flight needs. Some interviewees related to their seat location on the plane. Most participants were aware that due to evacuation regulations they are expected to be seated at the end of the plane, although they prefer a seat at the front, next to the exit door where there is more leg room. Some indicated that they would prefer an aisle seat in order not to inconvenience others. Some participants specifically indicated that they want to avoid unnecessary physical contact with others and reported a sense of discomfort as they often stumble on other passengers in the plane's narrow aisle. The findings indicate that blind people tend to minimise their in flight mobility. Additionally, some respondents indicated that occasionally, they needed assistance (e.g. finding the earphone outlet or differentiating between the identically packed salt and pepper). Some blind participants also claimed that they were unfamiliar with the safety information provided via crew members' explanations or by film at the beginning of each flight.

The hotel and its restaurants

The vast majority of respondents claimed that the hotel room's internal design frequently impairs free movement. To facilitate free movement, furniture needed repositioning. Participants reported on the necessity to re-arrange the room after the housekeeper's cleaning visit, as furniture had been repositioned in its original hotel-designed position. Participants also mentioned that within a few moments time they usually find the room easy to access, if the bell staff let them know where accessories are located. The participants also noted that the room number frequently does not protrude, leading to difficulties locating the room. Moreover, participants spoke of their problems with electronic keys. Specifically, they mentioned that they often swipe the key in the wrong direction and, thus, are not able to open the door.

In contrast to the relatively manageable room environment, the participants strongly criticised accessibility in hotels' public spaces. Participants mentioned that without assistance, when entering the hotel it is often impossible for them to locate the reception desk. Also, they mentioned that although reception clerks inform them of the location of the elevators and the rooms, it is often very difficult to find their way if not accompanied. Some participants also argued that many hotel lobbies are multi-level with connecting stairs, leading to potentially dangerous falls. An additional source of difficulties involves hotel elevators. Participants reported that not all elevators included floor numbers written in Braille. They also mentioned that in the larger hotels, each elevator may be designated to serve certain floors and their disability prevents them from reading signs and, thus, they often have no clue as to which elevator serves a particular floor.

> Try to imagine how you'd feel when you want to go to your room to use the bathroom, and you discover that you are in the elevator that only stops on floors ten to 20, and you are on the ninth floor. (Man, no. 7)

Regarding the hotel restaurants, almost no problems were reported when the serving style is personal, except for the need to read the menu and learn how the table is set and how the food is served on the plate. However, in a buffet style restaurant, participants reported that they were not able to find the plates, or the selection of dishes on the buffet tables. Moreover, even if assistance was available, the blind participants reported that the intense level of assistance necessary to navigate the buffet often caused embarrassment.

Art museums

The experience of visiting art museums is traditionally based exclusively on the sense of sight and involves looking at pictures and sculptures. Thus, a common assumption is that blind people will have minimal interest in visiting art museums. Surprisingly, a few blind participants asserted that they do indeed visit museums, although their experience is limited to feeling the exhibits. Participants indicated that touchable exhibits such as sculptures provide a sense of inclusion in the museum experience.

The findings showed that blind participants did not have high expectations of museum management and staff. Their general perspective was that since their abilities to fully experience museums are extremely limited, the museums need not make extraordinary attempts for inclusion:

> After all, it is impossible for us to see pictures, so with all due respect, art museums are not for us, as concerts are not for the deaf, and art museums should not invest time and money just for us. (Man, no. 2)

Participants suggested that in order to increase accessibility, large museums may consider exhibiting a small model of the museum layout which blind people can touch. In this way, blind visitors may locate the 'touchable' sculptures, elevators, restrooms and other service areas. Transport to and from museums was not mentioned as a major issue. The participants asserted that when visiting museums they are always accompanied ('if you are accompanied by someone, he is your eyes' (Man, no. 5)).

Staff behaviour

Three service-related issues were frequently mentioned as causing negative impact. Firstly, overly helpful and protective staff, who insisted on helping even in the absence of a real need, contributed to a feeling of being constantly watched. Participants indicated such behaviour annoys them and is viewed as an invasion of privacy. Also, some interviewees suggested that overprotective hotel staff prompt feelings of exaggerated dependency on others, which, in turn negatively affects self esteem. Secondly, participants highlighted that at times staff wanted to help them, however, they did not know how. The following comments illustrate the aforementioned:

> Sometimes I feel like a baby. The waiter decides that since she didn't have chance to help an old lady cross the street today, she will take care of me. I don't need this help. She doesn't need to cut the steak for me or twirl the spaghetti on my fork. Such acts are devastating. (Man, no. 6)

Thirdly, with respect to communication, participants indicated that staff, similar to much of general society, often assume that the blind have cognitive disabilities and hearing problems. Participants pointed out that on many occasions the staff preferred to approach the accompanying person, in lieu of the blind person. Additionally, staff tended to speak loudly, slowly and use very basic words, as if speaking to children.

> Someone should let the crew know that people who cannot see are not necessarily retarded [*sic*]. (Woman, no. 14)

Blind Tourists as a Unique Market Segment

The findings indicate that the study's participants faced difficulties before, during, and subsequent to their tourism experience. These difficulties may be explained by the physical as well as human environments. The study's findings are consistent with previous research about tourism and leisure experiences barriers, which emphasise both physical and personal constraints (e.g. Smith, 1987). That said, several issues emerging from the current study are worthy of discussion and comparison with the accumulated body of research.

The findings demonstrate that blind tourists, even when accompanied by another person, have unique needs. Moreover, the in-depth interviews revealed that blind tourists are indeed keen observers. For example, the participants indicated that they know when a staff member is not looking at them while speaking to them. Additional issues involved feelings of insecurity and, in certain cases, even to sensations of danger such as fear of falling.

The study findings reported here can be explained by Gladwell and Bedini's (2004) classification system. In their study, they highlight barriers not often mentioned in the literature such as emotional barriers, fear of the unknown, and loss of freedom. The findings of the present study indeed indicate that awareness of emotional barriers is essential to understanding people's responses. The blind participants clearly indicated that they fear the unknown as tourists in that they are confronted with new and unfamiliar terrain.

Studies on service experience clearly demonstrate the need for an appropriate balance between technical (what you get) and functional (how you get) aspects of service (Grönroos, 2001). The current study's findings indicate that participants assigned much importance to the functional, human dimensions of services; as such dimensions greatly affect their feelings. This is forcefully emphasised by the fact that the nature of the service encounter was a major factor in blind people's satisfaction of the flight/hotel as well as the museum experiences.

It is interesting to note that not all the participants in this study described themselves as 'disabled'. For example, blind individuals, when accompanied by someone who was able to effectively assist them, did not feel limited. This is consistent with Chou and Chao (2007) who found that accompanied individuals with impairments do not experience difficulties. This finding is also in line with studies demonstrating that people hard of hearing do not feel disabled amongst themselves (Altman & Barnartt, 2000).

Previous research findings highlighted the importance of information for people with disabilities (Eichhorn *et al.*, 2008; McKercher *et al.*, 2003). The providing of information in general and trustworthy information, in particular, was considered by participants as instrumental. The interviews indicated that blind people were interested in accurate verbal information so that, first and foremost, they would feel secure and safe. In fact, when compared to studies focusing on mobility challenged individuals (Poria *et al.*, 2009, 2010), it appears that the role of information is more substantial for blind individuals.

Physical appearance was also identified as meaningful in explaining communication and attitudes towards disabled people in the tourism and hospitality environments. Participants indicated that, in certain cases, the staff treated them as people with developmental disabilities. These reports are in line with studies that indicate that less physically attractive people are deemed to possess less desirable personal and social traits, and are less sociable, less dominant and with decreased mental well-being than attractive people (Ross, 2004).

Yau *et al.* (2004: 946) argue that 'people with disabilities have the same needs and desires for tourism as others'. The current study indicates that blind people have different needs as far as tourism and hospitality is concerned. The findings suggest that blind people are willing to cope with feelings of insecurity or even danger in order to enjoy the potential fruits of the expected tourism experience. Apparently, involvement in tourist activity is worthy of the physical and mental tolls. However, it seems that tourist organisations do not yet understand how to appropriately accommodate and host their enthusiastic blind guests.

Managerial implications

The implications for management of this current study are in line with Darcy's (2002) social model of disability, which emphasises the way society approaches people with impairments rather than viewing the disability as the person's shortcoming. Moreover, the managerial implications are based on the thought that it is the responsibility of the top level management as well as the State's, to be socially sensitive and responsive, by attempting to offer the blind tourist an attentive, and respectful experience.

It is common in the codes of practice of airlines, hotels and museums to emphasise the physical and technical aspects of the tourist space, ignoring the human service aspects (Shaw *et al.*, 2005; Yates, 2007). The finding highlights the need to also include human service elements in codes of practice, thus, taking into account the human as well as the physical environment.

The need for relevant information is crucial for blind travellers. Given the high noise level at airport terminals and individuals' language barriers, one recommendation involves allowing blind people free access to airport lounges where the staff can inform them on any scheduling changes. Another option is to facilitate the situation where the staff personally telephone the blind person on their cellular phone to relay scheduling changes or information. In the context of the hotel and the museum those who are trained to work with high expertise in communicating visuals to verbal text should be involved. Additionally, when participants related to various tourist attractions, such as museums, they mentioned that in some cases there were models of the attraction that helped them manoeuvre through the site (Poria *et al.*, 2009). This same concept can be applied in hotels. Such models can inform blind guests about the structure of the hotel, including the location of different restaurants and the public restrooms as well as the exact layout of the room. Another managerial implication is related to hotel elevators. It is suggested to expand the policy implemented in some hotels, where floor numbers are written in Braille and the elevator announces each floor upon arrival. It is also suggested to provide information during the check-in process about particular elevators directly reaching higher hotel floors.

Several issues concerning on-board flight service should be considered. First, it is suggested that attendants personally inform blind people of the safety-information procedures. Second, given that almost all participants reported feeling as if the flight crew approached them as if they were invisible, the crew should be appropriately trained to treat all people with disabilities as regular, fully-fledged passengers speaking with them in a normal manner, maintaining eye contact, and assuring swift problem solving. With regard to restaurants, the participants emphasised the importance of the quality of service provided and the need to provide blind people with personal service, even if the serving style is buffet.

The present study also illustrates the need for managers and researchers to directly consult with disabled persons using a qualitative research epistemology, in line with marketing literature dealing with segments of the population that differ from the 'normative' majority (e.g. Lee, 1993). In line with participants' suggestions, it is recommended that staff undergo simulation exercises and play the role of the disabled as part of their training. Such simulation exercises, suggested by the study participants, are useful for changing attitudes about minority groups (Grayson & Marini, 1996).

Given the significant role of staff behaviour in shaping blind people's tourist experience, the delicate balance between being aware of blind people's special needs vs. being over-protective, should be discussed in employee training and orientations. For example, housekeeping staff should be taught that blind guests may reposition furniture due to their specific needs and thus, they should not reposition the furniture in its original position during the daily cleaning. One obvious prerequisite is that housekeeping and other staff be informed that a particular guest is blind. Furthermore, all staff should be trained to communicate with blind people directly, without avoiding eye contact. In this context, hotel staff should provide very accurate information to people with disabilities. Clearly, erroneous or misleading information on available services can have a major effect on the actual experience.

Conclusion

The findings demonstrate that those managing hospitality and travel-related services should provide blind people with services tailored to their specific impairments. It should be noted that codes of practice relevant to blind travellers should capture not only the within flight/hotel/museum experience, but also the arrival and departure processes. Most of the above recommendations do not require considerable financial investments, but rather attentive and considerate attitudes and policies. From an academic perspective, researchers should recognise that tourism is not exclusively a visual experience. Blind people expect to have access to all tourist experiences and given the emerging recognition of their human rights and purchasing power, more attention will be focused on the needs of these people.

References

Abeyratne, R.I.R. (1995) Proposal and guidelines for the carriage of elderly and disabled persons by air. *Journal of Travel Research* 33 (3), 52–59.

Altman, B.M. and Barnartt, S.N. (2000) Introducing research in social science and disability: An invitation to social science to 'Get In'. In B.M. Altman and S.N. Barnartt (eds) *Expanding the Scope of Social Science Research and Disability* (pp. 1–30). Stanford: JAI Press.

Chou, S-H. and Chao, W-C. (2007) Seeing voices: Travel experience and individual risk of the hearing impaired. In L. Andreu, J. Gnoth and M. Kozak (eds) *Proceedings of the 2007 Advanced in Tourism Marketing Conference* (pp. 1–10), September 2007, Valencia, Spain.

Darcy, S. (2002) Marginalised participation: Physical disability, high support needs and tourism. *Journal of Hospitality and Tourism Management* 9 (1), 61–73.

Daruwalla, P. and Darcy, S. (2005) Personal and societal attitudes to disability. *Annals of Tourism Research* 32 (3), 549–570.

Eichhorn, V., Miller, G., Michopoulou, E. and Buhalis, D. (2008) Enabling access to tourism through information schemes? *Annals of Tourism Research* 35 (1), 189–210.

Gladwell, N.Y. and Bedini, L.A. (2004) In search of lost leisure: The impact of careering on leisure travel. *Tourism Management* 25 (6), 685–693.

Grayson, E. and Marini, I. (1996) Simulated disability exercises and their impact on attitudes towards persons with disabilities. *International Journal of Rehabilitation Research* 19, 123–31.

Grönroos, C. (2001) *Service Management and Marketing: A Customer Relationship Management Approach.* Chichester: John Wiley & Sons.

Hazel, N. (2005) Holidays for children and families in need: An exploration of the research and policy contexts for social tourism in the UK. *Children and Society* 19 (3), 225–236.

Kinney, W.B. and Kinney, W.B. (1992) Predicting life satisfaction among adults with physical disabilities. *Archives of Physical Medicine and Rehabilitation* 73 (9), 863–869.

Lee, R.M. (1993) *Doing Research on Sensitive Topics.* London: Sage.

McKercher, B., Packer, T., Yau, M.K. and Lam, P. (2003) Travel agents as facilitators or inhibitors of travel: Perception of people with disabilities. *Tourism Management* 24, 465–474.

Nicolle, C. and Peters, B. (1999) Elderly and disabled travelers: Intelligent transport systems designed for the 3rd Millennium. *Transportation Human Factors* 1 (2), 121–134.

Pakdil, F. and Aydin, O. (2007) Expectations and perceptions in airline services: An analysis using weighted SERQUAL scores. *Journal of Air Transport Management* 13, 229–237.

Poria, Y., Reichel, A. and Brandt, Y. (2009) People with disabilities visit art museums: An exploratory study of obstacles and difficulties. *Journal of Heritage Tourism* 4 (2), 117–129.

Poria, Y., Reichel, A. and Brandt, Y. (2010) The flight experiences of people with disabilities: An exploratory study. *Journal of Travel Research* 49 (2), 216–227.

Riley, R.W. and Love, L.L. (2000) The state of qualitative tourism research. *Annals of Tourism Research* 27 (1), 164–87.

Ross, G.F. (2004) Ethics, trust and expectations regarding the treatment of disabled staff within a tourism/hospitality industry context. *International Journal of Hospitality Management* 23, 523–44.

Shaw, G. and Coles, T. (2004) Disability, holiday making and the tourism industry in the UK: A preliminary survey. *Tourism Management* 25, 397–404.

Shaw, G., Veitch, C. and Coles, T.E. (2005) Access, disability and tourism changing responses in the United Kingdom. *Tourism Review International* 8 (3), 167–176.

Small, J. (2008) The absence of childhood in tourism studies. *Annals of Tourism Research*, 35 (3), 772–789.

Smith, R.W. (1987) Leisure of disabled tourists: Barriers to participation. *Annals of Tourism Research* 14, 376–389.

Takeda, K. and Card, J.A. (2002) U.S. tour operators and travel agencies: Barriers encountered when providing package tours to people who have difficulty walking. *Journal of Travel and Tourism Marketing* 12 (1), 47–61.

Turco, D.M., Stumbo, N. and Garncarz, J. (1998) Tourism constraints for people with disabilities. *Parks and Recreation* 33 (9), 78–85.

World Health Organization (2007) Disabilities. On WWW at http://www.who.int/topics/disabilities/en/. Accessed 19.11.2007.

Yates, K. (2007) Understanding the experience of mobility-disabled tourists. *International Journal of Tourism Policy* 1 (2), 153–166.

Yau, M.K–S., McKercher, B. and Packer, T.L. (2004) Traveling with a disability more than an access issue. *Annals of Tourism Research* 31 (4), 946–960.

Chapter 10

Demographic Drivers of Change in Tourism and the Challenge of Inclusive Products

G. SHAW and C. VEITCH

Introduction: Changes in Tourism Consumption

Tourism is an extremely dynamic sector with changes driven by shifts in consumption patterns related to lifestyles and demographics (Shaw, 2006), along with the rise of new tourism products and the impacts of technology (Buhalis & O'Connor, 2005). In addition, the consumption of tourism products is increasingly linked to what Pine and Gilmore (1999) have termed the 'experience economy'. This relates to the notion of services becoming experiences that involve consumers being presented with memorable offerings which are achieved through the customer participating in the creation of such offerings. These ideas in turn lead into a consideration of co-creation processes which are increasingly important in innovating new experiential services (Vargo & Lusch, 2006). Such processes which are related to the concept of service-dominant logic (Vargo & Lusch, 2006) are strongly embedded within tourist products and increasingly mark out the nature of post-modern tourism consumption. (Shaw & Williams, 2004). In such circumstances consumers become an integral part of the production process for holidays and other service offerings. Of course this in turn places responsibilities on both the consumer and the producer. In terms of the former, consumers need to be skilled in using the web, whilst producers need to consult with potential customers at different stages in the production process.

Such developments are of course influenced by certain market segments and demographics. Indeed the influence of particular lifestyle groups on the co-creation process is especially significant. In this context and in terms of the UK, Muirden and Martin (2004; see also Shaw, 2006) have identified the following consumer trends within tourism:

- The growth of mass customisation that includes consumer interest in perceived 'customised' experiences. This in part links to the ideas of 'McDonaldisation' or neo-Fordism (Shaw & Williams, 2004).

160

- An increase in consumers searching for quality experiences, ethical products (ecotourism), and spiritual awareness (volunteer holidays). This trend also covers the desire for self-improvement (sports, health and cultural tourism).
- A growth of what Muirden and Martin (2004) term 'tribing' which encompasses the idea of being part of well defined activity groups (defined by types of leisure activities or interests).
- Increased desire of 'pleasure' or fun holidays and experiences – especially within the youth market ('stag' and 'hen' breaks) holidays with strong hedonistic components.

In recognising these different groups it is also important to highlight those people within the UK who, for a number of reasons, are not part of these changes in service experiences; we can categorise these as 'leisure poor'. This term encompasses a number of deprived groups including many people with disabilities we can categorise as 'leisure poor'. It is this group that we are particularly concerned with in this chapter and we discuss them in two main contexts. The first is identifying the dimensions of this demographic and more particularly the characteristics of those people with disabilities that fall within this group. Second, we explore how such consumers can be embraced by the 'experience economy' through the co-creation of more inclusive tourism products which focus on the needs of the disabled.

The Leisure Poor and the Demographics of the Disabled

Within the UK approximately 40% of individuals do not participate in holiday taking during any one year (Shaw, 2007). These general, average figures conceal a range of reasons for not taking a holiday including; illness, lack of money and pressure of work (English Tourist Board, 1989). In a pioneering study Haukeland (1990) categorised such people as either 'constrained' or 'unconstrained', with the former wanting to take holidays but unable to do so. In contrast the latter group usually decide for various reasons not to go on holiday. As we shall see many of the disabled fall into the constrained category.

There are some 10 million people with disabilities in the UK with an estimated spend of £80b (Department of Work and Pensions, 2005). However such general figures, which have been used to encourage tourism businesses to focus on the disabled market, hide many significant variations. Indeed the general findings of the problems faced by the disabled are that they 'are more likely than non-disabled people to experience disadvantage' in many areas of life (Office for Disability Issues, 2008: 5). Furthermore, compared with the population as a whole the disabled tend to live in lower income households; 31% disabled compared with 16%

able-bodied (The Poverty Site, 2008). This is mainly because the disabled are less likely to be employed and if they are in employment it is much more likely to be in low wage jobs.

The characteristics of poverty and disability have been highlighted by a number of reports (Office for Disability Issues, 2008; Leonard Cheshire, 2008) which highlight the following:

- The disabled are twice as likely to live in poverty as non-disabled people.
- The disabled face extra costs relating to their impairment which is on average 25% above the normal expenditure of people who are not disabled.
- Due to such extra costs the disabled live on less than 60% of median national income – which further widens the gap between disabled and able-bodied. (Leonard Cheshire, 2008: 5)

In addition, the disabled tend to be older than the general population with 47% on state pension compared with 20% of the population. Furthermore, just over half of people with disabilities in a survey by the Office for Disability Issues (2008) reported that their impairment began before the age of 50, and 32% between 50–69 years old. In other words many of the disabled have experienced longer term disadvantages. The picture that emerges is of a disadvantaged group of consumers that tend to have low incomes. These problems of course not only impact on the individual but also the family unit. As Table 10.1 shows, the problems for single, disabled families with dependent children are extreme in terms of the percentage on low incomes.

Such disadvantages are compounded by the impairments these people have, with the problems of mobility being especially significant. Furthermore, the annual disability review undertaken by the charity Leonard Cheshire (2007) found that 89% of those surveyed 'felt that there was

Table 10.1 Types of low income households

Family Type	% of Households	
	Disabled adult	Non-disabled
Couples without dependent children	19	9
Couples with dependent children	31	18
Singles without dependent children	41	18
Singles with dependent children	54	43

Source: The Poverty Site (2008)

discrimination and prejudice towards disabled people' (p. 15). As the report goes on to argue this is a significant factor in what they call 'the poverty of expectation and poverty of opportunity' that the disabled experience (Leonard Cheshire, 2008: 8).

Clearly in terms of tourism consumption and notions of the 'experience economy' consumers with disabilities tend to be marginalised due to poverty, perceived discrimination and problems of mobility. The relationship between the disabled and tourism under these conditions is clearly going to be a rather strained and limiting experience for many people. Moreover, studies have highlighted the enhanced importance of holidays to both the disabled and their family members (Shaw & Coles, 2004). This is further supported by longer-scale surveys which showed that 79% of people with disabilities thought that holidays away from home every year were necessary for modern life, compared with just 55% of the general population (Leonard Cheshire, 2002). However, the same survey found that whilst 18% of the general population would like, but could not afford, such holidays, this figure rose to 47% for the disabled. Furthermore, even when access to holidays is possible many people with disabilities report on a poor level of service and experiences that hardly fit with the notions highlighted in the 'experience economy'.

The disabled group of consumers are often viewed as a single demographic and this is often dominated in thinking that this group are wheelchair users, a notion which the internationally recognised symbol for disability, a wheelchair user, perhaps reinforces. But of course they are comprised of many different segments based around age, family circumstances, employment, income and of course type of impairment. This lack of understanding by the tourism industry of a wider and varied audience with very differing needs can act as a barrier to product development. The misconception that disability equates primarily to wheelchair users can for some providers equate to them having to undertake structural adaptations and a large funding investment. Equally some of the segments who may have access needs, such as the aged, will not necessarily put a label of 'disabled' on themselves or necessarily look at additional access information where it is labelled, 'disabled or accessible'. There is therefore a need to consider the way in which information is presented for these different audiences and made to feel relevant to them and genuinely useful with the right level of information under the umbrella of accessibility.

It is difficult to identify market segments within the disabled demographic; mainly because so little attention has been given to such differentiations. Indeed, within the UK there is even some confusion over accepted definitions of the disabled as Meager and Hill (2005) have shown. Their work, following other studies (Grewel *et al.*, 2002; Hurstfield *et al.*, 2004), has drawn attention to two main definitions within the UK, namely:

- A definition used by the DDA which recognises those with a long-term health problem or disabilities which impact on normal day to day activities. As Meager and Hill (2005) point out, such a definition ignores those with past problems along with those having progressive problems that will impact at some future date.
- A definition specifically based on long-term health problems which impact on paid employment.

Using these broad definitions Meager and Hill have produced four further definitions of disability which in part may help to differentiate those with disabilities at least in terms of employment. We can therefore recognise a definition of the disabled used by official sources that utilises both the above perspectives. Using data compiled from official sources by Meager and Hill (2005) we can recognise some key differences within the disabled demographic. Table 10.2 highlights such variations for both the disabled and non-disabled. As Table 10.2 shows, gender differences in terms of the two groups are non-existent. However, important differences do emerge in terms of age groups, with, as expected, the disabled skewed towards the older age groups. The large differences in those with no qualifications in the disabled group gives us our first economic indicator and shows just how disadvantaged the disabled are across the working age profile. Such difficulties are highlighted in terms of those employed – which again shows large numbers of younger disabled people who are unable to work. This may be because of health problems or a lack of qualifications. As Meager and Hill (2005) show, this is not because of a lack of willingness to work; since 27% of all long-term disabled would like to work compared with 21% of non-disabled. Finally, the table shows the average hourly rates of pay to be substantially lower for the disabled reinforcing the poverty gap for these families.

Enhancing the Tourist Experience of the Disabled

The various surveys of people with disabilities and holiday taking reveal two major difficulties, namely:

- Problems of access to various tourism and travel products, ranging from accessible destinations, air flights and accommodation (Leonard Cheshire, 2005a, 2005b; VisitBritain, 2007). Such reports highlight the difficulties of physical access and rather less the impact of affordable holidays associated with low income households.
- Problems associated with poor service and limited experiences (Shaw, 2007; VisitBritain, 2007; Leonard Cheshire, 2005a).

Table 10.2 Characteristics of working age population (disabled and non-disabled)

		Disabled	*Non-disabled*
Gender	Male	51.7	51.3
	Female	48.3	48.3
Age	*Age Groups*		
	16–24	8.9	20.7
	25–34	13.3	22.8
	35–49	34.3	36.1
	50–64	43.5	20.4
Qualifications	*By Age*	*%with no qualifications*	*%with no qualifications*
	16–24	23.0	12.4
	25–34	16.2	7.3
	35–49	23.3	9.8
	50–64	32.3	17.0
	All	26.2	11.2
Employment Rates by Age		*% Employed*	*% Employed*
	16–24	42.1	59.8
	25–34	54.1	83.7
	35–49	55.6	88.3
	50–64	45.0	83.4
	All	49.6	80.3
Average Gross Hourly Pay		£	£
	Male	10.93	12.00
	Female	8.74	9.54
	All	9.84	10.81

Source: Modified from Meager and Hill (2005) and Labour Force Survey (2005)

To a degree both are interrelated in terms of creating a positive and rewarding experience for the disabled. We would also argue that to make experiences comparable for both the able-bodied and disabled consumers, there needs to be an attempt to deliver more inclusive tourism products. This is not new but we would go further and argue that to achieve this the process of co-creation that we discussed earlier also needs to encompass disabled consumers. In turn those marketing and developing tourism products need to be more aware of the different needs of the disabled, i.e. its various segments within the general demographic.

In terms of developing more inclusive tourism experiences it is easiest to view this via a case study approach based around the stages in tourist behaviour. This starts with information gathering and booking. It is at this level that perhaps most progress has been made. This is reflected in the growing number of travel websites aimed at people with disabilities. These include both commercial and charity-based sites offering a range of tourism products (Table 10.3). In part these are marketing to different types of tourists with disabilities and a number have blog sites which allow some element of consumer feedback. This is a very basic starting point for some degree of co-creation to occur in that experiences are shared with both producers and other consumers, enabling at least some of the disabled travellers to record their experiences. Interestingly, the use of these sites, in terms of feedback by those with disabilities, is low compared with more usage by the able-bodied of other social network sites.

An example of this move towards improving information for people with disabilities is the One Stop Shop to Accessible Tourism in Europe (OSSATE) project. The overall aim of this project, funded by the European Commission, was to create a new trans-national e-service in Europe, which would allow people with disabilities and their families to find information about the accessibility of tourist destinations within Europe. It brought together organisations from Austria, Belgium, Greece, Oslo, Spain and the United Kingdom in order to develop common standard templates to capture information about the tourism product such as accommodation and attractions. The project highlighted, however, the complexities which surround the relationship of people with disabilities and tourism such as:

- The level and depth of information varies from low to high according to personal requirements.
- The need for information to be independently verified increases where personal requirements are high.

Therefore the provision of accessible information is not a straightforward process. Tourism providers can probably be relied upon to

Table 10.3 Examples of websites dedicated to tourists with disabilities

Organisation	Date of foundation	Characteristics	Blog site
Your.com Commercial site founded by a disabled entrepreneur	2000	Wide range of holiday destinations and facilities	Discussion forum with users views
Tourism for All National charity, supported by regional tourist boards in the UK	2004 [this is when TFA merged with holiday care and individuALL	Information on UK holidays	User forum
Holiday Access Direct Commercial organisation, operated by people from within the travel industry – including some with disabilities	2005	Covers wide range of holidays and special-needs services	Widely used blog site
Fieldfare Trust Charity under the BT Countryside for All project	The trust was founded in 1986. Website 2004	Promotes and enables access to countryside	Blog site but poorly used
Endeavour Safaris Family-run commercial organisation	The company was established in November 2001. The first year was spent doing a lot of market research, promotions, etc. Tours have been fully operational since November 2002	Offers a range of holidays including adventure travel and mobility impairment tours	No blog site

provide basic low level information but anything more, such as measurements and more detailed information, usually requires trained independent assessors.

The issue with information reinforces how the market is segmented and suggests that this is an area that needs to be considered more when marketing products, as the majority of people with a low level of personal requirements are likely not to require as much as information as those with a higher level.

The availability of online information is seen as an important resource for those with disability hence the investment in the OSSATE project by the EU. However, there are at least three problem areas. The first concerns the actual physical access to the internet by having a home PC and broadband connections. Indeed the Department for Education and Employment (2001) found ownership of PCs and the internet much lower for the disabled than the total population. More recent work by Pilling *et al.* (2004) found online access by the disabled was limited by cost factors along with a lack of guidance. Thus, some 25% of the disabled stated they could not afford internet access and 40% of those using the internet had been unable to find suitable training. Secondly, there are difficulties of those visually impaired accessing websites due to their poor construction. In a study of 51 UK hotel–accommodation sites Williams *et al.* (2007) found that only 20% met the criteria to aid those with disabilities, the so-called Web Content Accessibility Guides (WCAG). Thirdly, there is clearly a division between sites directed at people with disabilities and those ones aimed at the general population which is the case for all holiday products. In this context the disabled tend to have a much more limited choice on offer even before the difficulties of access to resources comes into play.

In terms of the experience of the actual holiday then again a wide range of evidence suggests that the disabled are having quite different experiences than their able-bodied counterparts. Many of the complaints are about travel to destinations (57%) or even obtaining holiday insurance cover (22%) but even despite such difficulties 80% of those questioned by Leonard Cheshire (2005a) found holidays to be a rewarding experience. This probably says more about the low expectations of the disabled rather than anything to do with actual experiences. Indeed more systematic surveys by VisitBritain (2007) highlight those factors people with disabilities perceive as making a 'perfect' holiday, namely:

- Accessible accommodation – including detailed information about the whole area and particularly good customer service. The latter is of significance and encompasses the need for staff to have positive attitudes towards the disabled. This is in part encapsulated by the experiences of Pat (a married female with mobility impairments). Discussing the highs and lows of her holiday to Brittany she stated, 'Hubby pushed me in the wheelchair and I never felt more disabled in my life. Everyone stared. It was a down trip for me' (Different Strokes Discussion Board, 2008). Such views highlight some of the wider experiences that the disabled have on holiday.
- Suitable entertainment, a good mix of visitors.
- Carers were particularly concerned that their dependents were having an enjoyable time and were not being upset or dehumanised. In this context perceived problems came from insensitive and uncaring, poorly trained staff. Indeed the survey found that the most positive experiences occurred 'where there was a high level of customer service and awareness from staff'. (VisitBritain, 2007: 4).

The experiences of the disabled in terms of the hospitality industry are of particular importance and show there should be more inclusive products. However, audits highlight that much remains to be done despite the legal requirements of the Disability Discrimination Act (1995). As Table 10.4 shows there are wide variations in levels of disabled access amongst major hotels in the UK. The hotels were graded on scores along four main categories: reception and checking-in, quality of rooms, facilities and special assistance (Leonard Cheshire, 2005b). Of the 30 hotels surveyed by Leonard Cheshire (2005b) only 30% had lifts with Braille buttons whilst only one hotel had a text phone installed in its 'disabled room' to allow people with hearing impairments to use the phone.

There are of course exceptions; a notable one being the Inter-Continental Hotels Groups (IHG) which unfortunately did not figure in the survey by the Leonard Cheshire organisation. The IHG initiated an extensive staff training scheme to enhance the experiences of guests with disabilities. Under the title 'Confidence to Serve All', 9000 employees were given a short training course which became an integral part of staff development (IHG, 2004). As IHG's Chief Operating Officer (UK) stated, 'IHG doesn't want to single out disabled customers; it's more about giving employees the confidence to provide the same high level of customer service to all guests' (IHG, 2004: 1).

Table 10.4 UK hotels and accessibility

Hotel Types*	Accessibility Rating
Best Western	53%
Holiday Inn	82%
Marriott	68%
Premier Travel Inn	83%
Radisson	72%
Ramada Jarvis	52%
Thistle	84%
Travelodge	77%

Note: * survey was based on 30 hotels
Source: Modified from Leonard Cheshire (2005b)

Conclusion: The Challenge of Inclusive Tourism Products and Experiences

The struggle to provide access to tourism products for people with disabilities is clearly a difficult one. Increased legislation has set legal requirements – although even these are not always met within the tourism sector. Furthermore, the provision of tourism for people with disabilities is still very much seen as a different market. We have already argued that the so-called disabled market is itself segmented and many people with disabilities are within households that either have children or able-bodied adults. What most of the disabled want is to be offered more inclusive tourism products rather than something very different. Research by the European Travel Commission (ETC) confirmed that people with disabilities want to enjoy mainstream holiday experiences with their families (Veitch & Shaw, 2004). In the recent past much of the UK tourism providers were encouraged to make provisions for the disabled on economic grounds as various reports stressed the size of the market (Shaw, 2007). This approach in part has led to the separation of the market for the disabled as 'specialised' operators developed. Some companies like IHG have worked to embrace an inclusive product but such examples are still not commonplace.

In previous work we raised the issue of highlighting disabling and enabling factors impacting on the disabled visitor experiences (Veitch & Shaw, 2004). Table 10.5 summarises many of these issues in terms of stages in the tourist journey, a concept developed by Live Tourism, a tourism consultancy company. The enabling factors representing the issues of social inclusion provide a general blueprint for the range of inclusive products needed from information provision through to managing the visitor experience. At first glance the barriers to developing inclusive experiences seem somewhat intractable but in essence two key changes can act as enablers namely:

- Incorporating the needs and expectations of people with disabilities into the co-creation processes of product/service development. This would involve taking the views of the disabled into consideration at the outset, as happens with able-bodied consumers.
- Educating all staff involved in delivering tourism services, including at the destination. This is complex especially within the resort area itself and it may need to be tackled at a societal level. It can also be enabled through the use of social marketing initiatives that encourage all types of service providers to act in a more inclusive way.

The significance of using tourism as a means of enhancing the experiences of the disabled has been recognised by various charities but has still to be fully supported by government action. This needs to move

Table 10.5 Disabling and enabling factors impacting on the experiences of tourists with disabilities

Disabling Factors	KEY FACTORS AFFECTING THE VISITOR JOURNEY					
	1. Managing Communication and Information	2. Managing the Booking Process	3. Managing Access to the Destination	4. Managing the Visitor Experience	5. Managing the Visitor Exit	6. Managing the Quality of Visitor Memory
Disabling Factors	• Not represented in marketing images; • Information/marketing not in accessible format e.g. on web/print etc.; • Lack of authoritative and reliable information about product to help determine if personal needs can be met; • Unaware of organisations which can give support e.g. FHA and how to find out about them; • Perception that cannot share holiday experience easily with family and friends.	• Not able to access booking process easily; • Inaccessible website; • No Minicom contact or alternative; • Lack of product knowledge by provider to answer questions in relation to needs.	• Destination is not easily reached by public transport, (air, rail, coach); • Public transport is not perceived as accessible and convenient; • Inadequate or no facilities en-route to meet needs when using car or public transport; • Inadequate parking for private car at destination; • Transport costs are prohibitive.	• Attractions, retail, bars, restaurants etc. not accessible; • Little or no choice of accessible accommodation; • Infrastructure inaccessible e.g. poor pavements, road surfaces, signage etc.; • Difficult to move around; • Poor service/information due to lack of customer focus and needs not understood by staff; • Made to feel unwelcome.	• Not easy to return home by public transport; • Public transport is not perceived as accessible and convenient; • Inadequate or no facilities en-route when using car or public transport; • Not asked view of visitor experience and whether needs met or not.	• Negative relationship built between destination and user; • Needs not met; • Feelings of exclusion/not accepted, made to feel unwelcome; • Would not repeat visit to destination or recommend to others.
Enabling Factors	• Feel represented in marketing images; • Information/marketing in accessible format e.g. on web/print etc.; • Sufficient reliable and accurate information about product to help determine if personal needs may be met; • Aware of organisations that can offer support, where to find them and how to contact them; • Perception that holiday experience can be easily shared with family and friends.	• Able to access booking process easily; • Accessible website; • Minicom offered; • Full product knowledge by provider to answer and prompt questions to determine visitor's needs.	• Destination is easily reached by public transport, (air, rail, coach); • Public transport is perceived as accessible and convenient; • Good facilities en-route when using car; • Adequate parking for private car; • Transport costs are affordable.	• Accessible attractions, retail, bars, restaurants; • Choice of accessible accommodation; • Infrastructure accessible; • Easy to move around; • Good service/information, staff customer focused and aware of needs; • Made to feel welcome.	• Easy to return home by public transport; • Public transport is perceived as accessible and convenient; • Good facilities en-route when using car or public transport; • Asked views of visitor experience and if needs met to inform product development.	• Positive relationship built between destination and user; • Needs met; • Feelings of inclusion/acceptance, made to feel welcome; • Would repeat visit to destination and recommend to others.

Source: Modified from Veitch and Shaw (2004)

from legislation on access to a more fully comprehensive social tourism programme that enables the development of inclusive products.

References

Buhalis, D. and O'Connor, P. (2005) Information Communication Technology – Revolutionising Tourism. *Tourism Recreation Research* 30 (3), 7–16.

Department of Education and Employment (2001) ICT access and use report on the benchmark survey. London: HMSO research report 252. *Improving the Life Changes of Disabled People:* Prime Minister's Strategy Unit.

Department of Work and Pensions (2005) ICT access and use report on the benchmark survey. London: HMSO research report 252. *Improving the Life Changes of Disabled People:* Prime Minister's Strategy Unit.

Different Strokes Discussion Board (2008) *Holiday experience posted by Pat.* On WWW at http://www.differentstrokes.co.uk/egi-bin/config.pl?read=149732. Accessed 11.2008.

English Tourist Board (1989) *Tourism for All.* London: ETB.

Grewel, I., Joy, S., Swales, K. and Woodfield, K. (2002) Disabled for life? Attitudes towards and experiences of disability in Britain. Department for Work and Pensions, Research Report 173. Leeds: Corporate Document Services.

Haukeland, J. (1990) Non-travellers: The flip side of motivation. *Annals of Tourism Research* 17 (2), 172–184.

Hurstfield, J., Meager, N., Aston, J., Davies, J., Mann, K., Mitchell, H., O'Regan, S. and Sinclair, A. (2004) *Monitoring the Disability Discrimination Act 1995: Phase 3.* London: Disability Rights Commission.

Intercontinental Hotels Group (2004). On WWW at http://www.realising-potential. org/case-studies/goldcard-members/intercontinental.html. Accessed 11.2008.

Labour Force Survey (2005) Quarterly Supplement, National Statistics, April 2005 No. 29, UK. At http://www.statistics.gov.uk/Statbase/Product.asp?vLnk= 545&more=N.

Leonard Cheshire (2002) Inclusive citizenship: The Leonard Cheshire social exclusion report 2002. London: Leonard Cheshire.

Leonard Cheshire (2005a) Disabled people's holiday experiences. London: Leonard Cheshire.

Leonard Cheshire (2005b) No room at the inn: A report on UK hotels and accessibility. London: Leonard Cheshire.

Leonard Cheshire (2007) Disability review 2007. London: Leonard Cheshire.

Leonard Cheshire (2008) Disability poverty in the UK. London: Leonard Cheshire.

Meager, N. and Hill, D. (2005) The labour market participation and employment of disabled people in the UK. University of Sussex: Institute of Employment Studies (Working Paper 1).

Muirden, M. and Martin, B. (2004) *Future Trends in Lifestyles and Leisure.* Glasgow: Scottish Enterprise.

Office for Disability Issues (2008) *Experiences and Expectations of Disabled People.* London: Department of Work And Pensions.

Pilling, D., Barrett, P. and Floyd, M. (2004) *Disabled People and the Internet: Experiences, Barriers and Opportunities.* York: Joseph Rowntree Foundation.

Pine, B.J. and Gilmore, J.M. (1999) *The Experience Economy: Work is Theatre and Every Business a Stage.* Boston: Harvard University Press.

Shaw, G. (2006) Lifestyles and changes in tourism consumption: The British experience. In P. Reuber and P. Schnell (eds) *Postmoderne Freizeit und Freizeitraume.* Berlin: Schmidt.

Shaw, G. (2007) Disability legislation and the empowerment of tourists with disabilities in the UK. In A. Church and T. Coles (eds) *Tourism, Power and Space.* London: Routledge.

Shaw, G. and Coles, T. (2004) Disability, holidaymaking and the tourism industry in the UK: A preliminary study. *Tourism Management* 25, 397–403.

Shaw, G. and Williams, A.M. (2004) *Tourism and Tourism Spaces.* London: Sage.

The Poverty Site (2008) Households below average income. On WWW at http://www.poverty.org.uk/technical/hbai.shtml. Accessed 11.2008.

Williams, R., Rattray, R. and Grimes, A. (2007) Online accessibility and information needs of disabled tourists: A three country hotel sector analysis. *Journal of Electronic Commerce Research* 8 (2), 157–170.

Vargo, S.L. and Lusch, R.F (2006) Service-dominant logic: reactions, reflections and refinements. *Marketing Theory* 6 (3), 281–288.

Veitch, C. and Shaw, G. (2004) Understanding barriers to tourism in the UK. *Insights* May, A185–192.

VisitBritain (2007) Access consumer research. London: VisitBritain.

Chapter 11

Ageing Travellers: Seeking an Experience – Not Just a Destination

I. PATTERSON and S. PEGG

Introduction

Tourism is big business, especially for the increasing numbers of baby boomers and older adults who are becoming increasingly targeted by marketers and travel companies as a growing market. This is because many baby boomers are healthier, financially well off, better educated and have a greater desire for novelty, escape and authentic experiences than previous cohorts of retirees. The baby boomer generation in particular is a prime example of a niche market firmly embracing the notion that the next wave of successful tourism businesses will be those geared towards the experience economy. In recent years, 'boomers' have demonstrated that they are willing participants in new and adventurous forms of leisure and are opting for more physically challenging and authentic learning experiences more than ever before. In seeking to bring greater attention to this issue, this chapter seeks to first detail the changing leisure interests of today's older tourists before concluding with a discussion of key marketing considerations for this growing older cohort group.

The provision of tourism and leisure services is now increasingly becoming the domain of commercial operations. Part of the reason for this sectoral change has been linked to matters relating to the increased privatisation of public leisure and recreation services. More importantly, this has been due to the advent of greater entrepreneurial activity in the commercial recreation and tourism sectors. This is because there has been an industry wide acknowledgement of a significant and global market change that has occurred over the last decade, the growth of the older adult travel market.

As a result, this shift in the consumer mindset has forced tourism operators in particular to rethink about how they will provide services to a different type and age of their clientele. For instance, older travellers have recently shown a desire for more flexible and individualised travel packages that has necessitated a significant movement away from the pro-vision of traditional and somewhat generic ones. That is, many of the types of packages that were offered over 20 years ago to cater for the needs of what was then assumed to be a largely homogeneous group of older travellers are no longer seen to be attractive to them. The end result of this shift has been an industry wide movement towards the delivery of a new suite of package offerings that better reflect the needs and wants of the various heterogeneous niche travel markets that are evolving out of this growing (and rapidly ageing) cohort group.

Therefore, tourism businesses are now being forced to move away from a very product centric mindset to one that is now largely customer centred. Importantly, the market place has evolved to such a point whereby customers are no longer perceived as merely targets, they are now seen as humans to be served; marketing is no longer a game of persuasion, it is a service; customers are no longer data sets, they are human beings; and the focus is no longer on products but on experiences (Gilmartin, 2007). The business focus is now firmly on the customer experience as it is now the experience, and not the event or activity, that has become the critical motivation for consumers. This is because as new age consumers they stated, 'We want to escape, socialise, fantasise, be creative, learn new skills, engage in some form of physical activity or interact with the environment' (Grant, 2007: 30).

This was first acknowledged by Pine and Gilmore (1999) who stated that nowadays, people as paying customers will willingly buy an experience as they seek out opportunities to spend their leisure time enjoying a series of tailor made events that engage them in a memorable way. Experiences, in this context are considered to occur when a company '... intentionally uses services as the stage and goods as props to engage individual customers in a way that creates a memorable event' (Pine & Gilmore, 1999: 8).

Astute businesses who are mindful that this consumer shift is occurring are continually seeking out ways to attract new customers, as well as to retain old and valued ones. Importantly, experiences are the key, as they create added value by engaging and connecting with the customer in a personal and memorable way. As such, successful organisations in the tourism and leisure industries are the ones that are positively responding to this rapid transition from a service economy to a new experience economy (Fitzsimmons & Fitzsimmons, 2004). That is, those tourism operations considered best placed to do business in the new experience economy are those that have embraced the position that their mission is to stage experiences rather than deliver services, their buyers are guests rather than clients or customers, and their factors of demand are sensations and memories rather than tangible benefits (Pine & Gilmore, 1999). Clearly, tourism and leisure industries have now evolved to a stage where the better business operators are now very much about providing experiences (at a profit) for the pleasure of others. Yet, for one reason or another, not all businesses have yet made this transition. With this in mind, the aim of this chapter is to highlight the ways in which today's older adult consumers are changing their habits and their interests from that of the past. Importantly, this chapter also serves to detail the possibilities that the ageing traveller market now offers for those business entities willing to engage meaningfully in the experience economy. This is particularly the case for those operations which are willing to align their product and services offerings to a growing, but very discerning, consumer market, the older adult traveller.

The Leisure and Tourism Experience

The field of tourism and leisure research has also undergone major changes in recent years. In particular, the term leisure 'experience' is now more commonly used by tourism researchers and has replaced the use of other terms such as 'activities' or 'patterns' (Mannell & Iso-Ahola, 1987; Tinsley & Tinsley, 1986; Lee *et al.*, 1994). More recently, researchers have begun to refer to the leisure experience as multi-dimensional in nature and characterised by the variety of experiences that occur. For example, Lee *et al.* (1994) referred to the transitory, dynamic and complex nature of leisure experiences. To most people, leisure is seen as a mixture of pleasurable (and sometimes unpleasurable) experiences that are generally characterised by feelings of fun, enjoyment and relaxation.

As a result of this application of social psychological research, tourism researchers have now become more focused on studying the feelings, attitudes and motivations of people's leisure and tourist behaviour, rather than concentrating purely on participation rates or future leisure or tourism trends. In other words, the variety, frequency and quality of the 'experience' has become more important to study as a measure of overall life satisfaction, rather than the actual type of leisure or tourist activity that a person participates in (Smith & Godbey, 1991; Grant, 2007).

Furthermore, in recent years a number of tourism researchers have also become interested in studying the traveller's experiences. In 2002, Chris Ryan edited a text book titled *The Tourist Experience* because, as he noted, the industry is arguably devoted to the creation of satisfactory holiday experiences. Importantly, Ryan acknowledged that holidays represent special types of experiences such as a period of escape for some, as well as a catalyst for change for other individuals and communities alike. Yet, '... the process is partly based on the dreams and hopes about places and what they mean, and the manufacturing of images from industry sources' (Ryan, 2002: 8). Several researchers have also become interested in the differences between tourist and leisure experiences. Leontido (1994) and Carr (2002) found that tourists often behave in a more liberated and less restrained manner in contrast to their leisure time behaviour at home. Leontido (1994) claimed that individuals are influenced by the tourism atmosphere or, as it has been termed, the existence of a 'tourist culture' that is perceived to be different from their place of origin, and is responsible for less restrained and more hedonistic type of behaviour.

These hedonistic experiences were noted by Josiam *et al.* (1996) who reported that increased alcohol and drug consumption as well as increased levels of sexual activity occurred among a group of American students that travelled overseas. Eisner and Ford (1995) stated that the tourist '... sees oneself as a different kind of person when on holiday, less constrained by normal role demands and interpersonal obligations ... and more sexual activity was reported by those [tourists] who seemed to have felt more *disinhibited* within the holiday setting' (pp. 326–327). Importantly, in recent times the desire for new forms of tourist experience has seen a discernable shift in the motives and interests that are now driving tourist engagement. Where the current focus in tourism product development is focused on the technical properties of the product, the market is however now beginning to recognise the key consideration is actually to cater for the total experience of the customer (Haahti & Komppula, 2006). This point was also acknowledged by Gretzel *et al.* (2006) who noted that tourists today have evolved from being pure consumers, to co-producers of meaningful experiences who have embraced the new technologies available to them to ensure that they exercise a greater degree of control in terms of shaping the experience at their chosen tourism destinations and/or visitor attractions. Thus, critical to the shaping of the type and quality of the experience, and even the level of engagement from which they later drew personal meaning, was the consumer's 'modern' expectation of a meaningful consumption experience (Gretzel *et al.*, 2006; Shedroff, 2001).

Older adults including the 'baby boomer' cohort group (who were born between 1946 and 1964) have recently been identified as a new and emerging market for tourism activities. As argued by Gretzel *et al.* (2006), it is apparent that many in this cohort are today looking for more meaningful, challenging and authentic experiences when they travel as compared to the somewhat generic and inflexible offerings that were available to them in the recent past. Such a finding is consistent with recent analysis of the various tourism markets that reveals the fact that they are fragmenting, driven largely by a new-found consumer desire for self-expression and can only be serviced though the provision of a diverse and individualised range of tourism experiences (Cooper *et al.*, 2006). It is evident therefore, that the older adult tourist market is not a homogeneous group at all but represents, because of its size and ongoing development, a new and evolving niche market worthy of closer attention by researchers and industry alike.

The Older Market

The older travel market has continued to grow and evolve in recent years mainly because of the rapid increase in the numbers of older adults who are living longer and more healthier lives than previous generations. The United Nations has estimated that over 2 billion people will be aged 60 years and over by the year 2050. This will account for 22% (or one out of five) of the world's population, compared to only 10% in 2000, and this demographic shift will be seen across all continents (United Nations, 2000). On a global scale, the majority of industry and government stake-holders are becoming more aware of the significant impact that older adults will have on the tourism industry in the decades to come (Tourism Research Australia, 2008; World Tourism Organization, 2006). As noted by Moscardo (2006), the direct consequence of this ageing pattern is that seniors will now be responsible for a bigger share of all holiday and travel related spending. For example, in 1999, over 593 million international travellers were aged 60 years and over. At the time, this accounted for around a third of all holiday spending by this market segment. By 2050 this figure is projected to rise to be greater than 2 billion trips (World Tourism Organization, 2001). Baby boomer households (born between 1946 and 1964) generated the highest travel volume in the United States in 2003, registering 268.9 million trips, more than any other age group (Domestic Travel Market Report, 2004). In terms of the Australian setting, seniors spent an estimated $10.8 billion on domestic trips in 2002. This figure accounted for approximately 21% of the total expenditure on domestic travel in that year. Of this amount, senior travellers spent $8.5 billion on travel with some form of overnight stay element with a further $2.3 billion spent on day trips. Based on projected population forecasts the overall spend by travellers in Australia is expected to increase by $14.3 billion to $82.2 billion by 2022, with the senior cohort expected to account for approximately two thirds of this increase (Hossaain *et al.*, 2003).

This trend is beginning to have a notable impact on the type of holidays undertaken and the destinations that are being chosen (Alsnih & Hensher, 2003; Reece, 2004). For example, there is a strong likelihood that in the future the volume of beach holidays will fall markedly, while at the same time it is likely that educational and/or cultural holidays will increase as older people express a greater preference to take holidays where they learn something new, and/or embark on different historical and cultural experiences (Moscardo, 2006; World Tourism Organization, 2001). In the United States this shift in demand has already forced many operators in the active travel market to rethink their service offerings in an effort to attract new customers and retain the sizeable but ageing group of outdoor enthusiasts. For instance, Backroads, a 30-year-old bike tour company based in California, has recently unveiled plans to offer 22 new itineraries that involve none of the biking, hiking, rafting or strenuous walking that has long defined its trips. Rather, in the future, guests will be shuttled in vans to museums, markets, temples and vine-yards with travellers not required to walk more than two kilometres on any given day (Randall Travel Marketing, 2007: 8).

These future population projections imply that becoming older does not necessarily restrict people's desire to travel. Older travellers as a separate market to younger people are increasingly beginning to attract the close attention of tourism researchers and marketers. Because many older adults are increasingly healthy and affluent, they are travelling more, are more discerning and demanding and are continually looking for opportunities for special-interest travel as well as new and innovative experiences. Importantly, research clearly reinforces the fact that senior travellers will increasingly become a key market for many tourism and hospitality operators because this group tends to plan and go on holidays for longer periods of time than travellers in other age cohorts (Moscardo, 2006; Urhausen, 2008). For example, in Australia, senior travellers tend to stay away for an average of 5.5 nights per trip compared to only 3.5 nights by those aged 54 years and younger (Hossain *et al.*, 2003). They also tend to place a higher premium on quality, courteousness, and good service yet they still require value for money (Pritchard & Morgan, 1996).

There is little doubt that older people are placing travel as a higher priority in their retirement years mainly because they are feeling healthier, wealthier, better educated, more independent, have an abundance of leisure time and a lessening of social and family obligations than younger people (Martin & Preston, 1994; Zimmer *et al.*, 1995). They are seeking out new experiences and creative personal challenges in their travel and leisure, and are becoming skilful and knowledgeable consumers that seek value for their money. The interests of older adults are quite diverse and many require different types of travel packages and programmes. There is a growing market segment of relatively wealthy, frequent travellers who want to participate in special interest tourism and as a result are becoming more interested in adventure travel packages that take them to new, exciting and interesting places (Sorensen, 1993). In particular, special interest groups are seeking out niche markets that require specialised tours to serve their needs. There are now at least a dozen adventure travel companies that market primarily to the over 50-year-old traveller with a range of group package tours that are specialising in safaris, rafting trips, treks and sea kayaking.

Furthermore, many older people prefer the safety and convenience of package tours where their meals, hotels, admissions and baggage transfers are included in the one price, and where they can mix with other older people who have similar interests. The hospitality sector in particular has been quick to respond through the establishment of a small number of companies that promote special interest tourism, and which, by their operations, are fast become the cutting edge of what leisure travel buying will entail in the future. As a result, special interest package tours are helping the hotelier to increase occupancy rates in the low and shoulder seasons, as well as attracting more affluent tour groups through a diversification of the market.

The Desire to Buy an Experience

The tourism and leisure industry needs to respond not only to the changing demographics, but also the desire and demand that older consumers seek to ensure their own personal fulfilment (Grant, 2002). This desire to obtain the most they can out of their latter years as they perceive that their time is running out, suggests that older individuals are continually assessing their subjective age as being different from their chronological age. This perception has been supported by research that has shown that between 60% and 75% of people who have turned 60 years of age felt younger than their actual chronological age (Markides & Boldt, 1983).

Markides and Boldt (1983) found that the mean difference between people's felt age (subjective age) and their actual age (chronological age) was 11.2 years. That is, seniors typically felt a decade younger than their actual age and as a result are now placing greater importance on having fun and enjoyment in their lives, preferring to experience or enjoy vacation activities with younger people. Males in particular had a greater tendency than their female counterparts to prefer vacationing with much younger age groups, and often colour their hair and/or undergo cosmetic surgery procedures to enhance their appearance so as to lessen some of the physical signs of ageing. This perceived age difference becomes larger as the person ages. For example, research conducted by the Menlo Consulting Group found that, on average, US travellers who were aged around 80 years of age often thought of themselves as having a mean age of around 65 years (Smith & Jenner, 1997). This suggests that many older people do not perceive themselves as of 'retirement age' until they have actually reached around 75 years of age or older (Sherman & Cooper, 1988). These findings suggest that segmenting seniors by how old they 'feel', rather than how old they actually 'are' is a far better approach when marketing tourism products to this increasingly specialised and persona-lised niche market. Many older people want to feel young again, or at least to relive many of the pleasant experiences that characterised their youth. That is, they often want to reminisce about elements of their life, in some manner or other, that are connected to when they were younger and more active.

Because of these reasons, travel has now become a high priority among older age groups up to, and around, the age of 75 years. One of the main reasons for this is the intangible outcomes that are often derived from the travel activity that has become an important motivation. The fact that seniors often prefer to immerse themselves in worthwhile travel experiences rather than acquire material possessions is evidence to this effect. Many older travellers feel that travel helps to enrich their lives in some manner or other, and to help them feel young again. For example, the extreme adventure activity of jet boating in New Zealand is increasingly attracting many older customers (Cater, 2000). This was because Cater found that large numbers of older adults were attracted to this activity because it was considered to be highly risky by nature and as a result, enabled them to feel young again. This he concluded was related to the need for older people to rejuvenate their bodies through participation in adventure type activities, and that they were in some ways able to buy (or bring back) their youth, helping them to feel 'forever young'.

As a result, one of the emerging markets for older adults in recent years is adventure tourism that focuses on challenging, exciting and authentic experiences, and has become a new niche market for older individuals who have become bored with being a mass tourist and a passive sightseer.

Adventure Tourism Experiences

A new generation of retirees have emerged that are 'hungry to go off the beaten path' resulting in the adventure travel business growing to a $500 million segment at a rate of 30% per year, and this has been driven partly by '... more and more retirees with time, money, and a yen for the exotic' (Symonds, 1998: 102).

Many older adults want to escape the stress and boredom of their everyday routine and to spend their vacation time on pleasure filled trips with a range of exciting and new physically challenging experiences, as well as expressing their need to meet people and build new friendships. Gene Wellman, 71 years old, is a retired environmental consultant from Klamath Falls, Oregon, USA and typifies this type of traveller. 'Wellman has no desire to be herded onto sightseeing buses. So he and his wife, Genevieve, joined a small group trip to French Polynesia and Peru' to explore and experience these locales as they perceived they should (Symonds, 1998: 102).

The literature has supported the belief that many older individuals have a growing desire for self-fulfilling experiences that are physically challenging, more meaningful and authentic. They have more time to travel and one of the first things that they do on retirement is to take a trip, whether it is around Australia or overseas (Muller & Cleaver, 2000). A total of 21% of all trips taken in the USA were by people who were aged 55 years and older (Travel Industry Association of America, 1998). Their love for adventure tourism is particularly reflected in the comments of 74-year-old Elaine Carr:

> Over the last 10 years, I have slept in a mountain hut while climbing 19,300 ft Uhuru Peak on Mount Kilimanjaro and pitched a tent in a sandstorm in the Gobi Desert. I have been to Mongolia, Madagascar and Peru and I am already planning this year's trips to the Andes and Ethiopia. When I first began travelling after my husband died in 1993, my friends could not understand why I did not choose more relaxing vacations in Hawaii or California. I told them that these were very nice places, but I can visit them when I get older. (Bierman, 2005: 53)

The tourist industry needs to better cater for the very active, able, adventurous traveller who is also demanding that in addition, the travel experience becomes a learning adventure. Lipscombe (1995) stated that travelling is an important aspect of one's life adventure and exemplified the search for meaning in later life. He suggested that the taste for new adventures might be more intense and addictive as individuals grow older. Many older people are now indicating that they are craving new experiences with a substantial adventure component, and are requesting that they are part of the decision-making process choosing adventure travel that '... involves physical challenge, if not actual danger, travel that involves an inner journey, intellectual challenge, as well as exploration of new places and cultures' (Friedan, 1994, in Lipscombe, 1995: 44).

Muller and Cleaver (2000) concluded that older adults tended to prefer 'soft' adventure activities that are usually conducted under controlled conditions and are generally led by trained guides that supply the educational component that older people prefer. One older woman recounted a soft adventure experience with the Colorado-based company 'Walking the World':

> I made arrangements through the company for a seven-day hiking tour of the Canadian Rockies, specifically Banff and Jasper National Parks. I was in a group of six women and two men and two guides, a man and a woman. All of us were older than 60, nevertheless everyone was fit and had some hiking experience. Our guides were expert naturalists and planned daily walks that varied from four to six hours and took us to elevations of 2800 ft ... we all enjoyed the

trip very much. I thought many times during the trip that travelling with my contemporaries increased my enjoyment. The vistas were the same but the pace was more leisurely. My group of 'elderlies' out-walked many younger people, and good spirits and fitness carried us further on the trail than some other groups ventured. (Harnik, 1998: 42)

These findings suggest that older individuals prefer real life experiences where they can learn and broaden their minds. Many have attained higher levels of formal educational training than previous cohort groups, and now have the time to travel to diverse countries to visit, and learn about, different cultures through a variety of first hand experiences. They are more interested in enriching their lives through the gaining of knowledge rather than being entertained, so as to satisfy their needs for self-expression, creativity, and internal growth.

Educational Tourism Experiences

It has become evident that older adults are now placing a greater value on lifelong learning with the consequential flow-on being that many are seeking out educational experiences as, amongst other reasons, a way of adjusting to the challenges of moving into the third age of life (Adair & Mowsesian, 1993). Many older people are seriously concerned about the meaningful and satisfying use of leisure time after a lifetime of work. Cohen (2000) argued that all older people are capable of discovering their own creativity, whether it is a hobby such as arts and crafts, taking an educational course, or by volunteering. Cohen asserted that a person's creative spirit needs to find expression, despite the fact that many face such obstacles as poor health or disability that tends to increase with age. He insisted that the emphasis should not be on the quantity of time that is left for older people, but on the desire for quality use of this time. Thus, instead of lamenting that you are 'over the hill', the universal challenge for creative expression in life is that there is still 'another peak to climb' (Csikszentmihalyi, 1996).

Opportunities for senior adults to participate in formal and informal educational programmes have improved dramatically over the past 30 years. One way that older people have been able to rejuvenate this creative expression in their lives is through joining specialist educational organisations whose primary mission is to promote education for seniors. Because of this specialised need, Institutes for Learning in Retirement (ILRs) have been established in the United States and Canadian colleges and universities, while SeniorNet was also established as a National Association in the United States catering for mature aged computer users (Manheimer, 1998). Martin and Preston (1994) commented on the emergence of a new kind of older adult that will become commonplace in the 21st century. They described this older person as healthy and active, better educated and more financially secure than previous cohorts of older people.

As a result, larger numbers of older people are seeking out educational programmes and services that are specifically designed to meet their learning needs and many want to incorporate this with their travel opportunities. Research by Moscardo (2006) with respect to reef tourism in Australia, found that while senior travellers were not as physically active overall as their younger counterparts, nevertheless over 50% of the study group went snorkelling while more than 10% went scuba diving. Importantly, learning and education was rated by seniors as the primary motivation for visiting the reef with the opportunity to experience nature a close second.

Such opportunities have been termed educational tourism or 'edutourism' which has been defined as, '... a program in which participants travel to a location as a group with the primary purpose of engaging in a learning experience directly related to the location' (Bodger, 1998: 3). The emphasis in this case is on actually experiencing or seeing the subject matter in its natural context or original location.

A heightened interest in such activities by senior travellers has resulted in the development of Elderhostel (recently changed its name to Exploritas) educational travel programmes for older people aged 55 years and older in the USA and Canada. These have become extremely popular with numbers growing from 220 enrolments in 1975 to over 309,000 in 1999, using 2,300 campuses and institutions, as well as over 70 countries worldwide (Goggin, 1999). Generally, participants live in campus accommodation and eat in dining rooms although they do not have to do homework, sit exams or compete for grades. International programmes may run for up to two to three weeks' duration with classes lasting three one-and-a-half-hour sessions, as well as field trip excursions and social activities (Miller, 1997). Participants are more motivated to travel because of the 'seeking' and 'intellectual stimulation' motives rather than the 'escape' motive which was not found to be a strong motivator for the leisure or tourism behaviour of older adults undertaking Exploritas trips (Thomas & Butts, 1998).

Educational programming for seniors is regarded as one of the fastest growing areas, and is seen as a natural progression for resort activity departments to move toward, from purely fun activities to ones with educational components. Holdnak and Holland (1996) suggested that older participants want to take something educational home with them at the end of a vacation such as a lost or forgotten hobby, rather than merely participating in a variety of leisure activities. As a result, many travel agencies are now specialising in group tours to a range of educational destinations. For example, Siesta Tours in Florida provides guided tours to the historic centre of Mexico resulting in, 'Their clients being totally immersed in the history and culture of the region rather than just left sitting on the beach sipping margaritas' (Holdnak & Holland, 1996: 75).

The Disney Institute in Orlando, Florida, USA is another entity catering for this newly evolving educational market. Opened in 1996, the Institute now offers more than 80 hands-on learning programmes that range from culinary arts and topiary gardening to rock climbing and story telling. It also provides an artist-in-residence program and guest speaker forums so as to appeal to as wide a market as possible. Disney's goal is to encourage every guest who leaves to have more than just pleasant memories of pleasant experiences – they want to facilitate new knowledge, skills and a sense of 'expanded horizons' (Holdnak & Holland, 1996).

Because of this growing demand for adventure and educational experiences, tourist operators must quickly respond to this growing market so as to satisfy the changing needs of older consumers.

Marketing the Adventure Tourism Experience for Older Adults

Many tourism providers are scaling back the physical demands of their trips for older people, such as reducing the number of miles travelled per day, lighter backpacks, optional rowing on a white water trip, and providing the choice of vans or tents. Generally, tour companies warn clients that adventure travel can be taxing and even risky at times, and they need to be prepared for strenuous hiking and rustic conditions on five-day backpacking trips to such rugged locations. As a rule, many of these trips need to offer physical training programmes beforehand, especially for hiking and biking, as decent medical care may be many miles away.

Some firms are now requiring older tourists to complete a medical questionnaire before the trip, and may even request a physical examination if there are potential health problems (Silver, 1994). This assists travel companies to be more diligent and mindful about the physical capacity and health of older clients before sending them off to rugged destinations. They also need to heed older people's preferences for slower-paced tours, choosing their own food menus, and to avoid having too many early morning departures (Massow, 2000).

Marketing the Educational Tourism Experience for Older Adults

Older travellers are generally more interested in enriching their lives with educational experiences than through hands-off entertainment. As a consequence, tourism marketers should make a greater effort to understand older adults' attitudes, interests and opinions toward pleasure travel. Marketing campaigns need to focus on the experiential nature of the travel product, and to target older adults' preferences for the educational travel experience (e.g. self-exploration or enhanced knowledge of other cultures and people), and for the travel industry to develop unique products that older adult travellers seek out and purchase (Littrell *et al.*, 2004; Kersetter, 1993).

The success of the educational travel market will depend on tourism providers creating the right image and making it clear to older consumers that they offer 'added value'. This added value is related to offering something that is truly novel and different, i.e. the possibility of an in-depth study of a topic of personal interest with like-minded people under expert guidance and tuition. The successful educational providers of the future will be those that can create an image, offer value for money, provide exciting destinations and packages, and whose reputation for the provision of quality educational packages to cater for the needs of the older consumer is high.

Innovations are already beginning to be implemented such as Exploritas programs that are in some cases moving from college campuses to include a variety of different educational and outdoor centres and parks. In addition, new partnerships are also being forged between Exploritas and museums and other specialised institutions. The development of 'moving' courses are being planned and implemented where, for example, participants trace a pioneer trail learning about geography and period history along the way. In terms of the programming content, theme pro-grammes in which three courses that relate to one broad subject such as fine arts, music and creative writing are also becoming popular.

Exploritas is planning to offer programmes under a separate pro-gramme to appeal to baby boomers in their fifties, who are approaching retirement or pursuing options for enrichment and educational travel. Educational programs that include highly active, experiential learning opportunities will be selected for a new set of offerings. Plans are also presently underway to extend the Exploritas experience to older adults in other European countries, as presently participants in Exploritas pro-grams are solely from North America. An expansion to other parts of the world will follow as the organisation begins to serve a global market (Goggin, 1999).

Conclusion

Older people, and in particular those known globally as the 'baby boomers', are seeking out adventurous and authentic learning experi-ences more than ever before. It is true however that most prefer 'soft' adventure experiences under controlled conditions that are less physically demanding, and with the provision of trained guides who are employed to provide an educational component. The matching of needs against abilities requires some delicate balancing. To this end, travel companies need to be aware of the preferences of older clients with respect to a range of matters such as specific knowledge about each person's health needs, the level of physical intensity, the provision of slower-paced tours, the provision for choice in relation to food menus, and the provision of numerous social activities to encourage the group to mix and get to know each other. While it is apparent that a number of 'independent tourism businesses have begun to research and successfully target this new niche market, it is also evident that few destinations have yet to seriously consider how they might become more senior oriented' (Moscardo, 2006: 39). It is clear therefore that much still needs to be done in this regard.

The educational travel market is still quite small at this stage. However, academics are forecasting that as the population ages and baby boomers start to reach retirement age, the demand for educational programmes and services will dramatically increase over the course of the next 20 years or so. Already, lifelong learning is being recognised as an important educational need in many Western countries, resulting in a number of Institutes of Learning being established in North America, the United Kingdom and Australia that cater specifically for older adults who are aged 55 years and older.

Furthermore, the current baby boomer cohort group will take their educational values with them into retirement and be eager to combine them with overseas and domestic travel. This will create exciting opportunities for businesses that seek to offer a combination of overseas travel with cheaper accommodation at university campuses. Educational tourism provides older adults with the stimulation of gaining intellectually challenging experiences as well as learning through 'hands on' experiences about different cultures and ancient civilisations. It is this very type of engagement that is driving the current boom in the heritage tourism sector.

Over the next 10 years, adventure and educational travel will grow steadily and with more and more specialist holiday choices becoming available, it will soon be possible to choose preferred adventure activities and locations that individuals specifically want to go to. Multi-activity trips are also likely to become more popular, combining with such outdoor activities as trekking, rafting, diving as well as added cultural components. Visits can also be arranged for sightseeing purposes and to places of cultural or historical interest, either before or after the main adventure activity component of the programme.

References

Adair, S.R. and Mowsesian, R. (1993) The meanings and motivations of learning during the retirement transition. *Educational Gerontology* 19, 317–330.

Alsnih, R. and Hensher, D. (2003) The mobility and accessibility expectations of seniors in an aging population. *Transportation Research Part A: Policy and Practice* 37 (10), 903–916.

Bierman, F. (2005) For some, and adventuring never gets old. The New York Times, February 27, p. 5.3.

Bodger, D. (1998) Leisure, learning and travel. *The Journal of Physical Education, Recreation & Dance* 69 (4), 2–5.

Carr, N. (2002) The tourism-leisure behavioural continuum. *Annals of Tourism Research* 29, 972–986.

Cater, C. (2000) Can I play too? Inclusion and exclusion in adventure tourism. *The North West Geographer* 3, 50–60.

Cohen, G.D. (2000) *The Creative Age: Awakening Human Potential in the Second Half of Life.* New York: Harper Collins.

Cooper, C., Scott, N. and Kester, J. (2006) New and emerging markets. In D. Buhalis and C. Costa (eds) *Tourism Business Frontiers: Consumers, Products and Industry* (pp. 19–29). Oxford: Elsevier Butterworth-Heinemann.

Csikszentmihalyi, M. (1996) *Creativity: Flow and the Psychology of Discovery and Invention.* (Chapter 9, Creative Ageing). New York: Harper Collins.

Domestic Travel Marketing Report (2004) Baby boomers. On WWW at http://answers.google.com/answers/threadview?id=426311. Accessed 1.4.2009.

Eisner, J. and Ford, N. (1995) Sexual relations or holiday: A case of situational distribution: *Journal of Social and Personal Relationships* 12, 323–339.

Fitzsimmons, J.A. and Fitzsimmons, M.J. (2004) *Service Management* (4th edn). New York: McGraw-Hill.

Gilmartin, J. (2007) Baby boomer marketing & senior marketing. On WWW at http://www.comingofage.com. Accessed 30.11.2007.

Goggin, J.M. (1999) Elderhostel meets the silent revolution. *Tourism Recreation Research* 24, 86–89.

Grant, B. (2002) Over 65 and ready to play. *Australasian Leisure Management* 35, 37–38.

Grant, B. (2007) Searching for satisfaction. *Australasian Leisure Management* 62, 30, 32.

Gretzel, U., Fesenmaier, D. and O'Leary, T. (2006) The transformation of consumer behaviour. In D. Buhalis and C. Costa (eds) *Tourism Business Frontiers: Consumers, Products and Industry* (pp. 9–18). Oxford: Elsevier Butterworth-Heinemann.

Haahti, A. and Komppula, R. (2006) Experience design in tourism. In D. Buhalis and C. Costa (eds) *Tourism Business Frontiers: Consumers, Products and Industry* (pp. 101–110). Oxford: Elsevier Butterworth-Heinemann.

Harnik, E. (1998) Seniors seek adventure hiking Canadian Rockies. *Insight on the News* 14 (18), May 18, p. 41.

Holdnak, A. and Holland, S.M. (1996) EDU tourism: vacationing to learn. *Parks and Recreation* 31, 72–75.

Hossain, A., Bailey, G. and Lubulwa, M. (2003) Characteristics and travel patterns of older Australians: Impact of population ageing on tourism. Canberra: Bureau of Tourism Research.

Kersetter, D.L. (1993) The college educated older adult traveller. *Visions in Leisure and Business* 11, 26–35.

Josiam, B., Smeaton, G., Hobson, P. and Dietrich, U. (1996) Sex, alcohol and drugs on the beach: 'Where the boys are' in the age of AIDS. Paper presented at the 4th WLRA World Congress, Cardiff, Wales.

Lee, Y., Datillo, J. and Howard, D. (1994) The complex and dynamic nature of leisure experience. *Journal of Leisure Research* 26 (3), 195–211.

Leontido, L. (1994) Gender dimensions of tourism in Greece: Employment, sub-structuring and restructuring. In V. Kinnaird and D. Hall (eds) *Tourism: A Gender Analysis* (pp. 74–104). Chichester: Wiley.

Lipscombe, N. (1995) Appropriate adventure. Participation for the aged. *Australian Parks and Leisure* 31, 41–45.

Littrell, M.A., Paige, R.C. and Song, K. (2004) Senior travellers: Tourism activities and shopping behaviours. *Journal of Vacation Marketing* 10, 348–361.

Manheimer, R.J. (1998) The promise and politics of adult education. *Research on Aging* 20, 391–415.

Mannell, R.C. and Iso-Ahola, S. (1987) Psychological nature of leisure and tourism experience. *Annals of Tourism Research* 14, 314–331.

Markides, K.S. and Boldt, J.S. (1983) A structural modelling approach to the measurement and meaning of cognitive age. *Journal of Consumer Research* 19, 292–301.

Martin, L.G. and Preston, S.H. (1994) *Demography of Aging*. Washington DC: National Academy Press.

Massow, R. (2000) Senior sojourns. *Travel Agent* 299 (12), May 29, 1–2.

Miller, B. (1997) The quest for lifelong learning. *American Demographics* 19, 20–22.

Moscardo, G. (2006) Third-age tourism. In D. Buhalis and C. Costa (eds) *Tourism Business Frontiers: Consumers, Products and Industry* (pp. 30–39). Oxford: Elsevier Butterworth-Heinemann.

Muller, T. and Cleaver, M. (2000) Targeting the CANZUS baby boomer explorer and adventure segments. *Journal of Vacation Marketing* 6, 154–169.

Pine II, B.J. and Gilmore, J.H. (1999) *The Experience Economy: Work is Theater and Every Business a Stage*. Harvard Business School Press.

Pritchard, A. and Morgan, N.J. (1996) Marketing practice and opportunities in the tour operators' senior travel market: Beyond bowling and ballroom dancing. *Journal of Vacation Marketing* 3, 153–163.

Randall Travel Marketing (2007) *Top Ten Travel and Tourism Trends for 2007–2008*. Mooresville, NC: Author.

Reece, W. (2004) Are senior leisure travellers different? *Journal of Travel Research* 43, 11–18.

Ryan, C. (2002) *The Tourist Experience* (2nd edn). London: Continuum.

Shedroff, N. (2001) *Experience Design*. Indianapolis, USA: New Riders.

Sherman, E. and Cooper, P. (1988) Life satisfaction: The missing focus of marketing to seniors. *Journal of Health Care Marketing* 8, 69–71.

Silver, M. (1994) A trek on the wild side. *U.S. News and World Report* 116, 23, June 13, 102–3.

Smith, S.L. and Godbey, G.C. (1991) Leisure, recreation and tourism. *Annals of Tourism Research* 18, 85–100.

Smith, C. and Jenner, P. (1997) The seniors travel market. *Travel and Tourism Analyst* 5, 43–62.

Sorensen, L. (1993) The special-interest travel market. *Cornell Hotel and Restaurant Administration Quarterly* 34, 24–28.

Symonds, W.C. (1998) Far from the tour bus crowd: Track gorillas in Uganda, explore a rainforest, or pedal across France. *Business Week* 3587, July 20, New York, 102.

Thomas, D. and Butts, F. (1998) Assessing leisure motivators and satisfaction of international Elderhostel participants. *Journal of Travel and Tourism Marketing* 7, 31–38.

Tinsley, H.E. and Tinsley, D.J. (1986) A theory of the attributes, benefits and causes of the leisure experience. *Leisure Sciences* 14, 195–209.

Tourism Research Australia (2008) *Forecast 2008 Issue 2*. Canberra: Author.

Travel Industry Association of America (1998) *The Adventure Travel Report, 1997*. Washington DC: TIA.

Travel Industry Association of America (2001) *Newsline: February 2001*. Washington DC: TIA.

United Nations, Division for Social Policy and Development, Department of Economic and Social Affairs (2000) The sex and age distribution of the world populations: 1998 revision. On WWW at http://www.un.org/esa/population/publications/ageing/Graph.pdf.

Urhausen, J. (2008) Tourism in Europe: Does age matter? *Eurostat* 69, 1–7.

World Tourism Organization (2001) *Tourism 2020 Vision: Global Forecasts and Profiles of Market Segments, 7*. Madrid: World Tourism Organization.

World Tourism Organization (2006) *UNWTO World Tourism Barometer*. 4 (3) Madrid: World Tourism Organization.

Zimmer, Z., Brayley, R. and Searle, M. (1995) Whether to go and where to go: Identification of important influences on seniors' decisions to travel. *Journal of Travel Research* 33 (3), 3–10.

Chapter 12

Ageing Travel Market and Accessibility Requirements

Y. WANG

Introduction

As more people enter their 50s and 60s, mature travellers become more important to the tourism industry, and their importance grows as the segment increases in size and wealth (Reece, 2004). More than half of older adults aged 65+ take a vacation at least once a year (Capella & Greco, 1987). Longer vacations are taken after the age of retirement (Romsa & Blenman, 1989). A large number of trips that older adults take and the magnitude of trip-related expenditures that older adults spend on the road contribute to the development of the ageing travel market (Fleischer & Pizam, 2002). A combination of the above three major elements, namely, the growing size of potential mature travellers, the spending power of mature consumers, and the availability of spare time, determines the significance of the ageing travel market.

Age is a primary variable that defines the mature travel market: However, there is no uniform terminology of ageing population used in the field of leisure, tourism, and hospitality (Norman *et al.*, 2001). Various age standards (50+, 55+, 60+, or 65+) are used to define the older travellers. In this chapter, older adults, who are at or over 65 years of age, are frequently referred to as 'mature travellers' or 'aged travellers'. The chapter also refers to some other terms frequently used (see Table 12.1).

It has been an ongoing effort for almost 30 years that tourism researchers have tried to understand the mature travel market. Tongren's study in 1980 on pre and postretirement travel plan changes is regarded as 'the first serious investigation' of mature travel (Blazey, 1992: 772). The findings that retirees' travel activity had an emphasis on family are confirmed by many studies. It is acknowledged in literature that the mature travel market is not homogeneous. Mature travellers have been segmented and profiled based on different variables, e.g. socio-demographic variables, travel motivations, constraints, and benefits (Lehto *et al.*, 2001; Sellick, 2004; Shoemaker, 2000). Comparative studies have been conducted concerning age, gender, and retirement status (Anderson & Langmeyer,

Table 12.1 Glossary

Travel motivations	The 'set of needs which predispose a person to participate in a touristic activity' (Pizam *et al.*, 1979);
Travel constraints	The factors that prevent people from travelling or from enjoying travelling (Fleischer & Pizam, 2002);
Travel information sources	Sources from which mature travellers obtained related travel information, such as travel agents, newspaper, the internet, etc.;
Trip chaining	A sequence of trips that involve multiple purposes and multiple destinations so as to minimise travel and increase the number of activities performed due to time constraints (Hensher & Reyes, 2000).
Transportation mobility	Recognition of one or more of the following dimensions (Burns, 1999; Metz, 2000): (1) access to places of desire such as visiting family and friends; (2) the psychological benefits of travel where social contact and independence are important aspects of mobility; (3) the benefits of physical movement; (4) maintaining social networks; and (5) potential travel.
Social tourism	An objective which society must pursue in the interest of those citizens who are least privileged in the exercise of their right to rest (WTO, 1980).

1982; Blazey, 1992; Javalgi *et al.*, 1992; Moscardo & Green, 1999). Senior households travel farther than non-senior households (Reece, 2004). The oldest group of visitors was significantly more satisfied than the other age categories (Moscardo & Green, 1999). Furthermore, travel benefits have been recognised and documented, such as mature travellers had higher scores of life satisfaction compared to non-travellers (Blazey, 1987; LaForge, 1984).

However, the ageing travel market has to fulfil accessibility requirements before it can truly prosper. There is a well-established connection between disability and the ageing population of the US. As the population has aged, disability (morbidity) and death (mortality) among older adults has declined and level of functioning has as well. Older individuals are experiencing relatively high rates of disability – 50% for those 65 or older and 75% for those aged 80 and above (Alliance for Aging Research, 2002; Sheets & Liebig, 2005).

According to Lach (1999), the disabled group of the consumer segment is expected to double by the year 2030. Most of the rapid growth comes from the ageing baby boomers since more than 60% of the disabled in the US are 65 and older (Burnett & Baker, 2001). The 2000 census data in the US shows that 41.9% of people aged 65 and over, or a total of 1.4 million older adults, had sensory, physical, or mental impairments, or difficulty in taking care of themselves or going outside the home. According to data from the Centers for Disease Control and Prevention (CDC), about 3.3% of non-instituitionalised adults 65 to 74 years reported a physical limitation and needed person-to-person care. This number tripled to 9.6% for individuals aged 75 and older. More than forty percent (44%) of adults aged 75 and older reported being limited in their usual activities due to one or more chronic conditions (Adams *et al.*, 2007). The prevalence of disability, accompanied by activity limitations and the need for personal assistance, increases with age.

Therefore, the focus of this chapter is to introduce and describe the needs and constraints for the ageing travel market in general (including healthy older adults and older adults with disabilities), and more importantly, to explore and analyse the special accessibility requirements of the ageing travel market. This chapter also intents to develop a conceptual framework for the accessibility of the ageing travel market from a perspective of supply and demand.

Tourism Constraints of an Ageing Population

Studies have shown that many factors can prevent older adults from participating in tourism activities. These factors are closely related to the accessibility of travel activities. For example, older adults' travel tendency decreased as health status deteriorated (Fleischer & Pizam, 2002; Zimmer *et al.*, 1995). McGuire (1984) identified five such constraints: external resource, which refers to limitations in resources (i.e. lack of equipment, lack of facilities, lack of information, not having anyone to teach the activity, the amount of planning required, and lack of money); time factors (i.e. having more important things to do, not having enough time, being too busy with other activities, being too busy with work, and not wanting to interrupt a daily schedule); approval (i.e. fear of making a mistake, having to make too many decisions, a feeling family and friends would not approve, and fear of disapproval by others); abilities/social (i.e. not knowing how to do an activity, and not having the skills needed – ability-related; not having anybody to do the activity with and friends not doing the activity) and; physical well-being, which is related to health and well-being (i.e. lack of energy, health reasons, the weather, and fear of getting hurt). McGuire and Norman (2005) defined constraints as factors that inhibited the ability 'to narrow one's activity focus, to optimise engagement in activities, or to effectively compensate for loss' (p. 97).

The factors of expense, time convenience, physical and emotional costs, lack of information, health status, perceived disability are the most often identified and cited reason for not participating in leisure travel (Blazey, 1987; Mayo & Jarvis, 1985; McGuire *et al.*, 1986). Fleischer and Pizam's (2002) study confirmed the previous studies' results on constraints; but it was also found that the decision to take a vacation and the decision of the vacation length were affected by different constraints. Income and health were the constraints that influence seniors' decision to take a vacation; while the vacation length was affected by variables of income, health, past experience, and the parabolic function of age. The effect of the constraints on the vacation length changed with the age cycle. In the first cycle (55–65), it was found the number of vacation days positively correlated with leisure time and household income; while in the next cycle (65+), declining incomes and deterioration of health were found to cause a decrease of the vacation length. In a destination-based study, Wang *et al.* (2005) identified nine constraint factors for mature travellers, namely, fishing conditions, poor weather, time/work, environment, family/ spouse, reputation, children, safety/security, and seasonal constraints. Among them, fishing conditions and seasonal constraints were significant predictors of mature travellers' travel decision.

Accessibility Requirements

A supply-demand model regarding accessibility issues of the ageing travel market is proposed and illustrated as in Figure 12.1. Services that the travel market offer and supply include transportation (i.e. various transportation modes to move people from one location to another) and destination-based attributes (e.g. accommodation, food, attraction, recreation programs, etc.). These services cannot meet with the demand of less privileged older adults unless accessibility issues are properly addressed by each service provider. Three major accessibility issues include accessibility to facilities, availability and accessibility of information resources, and affordability of travel activities. The World Health Organization (WHO; 2007) provides a checklist of core age-friendly city features for each of eight areas of urban living, such as outdoor spaces and buildings, transportation, housing, social participation, respect and social inclusion, civic participation and employment, communication and information, and community support and health services.

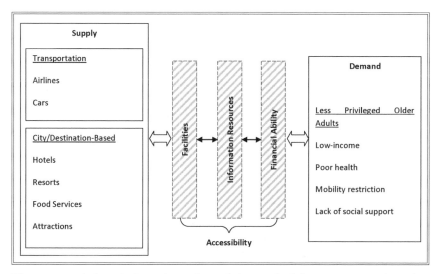

Figure 12.1 A description of supply and demand of the ageing travel market regarding accessibility requirements

Transportation

Cars, airline and coach buses are preferred transportation modes for older adults. Older adults have been used to depend on their own cars for their transportation needs, for example, trip chaining (Hensher & Reyes, 2000). Alsnih and Hensher (2003) found that older drivers, especially above 75 years of age, had increasing navigational problems when travelling through unfamiliar areas. Some improvements, such as eliminating traffic conflicts at intersections, ramps, roundabouts, and other trouble spot areas, could make the infrastructure for vehicles much more user friendly for older adults and the rest of the population as well (Coughlin, 2001).

However, the number of older adults whose major transportation mode is their own vehicle drops consistently and dramatically with an increase of age, while dependence on relatives, friends, and neighbours increases accordingly (Burkhardt, 2000). The decreased reliance on the personal car poses a high demand for a convenient and accessible public transportation system. London Transport (1993) developed a step-by-step guide to the underground system for elderly and disabled users. Petzall (1995) experimented on the design of entrances of taxis for elderly and disabled passengers. Alsnih and Hensher (2003) suggested that community-based educational programmes such as 'retiring from driving' needed to inform older drivers of the alternative transportation modes and also to increase the awareness of their potential mobility needs. Alternative transportation should be flexible as well, such as specialised door-to-door services.

As for long distance travel, tourism literature has long recognised the preference of air travel by mature travellers. Hawes (1988) found that the over-50 group were significantly more likely than under-50s to prefer air travel. Mature travellers rated 'convenience' as the most important attribute in selecting a tour package (Huang & Tsai, 2003). Abeyratne (1995) examined the widely adopted measures relating to air travel for older adults and disabled people and proposed guidelines that facilitate providing services to groups with special needs. These guidelines deal with various aspects of air travel, such as:

(1) contacts with airline reservations and ticket sales agents;
(2) specific fares, charges and related travel conditions;
(3) accessibility of aircraft; and
(4) movement, facilities and services on board aircraft. It is always a top priority for mature travel professionals to make air travel an experience of convenience and hassle-free.

Accommodation

According to Badinelli *et al.* (1991), the primary accommodation selection criteria for the mature travellers were cleanliness, convenience of location, room price, easy access from main roads, security systems, and parking lot lighting. Retired pleasure travellers placed more value on perception of cost, personal safety, and ease of movement when they chose a lodging facility to stay during their trips. Gustin and Weaver (1993) found various dimensions that were important for mature travellers to consider, such as comfortably secure, ambience, information aids, simplicity, consistency, price yet quality and non-smoking rooms. The top ten important attributes of hotels were cleanliness, value for money, comfort of bedroom, politeness of staff, efficiency of service, safety and security, responsiveness of staff, promptness of service, friendliness of staff, and location (Callan & Bowman, 2000). Some particular features that many mature travellers like include ramps and grab-bars in the bathroom and lift. Well-adapted hotel rooms with special features designed for older adults such as bath chairs and toilet raisers meet the mobility and accessibility requirements.

Restaurant services

Friendly service is the most important attribute for aged restaurant users, as indicated by various studies (Harris & West, 1995; Shank & Nahhas, 1994). Some other attributes of the restaurant such as clean bathrooms, wide variety menu, quiet dining area, and friendly greeting by host, were also very important for older customers (Harris & West, 1995). An open and comfortable seating area, specially designed for people with disabilities, is an amenity that may add value to customers' dining experiences. Adapted toilets offer convenience for older adults with some mobility difficulties.

Information search

Eichhorn *et al.* (2008) identified five interrelated informational need components, such as information reliability, information richness, appropriate sources, communication, and customer-oriented services. How to distribute the rich tourism-related information and make them accessible to the ageing market is a key to the success of accessible tourism. Besides traditional media to disseminate information, older adults start to adapt to Cyberspace. According to SeniorNet (2003), 55% of seniors searched for travel packages and services online, and 38% of seniors booked their trips online. Looking for travel information is the second primary usage of the internet for many older adults. The National Institute on Aging (NIA) and the National Library of Medicine (2002) developed and published a 'senior friendly' guideline for those websites targeting users 60+, entitled *'Making Your Web Site Senior Friendly: A Checklist'*, which aims to improve accessibility for the older adult internet user. This checklist consists of 25 empirically-based guidelines within four subject areas; namely:

(1) designing readable text for older adults;
(2) presenting information to older adults;
(3) incorporating other media; and
(4) increasing the ease of navigation.

Laurich (2002) developed an annotated bibliography of the most significant and useful websites dedicated to the older internet users. Elderhostel (Exploritas) was recommended as one of the travel sites, which offers various types of travel experience.

Price

Although over 60% of the world's international tourism expenditure came from mature travellers from North America and Europe (Fleischer & Seiler, 2002), lack of money is a major constraint for many older adults with a low and medium income. Declining incomes was one of the causes for a decrease in the number of vacation days taken in the older group (65+) (Fleischer & Pizam, 2002). Post-retirees were more price and security sensitive than pre-retirees when they travel (Hagen & Uysal, 1991). The probability to travel increased with the level of income (Fleischer & Pizam, 2002).

To make travel activities accessible and affordable for older adults, travel professionals need to address issues of price and perceived value. Many attractions and airline companies have senior discount programs, which encourage older adults to travel and participate in various recreational activities. Besides a lower price, a high perceived value can also promote the sales of travel products. A large variety of amenities and high-quality services can increase the perceived value of the desired travel product.

Future Trends and Conclusions

With an increase of the accessibility of travel-related facilities, a larger group of mature travellers are expected. Well-trained, qualified and friendly service providers are in need. Experienced mature travellers pay extra attention to the quality of the service that they pay for, other than merely comparing a base price. Mature travellers are conscious and interested in the benefits they may get from their travel experience.

Some countries and cities promote and practice social tourism by organising various associations to provide tourism products and activities that are accessible to older adults including those with mobility or financial difficulties. However, the concept of social tourism has not been widely recognised or practiced except in some European countries.

To conclude, the magnitude of the mature travel market demands improved access to travel and tourism services. Travel professionals need to consider the accessibility issue from various aspects, such as accommodation facilities with diverse assistance equipments, affordable travel packages of high value and good services, transportation infrastructures equipped with easy access for older adults, and information systems that older adults can easily navigate through. Older adults are one of the big groups who benefit the most from the development of accessible tourism.

References

Abeyratne, R.I.R. (1995) Proposals and guidelines for the carriage of elderly and disabled persons by air. *Journal of Travel Research* 33, 52–59.

Adams, P.F., Dey, A.N. and Vickerie, J.L. (2007) Summary health statistics for the U.S. population: National Health Interview Survey, 2005. National Center for Health Statistics. *Vital Health Stat 10* (233), 1–104.

Alliance for Aging Research (2002) *Medical never never land: Ten reasons why America is not ready for the coming age boom.* Washington, DC: Author.

Alsnih, R. and Hensher, D.A. (2003) The mobility and accessibility expectations of seniors in an aging population. *Transportation Research Part A* 37 (10), 903–916.

Anderson, B.B. and Langmeyer, L. (1982) The under-50 and over-50 travelers: a profile of similarities and differences. *Journal of Travel Research* 20 (4), 20–24.

Badinelli, K., Davis, N. and Gustin, L. (1991) Senior traveler survey. *Hotel & Motel Management* 206 (15), 31–34.

Blazey, M.A. (1987) The differences between participants and non-participants in a senior travel program. *Journal of Travel Research* 26 (1), 7–12.

Blazey, M.A. (1992) Travel and retirement status. *Annals of Tourism Research* 19, 771–783.

Burkhardt, J.E. (2000) Limitations of mass transportation and individual vehicle systems for older persons. In K.W. Schaie and M. Pietrucha (eds) *Mobility and Transportation in the Elderly*. New York, NY: Springer.

Burnett, J.J. and Baker, H.B. (2001) Assessing the travel-related behaviors of the mobility-disabled consumer. *Journal of Travel Research* 40 (1), 4–11.

Burns, P.C. (1999) Navigation and the mobility of older drivers. *The Journal of Gerontology* 54 (1), S49–S55.

Callan, R.J. and Bowman, L. (2000) Selecting a hotel and determining salient quality attributes: A preliminary study of mature British travelers. *International Journal of Tourism Research* 2, 97–118.

Capella, L. and Greco, A. (1987) Information sources of elderly for vacation decisions. *Annals of Tourism Research* 14, 148–151.

Coughlin, J. (2001) Transportation and older persons: Perceptions and preferences. A report on focus groups, Centre for Transportation Studies and Age Lab, AARP, Washington DC. At http://www.aarp.org. November 2002.

Eichhorn, V., Miller, G., Michopoulou, E., and Buhalis, D. (2008) Enabling access to tourism through information schemes? *Annals of Tourism Research* 35, 189–210.

Fleischer, A. and Seiler, E. (2002) Determinants of vacation travel among Israeli seniors: Theory and evidence. *Applied Economics* 34 (4), 421–430.

Fleischer, A. and Pizam, A. (2002) Tourism constraints among Israeli seniors. *Annals of Tourism Research* 29 (1), 106–123.

Gustin, M.E. and Weaver, P.A. (1993) The mature market: Underlying dimensions and group differences of a potential market for the hotel industry. *FIU Hospitality Review* 11 (2), 45–59.

Hagen, L.A. and Uysal, M. (1991) An examination of motivations and activities of pre-retirement (50–64) and post-retirement (65–98) age groups for a touring group. Proceedings of the Twenty-Second Annual Conference of the Travel and Tourism Research Association, Long Beach, California.

Harris, K.L. and West, J.J. (1995) Senior savvy: Mature diners' restaurant service expectations. *Hospitality Review* 13 (2), 35–44.

Hawes, D.K. (1988) Travel-related lifestyle profiles of older women. *Journal of Travel Research* 27 (2), 22–32.

Hensher, D.A. and Reyes, A.J. (2000) Trip chaining as a barrier to the propensity to use public transportation. *Transportation* 27, 341–361.

Huang, L. and Tsai, H.T. (2003) The study of senior traveler behavior in Taiwan. *Tourism Management* 24 (5), 561–574.

Javalgi, R.G., Thomas, E.G. and Rao, S.R. (1992) Consumer behavior in the U.S. pleasure travel marketplace: an analysis of senior and nonsenior travelers. *Journal of Travel Research* 31, 14–19.

Lach, J. (1999) Disability ? liability. *American Demographics* 2(June), 21–22.

LaForge, M.C. (1984) Elderly recreational travelers: A profile. *Cornell Hotel and Restaurant Administration Quarterly* 25 (August), 14–15.

Laurich, R. (2002) The platinum web: Sites dedicated to senior citizens on the internet. *Collection Building* 21 (4), 174–182.

Lehto, X.Y., O'Leary, J.T. and Lee, G. (2001) Mature international travelers: An examination of gender and benefits. *Journal of Hospitality & Leisure Marketing* 9 (1/2), 53–72.

London Transport (1993) *Access to the Underground: A Step-by-Step Guide to Each Station for Elderly and Disabled People*. London Transport: London.

Mayo, E.J. and Jarvis, P. (1985) *The Psychology of Leisure Travel*. Boston, MA: CBI Publishing.

McGuire, F.A. (1984) A factor analytic study of leisure constraints in advanced adulthood. *Leisure Sciences* 6, 313–326.

McGuire, F.A., Dottavio, D. and O'Leary, J.T. (1986) Constraints to participation in outdoor recreation across the life span: A nationwide study of limitors and prohibitors. _The Gerontologist_ 26, 538–544.

McGuire, F. and Norman, W. (2005) The role of constraints in successful aging: Inhibiting or enabling? In E.L. Jackson (ed) _Constraints to Leisure_. State College, PA: Venture.

Metz, D.H. (2000) Mobility of older people and their quality of life. _Transport Policy_ 7, 149–152.

Moscardo, G. and Green, D. (1999) Age and activity participation on the Great Barrier Beef. _Tourism Recreation Research_ 24, 57–68.

National Institute on Aging & National Library of Medicine (2002) Making your web site senior friendly: A checklist. Online document: At http://www.nlm.nih.gov/pubs/checklist.pdf.

Norman, W.C., Daniels, M.J., McGuire, F. and Norman, C.A. (2001) Whither the mature market: An empirical examination of the travel motivations of neo-mature and veteran-mature markets. _Journal of Hospitality & Leisure Marketing_ 8 (3/4), 113–130.

Petzall, J. (1995) The design of entrances of taxis for elderly and disabled passengers: An experimental study. _Applied Ergonomics_ 26, 343–352.

Pizam, A., Neumann, Y. and Reichel, A. (1979) Tourist satisfaction: Uses and misuses. _Annals of Tourism Research_ 6, 95–107.

Reece, W.S. (2004) Are senior leisure travelers different? _Journal of Travel Research_ 43, 11–18.

Romsa, G. and Blenman, M. (1989) Vacation patterns of the elderly German. _Annals of Tourism Research_ 16, 178–188.

Sellick, M.C. (2004) Discovery, connection, nostalgia: Key travel motives within the senior market. _Journal of Travel & Tourism Marketing_ 17 (1), 55–71.

SeniorNet (November 2003) SeniorNet survey on internet use. Online document. At http://www.seniornet.org/php/default.php?PageID=7284.

Shank, M.D. and Nahhas, F. (1994) Understanding the service requirements of the mature market. _Journal of Restaurant and Food Service Marketing_ 1 (2), 23–43.

Sheets, D. and Liebig, P. (2005) The intersection of aging, disability, and supportive environments: Issues and policy implications. _Hallym International Journal of Aging_ 7 (2), 143–163.

Shoemaker, S. (2000) Segmenting the mature market: 10 years later. _Journal of Travel Research_ 39, 11–26.

Tongren, H.N. (1980) Travel plans of the over-65 market pre and postretirement. _Journal of Travel Research_ 19 (2), 7–11.

Wang, Y., Norman, W.C. and McGuire, F.A. (2005) A comparative study of leisure constraints perceived by mature and young travelers. _Tourism Review International_ 8 (3), 263–279.

World Health Organization (2007) Global age-friendly cities: A guide. At http://www.who.int/ageing/publications/Global_age_friendly_cities_Guide_English.pdf.

World Tourism Organization (1980) Manila declaration on world tourism. At http://www.world-tourism.org/sustainable/doc/1980%20Manila-eng.pdf.

You, X. and O'Leary, J.T. (2000) Age and cohort effects: An examination of older Japanese travelers. _Journal of Travel & Tourism Marketing_ 9 (1/2), 21–42.

Zimmer, Z., Brayley, R.E. and Searle, M.S. (1995) Whether to go and where to go: Identification of important influences on seniors' decisions to travel. _Journal of Travel Research_ 33, 3–10.

Chapter 13

Heritage Sites: Attitudinal and Experimental Differences of Disabled and Able-Bodied Visitors

M. PEARN

Introduction

The polemic context of this chapter focuses on conservation within heritage settings as well as adopting an inclusive disability-centred approach. MacCannell's exploration of authenticity within tourist settings (1999) together with Wang's notions of authenticity (1999) form the conservational parameters, in terms of recommending caution to heritage bodies as to potential irreversible infringements on historic settings when considering improving disabled access to sites. In terms of Wang's 'objective' notion, this chapter's perspective attributes priority to the originality of traditional settings, thus warning against undue 'constructivist' changes. Crucially MacCannell's conceptual writings, particularly on 'front, back and reality' (1999), are prominent in this investigation, specifically, when gauging the differing settings for disabled and able-bodied visitors. For example, those with disabilities often experience more of the 'back regions' than other visitors, as barriers to access often deny them from using the 'front regions'. A hypothesis therefore could be: 'Does this lessen the visiting experience for patrons with disabilities?'

Disablist Perspective

Prior to investigating the ideological clash between disability and conservation, it is important to offer an explanation of what constitutes disability and how it is regarded by various quarters. The term disability encompasses a wide range of impairments including physical or mental conditions with either long-term or short-term effects. It is considered that the term 'impairment' is intrinsically linked to the conceptual nature of disability. A concise appreciation of the meaning of impairment is, according to Doyle (2003), not offered in disability legislation, nonetheless the meaning of it is vital to the understanding of all types of disabilities. The World Health Organization (WHO) in 1980 classified the meaning of impairment as 'any loss or abnormality of psychological, physiological, or anatomical structure or function' (WHO, 1980). This classification is still fundamentally relevant to today's understanding of impairment and is largely considered a helpful vehicle for debate.

The social model of disability, inaugurated by the Union of the Physically Impaired Against Segregation (UPIAS) in 1976, has been highly influential in the emancipation of people with disabilities. Critically, this has involved the transferring of attention from the constraints incurred by those with disabilities in respect of the barriers in society which curb the freedoms and independence of disabled people. Integral to this ideological shift was the transference from the 'tragedy model' to adopting an absolute inclusive standpoint, which regards people with disabilities as 'normal' and valid citizens.

Further to the medical and social models of disability, there is the 'tragedy principle' or 'charity model', which presents disability as an extremely negative issue. This extremist view, which dwarfs the medical model's pessimism, views disabled people as fundamentally flawed. The principle, according to Hevey (1993), uses a disability or any ailment as 'a metaphor and a symbol for a socially unacceptable person'. Unlike the inclusive agenda of the social model, it is negative misrepresentations of disability like the medical model that aim to alienate and practically demonise disabled people. Hevey sees this kind of ostracism as naturalising the exclusion of disability, which of course stalls the plight of the social model.

Tregaskis (2002), within the context of the recent escalation of the social model's emancipatory influence on disabled people's lives, discusses capitalist-based barriers against disabled people and how disability groups have been perceived as the 'deserving poor'. It seems that such oppression is borne from an out-dated narrow definition of disability, which has only been broadened during the late 1980s/1990s. It would appear that we have now entered an era whereby society is often willing to bend over backwards in the context of building an egalitarian societal construct without giving careful consideration to possible consequences and repercussions within other scenarios, in this case heritage and traditional environments. Indeed it is the well-intended plight of political correctness which could result in catastrophic affects on historic environments.

To illustrate the inappropriateness of some disability-orientated facilities, it is necessary to consider the potential clash of modernistic entities within an otherwise traditional setting. Religious settings such as cathedrals and churches are worthy examples of vulnerable environments. Facilities for disabled access, by definition, are symbols of modernity. By their mere presence within heritage environments some modernistic facilities could be interpreted as a 'fly in the ointment' effect, where an historical experience is tainted by a reminder of the present. An example of such a modern encroachment was the disability provision within Truro Cathedral, particularly in relation to the cathedral's internal ramp adjacent to the altar. The ramp, resembling a marine jetty, was garishly coloured in green and white and typified the inappropriate combination of modernity and gothic.

In contrast to the inappropriate provision within Truro Cathedral, Lanhydrock, a National Trust Property in Cornwall, has installed a lift within its 18th century house. The lift, when out of use, has been cunningly concealed behind original oak panelling, successfully disguising the 'modern intruder'.

Heritage Perspective

The essence of this chapter investigates how a consensus may be reached between conservational ideologies and the emancipation of disabled people. The formulation of a paradigm is therefore proposed whereby the interests of both conservational and inclusive ideologies are carefully considered. The emergence of such a multi-faceted paradigm could be interpreted in pragmatic terms by heritage sites which would ensure any facilities for disabled visitors to heritage sites did not cause negative infringements to the environment or the traditional aesthetics of sites.

This paradigmatic intervention would ensure a compromise is reached and, in the context of disability-orientated changes to heritage sites, would ensure a level of acceptability in terms of associated conflicts between societal inclusion ideologies and conservation. Current research into this ideological conflict is limited. Existing investigations, however, tend to favour a disability-centred approach, thus establishing how current policies and legislation can be applied to traditional settings, without fully appreciating the potential irreversible degrading consequences on the historical aesthetics of heritage environments.

Goodall sets out three scenarios by which planners and heritage bodies can determine whether increasing accessibility to historical sites can be 'conservationally' acceptable. These three scenarios are as follows:

- Sites where it is practical to make full access improvements.
- Sites where full accessibility cannot be achieved and compromise solutions are adopted.
- Sites whose fragility make it impossible to provide access without endangering their special values or the safety of visitors. (2005: 185)

Whilst this is possible for many heritage sites, particularly properties, to adhere to legislation such as the DDA, it is frequently impossible to adapt heritage sites, like monuments and ruins, in order to achieve greater disabled access. One typical example of this is Tintagel Castle, situated in North Cornwall, whereby access to the castle ruins was solely reliant on winding steps leading up a cliff, below which English Heritage have a very informative visitors' centre, complete with a video presentation of the ruins. However, the question here is raised as to how disabled visitors simply have to forego the experience, both physically and atmospherically, and also to what extent a visitors' centre can successfully supplement experience. It stands to reason that Tintagel Castle is an example of where a compromise has been reached, and where the autonomy of disabled visitors along with the fight for societal inclusiveness has to be surrendered.

A recent PhD study (Pearn, 2009) investigating the attitudes of disabled and able-bodied visitors to heritage sites in the South West of England, primarily aimed to establish a consensus between the access needs of visitors with disabilities along with the non-encroachment of associated alterations into the historical integrity of the sites. The investigation found a distinct willingness, particularly in the context of able-bodied visitor attitudes, as to the adoption of disability-orientated facilities. Despite their unquestionable respect for authenticity, able-bodied visitors were primarily willing to condone alterations, particularly in the knowledge of the disabled visitor experience being significantly enhanced.

Disabled visitors often achieve a very different experience to their able-bodied associates. This experience is frequently a 'watered down' experience due to many diversions and inaccessible areas. A classic example being the use of alternate access points for disabled visitors. Saltram House, a National Trust property in Plymouth, has installed a carefully constructed ramp to its main front entrance, enabling their disabled visitors to enter the house conventionally. In contrast, Lanhydrock provides an alternate entrance for its disabled visitors; the former servants' access point. As a consequence of this, Lanhydrock's disabled visitors forego the grandeur of entering the house conventionally and, whilst this has evidently been a pragmatic approach to the access quandary, a significant part of Lanhydrock's visitor experience is lost due to this alternate access point.

Among the theoretical concepts supporting this research was MacCannell's 'staged authenticity' (1976). Largely based around touristic settings, staged authenticity involves 'front' and 'back' regions, the front region being the focus of tourist gathering and activity and the back region being the part of the setting not permissible to tourists and where the contrived is far less prevalent. In applying MacCannell's staged authenticity to heritage settings, disabled visitors frequently have to divert from the conventional 'visitor route' thus experiencing back regions in order to avoid barriers to access.

Goffman's theory of 'performers' and 'performances' (1959) can be applied to staged authenticity in that the front regions are based around the performances. It is therefore possible to make further links from his well-established approaches to this comparatively modern assessment of disability perception within society. Goffman's term 'performance' refers to activities of an individual occurring under the observation of other people. In his insights into the 'individual', as someone who, like those with disabilities, is set apart from other members of society, Goffman focuses on the stigmatism of such individuals which leads to unwanted attention, acting as a distraction from another focal point. In the context of heritage settings, disabled visitors have the potential for being such distractions through their conspicuousness, caused by their disability.

The 'front' for the purpose of this investigation is the setting of a typical heritage site, for example a stately house, whereby the setting consists of able-bodied visitors (the observers) and one, or a number of visitors with disabilities (the individual/s). The visitors with disabilities are the unacquainted, and so, to a certain extent, taint the otherwise scenic surroundings. To reiterate, this portrayal is based upon the discriminatory opinions of a minority of visitors, and should not be an indicative representation of the majority. Using the terms of Goffman, visitors who possess wheelchairs or mobility aids often see these aids as an important part of their 'personal front'. Such apparatus exist as part of their identity and could therefore be termed as the individual's 'expressive equipment'.

Continuing this analogy, of 'expressive equipment', pre-judgemental attitudes towards disability in general can be linked to Goffman's interpretation of status in terms of 'appearance and manner' (1959). Wheelchair-users for example, may be regarded by some as having a lesser status than others because of the mere fact they are disabled. However, it must be noted that this interpretation is based on pure prejudice, before any social interaction takes place.

A Dual Experience

Paradoxically, the parameters of this study defy conventional attitudes in terms of human rights law. Monaghan (2005) discusses 'soft law' in relation to gender and nationality discrimination. The historical ineffectiveness of soft law within the context of disability legislation has resulted in disabled people not receiving the autonomy they rightfully deserve. However, the paradox comes within the context of heritage sites and the inappropriateness of current disability legislation in terms of its potential degradation of traditional aesthetics.

The crux of this investigation attempts to identify a compromise whereby disablist legislation is applied to places of historical significance sensitively, thus not incurring negative encroachments on the authentic and traditional visitor experience. This compromise involves a fundamental attitudinal shift which, if anything, will result in a slight reversal of inclusive ideologies such as those manifested by the social model of disability.

The tourism industry, being dominated by supply and demand patterns, is often torn between preservationist paradigms and the need to commoditise touristic environments. In discussing the dilemma of balancing conservation and enterprise, Silberberg (1995), in Apostolakis (2002), discusses the commercial development of a typical heritage site having to transfer from the mentality of 'being willing to take tourists to a stage of being able to accept tourists'. Applying Silberberg's philosophy to heritage sites accommodating visitors with disabilities, the dilemma of knowing how far to go without sanitising heritage environments is clear. The dilemma lies within being cautious against inadvertently 'repackaging what was once regarded as authentic'.

The obligation of many heritage sites and organisations to accommodate visitors with disabilities ultimately extends the commoditisation process in terms of transforming heritage sites to heritage attractions. A critical or even cynical approach would suggest that this transference even involves heritage sites entering into the realms of pseudo-escapism as discussed by Boorstin (1964). Considering this investigation from an accessibility perspective, one might feel that comparing disability-orientated alterations to commoditisation and pseudo-events may be somewhat overstated. However, those harbouring impassioned conservationist stances would be more inclined to support the curbing of external encroachments into the historical integrity of heritage sites.

Among these external encroachments, besides accessibility, are various interpretations of authenticity which, in their own right, depict the meaning of authenticity. In relation to Wang's Notions of Authenticity (1999), objectivist authenticity poses the greatest threat to traditionalist thinking and to the historical integrity of heritage environments. Pseudo-events and objectivist authenticity both occur when originality has been contrived, usually with the aim of creating a more enhanced experience. In relating these two originality opposers to accessibility, the resistance to change for traditionalism becomes increasingly challenged. It could further be argued that such resistance even curbs disabled visitors' quest for intra-personal authenticity, which arguably cannot be achieved within a society dominated by obstacles to access. Therefore, the pertinent question is whether people with disabilities should have their spontaneity and freedoms temporarily curtailed when visiting heritage sites.

The addition of disability-orientated provisions within heritage sites could be regarded as a method of commodifying heritage for the benefit of paying visitors. This process in essence is similar to the tourism industry commodifying indigenous cultures. Greenwood (1989) cites the case of local culture within the Basque region of Spain in which commodification has been instrumental in commoditising and belittling culture. He uses the Alarde, an ancient ritual of the Spanish town of Fuenterrabia to celebrate the town's victory over the French during a siege in 1638. The Alarde initially was very much a private ceremony, restricted to just Fuenterrabia's population.

However, the ritual became a victim of commercialisation on being exposed to large numbers of tourists, thus resulting in the 'collapse of cultural meanings' and traditional value. Greenwood comments: 'Making their culture a public performance took the municipal government a few minutes; with that act a 350-year-old ritual died' (1989: 180).

This investigation argues that, despite the feelings of able-bodied and disabled visitors, any alteration to a heritage site or property, no matter how charitable, is an infringement and commoditisation of heritage. As with the commercialisation of the Alarde, transforming a heritage site into a touristic attraction inevitably involves the extraction of authenticity.

In dealing with the conservation versus accessibility, and for that matter objectivist authenticity and pseudo-encroachments, schism, a balanced approach between able-bodied and disabled visitors is fully intended. It should therefore be stated that the investigation acknowledges that able-bodied visitors experience barriers too. Stumbo and Pegg put emphasis on barriers being wide-ranging and applicable to all social groups. These constraints, they say, 'are the elements of a tourism destination that stimulate visitation' (2005: 204). Stumbo and Pegg take a participatory approach to the experience of tourism and speak of the importance of inclusive leisure facilities 'without undue constraints'. However, a more balanced and moderate approach is reflected within this investigation which, in practical terms, places emphasis on reaching a compromise.

The Disability Perspective

The constructs of this investigation include establishing synergy between the disabled visitor experience within heritage sites being enhanced as well as supporting the preservation of authenticity. To gain a balanced approach, a brief analysis of society's current and past treatment of people with disabilities is necessary.

The transference from the medical model to the social model has involved a revolutionary attitudinal shift which has led to people with disabilities becoming valid members of all sections of society. This has recently been escalated through the passing of the Disability Discrimination Act 1995 (DDA), which has now made any discriminative behaviour towards disability illegal. Much of the legislation within the DDA can be heralded as a positive breakthrough in terms of the resulting autonomy rightfully awarded to people with disabilities. However, the heritage sector, namely historical sites and properties, is one of the few areas in which the powers of the DDA are less clear-cut. Statutorily the listed status of buildings has power and priority over the DDA and other disability-related legislation. The premise of this chapter and of a recent PhD is inclined to agree and support the promotion of conservational practices over and above the DDA and other disability-related philosophies.

It is therefore the ideological clash of conservation and social inclusion which is under scrutiny and a concept pioneered by the PhD pre-empting this chapter.

Legislative Framework

Before setting out the social model of disability's purpose, it is important to address the meaning of disability and the identity of disabled persons. An estimated 8% of the UK population are said to have a disability of some kind, and it is further estimated that 2% of visitors to heritage sites are registered as disabled. It could be surmised that one prominent reason for the percentage of disabled visitors being so low is because heritage sites, due to their nature, are not 'disabled friendly', particularly from an accessibility perspective. With the combined presence of the social model and the DDA, there could be a strong and justified argument for heritage sites to raise the disabled visitor quota by improving accessibility.

The term disability encompasses a wide range of impairments including physical or mental conditions with either long-term or short-term effects. It is considered that the term 'impairment' is intrinsically linked to the conceptual nature of disability. A concise appreciation of the meaning of impairment is, according to Doyle (2003), not offered in disability legislation, nonetheless the meaning of it is vital to the understanding of all types of disabilities. The WHO in 1980 classified the meaning of impairment as 'any loss or abnormality of psychological, physiological, or anatomical structure or function'. This classification is still fundamentally relevant to today's understanding of impairment and is largely considered a helpful vehicle for debate.

The Social Model and its Influence

This investigation sets out to interrogate how the 'social model of disability' can suitably be applied to heritage settings. Unusually, this involves a certain amount of 'watering down' of some of the concepts' ideals, particularly as the eradication of all barriers within heritage settings is conservationally unfeasible.

While maintaining many positive aspects of the social model, this investigation challenges and questions the model's practical application within sites of historical interest. For example, if the model were to be applied in its entirety, the destruction to historical integrity would be undesirable. Whilst the investigation by no means supports any ideal within the medical model of disability, it does call for sensible and realistic thinking and planning when imposing access amenities on any construction or environment classified as heritage.

A Historical Background

Fundamental meanings of disability have radically changed since the dominance of the medical model during the pre 1970s. Nowadays disability is regarded by most as not a medical or pathological deficiency, but a condition requiring changes within society in order to improve the lifestyles of those who are disabled. This viewpoint typifies the social model, its ramifications and its quest to bridge the disabilities/able-bodied divide. Watson (1998) in Swarbrooke and Horner (1999) advocates an 'interpretative analysis' which contextualises disability and related chronic conditions. This approach aims to shift the emphasis onto personal identity, rather than the focus being on the impairment. Watson's vision is an attempt to 'de-stigmatise' disability and, similar to the social model's position, can be seen as a viable pathway towards inclusion.

The ethos of the 'social model of disability' was introduced in Britain in 1976 by the Union of the Physically Impaired Against Segregation (UPIAS). However it was Oliver (1986) who claims to have interpreted and conceptualised the Union's assertions into the social model. Oliver's creation meant it was then possible to directly challenge the medical model. The social model's broad agenda asserts that society disables the impaired, as opposed to the disability itself being the hindrance.

The social model was introduced to challenge the ethos and re-percussions of the medical model. The medical model is the traditional definition of disability, and many see it as an outdated concept. This is mainly because of its narrow, 'disablist' vision. With the recent full inception of the DDA, it would appear that the UPIAS's vision is beginning to accelerate. However, there is still scope for criticism of the DDA, particularly because it contains too many legislative recommendations which are fundamentally based on the medical model rather than the social model.

There seems to be a plethora of now obsolete models which accompanied the medical model prior to the late 1970s. Disability policy consultant June Isaacson Kailes (Kailes, 2002) discusses the 'segregation' and 'rehabilitation' models in relation to the oppressive era of disability. The rehabilitation model, having distinct similarities to the charity model, made half-hearted attempts in the 1970s to medically cure disability by making ill-conceived efforts to include people with impairments. Kailes describes how society's attempt at rehabilitation and inclusion did not involve the removal of physical barriers. Such a lack of pragmatism involved disabled people faced with the impossible task of, for example, having to tackle flights of steps to reach a workplace, not being given the necessary provisions to enable them to work effectively, and a general lack of sensitivity in the able-bodied approach to disability. Aside from the rehabilitation model's drawbacks, there was at least the attempt to include those with disabilities.

Comparative Viewpoint

The social model adopts the necessary approach for an inclusive society which, from its inception, has emphasised the positive attributes of someone with a disability. McConkey and McCormack in arguing for changes in attitudes to people with disabilities say: 'People's negative stereotypes of disability can be counteracted by presenting opportunities for disabled people to demonstrate what they can do rather than dwelling on their limitations' (1983: 56).

McConkey and McCormack (1983) discuss the need for greater collaboration between disabled people and their able-bodied counterparts. The social model, along with McConkey and McCormack's call for greater inclusion, may potentially be without due consideration to the negative impact on heritage and culture.

Further to the medical and social models of disability, there is the 'tragedy principle' or 'charity model', which presents disability as an extremely negative issue. This extremist view, which dwarfs the medical model's pessimism, views disabled people as fundamentally flawed. The principle, according to Hevey (1993), uses a disability or any ailment as 'a metaphor and a symbol for a socially unacceptable person'. Unlike the inclusive agenda of the social model, it is negative misrepresentations of disability like the medical model that aim to alienate and practically demonise disabled people. Hevey sees this kind of ostracism as naturalising the exclusion of disability, which of course stalls the plight of the social model.

Hevey's perception of disability harks back to the way in which disability has been regarded historically. Before the emergence of the social model, the prejudice against people with disabilities was commonplace. The social model has reversed this preconception of disability and through its ethos, together with other emancipatory concepts and legislation, prejudice of disability has become far less prevalent.

The historical integrity of certain areas within society is, however, in danger of being impinged upon by this otherwise positive and egalitarian movement. The shift towards a more inclusive societal approach has involved a radical increase in disability-related legislature effectively instructing changes upon the physical constructs of society to enable greater autonomy amongst people with disabilities. According to the Approved Document Part M, which ensures planners and developers adhere to current building regulations, the requirements of the document are met by 'making reasonable provision to ensure that buildings are accessible and usable'. In reference to people regardless of disability, age or gender, the document legislates that they should be able to: 'gain access to buildings and to gain access within buildings and use their facilities, both as visitors and as people who live or work in them ...' (Approved Document Part M, 2000).

Part M is chiefly wholly acceptable within the majority of societal scenarios. However, the document, like the DDA, falls short of recognising the often inappropriateness of many accessibility recommendations within heritage settings. Despite the strict restrictions enforced by listed building statuses, there is a certain amount of flexibility and tolerance around such restrictions which allow for certain alterations to take place. Conservationists are even at times compelled to alter heritage sites for the greater good. A measured and balanced stance has to therefore be maintained in the interest of conservation to ensure well-meaning political correctness is not responsible for the diluting of otherwise enriched, meaningful and genuinely educative heritage experiences.

Conclusion

The fundamental aim of this investigation is to introduce synergy between disablist emancipation and preservation of historical places. This unique standpoint provides immense challenges to both heritage sites and the patience and understanding of people with disabilities. Where this synergy and subsequent balance exists is variable and determinant on the nature and scale of various heritage sites.

This investigation is still very much in its embryonic stages. Theoretically, the grounding and concepts of the investigation, both from a conservational and disability stance, have been broadly set. The next stage is the marrying of these theories pragmatically to the heritage industry, which would be followed by the adoption of 'best practice' approaches in terms of the sensitive installation of accessibility amenities. As with the disabled tourists attitudinal continuum (Appendix A), any such amenities have to be appreciative of both the valid experience provided for disabled visitors to heritage sites as well as being mindful of our duties as custodians of sites of historic interest. The second continuum (Appendix B) projects the need for a balanced approach in the maintaining of the integrity of heritage along with the onset of objectivist authenticity, in terms of Wang's approach. The continuum represents satisfactory levels of alterations imposed on heritage sites by accessibility amenities, whilst also representing at the opposing end levels of unsatisfactory infringement likely to cause irreversible inroads into traditional aesthetics.

By adopting a politically correct approach, some heritage sites, given the lack of advice as to how to sensibly adapt within this flexibility, could inadvertently be the perpetrators of their own downfall, in terms of causing irreversible degradation to their traditional aesthetics and identities. It is the avoidance of an ideological clash and the determining of an acceptable balance between the autonomy of disabled visitors and the integrity of heritage sites that custodians and society collectively should seek to achieve.

References

Approved Document Part M (2004) Access to and use of buildings. Office of the Deputy Prime Minister.

Boorstin, D.J. (1964) *The Image: A Guide to Pseudo-Events in America*. New York: Atheneum.

Doyle, B. (2003) *Disability Discrimination: Law and Practice* (4th edn). Bristol: Jordans.

Goffman, E. (1959) *The Presentation of Self in Everyday Life*. Garden City, New York: Doubleday.

Goodall, B., Pottinger, G., Dixon, T. and Russell, H. (2005) Access to historic environments for tourists with disabilities: A compromise? *Tourism Review International* 8 (3), 177–194.

Greenwood, D. (1989) Culture by the pound: An anthropological perspective on tourism as cultural commoditization. In V.L. Smith (ed.) *Hosts and Guests: The Anthropology of Tourism* (2nd edn) (pp. 171–185). Philadelphia, PA: University of Pennsylvania Press.

Hevey, D. (1993) From self-love to the picket line: Strategies for change in disability representation. *Disability and Society* 8 (4), 423–429.

HMSO (2003) The Disability Discrimination Act. On WWW at www.legislation. hmso.gov.uk/acts.html. Accessed 5.9.2008.

Kailes, J.I. (2002) Independent living and traditional paradigms. On WWW at www.jik.com/ilcpara.html. Accessed 26.11.08.

MacCannell, D. (1976) *The Tourist: A New Theory of the Leisure Class*. London: MacMillan.

MacCannell, D. (1999) *The Tourist: A New Theory of the Leisure Class*. New York: Schocken Books.

McConkey and McCormack (1983) *Breaking Barriers*. London: Souvenir Press.

Monaghan, K. (2005) *Blackstone's Guide to the Disability Discrimination Legislation*. Oxford: OUP.

Oliver, M. (1986) Social policy and disability: Some theoretical issues. *Disability, Handicap and Society* 1 (1), 5–17.

Pearn, M. (2009) The attitudes of disabled and able-bodied visitors to heritage sites – A case study of Devon and Cornwall. PhD thesis, University of Exeter.

Shakespeare, T. (1998) *The Disability Reader*. London: Cassell.

Silberberg, T. (1995) In A. Apostolakis (2003) The convergence process in heritage tourism. *Annals of Tourism Research* 30 (4), 795–812.

Stumbo, N.J. and Pegg, S. (2005) Travellers and tourists with disabilities: A matter of priorities and loyalties. *Tourism Review International* 8, 195–209.
Swarbrooke, S. and Horner, J. (1999) *Consumer Behaviour in Tourism.* Oxford: Butterworth-Heinenaan.
Tregaskis, C. (2002) Social model theory: The story so far ... *Disability and Society* 17 (4), 457–470.
Wang, N. (1999) Re-thinking authenticity in tourism experience. *Annals of Tourism Research* 26 (2), 349–370.
World Health Organization (1980) *International Classification of Impairments, Disabilities and Handicaps: A Manual of Classification Relating to the Consequences of Disease.* Geneva: World Health Organization.

Appendix A Continuum representing opposing societal treatment of people with disabilities

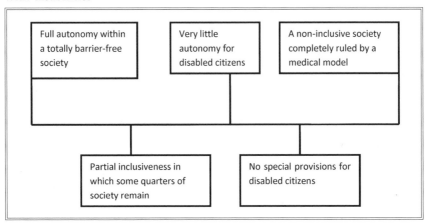

Appendix B Experiential continuum representing the opposing priorities attributed to disabled visitors and the conservational concerns of heritage sites

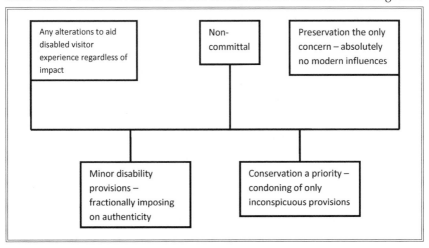

Chapter 14

Economic Contribution of Tourists with Disabilities: An Australian Approach and Methodology

L. DWYER and S. DARCY

This chapter presents the findings of a study into the economic contribution of tourists with disabilities to the Australian economy. The importance of including economic modelling within the research project is that rudimentary market estimates of tourists with disabilities in Australia were undertaken over a decade ago (Darcy, 1998). These estimates used a basic gross demand approach without having any detailed understanding of the expenditure patterns of the group. Further, while more detailed work has been undertaken in the US (HarrisInteractive Market Research, 2003, 2005) and Europe (Buhalis *et al.*, 2005; Neumann & Reuber, 2004) these continued to use basic gross demand estimates rather than any form of sophisticated economic modelling. The framework we use for estimating the economic contribution of tourists with disabilities to Australia employs the Australian Tourism Satellite Account (TSA). First, a brief overview of the data gathered from each of the steps used in the methodology will be presented. Second, an overview of the nature and usefulness of Tourism Satellite Accounting to estimate the economic contribution of a tourism market segment will be provided. Third, the summary findings of the economic modelling are presented, including the expenditure associated with tourists with disabilities and the economic contribution to tourism through Gross Value Added, Tourism Gross Domestic Product and Direct Tourism Employment.

Market Size and Economic Contribution

Globally there are over 650 million people with disabilities, equating to about 10% of humanity (United Nations, 2009). While the World Health Organization provides a framework for collecting disability statistics, the way that nation states define disability, operationalise the definitions, the regularity in which they collect the statistics and the rigour of the existing collections have all been identified as major methodological issues to accurately determining the number of people with disabilities (Fujiura *et al.*, 2005; Fujiura & Rutkowski-Kmitta, 2001). This has led to wide variations in estimating disability numbers particularly between the developed and the developing world. In the Australian context, approximately 20% of the Australian population, or four million people, identify as having a disability – twice the world average. Of these people 520,000 have a mobility disability, 480,000 are blind or vision impaired and 1 million are deaf or hearing impaired (Australian Bureau of Statistics (ABS), 2003). The numbers of people with disabilities are set to increase due to the ageing of the population. The World Health Organization (WHO) (2007) states that by 2020 there will be 1.2 billion people over 60 years of age. The 'greying' of the population has been well documented by the ABS, identified by Tourism Research Australia as a market opportunity (Tourism Australia, 2005), and is a phenomenon that affects all of our major inbound markets. These trends have considerable implications for global tourism (Dwyer, 2005; Dwyer *et al.*, 2004).

Reedy's (1993) seminal book on marketing to people with disabilities was the first to use the powerful population estimate of 43 million Americans to gain the attention of the US business sector. Similarly, Touche Ross (1993) and Keroul (1995) used estimates of disability in the European and Canadian populations to argue the market potential of the group. The first Australian market study was undertaken by Darcy (1998) where he estimated travel by individuals with disabilities was worth $AUS473 million, or their group travel was valued at $AUS1.3 billion. Darcy's (1998) study differed from earlier work by introducing empirical data on travel patterns of the group undertaken in the previous 12 months. His study was modelled on the Bureau of Tourism Research's domestic and international visitor surveys, and applied this to national survey data on the rates of disability in the Australian community (ABS, 1993).

Burnett and Bender-Baker (2001) drew attention to the discretionary income of these groups through nationally collected data. While not linked directly to an economic contribution, Burnett and Bender-Baker made a contribution of understanding people with mobility through their level of disability and the aids that they use. It was not until 2002 and 2005 that the US accessible tourism market used a commissioned market research study by the Open Doors Organisation, which collected travel patterns of people with disabilities. Through these figures it was estimated that people with disabilities contribute $US127 billion to the economy each year with $US13 billion directly attributed to travel (HarrisInteractive Market Research, 2005). Van Horn (2007) recently presented a more detailed analysis of this data as it related to the quantum of travel patterns, transportation generally and in air travel particularly. The study concluded by alluding to the market opportunity without developing the gross demand estimates any further. Similarly, Neumann and Reuber

(2004) estimated German tourists make a €2.5 billion contribution to the economy where the European Union countries' OSSATE (One-Stop-Shop for Accessible Tourism in Europe) research estimated that tourists with disabilities contribute €80 billion to the economy using gross demand estimates (Buhalis *et al.*, 2005). From an inbound perspective, it has been estimated that 7–8% of international travellers have a disability and it is this group who directly contribute to increased Gross Domestic Product (GDP) to the economy (Darcy, 2003; HarrisInteractive Market Research, 2005).

To this point, the only method that has been used is gross demand with the addition of applying specifically collected travel patterns. These methods are rudimentary, not based on expenditure patterns and are not regarded as economically robust (Dwyer *et al.*, 2004). This research project offered the opportunity to utilise the Tourism Satellite Accounts, National Visitor Survey and the Disability, Ageing and Carers Survey (Darcy, 2003; Dwyer *et al.*, 2007).

Research Design

This research project offered the opportunity to use the Australian Tourism Satellite Account (TSA) to estimate the economic contribution of accessibility tourism to Australia (Dwyer *et al.*, 2007). A number of steps and associated data sources required to accomplish the task are outlined in Table 14.1. The research design undertook the following steps:

Step 1: utilised the most recent ABS (2004) *Disability, Ageing and Carers* survey. Figure 14.1 illustrates the numbers and proportion of the Australian population with and without disabilities.

Step 2: updated the ABS (2004) statistics to the ABS (2007) Australian population estimates.

Step 3: drew on the Tourism Satellite Accounts to provide the expenditure associated with different tourist markets and the baseline contribution of tourism to the economy.

Step 4: utilised the National Visitor Survey, which included a disability module in 1998 and 2003, to undertake expenditure analysis in aggregate and on the goods and services purchased by tourists with disabilities. Tourism Research Australia provided the data in SPSS format.

Step 5: used the data from Steps 1–4, in association with the Australian TSA, to convert the expenditure data into estimated contribution in respect of key economic variables such as Tourism Direct Gross Value Added (TDGVA), Tourism Direct Gross Domestic Product (TDGDP) and tourism direct employment.

Table 14.1 Steps and data sources for economic modelling

Requirement	Source
1. Data must be available on Australians with disabilities	Disability, Ageing and Carers survey (ABS, 2004)
2. Data must be available on the Australian population estimates	Australian Demographic Statistics (ABS, 2007)
3. Data must be available on the overall economic contribution of tourism to Australia	(Tourism Research Australia, 2006),
4. Data must be available on the expenditure associated with tourists with disabilities both in aggregate and in respect of the types of goods and services that they purchase (i.e. their expenditure patterns)	National Visitor Survey (Bureau of Tourism Research, 2003)
5. The expenditure data must be converted into estimated contribution of key economic variables such as Gross Value Added (GVA), Gross Domestic Product (GDP) and employment	Carried out through TSA

Findings and Discussion

Figure 14.1 shows the numbers and percentages of the Australian population with and without disability and by type of disability. Some four million Australians or 20% of the population identified as having a disability. Of this group, half (9.8% of the population) have 'profound', 'severe' or 'moderate' levels of support needs to carry out activities of daily living.

Step 1: Australians with disabilities – Disability, Ageing and Carers survey 2003

The Disability, Ageing and Carers survey presents the most recent statistics on disability and ageing within the Australian population (ABS, 2004). Figure 14.1 illustrates the numbers and proportion of the Australian population with and without disabilities, while Figure 14.2 provides a breakdown of the level of core activity restriction of those identifying as having a disability on a spectrum of limitation from without to profound. What needs to be recognised is that the framework for collecting

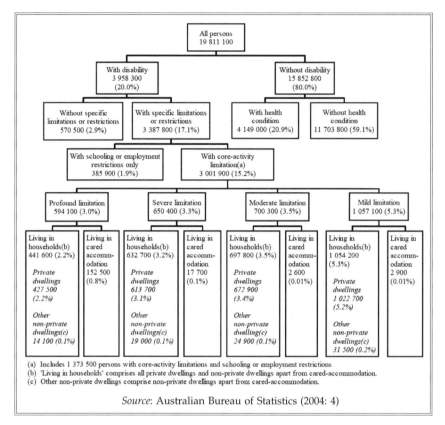

Figure 14.1 Australians with and without disabilities

these figures is based on the International Classification of Impairments, Disabilities and Handicaps (ICIDH) (WHO, 1997) and although the WHO had moved towards a bio-psychosocial approach (WHO, 2001) most national systems of data collection have retained the medical classification system of ICIDH.

To comprehend the statistics requires an understanding of the terminology of impairment, disability and dimensions of access. As discussed in Chapter 2, a person's impairment is conceptualised as the embodiment of the individual that within the statistics is referred to as the individual's limitations. Whereas *disability* is defined as a complex set of *social relationships* imposed on top of a person's impairment due to the way society is organised. Hence, disability is the product of the social relationships that produce *disabling barriers* and *hostile social attitudes* that exclude, segregate and oppress people with disabilities and deny them their rights of citizenship. The social model regards disability as the product of the social, economic and political relationships (*the social relations*) rather than locating it as the fault of an individual's impairment (embodiment). This approach to disability separates impairment from the social relations of disability (Oliver, 1990).

A social or citizenship approach would suggest that level of support needs refers to the support an individual requires for social participation. This re-conceptualisation of limitation to a social, economic and political issue focuses on supporting an individual through the creation of enabling environments and attitudes for social participation. As outlined within the ABS statistics the major area of support needs include: a) schooling/ employment; or b) core activities including meal preparation; property maintenance; housework; transport; paperwork; health care; cognition or emotion; communication; mobility and self care.

Further, as described by Darcy (1998, 2002), the support needs of people need to be seen in context of the dimension of access to facilitate social participation. The most common dimensions of access described in the literature include:

- mobility;
- sensory–hearing;
- sensory–vision;
- cognitive/learning/communication;
- environmental sensitivities (including asthma, chemical, etc.).

The dimensions of access provide a focus for enabling social participation. The complexity of understanding the market includes recognising that the individual's impairment may mean that an individual has multiple dimensions of access, which require multiple levels of accessibility for social participation. For example, a person with an impairment like cerebral palsy may have a mobility dimension and use a wheelchair or crutches; they may also have a communication dimension through an associated speech impairment for which they use a communication board. Depending on their level of independence with personal care, they may also travel with an attendant. This person requires an accessible physical environment as well as assistant technologies and social policy inclusions. This person's access requirements are different to a person with arthritis who has a basic requirement for a continuous pathway that includes handrails to assist in weight bearing, seats to provide a resting area, universal handles on doorways and taps to assist with reduced dexterity. As Figure 14.2 and Figure 14.3 demonstrate, of those identifying as having a disability there is a reasonably even proportion of each level of support needs.

Apart from demonstrating the potential market size of the group, the ABS data provides a sophisticated understanding of the market through what Buhalis *et al.* (2005) described as the disability pyramid. Figure 14.4

No Restriction 4.8%	Mild 5.3%	Moderate 3.5%	Severe 3.3%	Prof'd 3.0%
All with a Disability – 4.1 million or 20% of Population				

Source: Australian Bureau of Statistics (2004)

Figure 14.2 Level of support needs within the disability cohort

illustrates an adaptation of the disability pyramid concept, based on a scaled representation of the support needs identified in the ABS (2004) statistics. The shape may be more like a set of irregular Lego blocks than a 'pyramid' where each dimension of access can be considered a 'pillar' supporting the efforts of citizenship. The pillars have been extended to specifically refer to the relationship between ageing, seniors and disability as well as understanding that some disabilities are invisible. Invisibility refers to those people who do not have any external signifiers of their disability, for example, a person with learning disabilities is unable to be identified visually where a wheelchair user or a blind person with a guide dog can be visually identified as having a disability. While there is a focus on the dimensions of access, one of the most significant constraints identified across disability studies is the attitudes of non-disabled people and the industry towards people with disabilities.

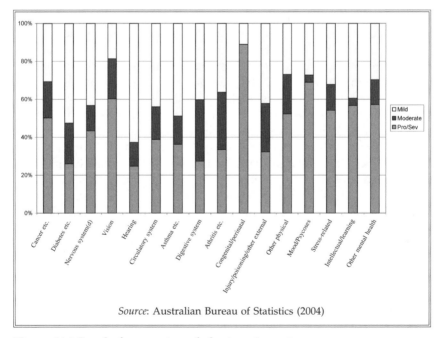

Source: Australian Bureau of Statistics (2004)

Figure 14.3 Level of support needs by impairment

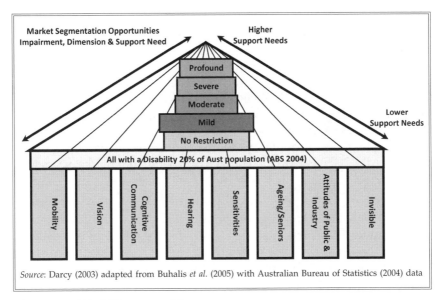

Figure 14.4 Disability pyramid

Step 2: Updated population estimate to the 2007 figures

Step 2 updated the ABS (2004) statistics to the ABS (2007) Australian population estimates, where the Australian population had increased to 20.6 million.

Step 3: Tourism satellite account's estimation of the contribution of tourism to the economy

Step 3 drew on the Australian TSA to provide the baseline contribution of tourism to the economy. This was regarded as the most valid and reliable source of tourism's contribution to the economy.

Tourism Satellite Accounts are based on the accounts for industries which are reported in the National Accounts. It is argued that tourism accounts for a proportion of the outputs of a range of industries which are explicitly recorded in the accounts. Thus tourism might account for 90% of 'Accommodation', 80% of 'Air Transport', 30% of 'Ground Transport' and say, 5% of 'Retail Trade'. Thus the outputs of these industries which can be attributed to 'Tourism' are estimated and aggregated, to obtain an estimate of the output of 'Tourism'. In a similar way, the Gross Value Added associated with tourism, the GDP, employment and other aggregates can be calculated. The result is a set of accounts documenting output, value added, employment and so forth for the tourism industry, consisting of the sum of the various parts of other industries which are attributable to tourism.

Satellite accounts allow an understanding of the size and role of activities which are not separately identified in the conventional national accounting framework. They enable the estimation of macroeconomic aggregates that describe the size and the economic contribution of tourism, such as Tourism Direct Gross Value Added (TDGVA) and Tourism Direct Gross Domestic Product (TDGDP), consistent with similar aggregates for the total economy, and for other productive economic activities and functional areas of interest.

The expenditure attributed to tourism from the Australian TSA for 2003–04 (ABS, 2005) is $75.793bn broken down into four market segments:

Overnight	$A40.9bn
Day trips	$A12.0bn
Inbound	$A20.5bn
Outbound	$A3.6bn

Step 4: National Visitor Survey expenditure patterns

Step 4 utilised the National Visitor Survey, which included a disability module in 1998 and 2003, to undertake expenditure analysis in aggregate and on the goods and services that tourists with disabilities purchased. Tourism Research Australia provided the data in SPSS format so that further statistical work could be undertaken. Part of the statistical work was to provide a comparison between people with disabilities and the general population.

The Australian Government's *White Paper* identified accessible tourism as part of its niche experiences that were comprised of people with disabilities and seniors. However, very little is known statistically about the accessible tourism market. Some limited *ad hoc* studies had been carried out on mainly people with mobility disabilities (Darcy, 1998; Murray & Sproats, 1990). More recently, there have been a number of studies that have investigated the experiences of people across the spectrum of disability groups (Access For All Alliance–Hervey Bay Inc., 2006; Darcy, 2003; Market and Communication Research, 2002). However, only one paper drew on the National Visitor Survey that included the disability module in 1998 (Darcy, 2003). Since that paper, the more recent National Visitor Survey 2003 data became available for analysis. This chapter draws on the expenditure of those people that identified as having a disability. Some comparative analysis between those identifying as having a disability and the non-disabled will now be presented as a lead in to the Australian TSA estimates.

Figure 14.5 shows the major market segments identified by the National Visitor Survey (2003) and presents the comparison between disability and the non-disabled. It shows that tourists with disabilities (referred to as PWD in Figure 14.5) are part of every market segment with variation

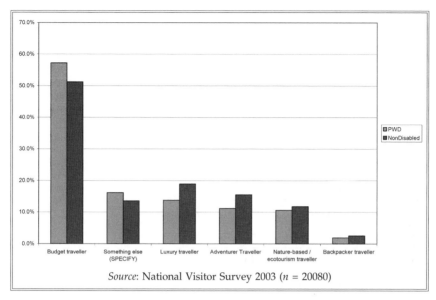

Figure 14.5 Market segment comparison – disability (PWD) and non-disabled

between the segments. Tourists with disabilities make up a higher proportion of budget travellers and 'something else', and make up notionally smaller proportions of luxury, adventure and nature-based travellers. Moreover, when a person with a disability travels on an overnight trip, they are in a group of between two to eight people ($\bar{x} = 3$) where they are the only member of the group with a disability. From a management perspective not being able to accommodate the person with a disability means that the business is missing out on the expenditure for the whole group, and not just that of the individual. While it is acknowledged that there are higher rates of underemployment for people with disabilities, their expenditure on overnight trips ($\bar{x} = \$444$) is less than their non-disabled ($\bar{x} = \$582$) counterparts. Proportionally, tourists with disabilities had 76% of the spend of their non-disabled counterparts. On average they had five trips away annually as opposed to seven trips to the non-disabled, where on average they spent 4.98 nights away as opposed to 4.22 nights for the non-disabled. The different patterns of travel between people with disabilities and the non-disabled, group size, total spend and nights away were all significant to the 99% level ($p = .000$).

As Table 14.2 and 14.3 demonstrate, based on the National Visitor Survey expenditure data, people identifying as having a disability had the following patterns of expenditure for overnight and day trips.

It should be noted that no pattern of expenditure data is available for inbound or outbound tourists with disabilities. However, it was decided that for the purpose of modelling expenditure for these groups, their

Table 14.2 Pattern of accessible tourist consumption (overnight)

Pattern of Domestic Tourist Consumption	*Percentage*
Taxis (including to/from airport)	0.81
Airline fares	9.95
Organised tours/side trips	1.33
Car hire costs (rental, leasing)	2.01
Fuel (petrol, diesel)	12.60
Vehicle maintenance or repairs	0.99
Other long distance transport costs (train, coach, ship etc.)	0.77
Other local transport costs (bus, train, tram, ferry etc.)	0.60
Accommodation (can include food e.g. breakfast if included)	21.62
Takeaways and restaurant meals	14.83
Groceries etc. for self-catering	6.77
Alcohol, drinks (not already reported with food above)	4.08
Shopping, gifts, souvenirs	11.59
Entertainment, museums, movies, zoos etc.	2.44
Horse racing, gambling, casinos	1.33
Conference fees	1.64
Education, course fees	0.41
Purchase of motor vehicles or any other major equipment	1.78
Other (phone, postage, medical expenses, repairs, dry cleaning etc.)	5.45
	100%

Source: Purchasing pattern percentages from National Visitor Survey (2003)

expenditure patterns would replicate that of overnight travel shown in Table 14.2. The next section presents the estimates of economic contribution based on this data.

Step 5: Estimating the economic contribution

Step 5 used the data from Steps 1–4, in association with the Australian TSA, to convert the expenditure data into estimated contribution in respect of key economic variables such as Gross Value Added (GVA), Gross

Table 14.3 Pattern of accessible tourist consumption (day trips)

Pattern of Day-tripper Consumption	*Percentage*
Package (e.g. transport and show)	0.12
Taxis (including to/from airport)	0.20
Airline fares	0.86
Organised tours/side trips	0.36
Car hire costs (rental, leasing)	0.07
Fuel (petrol, diesel)	22.07
Vehicle maintenance or repairs	0.54
Other long distance transport costs (train, coach, ship, etc.)	0.58
Other local transport costs (bus, train, tram, ferry, etc.)	0.69
Takeaways and restaurant meals	15.16
Groceries etc. for self-catering	8.06
Alcohol, drinks (not already reported with food above)	3.55
Shopping, gifts, souvenirs	31.36
Entertainment, museums, movies, zoos, etc.	2.55
Horse racing, gambling, casinos	1.61
Conference fees	0.57
Education, course fees	0.01
Purchase of motor vehicles or any other major equipment	2.18
Other (phone, postage, medical expenses, repairs, dry cleaning, etc.)	9.41
	100%

Source: Purchasing pattern percentages from National Visitor Survey (2003)

Domestic Product (GDP) and employment. We distinguish tourists with disabilities who are (1) inbound (international) visitors and (2) domestic visitors. Domestic visitation can be further divided into overnight visitation and day-trippers.

We have estimated the expenditure data associated with tourists with disabilities for each of these markets. Given the paucity of data related to expenditure by people with disabilities we use a combination of a 'top down' and 'bottom up' approach to estimating the economic contribution made by the accessible tourism market.

Overnight Visitation

Scenario 1: As set out in Appendix 1 Table A1, the National Visitor Survey data indicates that 11% of all people who took overnight trips in 2003 identified themselves as having a disability (Bureau of Tourism Research, 2003). Applying this figure to the national TSA data for domestic overnight tourism we derive a figure of $4822.390 million for expenditure associated with overnight tourism by tourists with disabilities. This information is set out in Table 14.4. We refer to the 11% scenario for overnight visitation as Scenario 1. This expenditure does not include expenditure by other members of the travel party.

Scenario 2: The number of people with disabilities in Australia is estimated to be 20% of the population (ABS, 2004). Based upon the 2007 population estimates, this implies that the potential number of tourists with disabilities who may travel domestically is 4,134,880 (ABS, 2007). Only a proportion of these people do in fact travel and only a proportion are overnight tourists. As set out in Appendix 1 Table A1, the National Visitor Survey data indicates that 22% of people with disabilities recall taking a trip in the past three months (Bureau of Tourism Research, 2003). However, this does not inform us as to how many trips were taken. People can make multiple trips and no information is provided on this. Accordingly, it seems appropriate for us to use the very same procedure as used in the TSA, that is, a pro rata method of allocation. Thus, assuming 20% of the population comes under the definition of having a disability one might expect that (other things equal) 20% of all overnight tourism would be by people with disabilities. Since the national TSA (ABS, 2005) indicates that for 2003–2004 overnight visitor expenditure in Australia was $43.8 billion then 20% of this is $8767.982 billion. This scenario represents the maximum expenditure associated with overnight tourists with disabilities as it assumes they have the same travel behaviour as the total population.

Day Trips

As set out in Appendix 1 Table A2, the National Visitor Survey data indicates that 13.3% of all day trips were taken by persons identifying as having a disability. Assuming that people with disabilities spend the same amount as other day-trippers we estimate day-tripper expenditure by persons with a disability as 13.3% of total day trip expenditure for Australia ($12.007 billion). This comes to $1.596 billion for the year 2003-04.

Table 14.4 shows the breakdown of expenditure using the data from the National Visitor Survey (2003). The main expenditure item is shopping items (souvenirs etc.) at 31.36%, followed by fuel (22.07%), which obviously mostly covers petrol expenses for car use on the day trips, and thence takeaway and restaurant meals (15.16%). These are the three sectors that gain most sales revenues from day-tripper tourists with disabilities, accounting for just under 70% of day-tripper expenditure on either scenario.

Outbound Tourism

The national TSA for 2003–2004 indicates that outbound tourism was $3269.0 million. As set out in Appendix 1 Table A3, the National Visitor Survey data indicates that the proportion of tourists with disabilities among all outbound travellers from Australia was 6.8%. Thus, it is estimated that expenditure associated to outbound tourists with disabilities is $222.29 million. No data is available on the expenditure patterns of outbound travellers who have a disability. Data on expenditure patterns for all outbound travellers was estimated by the Sustainable Tourism Cooperative Research Centre (STCRC) in its construction of TSA for Australia 2003–2004 (Dwyer *et al.*, 2007). In the absence of other data this expenditure pattern was used to allocate outbound tourism by tourists with disabilities to the expenditure items as shown in Table 14.4.

Inbound Tourism

While Australia has very detailed data on inbound tourism expenditure unfortunately there is no data available on either the numbers of inbound tourists who have a disability nor their expenditure in Australia. An assumption was made that the proportion of tourists with disabilities who visit Australia is unlikely to be less than 6.8% of all inbound visitation. This figure is also consistent with the proportion of tourists with disabilities who travel from Australia to international destinations (outbound). Further, this is consistent with the most recent US figures that suggest 7% of Americans with disabilities travel overseas each year (Open Doors Organization, 2005). In 2003, inbound tourism injected $20.5bn into Australia. Assuming for present purposes that tourists with disabilities spend 6.8% of the total amount of expenditure in Australia by international tourists, their expenditure is estimated to be $1.394bn. In the absence of any further data it was also assumed that their spending pattern conformed to the average for all tourists to Australia. Data on this is available from Tourism Research Australia (TRA) and used by the STCRC in its development of TSA for Australia. Estimated expenditure by inbound tourists with disabilities in total and by expenditure item is also shown in Table 14.4. Table 14.4 presents a summary of the expenditure of tourists with disabilities to overnight, day-tripper, out-bound and inbound travel; that constitute the accessible tourism market.

Table 14.4 Expenditure by tourists with disabilities, 2003–04, $m

Expenditure	Day	OVN (1)	OVN (2)	Outbound	Inbound	Total (1)	Total (2)
Travel agency and tour operator services	0.741	63.501	115.457	2.927	18.854	86.023	137.979
Taxi fares	3.204	38.676	70.319	1.783	9.462	53.124	84.768
Long distance passenger transportation	23.652	511.844	930.626	23.594	375.731	934.821	1353.603
Motor vehicle hire and lease	1.121	95.970	174.492	4.424	21.558	123.073	201.594
Accommodation services	0.000	1032.277	1876.867	47.583	172.747	1252.607	2097.198
Takeaway and restaurant meals	242.837	708.082	1287.422	32.639	125.007	1108.565	1687.905
Shopping (including gifts and souvenirs)	502.333	553.379	1006.144	25.508	171.750	1252.971	1705.736
Local area passenger transportation	11.334	28.650	52.091	1.321	19.708	61.012	84.453
Repair and maintenance of motor vehicles	8.650	47.269	85.944	2.179	1.281	59.379	98.054
Fuel (petrol, diesel)	353.523	601.603	1093.824	27.731	16.435	999.292	1491.513
Food products	129.107	323.245	587.718	14.900	98.896	566.148	830.621
Alcoholic beverages and other beverages	56.865	194.805	354.192	8.980	48.736	309.386	468.772
Motor vehicles, caravans, boats, etc.	34.920	84.990	154.527	3.918	12.451	136.279	205.816
Recreational, cultural and sports services	51.033	194.805	354.192	8.980	32.728	287.546	446.932
Gambling and betting services	25.789	63.501	115.457	2.927	14.443	106.661	158.617
Education	0.160	19.574	35.589	0.902	158.020	178.656	194.671
Actual and imputed rent on holiday houses	0.000	0.000	0.000	0.000	26.609	26.609	26.609
Other tourism goods and services	150.732	260.216	473.121	11.995	69.583	492.526	705.430
Total	1596.000	4822.390	8767.982	222.290	1394.000	8034.680	11980.272

Note: OVN (1) refers to scenario 1 (disabled OVN expenditure is 11% of total OVN); OVN (2) refers to scenario 2 (disabled OVN expenditure is 20% of total OVN). Total (1) is total figure using OVN (1) and Total (2) is total figure using OVN (2)

Purchasing Patterns

National Visitor Survey data is available on the purchasing patterns of tourists with disabilities in respect of both overnight tourists and day-trippers (Bureau of Tourism Research, 2003). This information was essential in allocating disability expenditure to relevant industries to estimate its economic contribution (see below). National Visitor Survey data categorises tourist expenditure as including (1) paid during the trip,

(2) paid before and/or after the trip and (3) paid for by an employer. For present purposes, since our interest is in total expenditure, the expenditure data was aggregated. The percentage allocations are reflected in the proportions of the expenditure items for overnight visitors and day-trippers. See Tables 14.2 and 14.3 which provide an itemised breakdown of the total expenditure of overnight tourists with disabilities for 2003. These percentages were applied to estimate the total expenditure allocated by overnight tourists with disabilities to individual products and services.

The main expenditure item for tourists with disabilities is accommodation (16.5%), followed by shopping (13.8%), takeaway and restaurant meals (13.90%) and fuel (12.3%). These are the sectors that gain most sales revenues from tourists with disabilities, accounting for around 57% of overnight tourism expenditure for tourists with disabilities.

In Table 14.4, the figure of $4822.39 for overnight tourist expenditure (Scenario 1) is based on the percentage of tourists with disabilities among all those who actually took trips in Australia in 2003. As such it can be regarded as a lower limit to the potential economic contribution of disability tourism to the Australian economy. On the other hand, the figure of $8767.982 million for overnight tourism for tourists with disabilities (Scenario 2) may be regarded as a 'maximum'. It assumes that tourists with disabilities have the same travel patterns for overnight visitation as the rest of the population. This figure provides a 'maximum' value for overnight tourism by tourists with disabilities and sets the potential to which stakeholders might aspire to if tourism experiences are to be accessed by people with disabilities to the same degree as the rest of the population.

Thus, we believe that these two scenarios reflect an 'actual' or 'best estimate' scenario and a 'maximum' scenario. Knowing the maximum potential for tourists with disabilities market is a useful indicator of possible lost opportunities to the tourism industry by not putting sufficient strategies in place to facilitate more tourism from this market.

Expenditure Associated with Tourists with Disabilities

To this point we have estimated the expenditure associated with tourists with disabilities in Australia for 2003–2004. In summary:

Scenario 1

Overnight tourism	$4822.390 million
Day-tripper tourism	$1596.000 million
Outbound tourism	$222.290 million
Inbound tourism	$1394.000 million
TOTAL Scenario 1	**$8034.680 million**

Scenario 2

Overnight tourism	$8767.982 million
Day-tripper tourism	$1596.000 million
Outbound tourism	$222.290 million
Inbound tourism	$1394.000 million
TOTAL Scenario 2	**$11,980.000 million**

Contribution to Tourism Gross Value Added

Contribution to Tourism GVA is the best available measure of the contribution of any tourism market to the tourism industry and the economy. Table 14.5 shows the contribution to Gross Value Added of each

Table 14.5 Contribution to tourism GVA by tourists with disabilities, 2003–04, $m

Industry	Day	OVN (1)	OVN (2)	Outbound	Inbound	Total (1)	Total (2)
Travel agency and tour operator services	0.430	36.856	67.010	1.699	10.943	49.927	80.082
Taxi transport	1.277	15.416	28.029	0.711	3.772	21.176	33.789
Air and water transport	10.762	166.271	302.312	7.663	121.648	306.344	442.385
Motor vehicle hiring	0.590	50.521	91.856	2.329	11.349	64.788	106.124
Accommodation	0.000	518.253	942.280	23.890	86.728	628.872	1052.898
Cafes, restaurants and food outlets	63.441	184.990	336.347	8.526	32.659	289.616	440.973
Clubs, pubs, taverns and bars	19.515	56.905	103.465	2.623	10.046	89.090	135.650
Other road transport	2.185	33.750	61.364	1.555	24.692	62.183	89.797
Rail transport	1.171	18.095	32.900	0.834	13.239	33.339	48.144
Food manufacturing	18.026	45.133	82.060	2.081	13.808	79.048	115.976
Beverage manufacturing	9.582	32.825	59.681	1.513	8.212	52.131	78.988
Transport equipment manufacturing	4.841	14.695	26.719	0.677	1.526	21.740	33.763
Other manufacturing	67.263	94.567	171.940	4.360	17.224	183.414	260.787
Retail trade	181.277	254.863	463.386	11.750	46.421	494.310	702.833
Casinos and other gambling services	4.099	10.094	18.352	0.465	2.296	16.954	25.213
Libraries, museums and arts	8.533	32.573	59.223	1.501	5.473	48.080	74.730
Other entertainment services	8.147	31.102	56.548	1.434	5.225	45.908	71.355
Education	0.110	13.520	24.582	0.623	109.143	123.395	134.457
Ownership of dwellings	0.000	0.000	0.000	0.000	21.757	21.757	21.757
All other industries	162.625	228.640	415.708	10.541	41.645	443.450	630.519
Total	563.875	1839.069	3343.765	84.774	587.806	3075.523	4580.219

of the separate markets for disabled tourism and also in total. The overall contribution to Gross Value Added is $3075.523 million (Scenario 1) or $4580.219 million (Scenario 2).

Total Contribution to Tourism Gross Value Added

Comparing our results with estimates of the contribution of Tourism to GVA we find that tourism by tourists with disabilities ranges between $3075.523 million (Scenario 1) and $4580.219 million (Scenario 2), or 10.47% and 17.39% of Tourism GVA, indicating its importance as a tourism market. The contribution of each market type to Tourism GVA is as follows:

Scenario 1

Overnight tourism	$1839.069 million
Day-tripper tourism	$563.875 million
Outbound tourism	$84.774 million
Inbound tourism	$587.806 million
TOTAL Scenario 1	**$3075.523 million**

Scenario 2

Overnight tourism	$3343.765 million
Day-tripper tourism	$563.875 million
Outbound tourism	$84.774 million
Inbound tourism	$587.806 million
TOTAL Scenario 2	**$4580.219 million**

The four most important sectors in terms of the contribution to Tourism GVA of tourists with disabilities were:

Accommodation	21%
Retail trade	16%
Air and water transport	10%
Cafes and restaurants	9%
(Non-tourism industries)	13%

Taken together, the five sectors comprised about 70% of the overall contribution to Tourism GVA by tourists with disabilities.

Contribution to Tourism GVA by Tourists with Disabilities by Type of Market

The five sectors that make the largest contribution to Tourism GVA from tourists with disability are set out below (with percentages).

Overnight	Day-tripper	Outbound	Inbound	Total
Accommodation 28%	Retail trade 32%	Accommodation 28%	Education 19%	Accommodation 21%
Retail trade 14%	Other manufacturing 12%	Retail trade 13%	Accommodation 15%	Retail trade 16%
Cafes, restaurants 10%	Cafes, restaurants 11%	Cafes, restaurants 10%	Retail trade 8%	Air and water transport 10%
Air, water transport 9%	Clubs, pubs, taverns 3%	Air, water transport 9%	Cafes, restaurants 6%	Cafes and restaurants 9%
Non-tourism 9%	Non-tourism 29%	Non-tourism 12%	Non-tourism 7%	Non-tourism 14%

Contribution to Tourism GDP

Table 14.6 sets out the contribution that tourists with disabilities make to Tourism GDP. As noted, Tourism GDP is tourism gross value added plus taxes paid less subsidies received on tourism related products as these are reflected in prices that visitors actually pay. Taxes on tourism products include the Goods and Services Tax (GST), wholesale taxes and excise duties on goods supplied to visitors. Tourism GDP will generally have a higher value than tourism value added. Tourism GDP is a satellite account construct to enable a direct comparison with the most widely recognised national accounting aggregate, GDP.

In sum, the contribution of tourists with disabilities to Tourism GDP is:

Scenario 1

Overnight tourism	$2324.989 million
Day-tripper tourism	$800.426 million
Outbound tourism	$107.173 million
Inbound tourism	$652.581 million
TOTAL Scenario 1	**$3885.168 million**

Scenario 2

Overnight tourism	$4227.256 million
Day-tripper tourism	$800.426 million
Outbound tourism	$107.173 million
Inbound tourism	$652.581 million
TOTAL Scenario 2	**$5787.435 million**

Table 14.6 Contribution to tourism GDP by tourists with disabilities, 2003–04, $m

	Day	OVN (1)	OVN (2)	Outbound	Inbound	Total (1)	Total (2)
Tourism GVA (i)	563.875	1839.069	3343.765	84.774	587.806	3075.523	4580.219
Net taxes (ii)	236.551	485.920	883.491	22.399	64.775	809.645	1207.217
Tourism GDP (i) + (ii)	800.426	2324.989	4227.256	107.173	652.581	3885.168	5787.435

Tourism GDP in Australia totalled $35262.0 million in 2003–04 (Australian Bureau of Statistics, 2005). Thus the contribution to Tourism GDP by tourists with disabilities is estimated to range between 11.01% (Scenario 1) and 18.26% (Scenario 2) of total tourism GDP in Australia.

Contribution to Direct Tourism Employment

Table 14.7 shows the contribution to Direct Tourism Employment of each of the separate markets for tourists with disabilities and also in total.

The contribution of each market type to Direct Tourism Employment is as follows:

Scenario 1

Overnight tourism	31,381 jobs
Day-tripper tourism	10,087 jobs
Outbound tourism	1446 jobs
Inbound tourism	8906 jobs
TOTAL Scenario 1	**51,820 jobs**

Table 14.7 Contribution to Direct Tourism Employment by tourists with disabilities, 2003–04, '000

Industry	Day	OVN (1)	OVN (2)	Outbound	Inbound	Total (1)	Total (2)
Travel agency and tour operator services	0.0071	0.6080	1.1054	0.0280	0.1805	0.8236	1.3210
Road transport and motor vehicle hiring	0.0618	1.3147	2.3903	0.0606	0.5804	2.0175	3.0931
Air and water transport	0.0848	1.3094	2.3806	0.0604	0.9580	2.4124	3.4837
Accommodation	0.0000	10.0944	18.3534	0.4653	1.6893	12.2489	20.5080
Cafes and restaurants	1.0933	3.1880	5.7963	0.1470	0.5628	4.9911	7.5994
Clubs, pubs, taverns and bars	0.4938	1.4399	2.6181	0.0664	0.2542	2.2543	3.4325
Rail transport	0.0074	0.1139	0.2070	0.0052	0.0833	0.2098	0.3029
Manufacturing	0.9789	1.8633	3.3879	0.0859	0.4150	3.3431	4.8676
Retail trade	5.1793	7.2818	13.2396	0.3357	1.3263	14.1231	20.0809
Casinos and other gambling services	0.0519	0.1278	0.2323	0.0059	0.0291	0.2146	0.3191
Libraries, museums and arts	0.1376	0.5254	0.9552	0.0242	0.0883	0.7755	1.2053
Other entertainment services	0.1872	0.7145	1.2991	0.0329	0.1200	1.0546	1.6392
Education	0.0022	0.2673	0.4859	0.0123	2.1575	2.4393	2.6580
All other industries	1.8015	2.5328	4.6051	0.1168	0.4613	4.9124	6.9847
Total tourism employed persons	10.0867	31.3809	57.0562	1.4465	8.9060	51.8201	77.4954

Scenario 2

Overnight tourism	57,056 jobs
Day-tripper tourism	10,087 jobs
Outbound tourism	1446 jobs
Inbound tourism	8906 jobs
TOTAL Scenario 2	**77,495 jobs**

The total contribution of tourists with disabilities to Direct Tourism Employment is 51,820 jobs (Scenario 1) and 77,495 jobs (Scenario 2). Direct Tourism Employment in Australia totalled 448,700 jobs in 2003–04 (Australian Bureau of Statistics, 2005). Thus the contribution to Direct Tourism Employment by tourists with disabilities is estimated to range between 11.55% (Scenario 1) and 17.27% (Scenario 2) of total Direct Tourism Employment in Australia.

Table 14.7 indicates that tourists with disabilities create jobs in all sectors of the economy. The sectors that most benefit from jobs sustained by the tourism industry are:

Retail trade	27.8%
Accommodation	22.0%
Cafes and restaurants	9.5%

That is, just under 60% of the jobs sustained by tourists with disabilities are in these three sectors. This of course reflects the purchasing behaviour of tourists with disabilities.

Conclusion

The paper has firstly brought together three significant secondary data sources to provide a valid and reliable foundation to model the economic contribution of tourists with disabilities. Significant numbers of Australians have disabilities and they still travel. However, the National Visitor Survey data conclusively showed that while tourists with disabilities and the non-disabled travel at the same level for day trips, there is a statistically significant difference in the travel patterns for overnight and for outbound trips. The reason for the difference in travel patterns can be attributed to the increasing complication of travel for tourists with disabilities when they have to stay away from home and require accessible accommodation, accessible transport and accessible destination experiences. The National Visitor Survey data has shown that while they spend comparatively less than the non-disabled they are still an important part of every major market segment. The relative proportion of tourists with disabilities as to the total travel market was determined through these figures and then used in conjunction with the tourism satellite accounts to estimate the economic contribution of tourists with disabilities. In Australia in 2003–04 the economic contribution of tourists with disabilities was estimated as:

- spent between $8034.68 million and $11,980.272 million;
- contributed between $3075.5243 million and $4580.219 million to Tourism Gross Value Added (12.27%-15.60 % of total tourism GVA);
- contributed between $3885.168 million and $5787.435 million to Tourism Gross Domestic Product (11.02%-16.41% of total);
- sustained between 51,820 and 77,495 direct jobs in the tourism industry (11.6%-17.3% of direct tourism employment).

Importantly, what the lower and upper economic estimate demonstrates is that there is a latent demand, with the market having the potential to grow to meet the demand if the barriers to participation are removed. Previous research in Australia and overseas has shown that the market experiences significant constraints above and beyond the general population. If government, the industry and the advocacy sector can develop universal and inclusive strategies to create a more enabling tourism environment, then the market potential can be realised. What this chapter demonstrates is that to undertake a valid and reliable estimation of the economic contribution of the accessible tourism market requires inclusion of disability within national statistical collection frameworks. As has been noted by this paper, Australia is one of the few countries where disability has been included as part of the demographic statistics and as a module by the statutory authority charged with tourism research. It must be conceded, however, that this has been done in an ad hoc fashion in a tourism context where virtually no comparison can be drawn between the 1998, 2003 and the proposed 2009 data sets.

Acknowledgements

The authors would like to thank the Sustainable Tourism Co-Operative Research Centre for the grant on which the research was completed. This chapter draws on the technical report produced from the grant (see references below for full details): *Technical Report 90064: Visitor accessibility in urban centres* by S. Darcy, B. Cameron, L. Dwyer, T. Taylor, E. Wong and A. Thomson.

References

Access for All Alliance (Hervey Bay) Inc (2006) *Survey into the barriers confronted by tourists with disabilities – When making travel arrangements, finding accommodation and visiting tourist venues.* Hervey Bay: Access for All Alliance (Hervey Bay) Inc.
Australian Bureau of Statistics (1993) *Disability, Ageing and Carers, Australia – Summary of Findings (Cat No. 4430.0).* Canberra: Australian Bureau of Statistics.

Australian Bureau of Statistics (2003) *Disability, Ageing and Carers, Australia – Summary of Findings (Cat No. 4430.0).* Canberra: Australian Bureau of Statistics.

Australian Bureau of Statistics (2004) *Disability, Ageing and Carers – Summary of Findings, 2003 (Cat No. 4430.0).* Canberra: Australian Bureau of Statistics.

Australian Bureau of Statistics (2005) *Australian National Accounts: Tourism Satellite Account (Cat. no. 5249.0).* Canberra: Australian Bureau of Statistics.

Australian Bureau of Statistics (2007) *3101.0 – Australian Demographic Statistics, Sep 2006.* Canberra: Australian Bureau of Statistics.

Buhalis, D., Michopoulou, E., Eichhorn, V. and Miller, G. (2005) *Accessibility Market and Stakeholder Analysis – One-Stop-Shop for Accessible Tourism in Europe (OSSATE).* Surrey, United Kingdom: University of Surrey.

Bureau of Tourism Research (2003) National visitor survey: travel by Australians. On WWW at www.btr.gov.au. Accessed 10.9.2007.

Burnett, J.J. and Bender-Baker, H. (2001) Assessing the travel–related behaviors of the mobility-disabled consumer. *Journal of Travel Research* 40 (1), 4–11.

Darcy, S. (1998) *Anxiety to Access: Tourism Patterns and Experiences of New South Wales People with a Physical Disability.* Sydney: Tourism New South Wales.

Darcy, S. (2002) Marginalised participation: Physical disability, high support needs and tourism. *Journal of Hospitality and Tourism Management* 9 (1), 61–72.

Darcy, S. (2003, 5–8 February) Disabling journeys: The tourism patterns of people with impairments in Australia. Paper presented at the Riding the Wave of Tourism and Hospitality Research, CAUTHE – Southern Cross University, Lismore.

Darcy, S., Cameron, B., Dwyer, L., Taylor, T., Wong, E. and Thomson, A. (2008) Technical Report 90064: Visitor accessibility in urban centres. Sustainable Tourism Cooperative Research Centre, Gold Coast. On WWW at http://www.crctourism.com.au/BookShop/BookDetail.aspx?d=626. Accessed 7.2007.

Dwyer, L. (2005) Trends underpinning global tourism in the coming decade. In W. Theobald (ed.) *Global Tourism* (pp. 529–545). Burlington, MA: Butterworth Heinemann.

Dwyer, L., Deery, M., Jago, L., Spurr, R. and Fredline, L. (2007) Adapting the tourism satellite account conceptual framework to measure the economic importance of the meetings industry. *Tourism Analysis* 12 (4), 247–255.

Dwyer, L., Forsyth, P. and Spurr, R. (2004) Evaluating tourism's economic effects: new and old approaches. *Tourism Management* 25 (3), 307–317.

Fujiura, G.T., Park, H.J. and Rutkowski-Kmitta, V. (2005) Disability statistics in the developing world: A reflection on the meanings in our numbers. *Journal of Applied Research in Intellectual Disabilities* 18 (4), 295–304.

Fujiura, G.T. and Rutkowski-Kmitta, V. (2001) Counting disability. In G.L. Albrecht, K.D. Seelman and M. Bury (eds) *Handbook of Disability Studies* (pp. 69–96). Thousand Oaks, CA: Sage Publications.

HarrisInteractive Market Research (2003) *Research among adults with disabilities – travel and hospitality.* Chicago: Open Doors Organization.

HarrisInteractive Market Research (2005) *Research among adults with disabilities – travel and hospitality.* Chicago: Open Doors Organization.

Keroul (1995) *Tourism for People with Restricted Physical Ability.* Quebec: Keroul.

Market and Communication Research (2002) *People with disabilities: A market research report.* Brisbane: Tourism Queensland – Special Interest Tourism Unit.

Murray, M. and Sproats, J. (1990) The disabled traveller: Tourism and disability in Australia. *Journal of Tourism Studies* 1 (1), 9–14.

Neumann, P. and Reuber, P. (2004) Economic impulses of accessible tourism for all (Vol. 526). Berlin: Study commissioned by the Federal Ministry of Economics and Technology & Federal Ministry of Economic and Labour (BMWA).

Oliver, M. (1990) *The Politics of Disablement*. Basingstoke, Houndmills: Macmillan.

Open Doors Organization (2005) *Researching Among Adults with Disabilities: Travel and Hospitality*. Chicago: Open Doors Organization, Travel Industry Association of America and Harrisinteractive.

Reedy, J. (1993) *Marketing to Consumers with Disabilities: How to Identify and Meet the Growing Market Needs of 43 Million Americans*. Chicago, IL: Probus Pub Co.

Touche Ross (1993) *Profiting from Opportunities – A New Market for Tourism*. London: Touche Ross & Co.

Tourism Australia (2005) Mature-aged travellers in Australia: Snapshot. On WWW at http://www.tourism.australia.com/Research.asp?lang=EN&sub=0361. Accessed 26.9.2006.

Tourism Research Australia (2006) Contribution of tourism to the Australian economy. On WWW at http://www.ret.gov.au/tourism/tra/Pages/default.aspx. Accessed 26.9.2007.

United Nations (2009) Fact sheet on persons with disabilities. On WWW at http://www.un.org/disabilities/default.asp?id=18. Accessed 1.3.2009.

Van Horn, L. (2007) Disability travel in the United States: Recent research and findings. Paper presented at the 11th International Conference on Mobility and Transport for Elderly and Disabled Persons (TRANSED) – 'Benchmarking, Evaluation and Vision for the Future', June 18–22, 2007, at the Palais des congrès de Montréal.

World Health Organization (1997) *International Classification of Impairments, Disabilities and Handicaps (ICIDH)*. Geneva: World Health Organization.

World Health Organization (2001) *International Classification of Functioning, Disability and Health (ICIDH-2)*. Geneva: World Health Organization.

World Health Organization (2007) Global age-friendly cities guide. At http://www.who.int/ageing/age_friendly_cities/en/index.html.

Appendix 1 Economic contribution tables

Table A1 People with disabilities taking an overnight trip in last 28 days

			Whether respondent has a disability			Total
			Yes	No	Refused	Yes
Had overnight trip in last 28 days	Yes (at least one in-scope trip)	Count	0	3823	23	4314
		% within had overnight trip in last 28 days	10.8%	88.6%	.5%	100.0%
		% within whether respondent has a disability	22.1%	27.8%	13.9%	26.9%
	No	Count	1651	9947	142	11740
		% within had overnight trip in last 28 days	14.1%	84.7%	1.2%	100.0%
		% within whether respondent has a disability	77.9%	72.2%	86.1%	
Total		Count	2119	13770	165	16054
		% within had overnight trip in last 28 days	13.2%	85.8%	1.0%	100.0%
		% within whether respondent has a disability	100.0%	100.0%	100.0%	100.0%

Source: National Visitor Survey 2003 data set analysed for this study–had overnight trip in last 28 days * whether respondent has a disability cross-tabulation

Table A2 People with disabilities taking a day trip in last 7 days

			Whether respondent has a disability			Total
			Yes	No	Refused	Yes
Had day trip in last 7 days	Yes (at least one in-scope trip)	Count	309	2009	9	2327
		% within had day trip in last 7 days	13.3%	86.3%	.4%	100.0%
		% within whether respondent has a disability	14.6%	14.6%	5.5%	14.5%
	No	Count	1810	11760	155	13725
		% within had day trip in last 7 days	13.2%	85.7%	1.1%	100.0%
		% within whether respondent has a disability	85.4%	85.4%	94.5%	85.5%
Total		Count	2119	13769	164	16052
		% within had day trip in last 7 days	13.2%	85.8%	1.0%	100.0%
		% within whether respondent has a disability	100.0%	100.0%	100.0%	100.0%

Source: National Visitor Survey 2003 data set analysed for this study–had overnight trip in last 28 days * whether respondent has a disability cross-tabulation

Table A3 People with disabilities taking an outbound trip in last 90 days

			Whether respondent has a disability			Total
			Yes	No	Refused	Yes
Had outbound trip in last 90 days	Yes (at least one in-scope trip)	Count	57	776	4	837
		% within had outbound trip in last 90 days	6.8%	92.7%	.5%	100.0%
		% within whether respondent has a disability	2.7%	5.6%	2.4%	5.2%
	No	Count	2063	12993	161	15217
		% within had outbound trip in last 90 days	13.6%	85.4%	1.1%	100.0%
		% within whether respondent has a disability	97.3%	94.4%	97.6%	94.8%
	Total	Count	2120	13769	165	16054
		% within had outbound trip in last 90 days	13.2%	85.8%	1.0%	100.0%
		% within whether respondent has a disability	100.0%	100.0%	100.0%	100.0%

Source: National Visitor Survey 2003 data set analysed for this study–had overnight trip in last 28 days * whether respondent has a disability cross-tabulation

Chapter 15

Developing a Business Case for Accessible Tourism

S. DARCY, B. CAMERON and S. PEGG

Introduction

The ongoing fallout from the recent global financial crisis has served to exemplify that business today is under significant internal and external pressures. Importantly, the nature of engagement of the consumer, and the expectations they have is also rapidly changing (Victorino *et al.*, 2008). It has become clear that in such a turbulent environment, traditional models and methods of product and service delivery have become largely ineffective or require significant reform. Such is the case in the tourism industry where industry leaders have recognised that significant change is now required, not only in terms of how the industry deals with crises but also with respect to the development of niche markets and offerings that will drive the industry forward in the short to medium term. It is argued that one such market that has continued to be underserved by the global tourism industry is that of people with disabilities. Part of this failure is rooted in the harsh reality that a great deal of research, much of it geared in recent times around the concept of sustainable tourism, has largely ignored social arguments with respect to ageing and disability. This is despite the fact that various government authorities throughout the world, for example the Australian Bureau of Statistics (ABS) (2004), have reported that a substantial number of people have or will likely acquire disabilities. Moreover, the actual level of disability in various communities throughout the world has substantially increased, from 15 to approximately 20% of the population in recent years.

Importantly, a significant component of the changing disability profile is as a direct consequence of the ageing of the population (Commonwealth of Australia, 2002). While this situation is reflected in all Western developed nations, it is particularly pronounced in Asian countries where the proportion of older adults, as a percentage of the wider population, is actually growing at a faster rate (Altman, 1975; World Health Organization, 2007). The relationship between disability and ageing is undoubted and it presents a considerable challenge for global tourism (Dwyer, 2005) given approximately 650 million people worldwide currently have some form of disability, and where this number will rise (Fujiura & Rutkowskikmitta, 2001).

In Europe and the United States, this new reality has already been recognised to a limited extent with the tourism industry in these regions now taking a more proactive effort to ensure that infrastructure and services are more accessible. To this end, it is argued that the design, planning and delivery of any service offerings can benefit substantially from their collective alignment with the principles of *universal design*. In so doing, tourism operators will effectively be ensuring the majority of people engaged in travel and leisure related activities, including the ageing population, parents with prams and employees, will benefit from these provisions as it incorporates appropriate functional design for a range of occupational health and safety requirements (Preiser & Ostroff, 2001).

However industry awareness of the substantial business and organisational benefits remains unrealised. While many businesses meet their legislative requirements – for example accessible parking and toilets – many do not consider the issue further (O'Neill & Ali Knight, 2000). This is unfortunate to say the least as it is clear that many operators in the tourism industry have yet to connect a high standard of access provision with other elements of corporate performance. In the accommodation sector for instance, many providers have not identified the benefits of accessible product provision and some have even anecdotally stated that 'disabled rooms' are a liability to their overall business (Australian Hotels Association, 1998). Part of the reasoning for this lies in the fact that there still pervades today a perception within the sector that the accessible tourism market is *low yield*. A consequence of long-held stereotypes that people with disabilities and seniors have significantly less disposable income due to the misconception that they are more likely to be dependent on a government pension, a misconception that is often raised in order to avoid investment in accessible tourism (Australian Hotels Association, 1998; Darcy, 2000, 2003, 2008; Healey, 2008; Pegg & Stumbo, 2008).

This chapter sets out to address these misconceptions by demonstrating that provision of accessible tourism infrastructure, products and services can indeed have a positive effect on business. Furthermore, it is argued that greater accessibility not only makes good financial sense but it also has the potential to promote social and environmental objectives as well. Conceptually therefore, the authors argue for a business case for accessible tourism grounded in the *triple bottom line* framework. Importantly, this framework is considered highly desirable as it acknowledges from the outset the ever increasing emphasis on sustainability in the tourism industry, the desire for businesses to grow and to succeed financially despite turbulent and often difficult economic times, and the significant growth potential in the largely untapped accessibility market where provision is premised on being as inclusive and equitable as possible.

This chapter draws largely from the findings of a research project carried out under the direction of the principal author, and under the auspices of the Sustainable Tourism Cooperative Research Centre (STCRC), with the aim of developing accessible tourism business case studies. The chapter begins with a discussion on universal design, with particular reference being made to it within the context of accessible tourism. This is then followed by a discussion of the value of business case studies and their function as a management tool for tourism ventures seeking to make their products more attractive to the accessible market. The research methodology was informed by a case study approach using the triple bottom line.

In setting out the parameters of this study five main objectives were set out:

(1) Identify a number of businesses offering accessible tourism experiences across a range of businesses, ownership structures or industry segments.
(2) Create a Business Case Instrument (BCI) based on the triple bottom line scorecard.
(3) Undertake a series of research tasks employing the BCI to gather data from the case study businesses and to present the information in a consistent and comparable format.
(4) Evolve or refine the BCI to produce an instrument which can be employed to seek, collate and document information for analysis and comparison.
(5) Identify areas of future research.

Accessible Tourism

In the Australian context, accessible tourism has been formally recognised by national tourism policy through the Commonwealth Department of Industry, Tourism and Resources (2003) with the release of Green and White Papers in which people with disabilities and seniors were formally acknowledged as an emerging market. Since the release of these papers, Tourism Australia (2005) has established accessible tourism as a niche experience. However, at this point in time, there has not been a research or, for that matter, an industry strategy developed to realise the opportunity that access markets offer. Furthermore, policy makers in Australia have yet to formally define or conceptualise *accessible tourism*. This being despite the best efforts of researchers such as Darcy (2001: 74) to generate debate about this issue by contending that 'access is not only about buildings; a truly accessible environment is one in which a person with a disability can freely express their independence, and one in which any impediment to integration is removed'.

The other term central to the development of accessible tourism is universal design. Universal design is a paradigm that extends the concepts of continuous pathways, access and mobility, and barrier-free environments to incorporate intergenerational and lifespan planning that recognises the nexus between ageing, disability and the continuum of ability of people over their lifespan (Aslaksen *et al.*, 1997; Steinfeld & Shea, 2001). Universal design has been defined as:

> the design of products and environments to be usable by all people, to the greatest extent possible, without the need for adaption or specialised design ... The intent of the universal design concept is to simplify life for everyone by making products, communications, and the built environment more usable by more people at little or no extra cost. The universal design concept targets all people of all ages, sizes and abilities. (Center for Universal Design, 2003)

Universal design is effectively about making all products, services and environments accessible to all people. Strategies that a tourism operator might use to better align themselves with the principles of universal design include:

- Incorporating a barrier-free design into the planning process.
- Acquiring knowledge of the appropriate laws and internationally recognised accessibility standards.
- Including people with disabilities as planning team members.
- Including an accessibility specialist on the planning team.
- Exceeding standards wherever possible.
- Extending accessibility beyond the parking lot.
- Incorporating accessibility into outdoor environments.
- Planning for a continuous path of travel.
- Considering aesthetics and environmental values when planning.
- Ensuring all materials used in the building process comply with suitable standards. (Moon *et al.*, 1995)

Importantly, the call for the tourism industry to adopt universal design principles as a foundation to achieving greater social sustainability as part of the triple bottom line is now growing (Rains, 2004). For instance the *Designing for the 21st Century III* conference on universal design included a stream on the travel and tourism industry and ended with delegates proposing the *Rio de Janeiro Declaration on Sustainable Social Development, Disability & Ageing* (Walsh, 2004). Together with the efforts of the World Health Organization (WHO) (2007) to formally recognise the right of all individuals to a positive quality of life, momentum has developed in a range of forums to place accessible tourism firmly on the globalised tourism agenda.

Also of particular note at this point is the reality that many businesses in the global tourism and hospitality sectors are today seeking to transform themselves into more efficient and effective operations, and businesses that are better placed to buffer themselves from the ongoing range of crises that continue to negatively impact the industry. Industry issues relating to governance, sustainability and effective destination management are known critical factors for business success, yet they have only been addressed in a piece-meal fashion by the majority of tourism and hospitality operators. Unfortunately, many businesses have sought to change their service and product offerings only on the basis of an alignment with better fiscal (or revenue-driven) business practices, be it related to the concepts of total quality management, organisational change or restructuring (Kotter, 1998). An issue identified as a real concern by Elkington (1997: 109) was that 'if any business was to prosper over the long term, it must continuously meet society's needs for goods and services without destroying natural or social capital'.

Too few operators have given any real attention to the broader concept of the triple bottom line (TBL). That is, business activities that are considered socially, economically and environmentally sustainable or, as Gilkison (1999: 2) described it, 'reporting that gives consideration to financial outcomes, environmental quality and social equity'. In discussing the issue, Dwyer (2005: 79–80) found that to date there had been little effort demonstrated by the tourism industry: 'why individual businesses should consider their environmental and social performance rather than their financial bottom line, or indeed, the role that individual businesses can play in achieving sustainable tourism development.' This is unfortunate to say the least as the tourism industry, in the Australian context, has become an important part of many regional communities as traditional industries have continued to decline in recent decades. As an industry, tourism has become important not only in terms of increased spending patterns in regional areas, but also because of the flow-on effects it accrues to community development, maintenance of transport, communications and training infrastructure (Commonwealth of Australia, 2002).

Business Case Studies: Providing a New Mechanism to Promote Accessible Tourism

MacLagan (2003) contends that the mavericks of today's business world are essential to championing new directions that create an organisation's future. To simply not adapt to change, or do nothing, is realistically no longer an option for the vast majority of business entities. Holbeche (2006) added that unless organisations continue to adapt to changes in their environment, they are likely to enter a phase of strategic drift which is best characterised by lack of clarity, confusion and deterioration of performance. In this context therefore, case studies are valuable in that they provide an insight into such mavericks who more often than not have a clear focus on elements of individualism, the power of reason, the value of argument and the base importance for managers and leaders alike of self-expression (Arnold *et al.*, 2005).

Kotter (1998) noted the most general lesson to be learned from the more successful case studies is that the change process is a series of phases that, in total, requires a considerable length of time. Skipping key sequential steps in the process only serves to give the illusion of speed yet rarely provides the desired outcomes. A second, and equally important, point argued by Kotter (1998: 3) is that making critical mistakes in any of the phases can have a devastating impact on operations in that momentum for positive change can be slowed and hard-won gains negated. While not all ventures are successful of course, each individual case study can nevertheless provide valuable insights for others as to what works, and what doesn't. They provide managers and owners of other operations with some guiding points as to what significant benefits can be derived by those operations that best align themselves with the broad notion of accessible tourism. Furthermore, case studies are deemed to be an invaluable aid for training and educating owners, managers and employees: this being particularly true with respect to awareness, attitude and/or technique training, and as a form of illustration for a particular point or issue.

Tourism case studies are commonly presented as a detailed account of a tourism operation, industry, person or project over a given period of time. While the format of the case study may vary depending upon its purpose, they commonly incorporate information and data pertaining to the aims and objectives of a given operation, its strategies, and any identified weaknesses and challenges to it as a business entity. Case studies are often used to chronicle the changes made by a given operation to best position itself in the competitive market place. As such, case studies highlight innovation and purposeful change.

Case studies on accessible tourism however are scant to say the least. In an academic sense, apart from the recent efforts of Darcy *et al.* (2008), there is no previously published work on this area of note. The limited work that has been produced comes from government statutory authorities charged with recreation and tourism provision. An Australian government organisation, NICAN (NICAN, 2010) produced a document outlining best practice principles for recreation provision citing a number of successful accessible tourism businesses (Culyer, 1997). NICAN then became part of a steering committee group for the Office of National Tourism (1998), which produced a series of fact sheets including 14 examples of tourism businesses that provide a high standard of service to people with disabilities. The best practice examples identified included five accommodation providers, three transport operators, three cultural/tourist attractions, two disability specialist tour operators, an interpretive trail, and a natural attraction. The commentary on each is limited to the inclusive best practice identified.

The UK Department for Work and Pensions (2008) has made available case studies across the tourism, hospitality, retail, finance and legal areas. These case studies were however limited to a number of paragraphs identifying inclusive practice but did detail some very good quotations from the business owners involved in the study. All up, the case studies detailed included four accommodation providers, two hotel/clubs, two outdoor recreation experiences, two farm stays and three attractions. They also included examples of their experiences of integrating employees with disabilities and tips for disabled customers for improving their service experiences. The UK examples provide a much more detailed account of the possible business outcomes that included: broadening the customer base, high occupancy of accessible accommodation, a customer base that was loyal, higher level of word-of-mouth recommendation, an investment that pays for itself, competitive advantage, contribution towards diversity profile, contribution towards winning a major tourism award, guarding against legal action and adding access to a new pool of potential employees. While the UK case studies have a higher level of detail there was no clear information on the metrics from which to evaluate business operations across the triple bottom line framework. Further, more detail of the inclusive practices are required to assist other potential business operators with their planning process.

In summary, it is argued that the case study process needs to provide an understanding of the position of accessible tourism within the overall business plan of the operator. As Leiper *et al.* (2008) noted, business cannot be truly regarded as tourism orientated unless it is specifically targeting tourists through its business, planning and collaborating with other businesses in the area to leverage the best possible outcome from tourists. Similarly, a great deal needs to be understood as to how accessible tourism fits in with overall business operations. Estimating the relative proportion of the business that is attributable to accessible tourism is a starting point. From this position, the investment into infrastructure, marketing and other considerations needs to be placed within the context of new business generated over stated periods of time.

Research Design: Developing the Cases

Due to the relative lack of attention to accessible tourism business case studies within academic and business research, an explorative qualitative research approach was applied (Morse, 1991: 121). This approach was employed using selected cases as the objects for study. The methodology was informed by case study approaches and the triple bottom line scorecard. The research design sought to expand the thinking in general business to consider performance beyond simply that of financial measures. The evaluation of environmental and social benefits has become part of core corporate reporting practice. The preliminary work utilised a Delphi group to identify a range of high standard of access product, across states, industry segments and a range of ownership structures. The next stage involved developing a *Business Case Instrument* to capture triple bottom line metrics. The metrics were collected and developed through reviews of management information systems, in-depth interviews with key informants and reviews of financial and performance information. The information sources included notes from the case study interviews, copies of documents and archival material sourced for the study. Tabular material was then generated from these sources. A matrix of categories or themes, placing the evidence collected within them, and developing, as appropriate, flowcharts and frequency tables facilitated a process of analysis and interpretation involving continual reflection about the data.

Findings: Measuring Business Performance

Initially 11 businesses considered to provide accessible tourism services were identified and contacted. Subsequently five businesses agreed to full participation from which the findings and analysis are based on.

TBL is operationalised as a reporting device and an approach to decision-making. It employs reporting tools to understand the economic, environmental and social implications of decisions for organisational activities (Gilkison, 1999; Savitz & Weber, 2006). TBL reporting is a quantitative summary that covers business performance across the three main components over the previous year (Storer & Frost, 2002).

As each industry sector is different the key indicators to be measured under the three main components are likely to differ as well. In order to understand the tourism sector specifically the Business Case Instrument was developed to capture triple bottom line metrics applicable to the industry (Darcy *et al.*, 2008). The outcome was a series of key indicators, or key result areas (as outlined in Table 15.1), that reflect good business practice that met the objectives as set out in the triple bottom line framework.

Tables 15.2–15.6 provide a summary of the findings from the fieldwork. The tables reflect an overview of the responses to the issues and measures outlined in the Business Case Instrument.

Table 15.1 TBL key indicators

A. Financial Report Card
An organisation's financial report card focuses on variations to budget, the cash position, profitability, balance sheet structure and viability. The annual financial report reviews: • Annual operating performance. • Cash management. • Debt management. • Short term viability of the organisation. • Long term viability of the organisation.
B. Environmental Report Card
An organisation's environment report card considers: • Recycling water, and solid waste (paper, cardboard, plastics etc.). • Energy conservation. • Environmental conservation.
C. Social Report Card
An organisation's social report card considers: • Enablers, inclusive practices and diversity of experience. • Employee and guest/visitor safety. • Business's support of the community. • Community partnerships.

Table 15.2 Commencement of triple bottom line activities

Business Case	Operations Began	Access	Social	Environ-mental	No. of Employees	Catchment
O'Carrollyn's		2000	2003	2000	3	International
Hervey Bay Whale Watch	1989/1995	2003	1990s	Early 1990s	17	International
Lakeside Holiday Park	1999	2000	NA	1999	15	International
Leisure Options	1990/1994	1990	1990	1990	1 FT 30 casual	International
Perth Convention Bureau	1972	2003				National & International

Table 15.3 Financial report card – funding, occupancy and activity

Business Finance Report Card Responses	O'Carrollyn's	Hervey Bay Whale Watch	Lakeside Holiday Park	Leisure Options	Perth Convention Bureau
Funding:					
Initial investment in establishing the business	Was not prepared to furnish this data.	>$1Million	Was **not** prepared to furnish this data.	<$100K	Beyond Compliance Initiative $50,000
Proportion of investment financed by debt		>75%		<25%	
Occupancy (Accomm):					
Average Occupancy – General	Provided substantial data detailing Occupancy, source of markets (domestic & inbound) and access.	NA	56% average	NA	NA
Average Occupancy – Accessible			'Occupancy figures for access is not tracked'		
Access Occupancy – Domestic tourism					
Access Occupancy occurring off-peak?	Detailed data & graphs are contained in the O'Carrollyn's Case Study.				
Management information systems/ observation of group visitation dynamic					
Groups of people with disabilities					
Activity (Attract):					
Change in total numbers (i.e. growth)	NA	Provided substantial data detailing Activity, Capacity from 2002–2006.	NA	Did not provide data.	18 conferences
Proportion of visitors seeking access					10,385 delegates.
Domestic visitors seeking access					Anticipated revenue $20M over three years.
Access activity occurring off-peak?		Detailed data & graphs are contained in the HBWW Case Study.			
Management information systems/ observation of group visitation dynamic					
Groups of people with disabilities					

Table 15.4 Financial report card – balance sheet and profitability

Business Finance Report Card Responses	O'Carrollyn's	Hervey Bay Whale Watch	Lakeside Holiday Park	Leisure Options	Perth Convention Bureau
Balance Sheet #: Equity to Total Assets % Current Assets to Total Assets % Current Liabilities to Total Liabilities % Retained Earnings to Total Equity %	Was prepared to submit this data but only under strict confidentiality	Was **not** prepared to submit this data	Was **not** prepared to submit this data	Was prepared to submit this data but only under strict confidentiality	NA
Profitability *: % Growth in Revenue % Growth in Net Profit Before Tax (NIBT) % Interest to NIBT % Depreciation to NIBT % Marketing and Advertising Expense to Total Income % M&A Expense Applicable to the Accessible Product	Was prepared to submit this data but only under strict confidentiality	Was **not** prepared to submit this data	Was **not** prepared to submit this data	Was prepared to submit this data but only under strict confidentiality	NA

Note: # Balance Sheet data questions were structured over three years. % data was sought as it offers a degree of protection of confidential raw financial information.
* Profitability data was sought over a three-year period to assist identifying any trends. % data was sought to protect confidential raw profitability information. Measures such as Return on Investment (ROI) were omitted for this same reason.

Analysis

All of the participating businesses, with one exception, began operations in the 1990s, with two having been in operation for in excess of 30 years. One organisation introduced their access provision progressively over the last decade with the business developing its accommodation component of operations from scratch using universal design principles. Only one of the businesses reviewed commenced operations specifically to service a clientele comprising people with disabilities, the remainder regarding disability as but one component of the business. All of the operators, except one, were categorised as being medium-sized enterprises with the majority operating with the use of a small core of full time employees supported by seasonal appointments/casuals. The one

Table 15.5 Environmental report card

Business	Recycling	Energy Conservation	Limit Greenhouse	Environmental improvements
O'Carrollyn's	Attempt to recycle water & solids Composts	Unit design, insulation	Limit washing machine use Limit water usage	Five star energy rating design Bush fire protected
Hervey Bay Whale Watch	Sewerage treatment	Vessel design saves fuel	Stopped smoking onboard 1999 Eliminated styrofoam cups	
Lakeside Holiday Park	Recycling stations around park (users tend to contaminate them) Rain water storage Bore water usage	Generators, power saving devices Emergency lighting Hot water services Energy saving replacement policy	Limit washing machine use	Reclaimed land replanted Landscaped with native vegetation
Leisure Options	Office-based recycling	Turn off power Use fluorescent lighting		
Perth Convention Bureau	Employment of business practices to minimise environmental impact	Committee established to monitor environmental impacts Recycling and carbon costed travel		

large-scale operator included in the review employed 36 full time and 30 casual staff across four businesses. All bar one of the businesses reviewed draw from both the domestic and international traveller markets with the disability specific service provider purpose funded to provide for the needs of Australians with disabilities.

A significant issue within the financial report card was the reluctance of management to provide financial data, with 40% declining to divulge this information to the research team. Trust was an important issue in this regard and where the researchers had previously liaised with a business the provision of information by management was considered less problematic, as long as the data was kept confidential and only used in the reporting of metrics. Some of the small to medium-sized enterprises were particularly

Table 15.6 Social report card

Business	Inclusive Enablers	Safety	Unexpected Outcomes	Community Support/Partnerships
O'Carrollyn's	Units, equipment, vehicle, pool, pathways	OH&S audit and emergency plans	Family/small child friendly	Access committee Koala Foundation Local operators, Tamboi Queen
Hervey Bay Whale Watch	Access onto and around vessel	Written safety instructions	Family/small child friendly Ageing friendly	Supports geographic area Local Government
Lakeside Holiday Park	Access Units Access en-suites & amenities block Access to lake, rockpool, barbecue	OH&S audit Staff training Signage, security lighting Security patrols, proxy access		Regional NSW groups Caravanners Organisational support
Leisure Options	Provision of accessible holidays Operates tours for people with disabilities	Safe lifting practices, equipment Mix of staff	Welcoming communities Impact on enjoyment & ability of the trip	Some operators welcome the business, others underestimate the opportunity
Perth Convention Bureau	Beyond compliance initiative a stated objective, cultural and community change as it relates to conferences and tourism			Supports conferences and organisers where issues are topical or important (e.g. Whaling Conferences) or have direct or indirect benefits to the broader community, or there is a societal demand to support a theme or conference

worried about possible unwanted attention being brought to bear on the business. Due to these concerns, some of the organisations declined to provide any financial data at all. Public companies, on the other hand, already publish this financial information and were much more amenable to this type of request.

In gaining an understanding of the financial position of an organisation and the relative position of accessible tourism within this context a series of measures were included in the instrument. Apart from confidentiality issues, information was requested on the movements between accounting periods or proportional to a base. For example indicators sought included: Depreciation/NIBT as a percentage, Growth in Revenue as a percentage, Growth Net Profit before Tax (NIBT) as a percentage etc. All of the measures are contained in the Business Case Instrument along with definitions but some operators said they were not clear about the way the ratios were calculated or the explanations given in the Business Case Instrument. All revealed substantial and significant growth in activity/ occupancy of the accessible aspects of their business. The relative level of quantification varied between the organisations. The Perth Convention Bureau was able to quantify the activity and financial benefit expected to accrue as a result from its access initiative.

The Environmental Report Card (ERC) is a series of indicators which are identified as having specific interest to an organisation reflecting organi-sational performance in respect to the environment. The ERC focuses on components such as waste water quality and recycling, recycled solid waste, weed and pest control, greenhouse gas emission reduction, reclamation and conservation projects all reflecting the enterprises' impact on the environment. All respondents (100%) had developed policies, strategies and implemented actions to recycle materials relevant to their area of operation. Two accommodation or resort operators conceded that the travelling public's attitude to recycling ranged from ambivalence to not caring. Similar to the response under Recycling all operators (100%) had developed responses appropriate to their business operations in respect to energy conservation. However, only one (Perth Convention Bureau) had gone so far as to develop the Carbon Costed Travel concept. Two accommodation or resort participants had spent significant time and effort in restoring and improving their environments. The drivers behind this, based on comments made over the course of the formal interview process, suggest a desire to meet the aspirations of their guests for a natural environment, often specifically involving fauna, 'critters and koalas'.

The Social Report Card (SRC) is a series of indicators which are identified as having specific interest to an organisation in reflecting organisational performance in respect to various social elements. The SRC focuses on components such as inclusive access practices, employee safety, workplace stability, community support, involving the community, community works and partnerships all reflecting the enterprises' impact on society and local community. All operators have provided access provisions to the basic components of their facilities, for example the accommodation providers had developed accessible accommodation, but they'd gone further and developed access to their full facility such as access to a rockpool, barbecues and a vehicle facilitating trips to the beach. Safety, and risk management more generally, was regarded by operators and participants alike as a high priority. As such, businesses reported that they had implemented the following in an effort to improve outcomes for visitors and reduce their possible exposure to unforeseen circumstances:

- OH&S audits and training.
- Emergency plans.
- Written safety instructions.
- Signage, security lighting.
- Security patrols, proxy access.
- Safe lifting practices, equipment.
- Mix of staff in situations.

Often the provision of access designed to facilitate participation of people with disabilities resulted in unexpected outcomes. For example, two accommodation providers noted that their accessible premises were patronised by families, particularly those with small children. They also noticed that these facilities were popular with members of the ageing population.

Each of the operators noted that over time they developed relationships with commercial operators, not-for-profit groups and other organisations. These relationships were found to contribute towards better destination experiences for their customers, increased customer loyalty, repeat visitation and word-of-mouth bookings. In particular, relationships with disability organisations and access committees provided a strategic approach to reaching large numbers of people with disabilities and the accessible tourism market.

The major outcomes and lessons learnt from the research include:

- The development of the business case instrument.
- A decision to use in-depth interviews and field visits rather than questionnaire style completion.
- Businesses providing a quality accessible experience are mature businesses that tend to have been in operation for about a decade before commencing their 'access activities'.
- Businesses providing a quality accessible experience are drawing their business from a Domestic and International market.
- Businesses are reluctant to provide financial data.
- Businesses providing a quality accessible experience demonstrate there is a market in accessible tourism and that market adds positively to their overall levels of activity/occupancy.
- All business demonstrated a high level of environmental responsibility. Key elements such as recycling, environmental rehabilitation and water conservation featured strongly in the majority of operations reviewed. This suggests strongly that a range of lessons can be gleaned by the environmental sector in terms of the style and

manner of how it communicates its messages to both businesses and consumers alike.

- The businesses had developed inclusive practices but gone beyond the basic access requirements; for example, as required by the Australian Standards for Access, and developed inclusive experiences that benefitted all parties involved.
- All businesses were highly aware of their safety obligations and often went much further, ensuring the safety of guests with disabilities.
- Families were an important component of business where one member of the family or group had a disability.
- Accommodation businesses found that family groups with a disabled member enjoyed the benefits of an accessible environment.
- There was significant disability group potential identified through a number of the businesses that provided opportunities during shoulder and midweek periods.
- Most businesses developed relationships in respect to their access provision, with community and regional groups and organisations.

Conclusion

Businesses providing a quality accessible experience demonstrate there is a market in accessible tourism and that market adds to their activity/occupancy. These businesses developed inclusive practices that went beyond the basic access requirements as outlined by the Australian Standards for Access. Businesses were surprised that other groups patronised the accessible features, particularly as it relates to accommodation.

The use of business cases for accessible tourism is an underdeveloped area. Typically this segment of the market is stereotyped by tourism providers as having less disposable income. Unfortunately, this view has also affected government tourism marketing authorities, who on the whole have avoided their responsibilities when it comes to the provision of equitable access to tourism experiences.

Until examples of good business practice are identified and promoted, the industry cannot be guided with any certainty as to the benefits in providing expanded accessible tourism products. This research project investigated five examples of business cases offering a high standard of accessible product. Key measures or indicators were developed and operationalised, within the TBL framework, in order to evaluate the key components of accessible tourism businesses. The insights provided by this investigation can be used to promote the benefits of accessible tourism product provision to the tourism industry.

While the number of businesses included in this research was small, the project provided scoping designed to point the way to additional research which has the potential to expand upon the key measures identified as important and informative. As well as generating important outcomes that can be built on in the future a number of gaps in our understanding of accessible tourism were revealed, these include: (1) greater analysis needs to carried out on accessible transport to and from tourism sites/accommodation, (2) due to the limited success in obtaining detailed financial data, more research is needed on this component which will require finding ways to satisfy participants' concerns about divulging this information, (3) a detailed analysis/breakdown of the international market currently attracted to accessible tourism in Australia, and (4) more defined sectoral analysis ensuring the benefits to each sector (transport, accommodation, experience/activities).

Acknowledgements

The authors would like to thank the Sustainable Tourism Co-operative Research Centre for the grant on which the research was completed. This chapter draws on the technical report Darcy, S., Cameron, B., Pegg, S. and Packer, T. (2008) Developing Business Cases for Accessible Tourism STCRC Technical Report 90042, Gold Coast Retrieved from http://www.crctourism.com.au/default.aspxg.

References

Altman, I. (1975) *The Environment and Social Behavior*. Monterey, CA: Brooks-Cole Publishing.

Aslaksen, F., Bergh, S., Bringa, O.R. and Heggem, E.K. (1997) *Universal Design: Planning and Design for All*. Oslo: The Norwegian State Council on Disability.

Arnold, M., Heyne, L. and Busser, J. (2005) *Problem Solving: Tools and Techniques for the Park and Recreation Administrator*. Champaign, IL: Sagamore Publishing.

Australian Bureau of Statistics (2004) *Disability, Ageing and Carers – Summary of Findings, 2003 (Cat No. 4430.0)*. Canberra: Australian Bureau of Statistics.

Australian Hotels Association (1998) *Catering for Guests with Disabilities: Survey of AHA Members*. Canberra: Australian Hotels Association.

Center for Universal Design (2003) Universal design principles. On WWW at http://www.design.ncsu.edu:8120/cud. Accessed 2.5.2008.

Commonwealth of Australia (2002) *Intergenerational Report 2002–03, Budget Paper No. 5*. Canberra: Australian Government Printing Service.

Commonwealth Department of Industry, Tourism and Resources (2003) *White Paper: The Medium to Long-Term Strategy for Tourism*. Canberra: Department of Industry, Tourism and Resources.

Culyer, B. (1997) *Making Anything Possible – Best Practice in Recreation Services for People with a Disability – Draft Report*. Canberra: NICAN.

Darcy, S. (2000) *Tourism Industry Supply Side Perceptions of Providing Goods and Services for People with Disabilities*. Sydney: New South Wales Ageing and Disability Department.

Darcy, S. (2001) People with physical disabilities and leisure. In I. Patterson and T. Taylor (eds) *Celebrating Inclusion and Diversity in Leisure* (pp. 59–80). Melbourne: HM Leisure Planning Pty Ltd.

Darcy, S. (2003) Access precincts: Understanding spaces and places for people with disabilities. In *6th Australia and New Zealand Association of Leisure Studies Biennial Conference – Leisure, Change and Diversity*. University of Technology, Sydney: Australia and New Zealand Association of Leisure Studies.

Darcy, S. (2006) *Setting a Research Agenda for Accessible Tourism*. Gold Coast, Australia: Sustainable Tourism for Cooperative Research Centre.

Darcy, S., Cameron, B., Pegg, S. and Packer, T. (2008) *Developing Business Case Studies for Accessible Tourism*. Gold Coast, Australia: Sustainable Tourism for Cooperative Research Centre.

Darcy, S. (2008) Valuing accessible rooms: Understanding accessible tourism accommodation information preferences. Paper presented at *Creating Inclusive Communities Conference – Association of Consultants in Access*, Adelaide, Australia.

Department for Work and Pensions (2008) *Working in the tourism sector – Questions for small to medium-sized businesses*. On WWW at http://www.dwp.gov.uk/employers/dda/case_tourism.asp. Accessed 1.4.2008.

Dwyer, L. (2005) Trends underpinning global tourism in the coming decade. In W. Theobald (ed.) *Global Tourism* (pp. 529–545). Burlington, MA: Butterworth Heinemann.

Elkington, J. (1997) *Cannibals with Forks: The Triple Bottom Line in 21st Century Businesses*. Oxford, UK: Capstone.

Fujiura, G.L. and Rutkowskikmitta, V. (2001) Counting disability. In G.L. Albrecht, K.D. Seelman and M. Bury (eds) *Handbook of Disability Studies* (pp. 69–96). Thousand Oaks, CA: Sage Publications.

Gilkison, B. (1999) *Accounting for a Clean Green Environment: Obligations and Opportunities for New Zealand Businesses and Their Accountants*. Nelson, NZ: Anchor Press.

Healey, B. (2008, 29–31 October) *The Australian Hotel Association position: Current status and future of tourist accommodation for people with disabilities*. Paper presented at the Creating Inclusive Communities Conference of the Association of Consultants in Access, Australia, Hyatt Regency, Adelaide.

Holbeche, L. (2006) *Understanding Change. Theory, Implementation and Success*. Boston: Butterworth-Heinemann.

Kotter, J.P. (1998) Leading change: Why transformation efforts fail. *Harvard Business Review* 2, 1–21.

Leiper, N., Stear, L., Hing, N. and Firth, T. (2008) Partial industrialisation in tourism: A new model. *Current Issues in Tourism* 11 (3), 207–235.

MacLagan, P. (2003) The change-capable organization. *Training & Development* 57 (1), 50–58.

Moon, S., Hart, D., Komissar, C. and Freidlander, R. (1995) Making sports and recreation activities accessible: Assistive technology and other accommodations. In K. Flippo, K. Inge and J. Barchus (eds) *Assistive Technology: A Resource for School, Work and Community* (pp. 187–198). Baltimore: Paul H. Brookes.

Morse, J.M. (1991) Approaches to qualitative-quantitative methodological triangulation. *Nursing Research* 40, 120–123.

NICAN website (2010) At http://www.nican.com.au.

Office of National Tourism (1998) *The Tourism Challenge: Access for All*. Canberra: Office of National Tourism.

O'Neill, M. and Ali Knight, J. (2000) Disability tourism dollars in Western Australia hotels. *FIU Hospitality Review* 18 (2), 72–88.

Pegg, S. and Stumbo, N. (2008) Creating opportunities and ensuring access to desirable heritage and cultural tourist services and leisure experiences. In B. Prideaux, D. Timothy and K. Chon (eds) *Cultural and Heritage Tourism in Asia and the Pacific* (pp. 250–256). New York: Routledge.

Preiser, W.F.E. and Ostroff, E. (2001) *Universal Design Handbook*. New York: McGraw-Hill.

Rains, S. (2004) Universal design and the international travel and hospitality industry. Paper presented at *Designing for the 21st Century III Conference*, Rio de Janeiro, Brazil.

Savitz, A.W. and Weber, K. (2006) *The Triple Bottom Line: How Today's Best-Run Companies are Achieving Economic, Social and Environmental Success – And How You Can Too*. San Francisco, CA: Jossey Bass.

Steinfeld, E. and Shea, S.M. (2001) Fair housing: Toward universal design in multifamily housing. In W.F.E. Preiser and E. Ostroff (eds) *Universal Design Handbook* (pp. 35.1–35.13). New York: McGraw-Hill.

Storer, C.E. and Frost, F.M. (2002) Triple bottom line reporting: It's relevance and application to agricultural production and marketing. In P.J. Batt (ed.) *From Farm to Fork: Linking Producers to Consumers Through Value Chains. Proceedings, Muresk 75th Anniversary Conference, 3–4 October*. Perth, Australia.

Tourism Australia (2005) *Markets – Australian experiences – Niche experiences*. On WWW at http://www.tourism.australia.com/Markets.asp?lang=EN&sub=0338. Accessed 20.5.2008.

Victorino, L., Verma, R. and Wardell, D. (2008) Service scripting: A customer's perspective of quality and performance. *Cornell Hospitality Report* 8 (20), 4–13.

Walsh, C.J. (2004) Rio de Janeiro declaration on sustainable social development, disability & ageing. Paper presented at *Designing for the 21st Century III* – An International Conference on Universal Design, Rio de Janeiro, Brazil.

World Health Organization (2007) Global age-friendly cities guide. On WWW at http://www.who.int/ageing/age_friendly_cities/en/index.html. Accessed 19.5.2008.

Chapter 16
Stakeholder Analysis of Accessible Tourism

E. MICHOPOULOU and D. BUHALIS

Introduction

Tourism is a highly networked industry dependant on cooperation and co-opetition (collaboration and competition) (Buhalis, 2003). The intense heterogeneity that characterises tourism is mainly due to the fact that many other industries and economical sectors, such as transportation, accommodation and sports play a critical role in the production process. There have been more than 30 industrial components identified that serve travellers (Sheldon, 1997). When accessibility is involved, all these components gain a new significance, making accessible tourism even more complicated to conceptualise and operationalise, because all these components need to be accessible for a journey to be accomplished (Darcy, 1998; Darcy & Daruwalla, 1999; Israeli & Mansfeld, 2003).

The dissemination of high quality, accurate, truthful and detailed information is key to creating travel opportunities for disabled persons (Cavinato & Cuckovich, 1992). However, the provision of specialised and detailed information tends to be inadequate, the higher the level of accessibility requirements (Miller & Kirk, 2002). Stakeholders involved in accessible tourism can be classified as mainstream, mixed and specialised, according to the detail of information provision.

This chapter elaborates on the stakeholders of accessible tourism, to allow for a better understanding of the nature and processes involved in the implementation and realisation of accessible tourism. The principal stakeholder parties are identified, and their interests and constraints in participating in accessible tourism are specified. The analysis of the impact on their products and customer base, strategies, and business models when participating in accessible tourism, reveals how each contribution is essential to sustain accessible tourism. Finally, an example of the classification for mainstream, mixed and specialised service providers for the disabled market provides the reader with an insight of the current market composition.

Relevant Stakeholder Groups

'Stakeholders are all the persons or groups who have interests in the planning, process(es), delivery and/or outcomes of the tourism service'. (Sautter & Leisen, 1999: 315)

The involvement of a wide range of stakeholders is considered crucial for the successful implementation, strategic development and dissemination of information on accessible tourism.

Accessible tourism, on the one hand, can help destinations to publicise their accessible products and services and, on the other hand, it conveys a significant social value for disabled and elderly citizens, who tend to be excluded from mainstream tourism services. Focus on improved accessibility gives a quality lift and greater flexibility of use for destinations, venues, facilities and accommodation providers. Better accessibility improves service levels for all, opens up new markets, stimulates more varied tourism offers, improves operational management and gives competitive advantage to providers (Eichhorn *et al.*, 2008).

For all these benefits to be delivered to the different stakeholder groups, cooperation and formulation of strategic partnerships are essential prerequisites. The existence of accessible tourism depends on the ability of the public sector actors to engage and work with a wide range of private sector and non-governmental organisation stakeholders, who are culturally diverse and whose infrastructures and resources vary widely.

Initially, the expected interested parties would include:

- National public and local authorities, national and regional tourism organisations.
- Tourism service providers, venue owners, hoteliers, restaurants, museums etc.
- Tourism intermediaries (tour operators, travel agents), associations of tourism and hospitality businesses such as HOTREC.
- European Tourism Commission.
- Disability NGOs.
- End users.
- Accessibility device and product vendors and distributors.
- Social partners (employers, trades unions, etc.).
- Vocational training sector.
- Media, the press.
- Investors, financial institutions, private and public.
- Corporate buyers: companies and organisations buying tourist services, the vast majority of them being SMEs.
- Professionals and professional associations: human resource managers, trainers, professional networks interested in professional development in accessible tourism.

Still, the most distinct financial and social benefits will affect the following broad categories:

Disability organisations and end users, as they will be able to offer valuable, accurate and reliable information, assisting the travel search procedure for disabled citizens. Hence, the tourism products will be more accessible for them, enhancing the choice options according not only to type of disability, but to personal preferences as well.

Destination related organisations and public authorities (NTOs, LTBs, etc.), as accessible tourism will add value to the current services, providing a more holistic overview of the destination and inclusive social service. Apart from capturing greater market share, destinations on local, regional or national level will be able to promote their diversity.

Tourism service providers and tourism vendors (hoteliers, caterers etc.), as the deployment of accessible tourism will open a new market numbering 600 to 900 million disabled people worldwide.

It is important to investigate what would be the major motives for them to finally engage in accessible tourism. In other words, what are the deficits in their current business models and where accessible tourism could add value to their business processes (Table 16.1).

Table 16.1 Target group anticipated requirements for accessible tourism

	Critical	*Very Important*	*Important*
Disability NGOs, end users	• Up to date accurate information on accessible destinations • Travel services promotions • On-demand services • Personalisation services	• Benchmarking • Sharing experiences • Networking	• Special interest groups
Destination management organisations and public authorities	• Up to date, accurate information • Market information	• User friendly admin tools • Benchmarking • Location based services	• Implementation models
Tourist service providers and tourism vendors	• User profile information • Networking • Market information	• Accessibility standards, procedures • User friendly admin tools	• Procurement guidelines

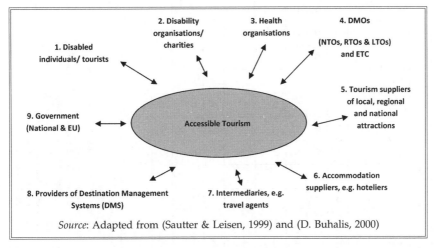

Figure 16.1 Stakeholder groups

There are a number of interests and constraints that implicate the engagement of these groups. Table 16.2 illustrates an analysis of these interests and constraints on an aggregated level, providing an overview of the extent of this implication. However, out of the wide range of stakeholders involved, nine categories are identified as the ones that should demonstrate mostly a strong interest in accessible tourism (Figure 16.1).

Matrix Analysis of Stakeholders

In this section, stakeholder groups are analysed in terms of the organisations' individual activities. For each activity/component, the value added is determined, thereby indicating if resources are used effectively and which areas actually provide competitive advantages for the organisation.

The matrix analysis in Tables 16.3–16.5, provides an overview of all stakeholder groups and their individual activities/components which leads to the identification of the value chain elements for each group at the aggregate level. Based on this, competitive advantages are identified for each group.

In order to break down each stakeholder group into its individual activities/components (deconstructing the value chain), the following business parameters are used: product and service offerings, target customer, operating countries, information gathering (suppliers), information organising (strategy), information synthesizing (variables, components, etc.) marketing/promotion, seasonality, information distribution (channels), business model (revenue sources) as well as competition/ cooperation amongst business players.

Table 16.2 Stakeholders' interests and constraints in accessible tourism

Stakeholder groups	Interests: 1	2	3	4	5	6	7	8	9	10	11	12	13	14	15	Constraints: 1	2	3	4	5	6	7	8	9
Disabled individuals/tourists	●	●	●	●	●	●				●						●								
Disability organisations/charities		●	●	○	●	●	●			●	○	○			●	●	●	○	○			○	●	●
Health organisations		●	●	●	●	○		●	●	●	○	○				○	●	●	●			●	●	●
DMOs (NTOs, RTOs & LTOs)		●	●	●	●	○	●	●	●	●	●	●	○	●	●				○	○		○	●	●
Suppliers of local, regional and national attractions				●	●	○	○	●	○	●	●	●	○	●	●			○		○			○	
Accommodation suppliers, e.g. hoteliers		○	●	●	●		○	●	○	●	●	●	●	●	●			○		●			○	
Intermediaries, e.g. travel agents			●	●	●	○	●	●	●	●	●	●	●	●	●			●		●				
Providers of Destination Management Systems			●	●	●	○	●	●	●	●	●	●	●	●	●		●	●			○			
Government (National & EU)	●	●	●	●	●	○	●						●	●	●	●	●	●	●	●		●		●

● = applicable   ○ = partially applicable

Interests:
1. Desire to travel for various reasons
2. Need to receive reliable information for travelling
3. Provide full range of services/tourism products at the destination to customer
4. Strengthen the destination's/organisation's image
5. Improve quality of service
6. Enhance organisational effectiveness
7. Potential for increasing customer knowledge/ market intelligence
8. Target new customer segments
9. Diversify and differentiate products
10. Personalise products and add value at all stages
11. Profit rationale: increase revenues/market share
12. Achieve cost-competitive advantage by creating value for money
13. Create competitive environment
14. Outperform competition in the long run
15. Reinvent new and innovative business practices

Constraints:
1. Cost constraints
2. Lack of content-rich information of destinations/ sites/venues
3. Lack of content-rich information on accessibility
4. Restricted legal status for generating profit
5. Lack of strong image for providing reliable information on accessible tourism
6. Lack of direct contact with customer
7. Lack of booking facilities
8. Low market penetration
9. Absence of strong advertising and promotion strategies

Table 16.3 Matrix analysis of stakeholders/business products and customers

Stakeholders/ Market players	Product & service offerings	Target customer	Operating countries
Disability organisations /charities	General information for disability issues. In some cases also advice on how to travel with a disability & access guides	Disabled people and other people with special ccessibility requirements	Depending on the organisation: either city, region or country-based
Health organisations	General information for health issues. In some cases also advice on how to travel with a disability & access guides	People with health concerns	Depending on the rganisation: either city, region or country-based
DMOs (NTOs, RTOs & LTOs)	Content-rich information on tourist destinations	Everyone	Either country/ region or city-based
Tourism Suppliers of local, regional and national attractions	Content-rich information on their attraction	Everyone	Either region or city-based
Accommodation suppliers, e.g. hoteliers	Content-rich information on their product (e.g. hotel)	Everyone	City-based
Intermediaries, e.g. travel agents	Tourism information on countries, regions, villages and all destination facilities they offer like hotels, museums or other places worth seeing	Everyone	Depending on intermediary. Generally high market penetration
Providers of Destination Management systems, e.g. Tiscover	Tourism information on countries, regions, villages and all destination facilities they offer like hotels, museums or other places worth seeing	Everyone Average Tiscover user: – 34 years old – male (61%) – has at least a B.A. (52%) – employee (> 40%) – from Austria or Germany – spends holidays at least once a year in Austria (64%)	Austria, Germany, Switzerland, Italy, Lichtenstein, South Africa, UK

Current Service Providers for the Disabled Market

In recent years accessible tourism has shown promising sign of expansion. Tour operators have started to appreciate the potential of a market that has traditionally been poorly served. Disability experts are joining forces through trans-national associations to exchange information, set up databanks, launch joint marketing campaigns and lobby for

Table 16.4 Matrix analysis of stakeholders and key functions

Stakeholders/ Market players	Info gathering: Suppliers	Info organising: Strategy/objectives	Info synthesizing: Variables, criteria, components, etc.	Marketing/promotion	Info distribution: Distribution channels
Disability organisations/ charities	Governmental bodies, authorities of public institutions as well as tourism suppliers (hotels, attractions, etc.)	Info is updated by DOs, charities, NGOs according to the existing and used scheme of the organisation	Different set of criteria/ scheme depending on the organisation	**Promotion:** fairs, work-shops, conferences, direct mailing, etc.	Internet, brochures, direct mailing, telephone, media, face to face contact, word of mouth
Health organisations	World Health Organization, hospitals, research and governmental authorities	Info is updated by health organisations according to the existing and used scheme of the organisation	Different set of criteria/ scheme depending on the organisationcol	**Promotion:** fairs, work-shops, conferences, (direct mailing)	Internet, brochures, telephone, face to face contact with personnel, word of mouth, direct mailing, media
DMOs (NTOs, RTOs & LTOs)	Tourism suppliers of the country/region or city	Info is updated by DMOs according to specific marketing themes (e.g. city trips/hotel/farm houses, etc.) In some cases regional content is delivered from RTOs to NTOs when using the same system	Components: Internet (for final customer) Generally info is structured into specific marketing/ promotion themes Extranet (for tourism suppliers) In some cases also an intranet for internal organisation	Wide range of marketing tools: **Advertising:** Web ads/ads in ordinary press/publications/brand image/dissemination material, etc. **Promotion:** fairs, work-shops, conferences, etc.	– Internet – Brochures – Direct mailing – E-mail newsletter – Telephone – Face to face contact – Tour operators – Incoming travel agencies – Media – DMSs (if existing)
Tourism Suppliers of local, regional and national attractions	*Not applicable*	Info is updated by themselves according to their product specification	Depending on their product specification and marketing aspects	Wide range of marketing tools depending on the size of the attraction	Internet, brochures, telephone, face to face contact with personnel, media Depending on the size of attractions also: Direct mailing, E-mail newsletter, tour operators, incoming travel agencies, DMSs, travel agencies
Accommodation suppliers, e.g. hoteliers	*Not applicable*	Info is updated by themselves according to their product specification	Depending on their product specification and marketing aspects	Wide range of marketing tools depending on the size of the supplier	Internet, brochures, telephone, face to face contact with personnel, media Depending on the size of attractions also: Direct mailing, E-mail newsletter, tour operators, incoming travel agencies, DMSs, travel agencies, CRS

Table 16.4 *Continued*

Stakeholders/ Market players	Info gathering: Suppliers	Info organising: Strategy/objectives	Info synthesizing: Variables, criteria, components, etc.	Marketing/promotion	Info distribution: Distribution channels
Intermediaries, e.g. travel agents	Tourism suppliers (accommodation, attractions, etc.) DMOs/DMSs	Intermediaries maintain their own database or use other tourism suppliers' databases Dynamic packaging	**Internet** **Content/Database Management System** Customers search for specific product offerings based on given search criteria **Extranet**	Online & offline	**Web** **WAP** **Web TV** **Call Center**
Providers of Destination Management systems: Tiscover	7,000 Tourism providers maintain information on 2,000 towns and villages and 40,000 accommodations Tiscover provides homepages for different types of suppliers: – accommodation providers – restaurants – towns and villages – skiing resorts – skiing schools – incoming travel agents	Tourism suppliers update their services on the Tiscover main database	Components: **Extranet:** For tourism suppliers: extent/update of information and prices, maintenance modules, booking report module, statistics/market information **Intranet:** Only for system provider: maintenance & configuration of whole Tiscover system **Public Internet:** Five Modules: Guide, book & search, report, magazines, route planer	online	**Web:** Information on tourism products flow into more than 400,000 web pages **WAP** **Web TV** **Call Center**

Table 16.5 Matrix analysis of stakeholders and business models

Stakeholders/ Market players	*Business model/Revenue sources:*	*Competition* *Co-opetition* *Cooperation amongst business players*
Disability organisations/charities	**Normally information only policies:** Revenues come from state funding, donations (and possibly from suppliers)	Cooperation with governmental bodies, authorities of public institutions and tourism suppliers
Health organisations	**Information only policies:** Revenues come from state funding and donations	Cooperation with World Health Organization, hospitals, research and governmental authorities
DMOs (NTOs, RTOs & LTOs)	**Information only policies:** Revenues come from state funding In some cases regions finance part of the NTOs funding **Information and booking policies:** DMOs that operate their own DMSs gain revenue from tourism suppliers for every booking that is made through the system	Cooperation with tourism suppliers of regions/cities, etc. DMSs that have a DMSs cooperate with providers of DMSs such as Tiscover
Tourism suppliers of local, regional and national attractions	**Information and booking policies:** Revenue comes from income generated through visitors If attraction is state-owned then from governmental funding	Cooperation with tour operators/incoming travel agencies/travel agencies/DMOs/DMSs
Accommodation suppliers, e.g. hoteliers	**Information and booking policies:** Revenue comes from income generated through customers	Cooperation with tour operators/incoming travel agencies/travel agencies/DMOs/DMSs/CRS
Intermediaries, e.g. travel agents	**Information and booking policies:** Revenue comes from merchant model/opaque pricing or commissions	**Partnership models with tourism suppliers**

Table 16.5 *Continued*

Stakeholders/ Market players	*Business model/Revenue sources:*	*Competition* *Co-opetition* *Cooperation amongst business players*
Providers of Destination Management systems: Tiscover	**Information and booking policies:** Revenue comes from tourism suppliers that pay Tiscover for using their marketing platform for their products and services: **– Hotels:** Annual fee for marketing, storage and world-wide distribution, provision of booking maintenance facilities: Premium model: €25 per available bed p.a. + 5% commission for every reservation Professional model: €12,5 per available bed p.a. +8% commission for every reservation **– Regions/cities (DMOs):** DMOs are charged an annual marketing fee depending on the number of overnight stays during year > 100,000 stays: €500 1 million to 2 million: €3000 **Software licenses:** €750 booking centre €750 room information €500 address management **Tiscover academy:** €750 training/seminars **Banners:** €750 36,34 per 1000 contacts (156 × 60 pixel)	**Partnership models:** Co-operation with market-dominating ISPs, search engines and travel portals, allowing destination marketing organisations and suppliers (hotels, SMEs, etc.) to benefit from even more distribution channels and increased levels of traffic

better services. At the same time, specialised travel agents and non-profit organisations have been cooperating by pooling what they have learned about the availability of special facilities in various countries.

Therefore, it is considered crucial to map the current provision of accessible tourism according to level of specialisation in serving the disability market. In Table 16.6, tourism players are classified by sector, into five clusters: tourism intermediaries, content providers, attractions, accommodation, and destination management organisations (DMOs). Then, they are divided into three categories, namely 'Mainstream', 'Mixed' and 'Specialised'. The categorisation is based on the information provision on accessibility. 'Mainstream' are mainstream companies that do not provide any kind of information related to accessibility. The companies that serve the bulk of the customer base, but provide some information on accessible tourism, are described as 'Mixed'. Finally, the purpose-built organisations aiming to serve the disabled niche market are characterised as 'Specialised'.

The content analysis of those providers demonstrates that people with severe disabilities are best served by the specialised players in the marketplace. These players not only have appropriate facilities but they also have adequately trained staff for serving this market. The mixed group has sufficient information to enable disabled travellers to decide the suitability of the facility. In most cases there is sufficient understanding of disability needs, and efforts are made to address the requirements of this market. Finally, most of the mainstream providers have limited facilities for the disabled market and are marginally capable of serving this market. Hence, the classification of the tourism supply into three categories allows the identification of appropriate strategies to get suitable content from those providers.

Conclusion

In conclusion, accessible tourism requires the cooperation of a variety of stakeholders to prove sustainable. It is essential that each stakeholder makes a unique contribution of an accessible component so that accessibility underlies the planning process, execution phase, and aftermath of a journey. While many stakeholders are relevant to accessible tourism, the most distinctively predominant are disability organisations and end users, destination-related organisations and public authorities, tourism service providers and tourism vendors. Accessible tourism can only be possible, coherent, and comprehensive when accessibility becomes a fundamental part of the value chain of the individual stakeholders and delivers benefits both to supply and demand.

Table 16.6 Analysis of stakeholders according to accessibility information provision (selected examples)

	Mainstream (purely mainstream Companies)	Mixed (mainstream but with sufficient provision for the disabled market)	Specialised (disability specific)
Tourism Intermediaries (TAs & TOs)	www.firstchoice.co.uk www.thomson.co.uk www.mytravel.com www.goingplaces.co.uk www.travelcare.co.uk www.thomascook.com www.tui.com www.kuoni.com www.lastminute.com www.opodo.com www.ebookers.com www.travelocity.com www.expedia.com www.priceline.com www.hrs.com	www.activehotels.com www.waingunga.com www.nattura.com www.buceoadaptado.com www.deporteydesafio.com	www.phicia.com/icare www.rollontravel.com www.valinet.org www.adistours.com www.rbtravel.es www.zafirotours.es www.alpe.com www.handiadventures.com www.roth-travel.ch www.cato-reisen.ch www.canbedone.co.uk www.accessibletravel.co.uk www.behindertenreisen.at
Content Providers	www.lonelyplanet.com	www.tiscover.com	www.bmaa.gv.at www.viennaairport.com www.oeamtc.at www.info.wien.at/wtv www.urlaubsvolltreffer.com

Table 16.6 *Continued*

	Mainstream (purely mainstream Companies)	Mixed (mainstream but with sufficient provision for the disabled market)	Specialised (disability specific)
Providers of tourist attractions (museums, theme parks, cultural heritage, etc.)	www.tivoligardens.com www.portaventura.es www.warnerbrospark.com www.gardaland.it www.alton-towers.co.uk www.casinomontecarlo.com	www.disneylandparis.com www.bpbltd.com www.europa-park.de www.liseberg.com www.efteling.nl/ www.bakken.dk www.louvre.fr www.thebritishmuseum.ac.uk www.vatican.va	www.oear.or.at www.octopus.or.at
Accommodation	www.bestwestern.com www.clubmed.com www.choicehotels.com www.summithotels.com www.medhotels.com www.marriott.com	www.accor.com www.hilton.com www.intercontinental.com www.hayatt.com www.radisson.com www.starwoodhotels.com	www.feriekompagniet.dk www.hotelfjordgaarden.dk www.propellen.dk www.skibelundkrat.dk www.hovborg-kro.dk www.labenbachhof.de www.mit-mensch.com/ www.eria-resort.gr www.disableds-resort.gr
DMOs	www.travelpoland.com www.tourism.lt www.visit-sweden.com www.tourismireland.com	www.visitbritain.com www.andalucia.com www.visitmalta.com www.gotland.se www.visitdevonandcornwall.com www.yorkshirevisitor.com	www.accessiblebarcelona.com

References

Buhalis, D. (2000) Marketing the competitive destination of the future. *Tourism Management* 21 (1), 97–115.

Buhalis, D. (2003) *e-Tourism: Information Technology for Strategic Tourism Management*. UK: Prentice Hall.

Cavinato, J.L. and Cuckovich, M.L. (1992) Transportation and tourism for the disabled: An assessment. *Transportation Journal* 31 (3), 46.

Darcy, S. (1998) *Anxiety to Access: Tourism Patterns and Experiences of New South Wales People with a Physical Disability*. Sydney, NSW: Tourism New South Wales.

Darcy, S. and Daruwalla, P. (1999) The trouble with travel: People with disabilities and travel. *Social Alternatives* 18 (1), 41–46.

Eichhorn, V., Miller, G., Michopoulou, E. and Buhalis, D. (2008) Enabling access to tourism through information schemes. *Annals of Tourism Research* 35 (1), 189–210.

Israeli, Y. and Mansfeld, Y. (2003) Transportation accessibility to and within tourist attractions in the Old City of Jerusalem. *Tourism Geographies* 5 (4), 461–481.

Miller, G.A. and Kirk, E. (2002) The Disability Discrimination Act: Time for the stick? *Journal of Sustainable Tourism* 10 (1), 82–88.

Sautter, E.T. and Leisen, B. (1999) Managing stakeholders: A tourism planning model. *Annals of Tourism Research* 26 (2), 312–328

Sheldon, P.J. (1997) *Tourism Information Technology*. Oxford: CABI Publishing.

Chapter 17

Web Design, Assistive Technologies and Accessible Tourism

F. PÜHRETMAIR and G. NUSSBAUM

Introduction

The concept of accessible tourism is based on the philosophy of Design for All. Touristic products and services, information materials and the complete environment and infrastructure should be designed in a way that they are usable for the largest group of tourists possible. Nevertheless Design for All is often misunderstood to be a 'Design for people with disabilities' (Darzentas & Miesenberger, 2005). The fact that Design for All intends to consider the requirements of many different user groups with and without disabilities within a single product or service clearly shows that this view is wrong. Quite the contrary, because Design for All intends to serve all customers it should become part of the mainstream design practice, rather being than identified as a design for 'the disabled' (Darzentas & Miesenberger, 2005). Applying the Design for All approach to the tourism industry means that everyone, regardless of whether they have any disabilities or not, should be able to travel to the country, within the country and to whatever place, attraction or event they should wish to visit (Neumann & Reuber, 2004).

There is a clear intention of people with disabilities to travel. Scientific studies (e.g. Neumann, 2002) have shown that the intensity of people with disabilities travelling in general is only a little below average, while the intensity of travelling within their native country is clearly above average. However the travel experiences of people with disabilities prove that their holidays are often negatively affected by physical inaccessibility of transportation, accommodation and infrastructure and incomplete or inadequate information materials including badly designed or inaccessible web pages (EDF, 2001). Due to their special requirements, the travel planning of people with disabilities is normally characterised by a more detailed information enquiry than known for travellers without dis-abilities (Pühretmair, 2004). The lack of reliable information has been identified as a main reason that prevents people with disabilities and other travellers with accessibility requirements from travelling (Stumbo

& Pegg, 2005). Frequently the unavailability of accessibility information results in the fact that a city or a region is less attractive for people with disabilities.

Within the last few years a serious technological and social change has taken place. This change has been pushed basically by the innovations of Information and Communication Technology (ICT) as well as by the fact that many technologies have become mainstream. The more Information and Communication Technologies and Assistive Technologies (AT) increase the potential to enable people with disabilities to take part in almost any area of the daily life, the more Inclusion and Accessibility become a common responsibility of the mainstream tourism industry. New media plays a significant and increasing role in the everyday life of the population. People with disabilities, especially, use the internet even more than people without disabilities (Huber & Vitouch, 2008). With respect to the tourism industry the internet is meanwhile the preferred information source for travel planning (Egger *et al.*, 2006). Therefore destinations, tourist services and service providers have the chance to use their online presence to increase competitiveness and to attract new target groups.

The success and the competitiveness of tourism destinations depend on customer perception, an effective customer acquisition, satisfying customer support and successful customer retention (Buhalis, 2000). The tourism industry is a very information intensive business where success depends heavily on the relevance of the content as well as on the quality and accuracy of the available information (Michopoulou & Buhalis, 2006; Egger *et al.*, 2006). Therefore the dissemination of reliable and accurate information over the internet, the information source preferred by tourists, is essential for the tourism industry. But to attract tourists with disabilities the information published on the internet must be:

(1) accessible for them;
(2) reliable, accurate and up-to-date.

A German study (Neumann & Reuber, 2004) has shown that 70.6% of travellers with disabilities stated that the organisation of their holiday, including the availability of information, is of special importance for their decision-making and destination selection; 38.9% percent of them pointed out that they encounter difficulties when organising their holidays and 37% said they had previously decided not to go on holiday due to a lack of accessible facilities, equipment or services.

Figure 17.1 shows a schematic diagram of the imbalance between information that is required by tourists with disabilities during travel planning and information that is provided by the tourism industry. The higher the degree of disability, the higher the degree of detailed

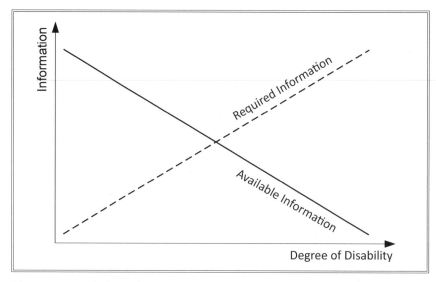

Figure 17.1 Imbalance between required and available information

information required by the tourists. Currently the reality shows the contrary; the higher the degree of disability, the less information is available. Further to the availability of information, the accessibility of existing information sources on the internet is an additional problem for people with disabilities. The information is in most cases available on web pages which are not accessible. In 2004 an analysis of national tourism web pages in the European Union (Oertel *et al.*, 2004) has shown that none of the destination management systems and tourism web pages tested presented their information in an accessible way: they did not even fulfil the lowest conformance level ('Single-A' according to the WCAG 1.0 guidelines (W3C, 1999)). A study commissioned by the United Nations (Nomensa, 2006) verifies that most of the web pages already fail in supporting the basic level of web accessibility. Due to a growing body of laws, regulations and policies which address accessibility of Information and Communications Technology (ICT), including the internet, as well as due to cutting-edge tourism businesses that have identified the potential of accessible tourism, there has been a slight improvement over recent years, but accessible tourism web pages are still rare.

Inaccessible tourism web pages imply that travellers are not able to use a service, to consume information or to book a trip. Typically, the cause is the inaccessible design and not the restricted information perception (visually, auditory, haptic) of people with disabilities, because people with disabilities use assistive technologies that enhance their ability to interact with computers and (partly) compensate for their disabilities.

Figure 17.2 Accessible homepage Nohandicap from Upper Austria Tourism (www.nohandicap.at)

Assistive Technologies

To control the computer, people with disabilities often have to use Assistive Technologies (AT) to facilitate input or enhance output and to bridge the gap between the standard user interface and the users' ability to interact. There is already a wide variety of AT available on the market. People with disabilities select the adequate AT according to their abilities, needs and preferences. For example, people with severe physical disabilities control their computers through devices other than a standard keyboard or pointing device. Such devices can be alternative keyboards and/or alternative pointing devices like joysticks, trackballs and head or eye trackers combined with on-screen keyboards.

Blind and visually impaired people often use Braille displays and/or audio output which are supported by screen reader software. The screen

Figure 17.3 Quadriplegic user using the IntegraMouse (Lifetool, 2009) to control the computer with lip movements and sip and puff clicking (Photo by Alexander Scheider)

reader software verbalises the content of the graphic user interface into text, including pure text, alternative text for graphics, buttons, links, lists, menus, etc. and makes them readable for blind people and adds additional information that is necessary to enable interaction.

People with disabilities rely on these technologies to operate the computer, to control software or to navigate on the internet. But assistive technologies are more than input and output devices for computers. People with disabilities use assistive technology daily to get around more easily, communicate better, live independently and become more active. There are many items that can be classified as assistive technology and many ways to think about categories of assistive technology. AT can be both 'low tech' like eating devices, mouth sticks, communication boards with pictures or big button phones and 'high tech' like environmental controls, computer control by eyemotion, head or lip movement, devices with voice recognition and screenreaders. ISO 9999 establishes a classification of assistive products especially produced, or generally available, for persons with disability. The top level classification of ISO 9999 (4th edition, 2007) differs between 11 different classes:

Class 04   Aids for personal medical treatment
Class 05   Aids for training in skills
Class 06   Orthoses and prostheses

Figure 17.4 Braille display

Class 09	Aids for personal care and protection
Class 12	Aids for personal mobility
Class 15	Aids for housekeeping
Class 18	Furnishings and adaptations to homes and other premises
Class 21	Aids for communication, information and signalling
Class 24	Aids for handling products and goods
Class 27	Aids and equipment for environmental improvement, tools and machines
Class 30	Aids for recreation

With respect to alternative input and output devices needed to control the computer the class 21 is the most important one. When using the computer people with disabilities can only profit from their AT if software or web pages are designed in an accessible way that considers specific requirements for each type of disability. Due to AT it is not exclusively a question of individual limitations, it is more and more a question of the design of tools and systems to leverage an individual's abilities and provide suitable interfaces to products, systems and services (Darzentas & Miesenberger, 2005).

The design guidelines of the Web Accessibility Initiative (WAI) of the World Wide Web Consortium (W3C) (WAI, 2008; W3C, 1999, 2008) clearly demonstrate that such an accessible design is possible and that accessible web pages support different users with different abilities using different input and output devices including Assistive Technologies.

Accessible Web Design

Accessible web design can be seen as the art of designing and implementing web pages in a way so that people with disabilities can use them (with or without AT) independently without the additional help of someone else. It is the art of designing web pages so that all information and functionality provided in them are accessible, and coping with different handling and presentation options that suit a variety of devices, situations of use and personal needs and preferences. People access content not only with their personal computer or laptop, they also access information with mobile devices like mobile phones and personal digital assistants (PDA), having small screens, or they use public web-kiosks. Blind people also use a screen reader on their mobile phone to navigate the menu or to read text messages. But not all generations of mobile phones support assistive technologies. For example new generation phones like the Apple iPhone or the Google G1 use operational concepts that are not usable for blind people. Furthermore their capacitive touch technology that measures the finger's electron flow cannot be used by people using a mouthstick, people with arm prothesis or with a gloved hand.

Additionally, the context of use includes situations where the users have low bandwidth making the download of huge content including videos and images slow. Furthermore, included are noisy environments (e.g. public web-kiosks) that make it difficult to perceive audio content or environments where the user is affected by optical reflections on the screen that make it difficult to see the information. These are everyday situations that people encounter when working, travelling or in leisure time. Furthermore there are some modes of interaction that are not socially accepted and that also affect the context of use, like talking on the mobile phone in the opera. When processing information the designer must pay attention to the fact that many users may operate in a context that is different to the designer's context. W3C (1999) summarise these problems and barriers as follows:

- People may not be able to see, hear, move, or may not be able to process some types of information easily or at all.
- People may have difficulty reading or comprehending text.
- People may not have or be able to use a keyboard or mouse.
- People may have a text-only screen, a small screen, or a slow internet connection.
- People may not speak or understand fluently the language in which the document is written.

- People may be in a situation where their eyes, ears, or hands are busy or interfered with (e.g. driving to work, working in a loud environment, etc.).
- People may have an early version of a browser, a different browser entirely, a voice browser, or a different operating system.

Accessible web design therefore means developing web pages that are accessible to the broadest user group possible. The W3C has identified four principles to satisfy the criteria of accessible web design:

- Content must be perceivable.
- Interface elements in the content must be operable.
- Content and controls must be understandable.
- Content must be robust enough to work with current and future technologies.

To also reach this aim the requirements of people with disabilities have to be considered. Unfortunately these requirements are quite often unknown and therefore ignored by web designers. The results are barriers which cannot be handled by the use of AT. Common barriers in web pages are, for example:

- Missing or inadequate alternative texts for images.
- Invalid source codes.
- Missing labels for input fields in forms.
- Wrong and inadequate usage of tables.
- Bad structure of the content, e.g. no headings.
- Information which is only conveyed by colour.
- Non-expressive link texts like 'read more'.
- Etc.

There already exist several rules and guidelines for creating accessible web pages, and the use of them is embodied in laws in many countries. The already mentioned Web Content Accessibility Guidelines (WCAG) of the WAI are the most comprehensive ones. These guidelines show how to consider accessibility in web pages regarding a wide range of disabilities like physical, visual, auditory, speech, language, learning, cognitive and neurological disabilities (W3C, 2008). WCAG 1.0 and 2.0 introduce the conformance levels A, AA and AAA. These three levels can be seen as the degree of accessibility.

- Level A must be satisfied to provide a basic accessibility of web pages to some groups.
- Level AA should be satisfied to remove significant barriers.
- Level AAA can be satisfied to further improve the accessibility (W3C, 1999).

Therefore it is strongly recommended to satisfy at least the conformance level AA. The guidelines demand, among others, equivalent alternatives for non-text (auditory, visual) content, good and consistent structure of the content (e.g. use of headings, lists), use of Cascading Stylesheets (CSS) for layout, use of labels for interactive elements, etc.

A very important criterion is the use of equivalent alternatives for non-text content like graphics, diagrams and images (a level A criterion). AT cannot identify the information non-text content transports but it can recognise the alt-text (alternative text) and present it to the user. Without alt-text a screen reader will just present the type of the non-text content, like 'graphic', to the user, which is almost no relevant information. The alt-text should be short (max. 150 characters), concise and should provide the core information of the non-text content. An example for a graphic is a conformance logo for the accessibility of a hotel (Figure 17.5). The alt-text should not describe the logo, this information is not important. The core information the conformance logo provides is the accessibility level of the hotel. Therefore the alt-text could be, for example, 'Conformance: good accessibility for wheelchair users'. If a graphic is just decoration and does not transport any relevant information then the alt-text attribute should stay empty.

Another important criterion is the adequate use of labels for interactive elements like radio buttons, check, select and text boxes and fields (a level AA criterion). Only a properly associated label makes the purpose of an interactive element clear. AT can recognise the label and present it to the user. Without labels a screen reader will just present the type of the interactive element but not its purpose, e.g. a screen reader will just say 'Text box' when the user enters a text box without an associated label. Is this text box for entering a postcode, a telephone number or an amount of money? (Figure 17.6) In this case a screen reader user cannot identify the purpose of the text box clearly.

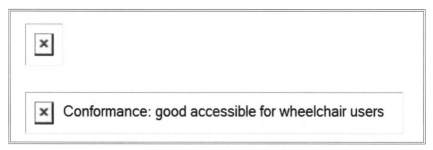

Figure 17.5 This figure shows the visualised presentation of two graphics in a web page, as shown to the user via a screen reader. Just the lower graphic has alt-text (alternative text). What information does the upper graphic impart?

Name:

Figure 17.6 This figure shows the visualised presentation of two text boxes. The lower text box has an explicitly associated label. The upper text box has no associated label. What is the purpose of the first text box?

The structuring of text is a criterion which is important for all users (a level AA criterion). Headings, for example, show where a new section or chapter starts. Furthermore the user very quickly gets a first impression of the content just by reading the headings. It is important, therefore, that headings are marked up in the proper way and hierarchy. AT such as screen readers can recognise the marked up headings and can present them to the user with additional information like 'heading level 1: Lorem Ipsun' (Figure 17.7). Without the mark up of headings this information gets lost. An additional value is that screen reader users can jump from heading to heading.

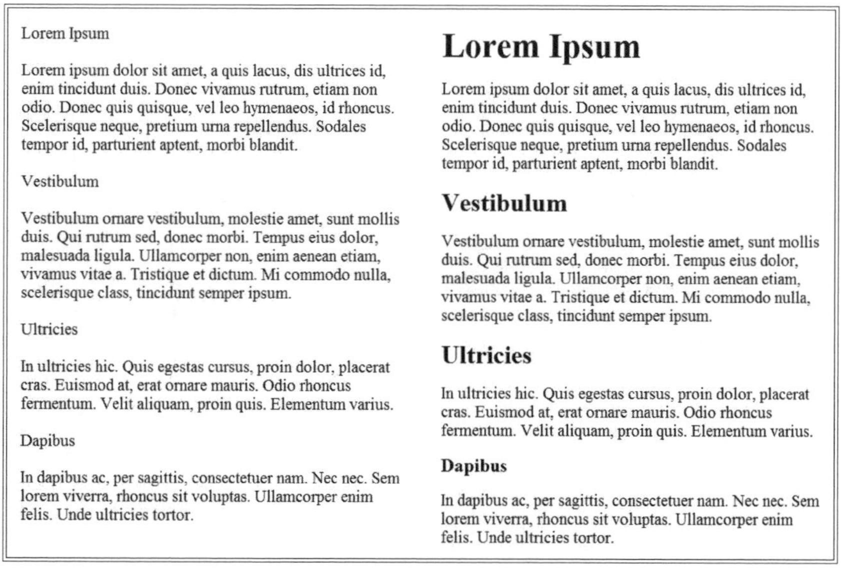

Lorem Ipsum

Lorem ipsum dolor sit amet, a quis lacus, dis ultrices id, enim tincidunt duis. Donec vivamus rutrum, etiam non odio. Donec quis quisque, vel leo hymenaeos, id rhoncus. Scelerisque neque, pretium urna repellendus. Sodales tempor id, parturient aptent, morbi blandit.

Vestibulum

Vestibulum ornare vestibulum, molestie amet, sunt mollis duis. Qui rutrum sed, donec morbi. Tempus eius dolor, malesuada ligula. Ullamcorper non, enim aenean etiam, vivamus vitae a. Tristique et dictum. Mi commodo nulla, scelerisque class, tincidunt semper ipsum.

Ultricies

In ultricies hic. Quis egestas cursus, proin dolor, placerat cras. Euismod at, erat ornare mauris. Odio rhoncus fermentum. Velit aliquam, proin quis. Elementum varius.

Dapibus

In dapibus ac, per sagittis, consectetuer nam. Nec nec. Sem lorem viverra, rhoncus sit voluptas. Ullamcorper enim felis. Unde ultricies tortor.

Lorem Ipsum

Lorem ipsum dolor sit amet, a quis lacus, dis ultrices id, enim tincidunt duis. Donec vivamus rutrum, etiam non odio. Donec quis quisque, vel leo hymenaeos, id rhoncus. Scelerisque neque, pretium urna repellendus. Sodales tempor id, parturient aptent, morbi blandit.

Vestibulum

Vestibulum ornare vestibulum, molestie amet, sunt mollis duis. Qui rutrum sed, donec morbi. Tempus eius dolor, malesuada ligula. Ullamcorper non, enim aenean etiam, vivamus vitae a. Tristique et dictum. Mi commodo nulla, scelerisque class, tincidunt semper ipsum.

Ultricies

In ultricies hic. Quis egestas cursus, proin dolor, placerat cras. Euismod at, erat ornare mauris. Odio rhoncus fermentum. Velit aliquam, proin quis. Elementum varius.

Dapibus

In dapibus ac, per sagittis, consectetuer nam. Nec nec. Sem lorem viverra, rhoncus sit voluptas. Ullamcorper enim felis. Unde ultricies tortor.

Figure 17.7 This figure shows the visualised presentation of two texts, as a screen reader would present them to the user. The text on the right side is structured with headings h1–h3. What is the structure of the text on the left side?

These three examples show how to create accessible content on the basis of three guidelines. But just implementing accessibility guidelines does not guarantee an accessible and also usable web page. A strong focus should be set on usability, too.

A very important criterion of accessible and usable web pages is their internal structure. Normally the layout divides a web page into several visible logical areas (e.g. header, main menu, sub-menus, content, search, footer, etc.). These logical blocks or page areas reflect the structure of the web page. A person can see and recognise this visible structure within the first second of entering the web page. A blind person cannot see the layout and the visual structure. In a worst case scenario the blind user has to read through every web page of a portal he enters to grasp the structure and the content, which can last up to several minutes and which is not satisfying, efficient or effective. For example, a blind person may have to spend a very long time trying to find a special hotel in a badly structured tourism portal. Therefore web pages should also have a good internal structure. A very efficient and already quite common method is to provide links (with accesskeys assigned) to the most important logical areas (e.g. content, menu, sub-menu, search, login) at the top of each page. The blind user can use these accesskeys to quickly jump from one page area to another page area without reading through the whole site (Nussbaum *et al.*, 2008) (see Figure 17.8). A good and consistent

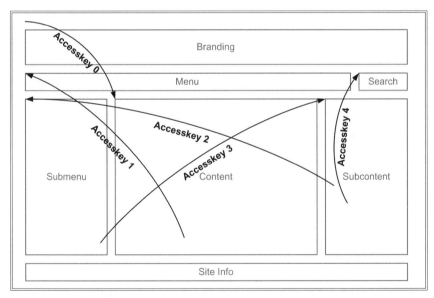

Figure 17.8 With the help of accesskeys associated to internal links which point to the logical areas of a web page, the user easily can jump between these areas

internal structure augmented with accesskeys can improve the usability of a web page for blind people and also people who exclusively handle their computer with a keyboard.

Only web pages which are accessible and usable will satisfy the user. Such web pages are much more efficient to use and the user will find the information he needs much faster.

Conclusion

The internet with its nearly unlimited offer of information, services and functionalities for communication has become an essential part of business and private life in the last few years. Recent information and communication technologies (ICT) together with the internet offer new impressive possibilities for people with disabilities. Unfortunately only a small percentage of web pages are implemented as accessible web pages. Consequently when browsing the internet people with disabilities often hit barriers or cannot retrieve inaccessible information.

Accessible design is not only a question of accessibility; most of the improvements needed for accessibility lead to better design and implementation overall. Approximately 10% of the population rely on accessibility, for about 30 to 40% accessibility is a necessity and for 100% it is comfortable (Neumann & Reuber, 2004). Therefore accessibility improvements can increase usability for all users, with and without disabilities. The forthcoming process of demographic ageing will lead to a growing number of people with needs for more accessibility and higher service quality also in tourism. The consideration of accessibility and usability issues improves accessibility, efficiency and structuring and significantly reduces the complexity of the web. It leads to more user-friendly web-systems that are essential for customer satisfaction, loyalty, quality and success (Pühretmair & Miesenberger, 2005).

The market for travellers with disabilities is lucrative (Neumann & Reuber, 2004), but still often neglected by the tourism industry. If the tourism industry wants successful access to this market potential, they must understand the needs of the people involved and support their needs in their business, services and information materials. Furthermore, the effort to support accessible tourism is worthwhile because accessible tourism is not only an indicator for quality and an image forming factor but can also be a competitive advantage.

References

Buhalis, D. (2000) Marketing the competitive destination of the future. *Tourism Management* 21 (1), 97–116.

Darzentas, J. and Miesenberger, K. (2005) Design for All in Information Technology: A Universal Concern. *Sixteenth International Conference on Database and*

Expert Systems Applications (DEXA 2005). IEEE Computer Society, Copenhagen, Denmark.

EDF – European Disability Forum (2001) EDF Position Paper on Tourism: Framing the Future of European Tourism. Doc. EDF 01/13 EN, Brussels, Belgium.

Egger, R., Hörl, J., Jellinek, B. and Jooss, M. (2006) Virtual Tourism Content Network TANDEM – Virtuelles Netzwerk zum Informationsaustausch im Tourismus, Werkstattbericht eTourism – Berichte aus Wissenschaft und Wirtschaft, pp. 4–13, Forschung Urstein GmbH, Zentrum für Zukunftsstudien, Puch/Salzburg.

Huber, W. and Vitouch, P. (2008) Usability and Accessibility on the Internet: Effects of Accessible Web Design on Usability. *11th International Conference on Computers Helping People with Special Needs (ICCHP 2008)*. ISBN 3-540-70539-2, Springer Verlag, pp. 482–489, Linz, Austria.

Lifetool – Lifetool IntegraMouse, mouse control by lip movements and sip and puff clicking. At http://www.lifetool.at/show_content.php?sid=217.

Michopoulou, E. and Buhalis, D. (2006) Developing an eTourism platform for accessible tourism in Europe: Technical challenges. In M. Hitz, M. Sigala and J. Murphy (eds) *Information and Communication Technologies in Tourism*. Lausanne, Switzerland: Springer Verlag.

Neumann, P. (2002) Barrierefreier Tourismus – Vom Tourismus für Menschen mit Behinderung zum Tourismus für Alle, Universität Paderborn, Germany.

Neumann, P. and Reuber, P. (2004) Economic Impulses of Accessible Tourism for All. Study commissioned by the Federal Ministry of Economics and Labour (BMWA), Berlin, Germany.

Nomensa Ltd (2006) United Nations Global Audit of Web Accessibility. At http://www.nomensa.com/resources/research/united-nations-global-audit-of-accessibility.html.

Nussbaum, G., Batusic, M., Fahrengruber, C. and Miesenberger, K. (2008) Proposal for a Structure Mark-up Supporting Accessibility for the Next Generation (X)HTML-Standards. *11th International Conference on Computers Helping People with Special Needs (ICCHP 2008)*. ISBN 3-540-70539-2, Springer Verlag, pp. 417–425, Linz, Austria.

Oertel, B., Hasse, C., Scheermesser, M., Thio, S.L. and Feil, T. (2004) Accessibility of Tourism Web Sites Within the European Union. Proceedings of the *11th International Conference on Information and Communication Technologies in Tourism (ENTER 2004)*. ISBN 3-211-20669-8, Springer Verlag, pp. 358–368, Cairo, Egypt.

Pühretmair, F. (2004) It's Time to Make eTourism Accessible. *9th International Conference on Computers Helping People with Special Needs (ICCHP 2004)*. Springer Verlag, pp. 272–279, Paris, France.

Pühretmair, F. and Miesenberger, K. (2005) Making Sense of Accessibility in IT Design – Usable Accessibility vs. Accessible Usability. Proceedings of the *Sixteenth International Workshop on Database and Expert Systems Applications (DEXA 2005)*. ISBN 0-7695-2424-9, IEEE Computer Society, pp. 861–865, Copenhagen, Denmark.

Stumbo, N.J. and Pegg, S. (2005) Travellers and tourists with disabilities: A matter of priorities and loyalties. *Tourism Review International* 8 (3), 195–209.

WAI – Web Accessibility Initiative (2008). At http://www.w3.org/WAI/.

W3C – World Wide Web Consortium (1999) Web Content Accessibility Guidelines 1.0. At http://www.w3.org/TR/WCAG10/.

W3C – World Wide Web Consortium (2008) Web Content Accessibility Guidelines 2.0. At http://www.w3.org/TR/WCAG20/.

Chapter 18
Technology Platforms and Challenges

E. MICHOPOULOU and D. BUHALIS

Introduction

In this chapter, assistive technology is defined and the underlying issues regarding its use and application are discussed. Once the relationship between disability, assistive technology and Information Communication Technologies (ICTs) is established, this chapter further elaborates on how this creates challenges for building an accessible tourism information system. There are four main challenges involved, namely: Interoperability, Content Integration, Personalisation and Accessible Design. By the end of this chapter, readers should have gained an understanding of the issues involved in designing technology for the disabled population in the particular context of accessible tourism.

Design for All and ICTs

One of the primary requirements of the disabled market with regard to technology is the 'design for all' principle which is defined as: 'The design of products, services and environments to be usable by all people, to the greatest extent possible, without the need for adaptation or specialised design' (ETSI, 2002a). This principle applies to all ICT products, services and environments. It is essential that 'design for all' is implemented throughout the development process but it is even more important to have accessibility in mind prior to initiating the process, to minimise unnecessary cost and effort. The importance of the 'design for all' principle lies within the fact that it enables disabled and elderly people to better integrate into society, with ICTs playing a significant role in that. Additionally, this principle is assistive for other markets as well, as for instance, a website 'designed for all' can be accessible to disabled as well as to PDA and mobile users. However, 'design for all' does not imply that all products and services following this principle will be utterly accessible to everyone; it rather conveys that designers ought to take under consideration the requirements of the disabled people at the very end of the pyramid (in contrast to the mainstream middle) and design interfaces that interoperate with their assistive technologies (ETSI, 2002a).

ICTs are not always designed to accommodate the needs of all users. Therefore often disabled people are forced to use a range of assistive technologies to be able to interact with ICTs. The interaction with ICTs requires a wide spectrum of media for data input and is also characterised by a number of output capabilities (ETSI, 2002a). For instance, input media can include different types of keyboards, voice input through microphone or pointing devices. Output media can be visual (e.g. display screens, light producing elements for presentation of state information), audio (e.g. loudspeakers for the presentation of audio communication, spoken text or state information), movement (e.g. vibration on mobiles), or a combination of the above.

Assistive Technologies

In 1998 in the US, the Assistive Technology Act (ATA, 1998) was introduced. With this act the US government recognised the importance of technology for the inclusion of people with disabilities in society, and acknowledged the failure of information system designers and tele-communication service providers to cater for the specific needs of persons with disabilities in the design, manufacture, and procurement of tele-communications and information technologies.

They were then prompted to follow universal design principles, so that the need for specialised assistive technology would be minimised because the resulting products or services would be compatible with the existing assistive technologies. However, the boundaries between mainstream and assistive technology are quite blurred. In general, assistive technology is defined as 'technology designed to be utilised in an assistive technology device or service', while assistive device can be regarded as 'any item, piece of equipment, or product system, whether acquired commercially, modified, or customised, that is used to increase, maintain, or improve the functional capabilities of individuals with disabilities' (ATA, 1998).

There are many types of disabilities with different extents, representing a continuum. Assistive technology comes to serve all people, regardless of their place on the type and degree of disablement. Still, it is considered more essential for people with severe or multiple disablement. It is then anticipated that in order to cater for the whole spectrum of special needs, a great number of assistive solutions must exist.

In fact, some organisations like AbleData in the US (www.abledata. com) have as their primary objective to collect and distribute information, solely on assistive technologies (Blasiotti *et al.*, 2001). A single query on the ABLEDATA database brings back as a result 29,000 assistive technology products and services. Hence, there is a huge number of assistive technologies deployed to enable people with disabilities to improve their lives. The international standard ISO 9999 provides a classification of existing assistive technologies, but this research is only interested in those relative to interaction with ICTs. Table 18.1 provides a description of the assistive technologies together with their ISO code (as cited in ETSI, 2002b).

Table 18.1 Relevant assistive devices in ISO 9999

Classification Code	Description
12 39 06	Electronic orientation aids
12 39 09	Acoustic navigation aids (sound beacons)
21 06 03	Image enlarging video system
21 06 06	Character reading machine
21 09 03	Input units (e.g. speech recognition)
21 09 06	Keyboard and control systems
21 09 09	Printers and plotters (e.g. Braille)
21 09 12	Displays
21 09 15	Devices for synthetic speech
21 09 27	Software for input and output modification
21 15 09	Dedicated word processors
21 15 15	Electric Braille writers
21 24	Aids for drawing and handwriting
21 33 09	Decoders for videotext
21 33 12	CCTV
21 36 06	Mobile phones and car telephones
21 36 09	Text telephones
21 36 10	Visual phones and videophones
21 42 09	Portable dialogue units
21 42 12	Voice generators
21 42 15	Voice amplifiers
21 45	Hearing aids
21 45 15	Tactile hearing aids
21 48 03	Door signals
21 51 03	Personal emergency alarm systems
21 51 06	Attack alarms for epileptics
21 51 09	Fire alarms
24 09	Operating controls and devices
24 12	Environmental control systems

This table is indicative rather than exhaustive and aims to demonstrate a wide range of assistive technologies that can interact with ICTs. It should be noted that some of the assistive devices (e.g. mobiles or fire alarms) are also mainstream devices used in a different context.

Disabled People and Assistive Technologies

Assistive technology (AT) is often perceived as a 'medical device'. This notion contradicts the very purpose of AT, which is to support independent living. It reflects the medical model view of disability, ignoring the social approach that focuses on community integration and inclusion (Ripat & Booth, 2005). It is important not to segment individuals into predetermined categories according to dysfunction, but to focus on functional abilities before looking at disability (Ripat & Booth, 2005). Technologies are most effective when they adequately attend to and fulfil users' functional and social needs, rather than solely address a physical limitation (Scherer, 2005). In fact, by addressing disabled people's limitations and enhancing their capabilities, assistive technologies remove psychosocial stressors resulting in higher confidence and self-esteem (Scherer, 2000, 2004).

The (prolonged) use of AT can be contributed primarily to the fact that it complies with the users values and emotions and secondarily to the functionality it may provide (Hocking, 1999). Even though there is an abundance of assistive technologies available to use, the majority are often discarded only after brief use. The main reason for this is that the evaluation occurring prior to launching new AT is insufficient in terms of contextualising the disabled person with the environment (Scherer, 2005). Hence, the starting point when designing AT should be the deployment of measures (Wessels *et al.*, 2000), to reveal the unique requirements, wants and needs of a disabled individual (Ripat & Booth, 2005), as well as the determination of characteristics of technology, and the relevant environments to ensure compliance between the user and AT (Cushman & Scherer, 1995; Kilgore *et al.*, 2001; Scherer, 2000, 2004; Scherer *et al.*, 2003). Also, financial, human and environmental factors are crucial and need to be considered carefully due to their effect on AT usage, as the lack of resources has been identified as a barrier to using AT effectively (Scherer, 2000).

The vast number of existing and most importantly the introduction of new AT reveal that there is substantial demand for it. One of the reasons is that the modern way of life requires increased information processing, time management, complex planning and technology comes to assist overloaded cognition of mainstream demand. Another reason can be that there is an increased recognition of the needs of people with cognitive disabilities (LoPresti *et al.*, 2004). The plethora of AT products and services imply that individual needs can be met, however, the process of identifying the appropriate AT for the person becomes highly complicated (Scherer, 2002, 2004).

Challenges for Accessible Tourism Information Systems

An accessible tourism information system should be designed to accommodate the informational and technical requirements of the target audience. However, designing such a system entails multiple challenges (Figure 18.1). While some of the challenges are generic and the tourism industry has faced them in many different cases, with regard to the disability market these challenges are enhanced and intensified.

Interoperability

Interoperability is a generic and much elaborated issue within the tourism industry. It is considered essential for the cooperation of the various stakeholders within the tourism system, in order to effectively promote and supply tourism products and services to customers. Only then can the tourism experience be successfully supported by all the involved tourism vendors from customer origin to destination. However, there are issues that complicate this process.

Tourism is not homogeneous; rather it exists by the compilation of more than 30 other identified sectors (Sheldon, 1997), such as education, agriculture and sports. The very essence of tourism lies within the network it consists of. All these sectors however, have different scope of service and therefore use different systems, which makes interoperability critical for the very creation of the tourism product. Research has shown that interoperability obstacles can be overcome at a semantic level, by specialised ontology development (Dongsong, 2004; Werthner & Fodor, 2005). Several attempts have been made by major industry players to provide standardisation guidelines for accessible facilities, including the HEDNA and activehotels.com checklists. Still, the need to assure interoperability amongst these diverse systems is immense. Interoperability must be ensured not only with the various stakeholders but with the end-users as well.

There is also a huge variation in the size of tourism companies. The bulk of tourism organisations comprise small and medium enterprises (SMEs) that compete together with the vast and well established brands. The implication of this is that all these organisations have disproportionate growth and the capital invested in technical infrastructure varies significantly. The differences can be traced in multiple areas, such as

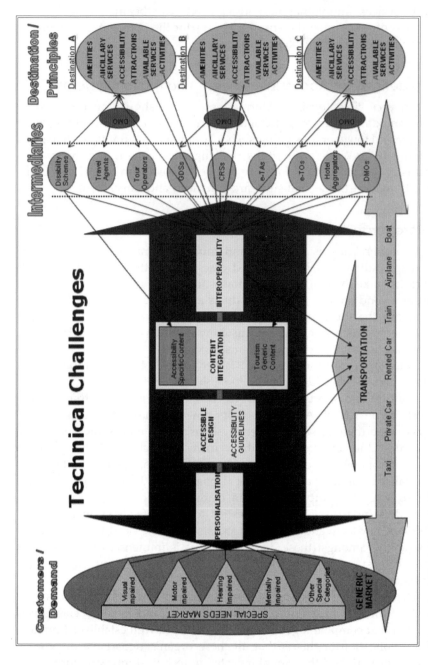

Figure 18.1 Technical challenges

type of technology deployment, system architecture, and information structure. Even similar services (e.g. accommodation) are supported by considerably dissimilar system designs creating a cooperation barrier for a variety of stakeholders within the tourism value chain.

Interoperability will be critical for creating an accessibility path, i.e. the interlinking of all accessible products and services required. Hence, inter-connecting value chain elements of the tourism industry and creating an accessibility path amongst accessible components will be critical for providing accessible tourism experiences. A comparative analysis of the database structure of three major European Accessibility Schemes, namely Visit Britain, Toegankelijk Vlaanderen Bureau and Association Nationale pour le Logement des Personnes Handicapées, revealed that there is a total of over 1200 different fields describing accessible tourism supply. Additionally, not more that 10% of the fields were found in common. Hence, there is a need to develop the accessibility tourism ontology to help the major players interoperate.

This problem is intensified when the multinational character of tourism is taken into account. Interaction, collaboration, and even regular business transactions are often obstructed by the language barrier that exists between countries. Interoperability is therefore a huge issue in tourism industry, which refers to technology infrastructure as well as the semantics involved in performing regular business processes.

Content Integration

Information has been called the 'lifeblood' of tourism (Sheldon, 1993), and this indicates its importance for the industry. The intangibility of the product makes information an essential prerequisite for travelling. With regard to disabled travellers, information is even more critical because the detail, depth and type of information determine the very decision to engage in travel. Hence, the integration of different types of content should enable disabled travellers to participate in tourism experiences. However, there are a number of issues that make content integration problematic.

Information is critical for disabled travellers to engage in travel. Their informational requirement is two-fold. On the one hand they need generic tourism information like any other able-bodied traveller, and on the other hand they need accessibility-specific information. Generic tourism information can be obtained from Destination Management Organisations (DMOs), local authorities, travel guides etc. Tourism suppliers (e.g. hotels, restaurants) may occasionally provide some sort of accessibility information regarding their respective facilities. More accessibility-specific information can usually be retrieved from disability related organisations, charities and accessibility schemes. Hence, the required information is scattered amongst a wide range of organisations, making the information gathering process for the disabled traveller difficult and time consuming.

Another complication is that each type of disability has different extents, and therefore requires different levels of detailed accessibility information. People with a low degree of disability have minimal accessibility information requirements, which are almost similar to able-bodied travellers. However, the higher the degree of disablement, the more detailed accessibility information is required. The existing content, provided by a wide range of organisations, varies considerably in terms of detail, accuracy and reliability. It has also been claimed that in fact, the provision of specialised and detailed accessibility information tends to be inadequate, the higher the level of accessibility requirements (Miller & Kirk, 2002). A survey on 43 Accessibility Schemes in 18 countries revealed that although these organisations provide accessibility-specific information, the content tends to focus mostly on mobility impairments, neglecting other types of disabilities.

The lack of comprehensive information provision regarding available and accessible travel and tourism opportunities is apparent in most countries (Stumbo & Pegg, 2005). Accessibility information, when available, is very fragmented and unevenly distributed within different geographical areas. The available content is also to be found in different languages and formats, setting an extra burden to the integration process that will enable reliability and consistency (Werthner & Ricci, 2004). The accessibility content can reflect coverage areas that include national, regional, city or even facility levels. Information is also often scattered amongst different industry players, including DMOs, national, regional or local Accessibility Schemes, and hotel aggregators.

Personalisation

'Personalisation is a technique used to generate individualised content for each customer' (Greer & Murtaza, 2003: 50) Organisations, in order to increase their overall value (Chin & Gopal, 1995) and profit (Cooper *et al.*, 2000), focus on the customers through personalisation. Finding the right content online can be hard and time consuming, especially for people seeking specific information. Personalisation allows internet users to specify their requirements and interests in order to access the required information in the desirable format. Travellers normally have a wide range of requirements and preferences and this has created the need for travel recommender systems (Ricci & Delgado, 2004). These may range from the preferred hotel chain to the language that the information should be presented in (Pierrakos *et al.*, 2003). The disabled traveller market, in particular, places additional requirements that relate to the *type* and *severity* of disability.

The disabled travellers' market has personalisation requirements that relate to the *type* of disability, and they need to be able to personalise their travel information search according to their needs. A blind person may therefore search only for places that have Braille displays whilst a full-time wheelchair user may want to access information only for the fully accessible hotels. Hence, personalisation needs to cater for all different types of impairments.

The actual need for personalisation is focused in filtering the information according to *severity* of disability. For instance, a mobility impaired person using a stick will be able to select a preferred tourism venue from a significant number of options ranging from almost inaccessible to totally accessible venues. Personalisation in this case is required to narrow down the available options. However, a tetraplegic full-time wheelchair user has limited options due to the high level of venue accessibility required. Personalisation is then needed to ensure that the search results include only the venues that actually meet the high level of accessibility requirement. Therefore, personalisation should act as a decision support mechanism by narrowing down available options as well as a verification mechanism, by assuring requirements-system/content fit.

Still, as type and severity of disability vary, users should be able to choose the products and services that best serve their individual abilities and preferences by *trading off* with parameters such as available facilities, venue location or price. Disabled travellers also need to be able to decide the compromises between travel elements and accessibility. Hence, a purpose-built tourism venue is not necessarily the best choice, when a person is willing to sacrifice ultimate accessibility for partial accessibility and better price or location. This is possible for a wide range of facilities, products and services that are not restricted by the 'veto principles' (Israeli, 2002). According to the 'veto principle', when a certain condition cannot be met then the venue in question cannot be considered as accessible for a particular type of disability. For example, a hotel with no elevator cannot be considered accessible for a full-time wheelchair user (veto principle applies) but can be suitable to a hearing impaired. Therefore, the provision of a flexible, personalised service should allow the end-user to make informed choices and compromises between different travel products according to their ability, preference and individualised criteria (De & Radha Krishna, 2002).

Accessible Design

Accessible design of websites is critical for both visually impaired as well as those using assistive technologies to navigate the site. The majority of governmental websites, Destination Management Organisations (DMOs), content aggregators and tourism suppliers websites are

Figure 18.2 Three column GUI layout

usually found to be inaccessible with very few exceptions, mainly those targeting exclusively the disabled audience. A positive correlation appears between disability content and accessibility, as the more generic the content is the more inaccessible the website.

One of the most common trade offs web developers are faced with is that of the web pages layout. Elements such as low colour contrast, rich graphics and animation components and pop-ups are not recommended or are even prohibitive for creating accessible websites (Han & Mills, 2006). An example of design trade offs is demonstrated in Figures 18.2 and 18.3. The three columns design approach, as illustrated in Figure 18.2, is most common amongst the mainstream travel websites. It looks

Figure 18.3 Two column GUI layout

professional and appealing to end users as they are familiar with this design. It also provides sufficient space for presentation on the landing page. However, from an accessibility point of view, this layout has some inherent drawbacks. In particular, when attempting to increase the font size, the columns either get out of proportion resulting in a damaged layout, or they retain their size and the larger font-sized content cannot fit within the same space.

On the other hand, the two content column approach may not be as appealing but ensures accessibility (Figure 18.3). In particular, when increasing either the font size or even the window size, the layout remains consistent. Text and images take up any additional space and adapt to the initial layout.

Conclusion

In order to interact with ICTs disabled people often need to utilise additional technology that consists of a wide range of input and output devices, such as specialised keyboards and screen readers. Known as assistive technology, it aids the inclusion of disabled people in the digital arena.

However, the number of available assistive products and services is vast, and the reason for this is two-fold. On the one hand, as new technologies constantly emerge, interoperability and compatibility issues appear, and therefore new assistive products keep entering the market-place. The number of new entries is likely to be reduced since initiatives and principles such as 'Design for All' have been introduced. 'Design for All' suggests that new products are designed with accessibility in mind, but it is unrealistic to expect that all new products and services are utterly accessible to everyone. On the other hand, people with different types and severities of disability have diverse needs and require alternative assistive technologies. For all these requirements to be adequately addressed, a wide range of assistive technologies is required.

The life expectancy of AT is often very short and this is due to poor evaluation prior to launching. When developing technology for the disabled, financial, human and environmental factors should be taken into consideration, to identify the appropriate user requirements. People have individual sets of requirements and priorities, which can change with age, experiences and exposure to technologies. Technology needs to be adequately customisable to address these requirements and result in satisfaction and acceptance.

Building an accessible tourism information system needs to take into account the technical requirements of the target audience, however the process can be impeded by four critical challenges, namely: interoperability, content integration, personalisation and accessible design.

There are many ways to overcome these challenges (such as creating specialised information collection tools; designing a scalable database to store and manage the data, deploying technologies such as RSS and Portlets to deliver dynamic, specialised content to the end-users, etc.), but it is up to the system architects and other stakeholders to see the best fit for each particular system. A successful accessible tourism system, however, should allow accessible travel suppliers to 'plug and play', creating a pool of resources, and give disabled consumers the ability to customise the way they retrieve and interact with information.

References

AbleData website (2006) On WWW at www.abledata.com. Accessed 5.12.2006.
ATA (1998) Assistive Technology Act of 1998. At http://www.section508.gov/docs/AT1998.html.
Blasiotti, E.L., Westbrook, J.D., Kobayashi, I., Albrecht, G.L., Seelman, K.D. and Bury, M. (2001) Disability studies and electronic networking. In G.L. Albrecht, K.D. Seelman and M. Bury (eds) *Handbook of Disability Studies*. Thousand Oaks, CA: Sage.
Chin, W. and Gopal, A. (1995) Adoption intention of GSS: Relative importance of beliefs. *Data Base Advances* 26 (2), 42–61.
Cooper, B.L., Watson, H.J., Wixom, B.H. and Goodhue, D.L. (2000) Data warehousing supports corporate strategy at First American Corporation. *MIS Quarterly* 24 (4), 547–567.
Cushman, L.C. and Scherer, M.J. (1995) *Psychological Assessment in Medical Rehabilitation*. Washington, DC: APA Books.
De, S.K. and Radha Krishna, P. (2002) Mining web data using clustering technique for web personalization. *International Journal of Computational Intelligence & Application* 2 (3), 255–265.
Dongsong, Z. (2004) Web services composition for process management in e-business. *Journal of Computer Information Systems* 45 (2), 83–91.
ETSI (2002a) *Guidelines for ICT products and services; 'Design for All'* (No. ETSI EG 202 116 V1.2.1 (2002–2009)).
ETSI (2002b) *Requirements for assistive technology in ICT* (No. ETSI TR 102 068 V1.1.3 (2002–2011)).
Greer, T.H. and Murtaza, M.B. (2003) Web personalization: The impact of perceived innovation characteristics on the intention to use personalization. *Journal of Computer Information Systems* 43 (3), 50–55.
Han, J. and Mills, J. (2006) The mutual designing of travel websites: Perceptions of the visually impaired. Paper presented at the *ENTER 2006*, Lausanne, Switzerland.
HEDNA website At http://www.**hedna**.org.
Hocking, C. (1999) Function of feelings: Factors in abandonment of assistive devices. *Technology & Disability* 11 (1–2), 3–11.
Israeli, A.A. (2002) A preliminary investigation of the importance of site accessibility factors for disabled tourists. *Journal of Travel Research* 41 (1), 101–104.
Kilgore, K.L., Scherer, M.J., Bobblitt, R., Dettloff, J., Dombrowski, D.M., Godbold, N., Jatich, J.W., Morris, R., Penko, J.S., Schremp, E.S. and Cash, L.A. (2001) Neuroprosthesis consumers' forum: consumer priorities for research directions. *Journal of Rehabilitation Research and Development* 38 (6), 655–660.

LoPresti, E.F., Michailidis, A. and Kirsch, N. (2004) Technology for cognitive rehabilitation and compensation: State of the art. *Neuropsychological Rehabilitation* 14 (1–2), 5–39.

Miller, G. and Kirk, E. (2002) The Disability Discrimination Act: Time for a stick? *Journal of Sustainable Tourism* 10 (1), 82–88.

Pierrakos, D., Paliouras, G., Papatheodorou, C. and Spyropoulos, C.D. (2003) Web usage mining as a tool for personalisation. *User Modeling and User-Adapted Interaction* 13 (4), 311–372.

Ricci, F. and Delgado, J.E. (eds) (2004) *Information Technology and Tourism (Special Issue on Travel Recommender Systems)* (Vol. 6): Cognizant Communication Corporation.

Ripat, J. and Booth, A. (2005) Characteristics of assistive technology service delivery models: Stakeholder perspectives and preferences. *Disability and Rehabilitation* 27 (24), 1461–1470.

Scherer, M.J. (2000) *Living in the State of Stuck: How Technology Impacts the Lives of People with Disabilities*. Cambridge, MA: Brookline Books.

Scherer, M.J. (2002) *Assistive Technology: Matching Device and Consumer for Successful Rehabilitation*. Washington, DC: APA Books.

Scherer, M.J. (2004) *Connecting to Learn: Educational and Assistive Technology for People with Disabilities*. Washington, DC: APA Books.

Scherer, M.J. (2005) Assessing the benefits of using assistive technologies and other supports for thinking, remembering and learning. *Disability, Handicap & Society* 27 (13), 731.

Scherer, M.J., Coombs, F.K. and Hansen, N.K. (2003) Policy issues in evaluating and selecting assistive technology and other resources for persons with disabilities. Paper presented at *Bridging Gaps: Refining the Disability Research Agenda for Rehabilitation and the Social Sciences*.

Sheldon, P. (1993) Destination information systems. *Annals of Tourism Research* 20 (4), 633–649.

Sheldon, P.J. (1997) *Tourism Information Technology*. Oxford: CABI Publishing.

Stumbo, N.J. and Pegg, S. (2005) Travellers and tourists with disabilities: A matter of priorities and loyalties. *Tourism Review International* 8 (3), 185.

Werthner, H. and Fodor, O. (2005) Harmonise: A step towards an interoperable tourism marketplace. *International Journal of Electronic Commerce* 9 (2), 11–39.

Werthner, H. and Ricci, F. (2004) E-commerce and tourism. *Communications of the ACM* 47 (12), 101–105.

Wessels, R., deWitte, L., Andrich, R., Ferrario, M., Persson, J., Oberg, B., Oortwijn, W., VanBeekum, T. and Lorentsen, Ø. (2000) IPPA, a user-centred approach to assess effectiveness of assistive technology provision. *Technology & Disability* 13 (1), 105–115.

Chapter 19

Conclusion: Universal Approaches to Accessible Tourism

S. DARCY, I. AMBROSE, S. SCHWEINSBERG and D. BUHALIS

Introduction

This book aimed to explore and document the current theoretical approaches, foundations and issues in the study of accessible tourism. As has already been alluded to in a number of chapters, the tourism industry interest in accessible tourism has accelerated in recent years as stakeholders wrestle with notions of accessibility, 'tourism for all', and the way in which these ideas can be incorporated into business practices. What should become apparent from a reading of the chapters is that accessible tourism is by its very nature multifaceted, which is conceptualised through a range of diverse theoretical discourses and networks. Due to this, it would be hubris for us to suggest in the course of this concluding chapter that a book such as this can ever hope to offer a comprehensive appraisal of the scope of accessible tourism as a developing and dynamic field. Instead, we will confine ourselves in these concluding remarks to stating that the current book offers the collective insight into the way in which one group of authors has approached the accessible tourism phenomena. The strengths of the approaches contained in the chapters will be evaluated by others in due course.

A central argument of this book is that disability is first and foremost a social construct. In Chapter 1 Darcy and Buhalis observed that disability is created through the disabling social environment that requires social action to change and it is the collective responsibility of society to make the environmental and attitudinal modifications necessary to encourage the full participation of people into all areas of citizenship. The editors believe that social participation can best be operationalised by seeking to incorporate the principles of universal design into planning, design, operations and research agendas. Universal design moves beyond accessibility and inclusive practices to incorporate:

> ... the design of products and environments to be usable by all people, to the greatest extent possible, without the need for adaptation or specialised design ... The intent of the universal design concept is to

simplify life for everyone by making products, communications and the built environment more usable by more people at little or no extra cost. The universal design concept targets all people of all ages, sizes and abilities. (Center for Universal Design, 2009)

The concept is immensely appealing to developing the potential of social participation of all embodiments over lifespan and across cultural divides (Ginnerup, 2009). It seeks to move beyond building codes and standards for access and mobility to the far more encompassing whole of life approach to embodiment. Of course, it must be implemented through the international human rights agreements and then implemented by nation states through disability discrimination legislation. Yet many countries do not actively implement human rights legislation and national building codes and standards – the outcome of which means that if universal design principles are not incorporated within national frameworks then they are rarely implemented. In reviewing the literature, the most common discussion about universal design is in relation to the components of built environment accessibility. While this is not a criticism, it does not fully reflect the complexity of implementing universal design to its fullest intent. Not surprisingly a great deal of the discussion about universal design and tourism has largely been left to its potential and conceptualisation rather than its operation (Darcy & Dickson, 2009). These brief concluding remarks will not, it must be said, seek to redress this situation but our aim will be to illustrate the ways in which the contributions have furthered our understanding of the component parts of universal design when it is applied to accessible tourism. Major benefits of universal design approaches are taken up in the accompanying book: *Accessible Tourism Practice: International Best Practice* which seeks to operationalise these concepts with practical solutions.

Universal Design and Tourism – The State of Play

Any work that seeks to establish the nuances of universal design in relation to tourism is important because of the conceptual state of the current literature. Yet in related fields such as architecture, universal design is a well developed body of knowledge, which is used to create enabling environments for all types of embodiments (Baucom & Grosch, 1996; Goldsmith et al., 2000; Lidwell et al., 2003). There has been some limited use of the concept as part of the development of information systems for tourist wayfinding from a computer science perspective (Zarikas et al., 2001), within the broad features for the accommodation sector (BDE Ltd, 2006; Goldsmith et al., 2000; Rossetti, 2009) and within calls for policy inclusion for the tourism industry globally (Rains, 2004, 2006a, 2006b, 2009a, 2009b). In fact, the World Tourism Organization, amongst others, has enshrined universal design within its overall vision

(Japan Tourism Marketing Co., 2009; World Tourism Organization, 2010), but on closer examination they have not operationalised universal design within detailed policy or funding arrangements. Similarly, other authors use the terminology but employ an access auditing methodology that limits itself to mobility access (Horino *et al.*, 2007). Probably the major use of universal design principles has been through the operationalisation of W3C protocols for website accessibility (Foggin *et al.*, 2003; Foggin *et al.*, 2004; Shi, 2006; Williams & Rattray, 2005; Williams *et al.*, 2006; Zhou & DeSantis, 2005).

On a policy level, universal design was an important component of the Australian national research agenda for accessible tourism, which called for the industry to 'operationalise universal design and easy living principles within tourism product development' (Darcy, 2006: 6). To date the major area where research has been carried out is with respect to the accommodation sector. In a policy context, the One-Stop Shop for Accessible Tourism Europe (OSSATE, 2005) and Europe for All (Europe for All, 2007a, 2007b) operationalised the major components for the accommodation sector through an accessibility assessment template (Europe for All, 2007b). This project was based on a stakeholder analysis of developing an information system for accessible tourism (Buhalis, Eichhorn, Michopoulou & Miller, 2005; Buhalis, Michopoulou, Michailidis & Ambrose, 2005; Buhalis *et al.*, 2006) and resulted in a seminal paper in the area (Eichhorn *et al.*, 2008). The European work provided a robust approach to developing tourism information to satisfy the needs of the accessible tourism market.

However, the specifics of universal design within tourism require quite detailed approaches to understand the way spaces and places are used. This type of research has largely been absent in the literature except for broad brush approaches to understanding accessibility (Israeli, 2002a). One area where preliminary work has been carried out is in the accommodation sector where the principles and how they relate to the building codes, standards and the way that the information needs to be presented has been undertaken (Darcy, 2007, 2010; Darcy & Cameron, 2008a, 2008b). In particular, the *Hotel Accessibility Scale* (HAS) sought to bring together all the components required under the building codes and the standards for people with mobility, hearing and vision dimensions of access (Darcy, 2010).

An understanding of the nuances of universal approaches for accessible tourism is a necessary precursor to any move to operationalise the concept for the tourism industry. Figure 19.1 demonstrates that an understanding of disability requires knowledge of four concepts, namely:

- types or dimensions of disability;
- levels of support needs;

- access enablers; and
- universal design.

These four concepts and their interdependence form the basis of a comprehension of disability and tourism and hence, what is known as *accessible tourism*. As Packer *et al.* (2006) suggest, there is a complex inter-play between the individual, the environment and the tourism context, which demonstrates how people with disabilities can be excluded in tourism. At one or more of these interfaces, people can become margina-lised through a series of structural constraints that may require a series of institutional responses to provide an enabling tourism environment (Darcy, 2002; Daniels *et al.*, 2005).

Relatively little research has empirically examined how these inter-faces create social inequality with most research on disability and tourism limited to a focus on the experiences of people with disabilities and, more specifically, mobility disabilities. For example, Israeli's (2002a) study

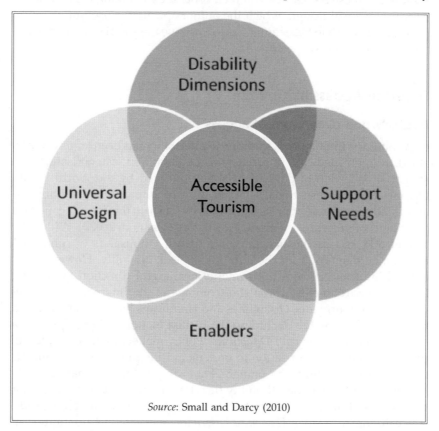

Source: Small and Darcy (2010)

Figure 19.1 Concepts for developing an understanding of accessible tourism

which identified some seven basic considerations for destination site accessibility for mobility. However, as identified by Packer *et al.*'s (2006) research, accessible tourism is more complex. To this end, others identified impairment, independence, level of support needs and aids used as statistically significant determinants of a person's likelihood to travel and how often they travelled (Burnett & Bender-Baker, 2001; Darcy, 2002). Similarly, Bi *et al.* (2007) found that level of support needs and functional ability were major influences on the perceptions of accessibility and attitudinal barriers to transport, accommodation, hospitality and attractions.

In summary, the literature suggests that the disability/dimensions of access, the support needs and the accessibility of the environment (enablers) are important to understanding the tourism experiences of people with disabilities. These concluding remarks will now illustrate the ways in which the chapters in this book have increased our understanding of these issues. We will then conclude by linking the discussion back to universal design, which the authors posit as a useful theoretical position on which to base initiatives to improve the social sustainability of the accessible tourism sector.

Facets of Accessible Tourism

Disability and dimensions of access

As outlined in Chapter 2, traditionally disability has been largely understood through medical approaches in the definition, categorisation and statistical collection of data on disability outlined by the World Health Organization's International Classification of Impairments, Disabilities and Handicaps. These approaches primarily focus on the disabling medical conditions of individuals (World Health Organization, 2002b). Within the frameworks of classification there are literally thousands of conditions that can be diagnosed for the individual's lack of ability. However, this type of information does not provide meaningful direction to creating enabling environments. These shortcomings of the International Classification of Impairments, Disabilities and Handicaps have been recognised by many commentators including the United Nations' (2006) *Convention on the Rights of People with Disabilities*. Policy makers have attempted to provide a better categorisation to understand the practical requirements of creating an enabling environment. For example, the way that disability is defined under national disability discrimination legislation focuses far more on the dimensions of disability as an outcome of their access needs. As such, the Australian *Disability Discrimination Act 1992*'s definition of disability aggregates major dimensions rather than focusing on individual conditions. In doing so it identifies: physical (mobility); sensory (hearing and vision); intellectual; psychiatric; neurological; learning, physical disfigurement; and the presence in the body of disease-causing organisms. Research in accessible tourism presented in this book suggests that inclusive industry practices need to be cognisant of the following dimensions and requirements for access:

- Mobility.
- Vision.
- Hearing.
- Cognitive/learning – involving issues of speech or understanding.
- Mental health.
- Sensitivities – including respiratory, food and chemical.
- Other.

The advantage of the above conceptualisation is that the focus is on the provision of the broad dimensions for access to create enabling environments, as advocated by social approaches to disability (Oliver, 1990, 1996; Swain et al., 2004; Thomas, 1999, 2007; Thomson, 1997; Eichhorn et al., 2008).

Level of support needs

The next layer of complexity lies in the requirements of the individual with a disability. Any person has needs in everyday living. The level of support needs of individuals with disabilities can be identified on a continuum. At one end of the continuum are those who live independently in the community, with no support required. At the other extreme are those who require a high level of one-on-one support, 24 hours a day. The level of an individual's support needs directly affects their social participation. In disability statistics, this has been referred to as the relative 'severity' of a person's disability or their functional ability (World Health Organization, 2002a). For the purposes of this book, authors have referred to this as 'medical' conceptualisation that focuses on 'loss' rather than social approaches that recognise support needs as an area requiring inclusive social responses. The level of support needs is generally described in the following terms: Independent (no support needs); Low; Medium; High; Very High (requires 24hr support). By combining both the dimensions of access and the level of support needs, we start to get a greater understanding of the experiences of travel that became one of the main themes of enquiry in the book.

Studies which examine tourist experiences through phenomenological approaches are an essential part of the accessible tourism research landscape. Several contributors to this book have focused in depth on the tourism experience of people with disabilities. From these studies comes a striking catalogue of interactions or 'negotiations' between the disabled visitor and the many constraints – personal, social, informational, physical ... that they confront when travelling. Crucially, in a world which is largely *not* designed for people with disabilities, it has been documented that those who need appropriate social responses are faced with multiple constraint negotiations and ongoing decisions about when, where and how to travel. When one has a disability, being a tourist and deciding where to go and stay is not a simple matter of holiday preference or financial means (although, as always, money *might* help) but an ongoing search for enabling destinations. Being able to travel (or not), as a disabled person is, rather, the result of a complex process of decision-making composed of many parts, and invariably includes a number of unknown factors. It is about 'personal risk management', in a very real and practical sense.

Darcy and Buhalis's Conceptualising Disability and the social model of disability (see Chapter 2) proposes that the environment play a fundamental role in the experience of being disabled. By removing or minimising access barriers in architecture, transport and information systems, tourism providers can effectively allow travel possibilities for people with disabilities. Failure to address or remove barriers means that tourism is simply impossible for many citizens, excluding these consumers from leisure activities and depriving the industry from a major market. Complicating this situation is the reality that access barriers are not always visible or immediately tangible whilst information is not always available, in the right format or language. Foggin, in Chapter 6, reported on a study of tourism as a facet of life of people with disabilities, showing how travel can be an expression of the breaking of personal boundaries, taboos and social barriers. In this way tourism can be an important part of improving self-esteem, expanding one's life skills and living life to the full. Fullagar's study of women with depression (Chapter 7) takes up this issue, demonstrating how travel can be a means of escape for women from ambivalent relationships with home and work.

With regard to future directions for tourism research, the experience-based studies in this book (see Chapters 4–12) point to the continuing importance of phenomenological research, not least as a means for the tourism industry to better understand its customers. There is certainly a need for investigating further the experiences of many diverse groups of people who may not be tourists – or who may participate given the chance. Research needs to examine their motives and their decision-making processes for destination choice. In addition, *ex-post* studies may be directed towards evaluating visitors' experiences of those that demonstrate good practice in visitor access. Results of such studies would indicate how visitors' needs can be satisfied and their experiences enhanced, while raising awareness more generally in education and practice about the target groups that benefit from greater accessibility in tourism.

Access enablers

The discussion so far has focused on the intersection between disability and level of support needs and has shown the complexity of an under-standing of disability. A further layer to this understanding can be found through the disability studies literature which seeks to change disabling environments to enabling environments (Swain, *et al.*, 2004). The pre-cursor to this change is focusing on the lived experience of people with disabilities and the constraints that they face in their everyday living. Understanding their access needs is the first step of implementing often minor amendments that improve access massively. While no chapter focused on the well-developed body of leisure constraints research and the application to tourism (Daniels *et al.*, 2005; Darcy, 1998; Turco *et al.*, 1998) many of the chapters and the references used implicitly dealt with this body of work but through the theoretical frameworks (e.g. Burnett & Bender-Baker, 2001; Darcy, 2002; Israeli, 2002b; Ray & Ryder, 2003). With respect to the body of literature on leisure and tourism constraints, access enablers can be regarded as the antidotes to constraints and can be conceptualised in three broad categories:

- Intrapersonal or interpersonal: adaptive or assistive technology or attendant support that maximises the abilities of people with disabilities.
- Structural environment and institutions: in their most basic form, enablers require a continuous pathway for people to experience environments.
- Attitudes/Behaviour of others: a significant area of consideration goes beyond adaptive equipment and environmental enablers to challenge disabling individual and institutional attitudes towards people with disabilities and accessible tourism inclusion.

The fragmented nature of the tourism sector means that the attitudes/behaviour of other stakeholders can have a direct influence on the degree to which tourism industries are enabling for people with disabilities. Michopoulou and Buhalis in Chapter 16 provide a breakdown of the principle stakeholder groups involved in the study of accessible tourism, focusing on their interests and constraints in participating in accessible tourism. One of the groups which are considered is destination manage-ment organisations and public authorities. Destination management organisations such as parks agencies are subject to a range of competing management considerations, which often result in tension between conservation and accessibility objectives. Pearn in Chapter 13 writes that:

> It would appear that we have now entered an era whereby society is often willing to bend over backwards in the context of building an egalitarian societal construct without giving careful consideration to possible consequences and repercussions within other scenarios, in this case heritage and traditional environments. Indeed it is the well-intended plight of political correctness which could result in catastrophic affects on historic environments.

To ensure that people with disabilities are genuinely empowered in their negotiations with other tourism stakeholders, countries such as the United Kingdom have introduced specific disability discrimination legislation (see Shaw and Veitch, Chapter 10). In the United Kingdom the *Disability Discrimination Act* has been in place since 1995. However in spite of the presence of this law Shaw and Veitch note that the tourism industry in the UK is still lacking in terms of the provision of high quality tourism experiences for people with disabilities. One area which was identified relates to the provision of information on accessible accommodation.

Chapters 17 and 18 consider the issue of visitors' access to information and its role in ensuring the social sustainability of the disabled tourism market. This is an area of research which addresses, especially, the lack of attention paid by designers and managers of tourism information systems to access issues. This can be to the detriment of visitors who require reliable access information and also to those who may have difficulty in accessing certain kinds of content, such as web pages and other electronic services. Pühretmair and Nussbaum (Chapter 17) describe how everyday challenges faced by people with disabilities can be overcome by the use of assistive technologies, in combination with 'enabling' environments (designed to reduce barriers) and services that may be provided either on site or accessed remotely via Information and Communication Technologies (ICTs). In Chapter 18 Buhalis and Michopoulou give an account of the four main challenges involved in the creation of information and technology platforms, particularly where the needs of people with disabilities are concerned, namely: Interoperability, Content Integration, Personalisation and Accessible Design. An important underpinning of these chapters is the recognition of the significance of ensuring that online information channels are both accessible to and contain accessible information for people with disabilities. It is clearly essential that the content which describes the physical access of venues, transport and their related services is equally accessible and accurate, based on the needs of visitors with disabilities and other access requirements. Making web content accessible and user-friendly is a means for providers to engage a larger market and thereby also to promote greater participation in tourism. The consideration of accessibility and usability issues improves accessibility, efficiency and structuring and significantly reduces the complexity of the web. It leads to more user-friendly web-systems that are essential for customer satisfaction, loyalty, quality and success (Pühretmair and Nussbaum – Chapter 17). The use of assistive technologies may be unfamiliar territory to the average tourism provider, yet people with disabilities and an increasing number of older people benefit from having equipment which extends their independence and increases their mobility, security, ability to communicate and comfort. In addition, accessibility optimised web sites are also accessible and adaptive to new platforms such as smart phones, games consoles etc. adding to the reasons for using accessibility compatible practices. For this reason future research in this area should focus on all tourism stakeholders that are able to work with the tourism sector, enabling providers to deliver appropriate support services to customers who need assistive technologies. Technical research is also needed to identify and help develop new services and systems specifically for tourists. These could include, for example, mobile applications for communication, navigation, augmented speech and language, and health monitoring.

This book, as well as the accompanying book *Accessible Tourism Practice: International Best Practice*, has approached the issue of environmental or structural enablers by proposing that the supply side of accessible tourism can be conveniently conceptualised across the tourism system to focus on four key areas, namely:

- Accessible infrastructure and facilities.
- Accessible transport.
- Accessible services.
- Accessible information.

In all these areas, tourism providers need to have some basic knowledge, skills and competencies to meet the expectations of tourists with disabilities and other groups that need better access, such as older people and families with small children. In any visitor journey, the infrastructure, transport, services and information as well as the links between them must all be accessible, making what is sometimes referred to as a 'chain of accessibility', indicating that accessible tourism should be a holistic experience or value system. This is, of course, only as strong as its 'weakest link' and all too often it is the disabled customer who is left to discover the weaknesses or breaks in the chain, while travelling. Providers can only develop their understanding of the needs of disabled customers by working directly with them, and by evaluating and improving their facilities. Reaching a good understanding of how to serve customers with particular access needs may not be easy for providers, especially when major architectural improvements are required. However, minor and cost effective amendments can often make a real difference in accessibility when there is a positive attitude towards change. The relationship between providers and disabled customers is typically fraught with tension, due to providers' initial lack of understanding of the customer's situation and requirements and often to the customer's lack of tolerance. On the one hand suppliers may be unwilling to admit their ignorance and, on the other hand, consumers may be embarrassed or uncomfortable about explaining what exactly they require. Studies reported in this book have provided useful research models for exploring the provider's relationship to disabled customers, and numerous substantive results.

An important finding that contributing authors have noted is that when exploring interactions between customers and staff it is necessary to consider the roles of different employees in the service chain. The study by the late Esa Arola (Arola, Cooper and Cooper) notes that in accessible tourism, as well as tourism in general, knowledge of customers' needs is the key to providing good service. In spite of this, Arola reports that often 'distinctions and tensions were evident between the attitudes of management and their front-line staff towards their disabled customers' (Arola, Cooper and Cooper – Chapter 8).

In Chapter 13 Pearn explores the related idea of tensions between conservation management objectives and accessibility. In doing so he clearly articulates the challenges for custodians of heritage sites when they seek to develop inclusive accessible tourism infrastructure. The apparent ideological clash between conservation and social inclusion which Pearn describes is perhaps only a variant of the more general concern that some historical sites and artifacts must be protected from *any* encroachment or direct access by tourists, due to their fragile or otherwise sensitive condition. The removal of access barriers therefore, like any other environmental intervention, requires a balanced approach, taking into account not only the rights of the visitors and the obligations of conservationists (or owners) but also the technical means that are available to create workable and acceptable solutions.

Strategic approaches to address the apparent impasse, which is described by Pearn, do exist. When one is considering future measures to improve access provisions in tourism; one potentially fruitful avenue of enquiry is to examine how the specific access demands of certain user groups are developed and integrated within 'mainstream' venues and offers. Such research would examine not only the *technical* solutions on offer but also the existence or otherwise of appropriate standards and the planning and management tools which influence the strategies and choices adopted by tourism providers. As long as accessibility is thought of and erroneously promoted as being only for visitors with extensive 'special needs', there will continue to be an economic and functional schism between the markets of disabled and non-disabled customers. Chapter 14 in this book offers a discussion of the economic contribution of tourists with a disability. Any simplistic division of the market is not efficient nor is it helpful either to providers or customers, as it perpetuates the existence of less than optimal provisions for disabled tourists, and inhibits (or at least delays) the introduction of inclusive, accessible solutions in tourism destinations, venues and offers. With this in mind the principles of universal design may offer a way forward for those interested in developing infrastructure, transport, services and information systems, so as to include the needs of the full range of stakeholders in the accessible tourism spectrum.

A Way Forward Through Universal Design

As introduced in Chapter 1, universal design is a paradigm that incorporates intergenerational and lifespan planning, recognising the nexus between ageing, disability and the continuum of ability of people (Alaksen *et al.*, 1997; Steinfeld & Shea, 2001). Universal design is based on seven principles to facilitate equitable access across the lifespan that are (Center for Universal Design, 2003, 2009; Preiser & Ostroff, 2001): Equitable Use; Flexibility in Use; Simple and Intuitive Use; Perceptible Information; Tolerance for Error; Low Physical Effort; Size and Space for Approach and Use (Center for Universal Design, 2009).

This book has established that making universal design central to the development process would normalise disability, ageing and access, and, hence, create enabling accessible tourism environments. The global economic recession may also serve as a further catalyst encouraging the tourism industry to look more closely at this market, as explained by Darcy, Cameron and Pegg, in their chapter on the business case for accessible tourism (see Chapter 15). Universal design is not only a catalyst for accessible tourism but also it supports operational management of facilities and reduces operational costs.

The ultimate aim of universal design is to extend and evolve the concepts of a continuous pathway and barrier-free environments (Goldsmith, 1997; Holmes-Siedle, 1996). A nexus was established where universal design was firmly founded on the tourism industry achieving a greater social sustainability as part of triple bottom line accounting (Rains, 2004). The Rio de Janeiro Declaration on Sustainable Social Development, Disability & Ageing was the formal recognition of this goal (Walsh, 2004). This was a proactive and significant declaration given the recent work on developing a UN Convention on the Rights of People with Disabilities (United Nations, 2006) together with the UN Millennium Development Goals (United Nations, 2009). Yet, declarations and conventions belie the fact that in many countries, the framework for developing accessible tourism or implementing universal design is not embedded in building codes and the accessibility standards to ensure a right to basic access. The intersection of disability type, access dimension, levels of independence and enablers create a series of complexities to operationalising universal design principles within enabling accessible tourism environments.

Epilogue

With these challenges in mind, the editors and contributing authors submit this book to the broader community of scholars to encourage and stimulate further dialogue. As Figure 19.2 suggests, the notion of applying universal design principles to the study of accessible tourism is likely to raise a number of issues for tourism scholars, managers and operators in equal measure. Considerations surrounding visitor access go to the very core of tourism such as: customer relationship management, quality in tourism, sustainability, corporate social responsibility, product and service

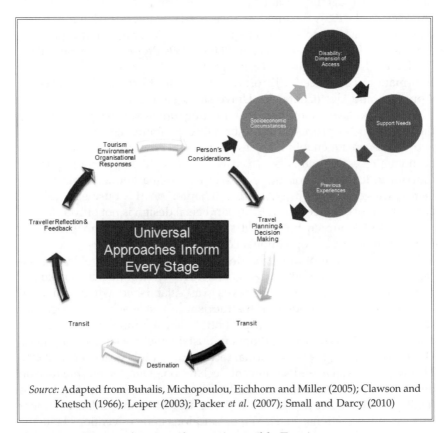

Source: Adapted from Buhalis, Michopoulou, Eichhorn and Miller (2005); Clawson and Knetsch (1966); Leiper (2003); Packer *et al.* (2007); Small and Darcy (2010)

Figure 19.2 Universal approaches to Accessible Tourism

design, hotel design, destination management and online marketing etc. It is only through the collaboration of the full range of interested stakeholders that the accessible tourism sector can break down traditional research silos and pursue a truly all-encompassing agenda for the sustainable development of this important industry sector.

References

Alaksen, F., Bergh, S., Bringa, O.R. and Heggem, E.K. (1997) *Universal Design: Planning and Design for All.* Oslo: The Norwegian State Council on Disability.

Baucom, A. and Grosch, R. (1996) *Hospitality Design for the Graying Generation: Meeting the Needs of a Growing Market.* New York, NY: John Wiley & Sons Inc.

BDE Ltd. (2006) *International Best Practices in Universal Design: A Global Review.* Canada: Betty Dion Enterprises Ltd.

Bi, Y., Card, J.A. and Cole, S.T. (2007) Accessibility and attitudinal barriers encountered by Chinese travellers with physical disabilities. *International Journal of Tourism Research* 9, 205–216.

Buhalis, D., Eichhorn, V., Michopoulou, E. and Miller, G. (2005) *Accessibility Market and Stakeholder Analysis.* Surrey: University of Surrey.

Buhalis, D., Michopoulou, E., Ambrose, I. and Michailidis, S. (2006) An eTourism portal for the disabled tourism market in Europe: the OSSATE portal design (One-Stop-Shop for Accessible Tourism). Paper presented at the *CAUTHE Conference.*

Buhalis, D., Michopoulou, E., Eichhorn, V. and Miller, G. (2005) *Accessibility Market and Stakeholder Analysis – One-Stop-Shop for Accessible Tourism in Europe (OSSATE).* Surrey, United Kingdom: University of Surrey.

Buhalis, D., Michopoulou, E., Michailidis, E. and Ambrose, I. (2005) Developing a one-stop-shop for accessible tourism in Europe (OSSATE Portal) for the disabled tourism market: technical and business challenges. Paper presented at the *eChallenges Conference.*

Burnett, J.J. and Bender-Baker, H. (2001) Assessing the travel-related behaviors of the mobility-disabled consumer. *Journal of Travel Research* 40 (1), 4–11.

Center for Universal Design (2003) Universal design principles. On WWW at http://www.design.ncsu.edu/cud/about_ud/about_ud.htm. Accessed 20.5.2009.

Center for Universal Design (2005) Universal design principles. On WWW at http://www.design.ncsu.edu/cud/about_ud/about_ud.htm Accessed 20.5.2009.

Center for Universal Design (2009) Universal Design Principles. On WWW at http://www.design.ncsu.edu/cud/about_ud/about_ud.htm. Accessed 20.5.2009.

Clawson, M. and Knetsch, J.L. (1966) *The Economics of Outdoor Recreation.* Baltimore: Johns Hopkins Press.

Daniels, M.J., Drogin Rodgers, E.B. and Wiggins, B.P. (2005) 'Travel Tales': An interpretive analysis of constraints and negotiations to pleasure travel as experienced by persons with physical disabilities. *Tourism Management* 26 (6), 919–930.

Darcy, S. (1998) *Anxiety to Access: Tourism Patterns and Experiences of New South Wales People with a Physical Disability.* Sydney: Tourism New South Wales.

Darcy, S. (2002) Marginalised participation: Physical disability, high support needs and tourism. *Journal of Hospitality and Tourism Management* 9 (1), 61–72.

Darcy, S. (2006) Setting a research agenda for accessible tourism. In C. Cooper, T.D. Lacy and L. Jago (eds) STCRC Technical Report Series, pp. 48). At http://www.crctourism.com.au/BookShop/BookDetail.aspx?d=473.

Darcy, S. (2007, 11–14 February) A methodology for assessing class three accessible accommodation information provision. Paper presented at *Tourism – Past Achievements, Future Challenges*, Manly Pacific Novotel, Manly, Sydney Australia.

Darcy, S. (2010) Inherent complexity: Disability, accessible tourism and accommodation information preferences. *Tourism Management* 31 (6), 816–826.

Darcy, S. and Cameron, B. (2008a) Accessible accommodation assessment template [Software template]. Sydney: University of Technology, Sydney and Easy Access Australia.

Darcy, S. and Cameron, B. (2008b) Accommodating tourism: Hotel accommodation, accessible tourism and market principles – Evidence-based research. [Research note]. *Independent Living: Official Journal of Independent Living Centres Australia* 24 (4), 24–28.

Darcy, S. and Dickson, T. (2009) A Whole-of-Life Approach to tourism: The case for accessible tourism experiences. *Journal of Hospitality and Tourism Management* 16 (1), 32–44.

Eichhorn, V., Miller, G., Michopoulou, E. and Buhalis, D. (2008) Enabling access to tourism through information schemes. *Annals of Tourism Research* 35 (1), 189–210.

Europe for All (2007a) Europe for All – Better information for discerning travellers. On WWW at http://www.europeforall.com/. Accessed 1.1.2008.

Europe for All (2007b) Tourism providers report on the Europe for all self-assessment questionnaire: For owners/managers of hotels and self-catering establishments and the Europe for all photo and measurement guide. (Vol. 2008). At http://www.europeforall.com/tourismProviders.seam? conversation Propagation=end&conversationId=162076.

Foggin, S.E.A., Cameron, B. and Darcy, S. (2004, 6–9 July) Towards barrier-free travel: Initiatives in the Asia Pacific Region. Paper presented at the Refereed conference proceedings of *Developing New Markets for Traditional Destinations' – Travel and Tourism Research Association (TTRA) Canada Conference 2003*, Ottawa.

Foggin, S.E.A., Darcy, S. and Cameron, B. (2003) Vers un tourisme sans barrières: Initiatives dans la région Asie-Pacifique. *TÉOROS: Revue de recherche en tourisme* 22 (3), 16–19.

Ginnerup, S. (2009) *Achieving Full Participation Through Universal Design*. Council of Europe.

Goldsmith, S. (1997) *Designing for the Disabled: The New Paradigm*. Boston, MA: Architectural Press.

Goldsmith, S., Dezart, J. and Architects, P. (2000) *Universal Design: A Manual of Practical Guidance for Architects*. Architectural Press.

Goldsmith, S. and PRP Architects (Firm) (2000) *Universal Design: Manual of Practical Guidance for Architects*. Boston, MA: Architectural Press.

Holmes-Siedle, J. (1996) *Barrier-Free Design: A Manual for Building Designers and Managers*. Oxford: Butterworth Architecture.

Horino, S., Mori, M., Kubota, N., Gennai, S. and Kogi, K. (2007) Participatory universal design practice at the international and historic tourist city of Kamakura: On-site study on an accessible city design and development of a barrier-free road map for wheelchair visitors around the JR Kita-Kamakura station. DBpia, Korea 2007, 27–29 (3).

Israeli, A. (2002a) A preliminary investigation of the importance of site accessibility factor for disabled tourists. *Journal of Travel Research* 41 (1), 101–104.

Israeli, A. (2002b) A preliminary investigation of the importance of site accessibility factors for disabled tourists. [Swetswise]. *Journal of Travel Research* 41 (1), 101–104.

Japan Tourism Marketing Co. (2009) Focus on tourism policy: Accessible tourism. *UNWTO Asia Pacific Newsletter,* 17 (1), 33–35.

Leiper, N. (2003) *Tourism Management* (3rd edn). Sydney: Hospitality Press.

Lidwell, W., Holden, K. and Butler, J. (2003) *Universal Principles of Design.* Rockport Publishers.

Oliver, M. (1990) *The Politics of Disablement.* Basingstoke, Houndmills: Macmillan.

Oliver, M. (1996) *Understanding Disability: From Theory to Practice.* Basingstoke, Houndmills: Macmillan.

OSSATE (2005) One-Stop-Shop for Accessible Tourism in Europe. On WWW at http://www.ossate.org/index.jsp. Accessed 1.9.2005.

Packer, T., McKercher, B. and Yau, M. (2006) Understanding the complex interplay between tourism, disability and environmental contexts. *Working Paper.*

Packer, T.L., McKercher, B. and Yau, M. (2007) Understanding the complex interplay between tourism, disability and environmental contexts. *Disability & Rehabilitation* 29 (4), 281–292.

Preiser, W.F.E. and Ostroff, E. (2001) *Universal Design Handbook.* New York: McGraw-Hill.

Rains, S. (2004) Universal design and the international travel & hospitality industry. Paper presented at the *Designing for the 21st Century III,* Rio de Janeiro, Brazil: 7th–12th December, 2004.

Rains, S. (2006a) Forum: Travel and tourism, through the lens of disability studies. *The Review of Disability Studies: An International Journal* 2 (2).

Rains, S. (2006b) Introduction to forum: Travel and tourism, through the lens of disability studies. *The Review of Disability Studies: An International Journal* 2 (2).

Rains, S. (2009a, 17–19 April) Inclusive tourism – Participant/observer – Notes on the global paradigm shift toward solutions. Paper presented at the *Neurology of the Third Millenium: For Well-Being in Disability – Quality of Life from Rehabilitation to Accessible Tourism,* Milan.

Rains, S. (2009b, 17–19 April) Second policy roundtable – Accessible tourism for well-being in disability. Paper presented at the *Neurology of the Third Millenium: For Well-Being in Disability – Quality of Life from Rehabilitation to Accessible Tourism,* Milan.

Ray, N.M. and Ryder, M.E. (2003) 'Ebilities' tourism: An exploratory discussion of the travel needs and motivations of the mobility-disabled. *Tourism Management* 24 (1), 57–72.

Rossetti, R. (2009) A universal design approach for the hospitality industry. Paper presented at the *Hospitality Design 2009 Expo & Conference.*

Shi, Y. (2006) The accessibility of Queensland visitor information centres' websites. *Tourism Management* 27 (5), 829–841.

Small, J. and Darcy, S. (2010) Chapter 4: Tourism, disability and mobility. In S. Cole and N. Morgan (eds) *Tourism and Inequality: Problems and Prospects* (pp. 1–30). Wallingford CABI.

Steinfeld, E. and Shea, S.M. (2001) Fair housing: Toward universal design in multifamily housing. In W.F.E. Preiser and E. Ostroff (eds) *Universal Design Handbook* (pp. 35.31–35.13). New York: McGraw-Hill.

Swain, J., Finkelstein, V., French, S. and Oliver, M. (2004) *Disabling Barriers – Enabling Environments* (3rd edn). London: Sage Publications Ltd.

Thomas, C. (1999) *Female Forms: Experiencing and Understanding Disability.* Buckingham: Open University Press.

Thomas, C. (2007) *Sociologies of Disability and Illness: Contested Ideas in Disability Studies and Medical Sociology*. Houndmills, Hants.: Palgrave Macmillan.

Thomson, R.G. (1997) *Extraordinary Bodies: Figuring Physical Disability in American Culture and Literature*. New York: Columbia University Press.

Turco, D.M., Stumbo, N. and Garncarz, J. (1998) Tourism constraints – People with disabilities. *Parks and Recreation Journal* 33 (9), 78–84.

United Nations (2006) Convention on the rights of persons with disabilities. New York. On WWW at http://www.un.org/esa/socdev/enable/rights/convtexte. htm. United Nations General Assembly A/61/611 – 6 December 2006.

United Nations (2009, 2 June) Enable. At http://www.un.org/disabilities/. (2009, 2 June) Millenium Development Goals. On www at http://www.un.org/milleniumgoals/. Accessed 14.2.2010

Walsh, C.J. (2004) Rio de Janeiro Declaration on Sustainable Social Development, Disability & Ageing. Paper presented at the *Designing for the 21st Century III* – An international conference on universal design, Rio de Janeiro, Brazil: 7th–12th December, 2004.

Williams, R. and Rattray, R. (2005) UK hotel web page accessibility for disabled and challenged users. *Tourism & Hospitality Research* 5 (3), 255–267.

Williams, R., Rattray, R. and Grimes, A. (2006) Meeting the on-line needs of disabled tourists: An assessment of UK-based hotel websites. *International Journal of Tourism Research* 8 (1), 59–73.

World Health Organization (2002a) *ICF CHECKLIST: Version 2.1a, Clinician Form for International Classification of Functioning, Disability and Health*. Geneva: World Health Organization.

World Health Organization (2002b) *Towards a Common Language for Functioning, Disability and Health – ICF*. Geneva: World Health Organization.

World Tourism Organization (2010) *Declaration on the Facilitation of Tourist Travel*. Madrid, Spain: World Tourism Organization.

Zarikas, V., Papatzanis, G. and Stephanidis, C. (2001) *An Architecture for a Self-Adapting Information System for Tourists*. Citeseer.

Zhou, Q. and DeSantis, R. (2005) Usability issues in city tourism website design: a content analysis. Paper presented at the *Professional Communication Conference*.

ASPECTS OF TOURISM
Series Editors: Chris Cooper, *Oxford Brookes University, UK*, C. Michael Hall, *University of Canterbury, New Zealand* and Dallen J. Timothy, *Arizona State University, USA*

Aspects of Tourism is an innovative, multifaceted series, which comprises authoritative reference handbooks on global tourism regions, research volumes, texts and monographs. It is designed to provide readers with the latest thinking on tourism worldwide and push back the frontiers of tourism knowledge. The volumes are authoritative, readable and user-friendly, providing accessible sources for further research. Books in the series are commissioned to probe the relationship between tourism and cognate subject areas such as strategy, development, retailing, sport and environmental studies.

Full details of all the books in this series and of all our other publications can be found on http://www.channelviewpublications.com, or by writing to Channel View Publications, St Nicholas House, 31-34 High Street, Bristol BS1 2AW, UK.

Accessible Tourism

MIX
Paper from
responsible sources
FSC® C016379